Notes From Our Contributors

"What a treasure trove! The fact that these stories are all written by women makes this book even more intriguing. How wonderful to be part of this vibrant and beautiful anthology."

—Susan Orlean, author of The Orchid Thief.

"This is the collection I wish I'd had when I was starting out as a writer. Back then, non-fiction was the purview of men; here's an unequivocal affirmation that it no longer is."

—Elizabeth Kaye, author of Lifeboat No. 8.

"One of the many beauties of nonfiction as a genre is that it invites diversity in the stories it seeks to tell and, by extension, in the practitioners who tell those stories. At long last, the contributions of women as leaders in this field are being fully acknowledged."

— Madeleine Blais, author of To the New Owners.

Here's the book you've been missing, the only one you'll need for the next week or two, brimming with tall tales, hairpin turns, and poignant moments, all of them true, and with deftly-captured personalities brought vividly to life in these pages.

— Melissa Fay Greene, author of Praying for Sheetrock.

This is an amazing collection of journalists who just happen to be female—it's a must read for any and all young writers, a much-needed road map for how to report, write, and think about stories.

—Mimi Swartz, author, editor and two-time National Magazine Award winner.

I'm so honored to be included in these pages with some of the true masters of our genre. I've been waiting for a book like this for longest time. *The Stories We Tell* belongs in the permanent collection of anyone who loves reading and writing reported stories and essays.

— Jeanne Marie Laskas, author of Concussion.

"I won't be here to witness it, but won't it be a fine day when anthology specifically focused on women journalists won't make any sense?"

— Adrian LeBlanc, author of Random Family.

More Intriguing Text/Anthologies from The Sager Group

Newswomen: Twenty-five Years of Front Page Journalism

•

Janet's World: The Inside Story of Washington Post Pulitzer Fabulist Janet Cooke

•

Next Wave: America's New Generation of Great Literary Journalists

•

Artful Journalism: Essays in the Craft and Magic of True Storytelling

•

Everyone Leaves Behind a Name: True Stories by Michael Brick

•

Danny Yukon and the Secrets of the Amazing Lamp

THE Stories WE TELL

CLASSIC TRUE TALES BY AMERICA'S GREATEST WOMEN JOURNALISTS

The Stories We Tell: Classic True Tales by America's Greatest Women Journalists

Published in the United States of America.

Cataloging-in-Publication data for this book is available from the Library of Congress.
ISBN-13: 978-0-9980793-1-8
ISBN-10: 0-9980793-1-6

Cover Designed by Stravinski Pierre and
Siori Kitajima, SF AppWorks LLC
www.sfappworks.com
Formatted by Ovidiu Vlad
Published by The Sager Group LLC
www.TheSagerGroup.net
info@TheSagerGroup.net

THE Stories WE TELL

CLASSIC TRUE TALES BY AMERICA'S GREATEST WOMEN JOURNALISTS

EDITED BY PATSY SIMS

With Research By Jamie Ballard and Caitlynne Leary

We tell ourselves stories in order to live.

—Joan Didion, *The White Album*

Table of Contents

Introduction

The Stories We Tell celebrates the work of twenty women who have made major contributions to American longform journalism over the past half-century.

All counted, they have garnered at least four Pulitzer Prizes, seven Guggenheim fellowships, five Woodrow Wilson fellowships, three National Magazine Awards, four National Book Awards for nonfiction, three National Book Critics Awards—among many other honors. The National Book Foundation presented its Medal for Distinguished Contributions to American Letters to Joan Didion in 2007; Adrian Nicole LeBlanc was named a 2006 MacArthur Fellow.

While each has her own style, the women in these pages share the attributes of all good writers: meticulous research and reporting, careful attention to detail, a talent for choosing the perfect noun or verb. Above all, they are astute observers and sticklers for accuracy. Over the years, they have been both prolific and versatile, writing about a wide range of topics, as demonstrated by the selections here, which take us from Suzannah Lessard's look at the cultural divide in a New York neighborhood, where trendy shops and residences give way to housing projects; to Isabel Wilkerson's interview with civil rights activist Stokely Carmichael; to Janet Malcolm's profile of the brilliant and stylish young pianist Yuja Wang; to Robin Marantz Henig's poignant account of the determination of one Alzheimer's victim to end her life on her own terms.

Many of the writers spent long periods of time with their subjects. To profile Rudolf Nureyev, Elizabeth Kaye traveled with the famed ballet dancer for nearly a year; she stayed in the same hotels and spent time with him as he played the piano and watched movies into the wee hours. "I was there late, and I was there early, and I saw a lot," she recalls. "It was incredibly generous of him, and trusting."

In Lis Harris's case, it took more than a year just to find the ideal Hasidic family for her profile, a search made more difficult by her insistence that the family include a teenager. She spent another year observing their lives.

"I thought, where there are teenagers, there is rebellion," she explains. "I rejoiced when I finally found the family I wrote about because they had five teens in the clan. But surprise! There was no rebellion. It was one thing to rebel against your mom and dad, quite another to rebel against your parents, your entire community, the Rebbe—and God!"

Gerri Hirshey looks back on her month-long series of conversations aboard the private tour bus of the late B.B. King as "a music journalist's fever dream." She remembers King, who was seventy-three at the time, as a wise, compassionate man, "a combo of a funky Yoda and the Dalai Lama." Her story won that year's ASCAP-Deems Taylor/Virgil Thompson Award.

By contrast, Joan Didion didn't arrive in San Bernardino until a year after the trial ended in the tabloid-style murder case she chronicles in "Some Dreamers of the Golden Dream," considered one of the classics of literary journalism. Nevertheless, with the help of trial transcripts, news clips, interviews, her observations of the community, and even Chamber of Commerce handouts—the basic tools of the reporter's trade—she reconstructs a story that brings readers into real time.

Gloria Steinem's 1964 profile of Jacqueline Kennedy provides another example of a writer who, without benefit of extended access to her subject, combined reportorial ingenuity with literary skills to construct a look at the former First Lady one year after the assassination of her husband, President John F. Kennedy.

Gaining face time with celebrities often takes as much creativity as actually writing the stories. When Susan Orlean set out to profile Christina Sanchez, she was convinced the only way to get to the popular Spanish bullfighter was through her agent, a man who assured Orlean of a meeting. The man, however, turned out to be an imposter and was no longer answering his phone by the time she arrived in Madrid.

"I was so embarrassed and frustrated that I prepared to leave on the next flight, but my editor urged me to use some ingenuity and try to get to her on my own," Orlean recalls. "I managed to figure out where her mother lived and decided to go visit, in hopes she would plead my case to Christina. As luck would have it, when I arrived at her mother's, Christina was there, taking a short break from her travels, and she invited me to follow her for the next several days."

Orlean's lesson learned: persevere.

While a number of stories in this collection focus on well-known subjects, many more are about ordinary people: Madeleine Blais writes about a girls' high school basketball team battling to win the state championship; Adrian Nicole LeBlanc focuses on a group of teenage boys struggling to fit in at school; Melissa Fay Greene follows the training of service dogs for children with autism and other cognitive disabilities. Susan Sheehan's article brings readers into the lives of a twelve-year-old boy and his family trying to live on $21,723 a year. Jeanne Marie Laskas writes about the recipient of a face transplant. E. Jean Carroll offers a haunting account of a series of mysterious teenage deaths in a small upstate New York town. Mimi Swartz chronicles the long political battle over reproductive rights in Texas.

Only two of the anthology stories are intensely personal: Joyce Wadler's "My Breast: One Woman's Cancer Story," and Jill Lepore's "The Prodigal Daughter."

At the outset, Wadler says, she had no intention of writing about her fight against cancer. "I was focused on getting the best medical treatment I could and saving my life," she says. "But it was a story that wanted to be written and several months after surgery the first sentence popped into my mind: 'I have a scar on my breast.' After that, it felt like the story was writing itself."

Lepore sees herself as more of an historian than a personal essayist, and yet, in "Prodigal Daughter," she goes against her rule of not writing about herself, combining research for her book on Ben Franklin's sister with memories of her recently deceased mother to beget a powerful piece of nonfiction.

As a journalist who has worked for decades alongside these great women in the same male-dominated field, it gives me a great deal of satisfaction to bring them together under one cover. All of the writers collected herein had a hand in choosing the stories featured. In the emails and telephone calls we shared, all expressed their delight that such a volume was being compiled.

While male bylines still outnumber those of females in American magazines, the trend is changing, so much so that narrowing this anthology to twenty women has not been easy. As a result, The Sager Group is compiling a second collection of longform magazine writing by a younger generation of women—many of them inspired by the writers featured here.

Patsy Sims

Madeleine Blais

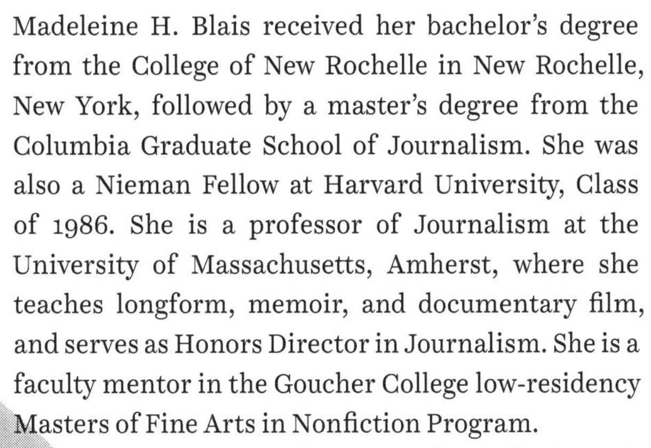

Madeleine H. Blais received her bachelor's degree from the College of New Rochelle in New Rochelle, New York, followed by a master's degree from the Columbia Graduate School of Journalism. She was also a Nieman Fellow at Harvard University, Class of 1986. She is a professor of Journalism at the University of Massachusetts, Amherst, where she teaches longform, memoir, and documentary film, and serves as Honors Director in Journalism. She is a faculty mentor in the Goucher College low-residency Masters of Fine Arts in Nonfiction Program.

From 1979-1987 she was on the staff of *Tropic Magazine* of *The Miami Herald* where she won many awards, including a Pulitzer Prize for feature writing. She is the author of *The Heart Is an Instrument*, a collection of journalism, and *In These Girls, Hope Is a Muscle,* which was chosen as a finalist in general nonfiction by the National Book Critics Awards and was cited by *ESPN* as one of the top one hundred sports books of the twentieth century. Her most recent book is *To the New Owners: A Martha's Vineyard Memoir.* She is currently at work on a biography of tennis great Alice Marble.

Her essays have appeared in *Superstition Review, Cogniscenti,* and *The New Guard* as well as in books such as *Bad Girls: 26 Writers Misbehave* edited by Ellen Sussman, *Our Boston: Writers Celebrate the City They Love* edited by Andrew Blauner, *A Story Larger than My Own* edited by Janet Burroway, and *Double Take: Portraits Over Time* by Maggie Evans Silverstein. She is on the editorial board of *River Teeth Magazine.*

They Were Commandos

After near-perfect seasons tarnished by losses in the state championships, the Amherst High School girls' basketball team might finally change its story.

The voice of the coach rises above the din of shuffling footsteps, loud greetings, the slamming of metal, the thud of books. "Listen up. I want you to check right now. Do you have your uniforms? Your shoes and your socks? Do you have any other items of clothing that might be needed?"

Coach Ron Moyer believes it's possible to pack abstractions along with one's gear, intangibles like "intensity" and "game face" and "consistency" and "defense." As the members of the Amherst Regional High School girls' basketball team prepare to board the Hoop Phi Express on their way to the Centrum in Worcester more than an hour away for the Massachusetts state championship, he tells them, "Today, I want you to pack your courage."

The team is 23–1 going into this game, losing only to Agawam, which, like the Haverhill team they are facing this evening, has some real height. Haverhill, known for aggressive ball, nothing dirty but just short of it, has two girls over six feet nicknamed the Twin Towers. Moyer has prepped his team with a couple of specialized plays, the Murphy and the Shoelace, and he tells them: "Expect to play a little football." Amherst girls have a reputation for being afraid to throw their elbows, but this year they have learned to take the words "finesse team" as an insult. Although Coach has been careful to avoid saying "state championship" to goad his team, last fall he did tell one aging gym rat in town: "I have the two best guards in the state and probably the nation, but it all depends on the girls up front. There's an old saying— 'Guards win games, but forwards win championships.' We'll have to see."

At six foot six, Moyer looms over his players. With a thick cap of graying brown hair and bangs that flop down over his forehead, he resembles a grizzly bear on spindly legs. The girls are more like colts. For Moyer, turning them into a team has nothing to do with breaking their spirit and everything to do with harnessing it.

As Jen Pariseau listens to Coach before leaving for Worcester, her legs can't stop twitching. One of the six seniors on the team playing high-school hoop together for the last time, she has thick, dark eyebrows and long, lanky limbs. For her, tonight's game is the perfect revenge, not just against Haverhill but also against some of the rebuffs she suffered as an athlete on the way up. For three years, she played on one of Amherst's Little League teams, the Red Sox. She was pitcher, shortstop, and first baseman. When it was time to choose the all-star league, she was told her bunts were not up to par.

Jen's teammates are just as hyped up. Half of them are giving the other half piggybacks. There are lots of hand-slapping and nudges. They swirl around one another, everyone making a private point of touching Jamila Wideman, Jen's co-captain, as if one dark-haired, brown-eyed girl could transmit the power of her playing to all the others. Jamila is an all-America, recipient of more than 150 offers of athletic scholarships. On the court, the strong bones on her face are like a flag demanding to be heeded; she is a study in quickness and confidence, the ball becoming part of her body. Her nickname is Predator.

Jen Pariseau is two-time all-Western Mass, and together the two guards delighted fans all season with the way they delivered the ball to each other, sometimes in a dipsy doo behind the back or between the legs, often resulting in an open shot. JennyandJamila. In Amherst, it's one word.

Coach pauses. He looks as though he is about to rebuke the girls for all the squirming, but he shrugs and gives a big smile. "Let's go." Then, perhaps more to himself than to them: "While we're still young."

Shortly after five in the evening, the sky is thick and gray and hooded, the cloud cover a welcome hedge against what has been a bitter New England winter. The bus the girls board is different from the usual.

"Hooked up and smooth," says Jen Pariseau, admiring the special features, including upholstered seats, a toilet, four television sets, and a VCR mounted on the ceiling—a definite step up from the yellow tin cans they have taken to every other game. There are some cheerleaders on the bus as well as Tricia Lea, an assistant coach with her own high-school memories about what it was like to go up against those Hillies from Haverhill in their brown and yellow uniforms with the short shorts. "Haverhill. I don't know what they eat up there, but they can be slightly ruthless. Sportsmanship does not run very deep in that town."

A few years back, Coach had trouble convincing players and their families of the seriousness of the commitment to girls' basketball. JennyandJamila remember playing in varsity games five and six years ago when the gym would be empty of spectators except for their parents and maybe a few lost souls who had missed the late bus. Coach remembers girls who would cut practice to go to their boyfriends' games, and once during the playoffs, a team captain left to go on a school-sponsored cultural exchange for three weeks in the former Soviet Union. As far as he's concerned, the current policy could not be clearer: You want cultural exchange? You can have it with Hamp.

Tonight, Amherst is sending three "pep" buses to the game, unprecedented support for an athletic event, boys' or girls'. Amherst is a place that tends to prize thought over action, tofu over toughness. It prefers to honor the work of the individual dedicated to a life of monastic scholarship rather than some noisy group effort. But this season, there were sellout crowds. There was even that badge: a wary cop on the premises for the first time in the history of a girls' event.

Amherst is a college town, with the usual benign ineffectuality that makes most college towns as maddening as they are charming and livable. When the Chamber of Commerce sponsored a contest for town motto, Moyer submitted one that he still thinks should have won—"Amherst: Where sexuality is an option and reality is an alternative."

Amherst is, for the most part, smoke-free, nuclear-free, and eager to free Tibet. Ponchos with little projectiles of fleece have never gone out of style. Banners stretch across South Pleasant Street at the town common, including the vintage "Spay or Neuter Your Pet, Prevent Abandonment & Suffering." This is a town that saves spotted salamanders, creating love tunnels (at taxpayers' eager expense) so that they can all descend from the hills in early spring and migrate to the marshy areas for sexual assignation without being squashed on Henry Street. There's a new band called Salamander Crossing; heavy metal it's not. A famous local headline: "Well-Dressed Man Robs Amherst Bank." Amherst is an achingly democratic sort of place in which tryouts for Little League, with their inevitable rejections, have caused people to suggest that more teams should be created so that no one is left out. There are people in Amherst who still think "politically correct" is a compliment. The program notes for the spring musical *Kiss Me, Kate* pointed out politely that *The Taming of the Shrew*, on which it is based, was "well, Shakespearean in its attitude toward the sexes."

The downtown area seems to support pizza joints, Chinese restaurants, ice-cream parlors, and bookstores and not much else. It's hard to find a needle and thread, but if you wish you can go to the Global Trader and purchase for $4 a dish towel with a rain-forest theme. The surrounding communities range from the hard and nasty inner-city poverty of Holyoke, the empty factories in Chicopee and the blue-collar scrappiness in Agawam to the cornfields and asparagus patches in Whately and Hatfield and Hadley and the shoppers' mecca that is Northampton. They tend to look on Amherst with eye-rolling puzzlement and occasional contempt as the town that fell to earth.

The girls on the Hurricanes know they live in a kindly, ruminative sort of place. Sometimes they joke about how if they weren't playing ball, they'd be "tipping cows"—a basically useless activity necessitated by the unfortunate tendency of cows to sleep standing up.

With the playoffs looming, the six senior girls—JennyandJamila, Kathleen Poe, Kristin Marvin, Patri Abad, and Kim Warner—were treated to a late lunch by Jamila's father, John Edgar Wideman, winner of two PEN/Faulkners as well as numerous other awards, and author of the nonfiction meditation *Brothers and Keepers*; *Philadelphia Fire*, a fictional visitation of the Move bombing in 1985; *The Homewood Trilogy*, about growing up black in Pittsburgh.

It was at that lunch that the team's center, Kristin, in trying to sum up the peculiar, almost consoling, lack of outward drama in a town like Amherst, confessed that the night before she had a dream.

"My Mom and I, we went to Stop and Shop and while we were there, we went down, you know, all our usual aisles in the regular order, picking out all the things we usually buy, and after that we got in line to check out."

"That's it?" said the other girls.

Jamila's father thought maybe the dream had another layer and so he tried a gentle psychoanalytic probe. He had a quicksilver face, his expression changing in a flicker from stormy to melancholy to soft and forgiving. Now it was contemplative.

"Did you run into any unusual people?"

"No."

"How about money? Did you run out of money or anything?"

"No."

"Kristin," said her teammates, "that's so sad."

Kathleen, who is in the top ten academically in her class of 250, told Jamila's father that she tried reading a collection of his short stories, "the one called 'Jungle Fever.'"

"I'm not Spike Lee. It was just *Fever*."

"Mr. Wideman, I tried reading it," said Jen Pariseau, also in the top ten academically. "I found the shortest story I could, and you know what? I think I understood it. I can't guarantee it, but I think I did."

He looked at his guests at the table, a blur of happy faces and ponytails. Their teasing was a joy. He is a former basketball player for the University of Pennsylvania and a Rhodes scholar who played at Oxford, and his passion for the game is such that Jamila tells people she was born playing basketball. Girls' basketball is not boys' basketball being played by girls. It's a whole new game. There's no dunking. They can't jump as high. They can't play above the rim. But they can play with every bit as much style. And there's that added purity, that sense of excellence for its own sake. It's not a career option for girls; after college the game is over, so there is none of the desperate jockeying for professional favor.

As a black man, Wideman knows only too well the shallow triumph of token progress. He had told Kathleen's father, "This is just one team in one season." It alone cannot change the discrimination against girls and their bodies throughout history. But here in these girls, hope is a muscle.

"Here's to the senior girls," he said, looking at all of them.

They hoisted their ritual glasses of water.

"This is," he said, "as good as it gets."

To look at them, these six seniors on the team, who all appear to be lit from within, one would assume that their lives have been seamless journeys. In fact, as Jen Pariseau puts it, she does not come from a "Dan Quayle kind of family"—and neither do most of the others. Whatever sadness or disruption they've been dealt, an opposite force follows them onto the court. JennyandJamila have not gone it alone; they have had Kathleen's strong right hand, an almost irresistible force heading toward the basket. She never wastes a motion: The ball is in her hands one second, then quietly dropping through the hoop the next, without dramatics, almost like an afterthought. There's Kristin. Her flushed cheeks are not a sign of exhaustion but of some private fury. When the ball comes curling out of the basket, more often than not it is Kristin who has pushed and shoved her way to the prize.

The only underclass starter, Emily Shore, is so serious about her chance to play with the famous JennyandJamila that she spent the bulk of her summer lifting weights and battling in pickup games on Amherst's cracked and weather-ravaged outdoor courts with a succession of skeptical and then grudgingly appreciative young men.

They have become what every opponent fears most: a team with a mission.

As good as it gets. That is, of course, the exact sentiment the girls feel toward their fancy bus.

"Fasten your seat belts," says Coach. "Beverage service will commence shortly after takeoff. There'll be turbulence coming to Haverhill when the Hurricanes hit Worcester." Then he announces the people to whom he would like them to dedicate the entire season. "And that's to the 140 girls who are now playing youth basketball in Amherst for the first time this year."

Jen Pariseau says she wants to read a letter from Diane Stanton, the mother of Chris Stanton, the star of the boys' basketball team.

"Jenny and Jamila," the letter began. Diane Stanton said she was addressing them because she knew them the best, but the letter was for the whole team. "Your existence as a team represents a lot of things to a lot of women like me. . . . As a young girl I remember standing outside the Little League fence and watching the boys and knowing that I could hit and catch better than at least a third of them. When our high-school intramural field hockey team and softball team asked for leagues, we were told flatly—NO, because there was no money. . . . When this group of girl athletes got together to form an intramural basketball team, we were subjected to ridicule and anger from some of the student body. . . . I lost courage, I'm embarrassed to admit, in my junior year and would no longer play intramural sports. Part of it was a protest against the failure of my school. . . to recognize that we needed to play as much as boys. I know the struggle."

Coach gives the driver a signal and the vehicle starts to roll. A police car just ahead suddenly activates its lights and in a slow ceremony leads the vehicle to the corner of Main and Triangle Streets, where another officer has been summoned to stop all traffic. Coach is beaming and silently thanks his old pal, Captain Charlie Scherpa, over in the Police Department for coming through. In addition to being a guidance counselor, Moyer has been the girls' coach off and on since 1981, a task he enjoys because unlike with boys, whose arrogance and confidence often have to be eroded before he can get the team to work, this is all constructive. The way to build a girls' team is to build their individual self-confidence.

The bus heads down Main (a street that is most famous for being the site of the house where Emily Dickinson was born, where she lived, died, and wrote her poetry) to the corner of Northeast, where they get to run a red light, turning in front of Fort River Elementary School, then heading out to Route 9, where the escort lasts all the way to the town line. In an instant, the sign that says "Entering Pelham" appears, and in another instant a new one looms ahead that says "Entering Belchertown."

The girls watch the film they had chosen unanimously to pump them for the game—"A League of Their Own." The six seniors are lost in their own thoughts.

Kim Warner knows her mother, who works in personnel at the University of Massachusetts, will be at the game, plus her two sisters, plus her boyfriend's family. Her father lives in Florida, and although she sends him news accounts of all the games, he has never seen her play. She hasn't seen him since the tenth grade. She plans to go to Westfield State and major in early childhood education. On the way to the game, Kim writes a fantasy letter in her head: "Dear Dad, At long last a lot of hard work paid off."

Patri Abad's mother, a bilingual teacher, has to be at work, and although Patri will miss her, she knows she can count on a large cheering section of friends. She almost didn't get to play this year. During her junior year, she had moved to Chicago with her mother and her new stepfather. Patri, who is Cuban on her father's side and Puerto Rican on her mother's, prayed incessantly to the Virgin. She received constant mail from teammates like Lucia Maraniss, back when Lucia was a gushing eighth grader: "Patri, I will always remember you as one of the wisest, most caring and compassionate people I've ever met. I'm going to miss you very, very, very, very, very, very, very, very, very, very, very, very, very, very much."

Whether it was divine intercession or that fourteenth "very" from Lucia, the resolve of Patri's mother to stay in Chicago eventually vanished. They returned to the Happy Valley, as Amherst is called, and Patri could finish her senior year as a member of the Hurricanes. She has been accepted at Drew, Clark, and the University of Massachusetts, pre-med.

Kristin Marvin, also known as Jolly, Jolly Green, and Grace (her teammates have misinterpreted her tenacity as clumsiness), is going to Holy Cross College, pre-med. She likes medicine because it has a strong element of knowability. Her parents were divorced when she was young and she lived with a lot of uncertainty. Her mother has since married a builder whose first wife married Kristin's father, who works in Connecticut and often rushes to the games after work in his business suit. The marital realignment has created a circumstance in which the daughter of her stepfather and stepmother is Kristin's double stepsister.

Coach calls Kathleen Poe his silent assassin—the girl with two distinct personalities. The demure senior with the high grades, with applications at Williams, Haverford, Duke, and Dartmouth, is Kathleen; the girl on the court is her ferocious twin, Skippy. He concocted the dichotomy because when Kathleen first started playing she said "Excuse me" all the time and would pause to pick her opponents up off the floor. She wants to be like Jamila: someone you don't want to meet on the court but who will be a good friend off it.

Jamila plans to study law and African American studies at Stanford. Like her mother, Judy Wideman, who is in her second year of law school, she hopes to be a defense attorney. As a child of mixed races, she has told interviewers she identifies not with being black or white but with being herself. Still, her bedroom has pictures of Winnie Mandela, Jesse Jackson, and the children of Soweto. After the riot in Los Angeles, she wrote several poems that reflected her feelings.

In "Black," she wrote:

I walk the tightrope between the fires
Does anyone know where I fall through?
Their forked daggers of rage reflect my eye
Their physical destruction passes me by
Why does the fire call me?

Jen is known locally as the best thing that ever happened to Pelham, which is that little twinge on the highway on Route 9. Since Jen was two and her brother, Chris, was four, they have lived with their father, who is a manager of reservoirs and water treatment in Amherst. She is planning to play ball for Dartmouth and to major in engineering. She turned down Princeton, especially after the recruiter, who made a home visit, would not let her father, who had a stutter, talk.

The door to her room is plastered with Nike inspirational ads. She calls the wall above her bed her "strong women wall," and it is filled with pictures of her favorite role models, including Ann Richards and Toni Morrison. By her bedside, she keeps a clothbound book—given to her by her teammate Rita Powell—in which she writes favorite quotes, a customized Bartlett's.

Marilyn Monroe: "If I'm going to be alone, I'd rather be by myself."
Colette: "You will do foolish things, but do them with enthusiasm."
Zora Neale Hurston: "The dream is the truth."

The team bonding among these six seniors and the ten younger girls is one reason they have played so well: the sisterhood-is-powerful quest for unity. They have a team song, "Real Love," and they have team trinkets (beaded necklaces with their names and plastic rings and scrunchies with basketballs), team teddy bears, team towels. At team dinners, Jamila's mother carbo-loads them with slivered chicken cooked in garlic and oil and lemon and served on a bed of noodles. The meals often conclude with a dozen or so girls linking arms in a tight circle, swaying, singing, shouting, "*Hoop Phi!*"

To witness adrenaline overload at its most frenetic, nothing beats the atmosphere on one of those yellow buses on the return home after a victory over Hamp. Northampton is a fine town, birthplace of Calvin Coolidge, home of Smith College. But, as Jen Pariseau says: "Something happens when we play Hamp. Both teams become brutes." Hamp fans are always trying to demoralize JennyandJamila with the scornful chant: "You're overrated; you're overrated."

A victory against Hamp, especially on their territory at Feiker gym, especially in front of at least one thousand people with several hundred more turned away at the door, was a great moment to whoop and cheer the whole way home, to sing Queen's famous anthem, "We Are the Champions," to slap the ceiling of the bus, to open the windows and to shout:

> *Who'll rock the house?*
> *The Hurricanes will rock the house.*
> *And when the Hurricanes rock the house*
> *They rock it all the way down.*

But even though they beat Hamp in the Western Mass Regional finals, they weren't really champions—not yet. Do they have what it takes, these sweet-looking girls reared in maple syrup country on land that includes the Robert Frost trail? Playing before a few thousand fans in what is almost your own backyard is nothing compared with a stadium that seats 13,800, where real pros play. Rocking Feiker is one thing, but the Centrum?

When the bus finally pulls in front of the Centrum and it is time to leap off, the girls have faces like masks. To the world, they are a bunch of teen-age girls; inside their heads, they are commandos. To the world, these teen-agers have pretty names: Patri, Kristin, Jen, Kathleen, Kim, Jamila, Sophie, Jade, Emily J., Emily S., Jan, Lucia, Carrie, Rita, Jessi, Julie. But as far as these girls are concerned, they *are* the codes that encapsulate their rare and superb skills, their specialty plays, their personal styles. They are Cloudy and Cougar and Jones-bones and Gumby and Grace and Skippy and Predator. They are warriors.

The girls crowd into a locker room. With much less commotion than usual, they dress in their baggy knee-length uniforms. They slap hands and stand tall. Meanwhile the arena is redolent of hot dogs, popcorn, sweat, and anticipation, one side of the bleachers filled with their people and the other side with the fans from Haverhill.

The girls walk out wordlessly. They look up.

You have to live in a small town for a while before you can read a crowd, especially in New England, where fences are deep in the soil. But if you've been in a town like Amherst for a while, you can go to an out-of-town game, even one in as imposing and cavernous a facility as the Centrum, and you can feel this sudden lurch of well-being that comes from the soothing familiarity of faces that are as much a part of your landscape as falling leaves, as forsythia in season, as rhubarb in June. You scan the rows, and for better, and sometimes for worse, you know who's who. You know whose parents don't talk to whom else and you know why. You know who has had troubles that never get discussed.

You see the lawyer that represented your folks or one of their friends in a land dispute or a custody case. You see the realtor who tried to sell a house next to the landfill to the new kids in town. You see the doctor who was no help for your asthma and the one who was. You see the teacher who declared your baby brother a complete mystery and the teacher who always stops to ask what your remarkable brother is up to now. You know which man is the beloved elementary-school principal, now retired. You recognize the plump-cheeked ladies from the cafeteria who specialize in homemade cinnamon buns for sixty-five cents. You see your family and you see the fathers and mothers and stepfathers and stepmothers of your teammates. You know whose brother flew in from Chicago for the game; whose step-grandparents came from Minnesota.

But what is most important about all this is how mute it is. The commonality is something that is understood, as tacit as the progression of the summer to fall to winter to spring, and just as comforting. Usually there is a buzz of cheering at the start of a game, but this time the Amherst crowd is nearly silent as the referee tosses the ball.

The Haverhill center taps the ball backward to her point guard. She comes down the court, swings the ball to the wing, who instantly dishes it inside to the center. Easy layup. Amherst blinks first. Two-nothing. In the Haverhill stands, the crowd cheers. It is the only pure cheer they will get.

Within a few seconds, the score is 6–4 Amherst, and something truly remarkable takes place. The Hurricanes enter into a zone where all of them are all-Americans. It's a kind of controlled frenzy that can overtake a group of athletes under only the most elusive of circumstances. It's not certain what triggers it, perhaps it's Jamila's gentle three-pointer from the wing, or more likely, when Jen drives the baseline and as she swoops beneath the basket like a bird of prey she releases the ball back over her head, placing it like an egg against the backboard and through the hoop. It may have been ten seconds later when Jamila steals the ball, pushing it down court in a three-on-one break, makes a no-look pass to Jen who just as quickly fires the ball across the lane to Kathleen for an uncontested layup. Whatever it is that started it, there is nothing Haverhill can do to stop it, and time-outs repeatedly called for by their hapless coach only fuel Amherst's frenzy further.

Even the sportscasters can't remember a 37 to 0 run in a state championship game. The halftime score is 51–6.

An astonished Amherst can hardly even cheer. One Amherst fan shouts: "Where's Dr. Kevorkian?" Another makes the very un-Amherst comment: "They should bring on the Haverhill boys for the second half."

Among the spectators is Kathleen's father, Donald Poe, an associate professor of psychology at Hampshire College, who saw how her defense, along with that of Kristin and Emily Shore, kept Haverhill's score so low. When his son, Chris, was an infant, Donald Poe tried to teach him to say "ball" as his first word, until he was told that "b" is a hard sound for a baby. He expected a son to be an athlete, and when Kathleen came along he didn't have that expectation. Yet whenever they go into the yard and she pitches a ball to him, it takes only five minutes before his hand hurts. She throws a heavy ball.

To him, what's important is not that Amherst win, but that the spirit of girls' sports endures. Next year, it doesn't have to be Amherst; it might be Westside in Springfield. Its junior varsity is undefeated. When he was in W. T. Woodson High School in Fairfax, Virginia, the girls were not allowed to use the boys' gym, which was fancy and varnished with a logo in the middle of the floor. The girls had a little back gym, without bleachers. After a game, whenever he saw the little kids asking his daughter for autographs, he was glad to see the girls, pleased that they now had models. But he was just as glad to see the boys asking; to him their respect for the girls' team was just as important.

The final score is 74–36.

After receiving the trophies and after collapsing in one huge hysterical teen-age heap, they all stand up. First they sing "Happy Birthday" to Kristin Marvin, who turns eighteen this day. Then they extend their arms toward their parents, teachers, brothers, sisters, even to some of those 140 little girls whose parents have allowed them a school night of unprecedented lateness, and in one final act as a team, these girls shout, in the perfect unison that has served them so well on the court, "*Thank you.*"

Back in the locker room, Kristin Marvin sucks on orange slices and sloshes water on her face. She then stands on a back bench, raises her right fist, turns to her comrades and shouts: "Holy #@&*! We're the *@#&*@# champions!" And then she loses it. For the next half-hour, she throws herself into the arms of one teammate after another. She cries and hugs, and hugs and cries, and so do they.

Coach keeps knocking at the door, trying to roust the stragglers. Finally, he announces he is coming in and what greets him is a roomful of girls who return his level gaze with eyes that are rheumy and red as they sputter "last . . . final . . . never again."

He looks right at them and says: "You're wrong. This isn't the last. There will be more basketball." His tone is conversational, almost adult to adult.

"But. . ." they start to say.

"I promise you. There will be lots more basketball."

Still they regard him with disbelief. They can't decipher his real message, at least not at this moment. They can't fathom how the word "basketball" might have more than one meaning.

Over. The game was over. On the way home, they watched a videotape of the game. Jen was stunned at how it had all fallen into place: "We were so fluid it was scary." While they watched themselves, television viewers all over the state were witnessing recaps of the highlights and hearing the verdicts of professional commentators who claimed these girls had wandered into the wrong league: They shoulda been playing Calipari's men at U Mass; they coulda taught the Celtics a thing or two.

The girls would hear all that in the days to come, but at this moment they were mostly thinking about the present—when truth itself had become a dream. The bus was going backward, retracing its earlier path, down the Pike back through Palmer, where the only sense of abundance is in the fast-food stores, then through Bondsville with its gin mill and the sunken rusty playground with a metal fence, back through the center of Belchertown, a singularly flat stretch in a town with a singularly unfortunate name, and back in and out of Pelham—thanks to Jen, on the map at last.

Kathleen Poe wished that the whole team could sleep that night in the gym at the high school, the coziest, most homey, softest place she could now imagine, that they could all sink into its floor, become part of it forever. She kept trying out rhymes in her head, phrases popping into her mind like sudden rebounds: top and stop, pride and ride, forever and sever, heart, smart, true, you.

> *Hoop Phi is one of an intangible, untouchable breed,*
> *It satisfies the soul, and a life-long need.*
> *We represented our school, represented our sex,*
> *Now maybe both will get some well-earned respect.*

No one really wanted the ride to end. The bare trees, the velvety night air, the cocoon of the bus itself.

At the town line there awaited another police escort, this time back into town. The cruiser was once again full of proud, slow ceremony. At the corner of Main and Triangle, the cruiser seemed to lurch right to take the short-cut back to the school, but then as if that was only a feint, it continued to move forward, so that the girls would be brought through town the long way.

The bus, boisterous in its very bigness, moved past the red-bricked Dickinson homestead with its top-heavy trees, tall and thin with a crown of green: *We're somebody; who are you?* Downtown was almost empty save for a couple of pizza eaters in the front window of Antonio's and a lone worker sweeping in the back shadows of Bart's Ice Cream. As the strobe lights from the cruiser bounced off the storefronts, the bus wheezed past St. Bridget's and the bagel place, turning right, then left, finally pulling into the school parking lot a few minutes shy of midnight.

All of a sudden one of the players shouted: "There are people there, waiting for us!" And, indeed, in the distance was a small crowd standing in the cold and in the dark, clapping.

When the bus came to a stop, Coach stood up. "I promise it won't be mushy. There's just one thing you should know. When you're the state champions, the season never ever ends. I love you. Great job. And now, I'd like everybody else on the bus to please wait so that the team can get off first."

Often the Hurricanes will bound off a bus in a joyous squealing clump. On this night, they rose from their seats, slowly, in silence. *State champs!* For the final time this season, with great care bordering on tenderness, the teammates gathered their stuff, their uniforms, their shoes, their socks, their game faces, and their courage. And then in a decision that was never actually articulated but seemed to have evolved as naturally as the parabola of a perfect three-pointer, the Hurricanes waited for captain Jen Pariseau to lead the way, which she did, and one by one the rest of the women followed, with captain Jamila Wideman the last of the Hurricanes to step off the bus into the swirling sea of well-wishers and winter coats.

Overhead the sky was as low-hanging and as opaque as it had been earlier in the evening, but it didn't need stars to make it shine.

E. Jean Carroll

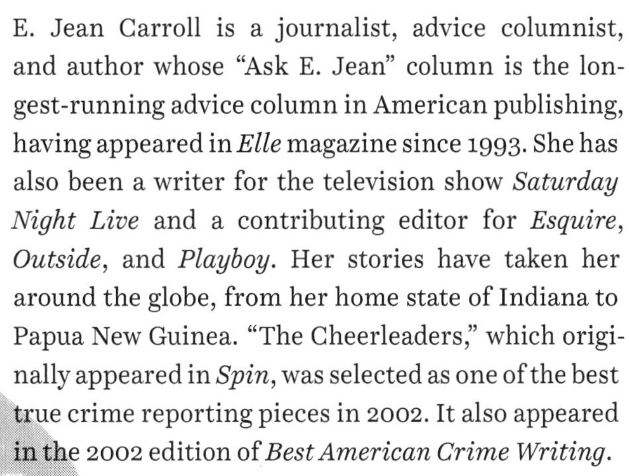

E. Jean Carroll is a journalist, advice columnist, and author whose "Ask E. Jean" column is the longest-running advice column in American publishing, having appeared in *Elle* magazine since 1993. She has also been a writer for the television show *Saturday Night Live* and a contributing editor for *Esquire*, *Outside*, and *Playboy*. Her stories have taken her around the globe, from her home state of Indiana to Papua New Guinea. "The Cheerleaders," which originally appeared in *Spin*, was selected as one of the best true crime reporting pieces in 2002. It also appeared in the 2002 edition of *Best American Crime Writing*.

Carroll is the author of four books: *Female Difficulties: Sorority Sisters, Rodeo Queens, Frigid Women, Smut Stars, and Other Modern Girls*; *A Dog in Heat Is a Hot Dog and Other Rules to Live By*; *Hunter: The Strange and Savage Life of Hunter S. Thompson*; and *Mr. Right, Right Now*.

In 2012 Carroll founded the matchmaking service Tawkify. She also developed the mobile app, Damn Love, a send-up of modern dating apps where players can ruin (virtual) relationships. A native of Fort Wayne, Indiana, she attended Indiana University in Bloomington. She currently lives in upstate New York.

The Cheerleaders

The tiny town of Dryden, New York, endures a strange, five-year string of murders, car accidents, and suicides—all of it tied to two popular high school cheerleaders.

Welcome to Dryden. It's rather gray and soppy. Not that Dryden doesn't look like the finest little town in the universe—with its pretty houses and its own personal George Bailey Agency at No. 5 South Street, it could have come right out of *It's a Wonderful Life*. (It's rumored the film's director, Frank Capra, was inspired by Dryden.) But the thriving, well-heeled hamlet is situated on the southern edge of New York's Finger Lakes region, under one of the highest cloud-cover ratios in America. This puts the nineteen hundred inhabitants into two philosophical camps: those who feel the town is rendered more beautiful by the "drama" and "poetry" of the clouds and those who say it's so "gloomy" it's like living in an old lady's underwear drawer.

If you live in Dryden, the kids from Ithaca, that cradle of metropolitan sophistication fifteen miles away, will say you live in a "cow town." ("There's a cow pasture right next to the school!" says one young Ithacan.) But Dryden High School, with its emerald lawns, running tracks, athletic fields, skating pond, pine trees, and 732 eager students, is actually a first-rate place to grow up. The glorious pile of salmon-colored bricks stands on a hill looking out on the town, the mountains, the ponds, and the honey-and-russet-colored fields stretching as far as the eye can see. In the summer, the Purple Lions of Dryden High ride out to the fields and the ponds and build bonfires that singe the boys' bare legs and blow cinders into the girls' hair.

In the summer of '96, many bonfires are built. The girls are practicing their cheerleading routines and the boys are developing great packs of muscles in the football team's weight room; everybody laughs and everybody roars and the fields around town look like they've been trampled by a pride of actual lions. In fact, the Dryden boys display such grit at the Preseason Invitational football game that fans begin to believe as the players do: that the upcoming season will bring them another division championship. This spirit lasts until about 6:30 p.m. on September 10, when Scott Pace, one of the most brilliant players ever to attend the school, the unofficial leader of the team, a popular, handsome, dark-haired senior, rushes out of football practice to meet his parents and is killed in a car crash.

It is strange. It is sad. But sadder still is the fact that Scott's older brother, Billy, a tall, dazzling Dryden athlete, as loved and admired as Scott, had been killed in a car crash almost exactly one year before. The town is shaken up very badly. But little does anyone dream that Scott Pace's death will be the beginning of one of the strangest high school tragedies of all time: how, in four years, a stouthearted cheerleader named Tiffany Starr will see three football players, three fellow cheerleaders, and the beloved football coach of her little country school all end up dead.

At a home football game, Friday evening, October 4, 1996, three weeks after the death of Scott Pace, townspeople keep talking about the team and the school "recovering" and "pulling together," but the truth is, nobody can deal. To the students of Dryden High, it just feels as if fate or something has messed up in a major way, and everybody seems as unhappy as can be.

The game tonight, in any case, is a change. Tiffany Starr, captain of the Dryden High cheerleaders, arrives. The short-skirted purple uniform looks charming on the well-built girl with the large, sad, blue eyes. Seventeen, a math whiz, way past button-cute, Tiffany is on the student council, is the point guard on the girls' basketball team, and has been voted "Best Actress" and "Class Flirt." She hails from the special Starr line of beautiful blonde cheerleaders; her twin sisters, Amber and Amy, graduated from Dryden two years before. Their locally famous father, Dryden High football coach Stephen Starr, has instilled in his daughters a credo that comes down to two words: "Be aggressive!"

And right now the school needs cheering. Though her heart is breaking for Scott, Tiffany wants to lead yells. But as she walks in, the cheerleading squad looks anxiously at her, and one of them says, "Jen and Sarah never showed up at school today."

"What?" says Tiffany.

Tiffany taught Jennifer Bolduc and Sarah Hajney to cheer, and her first thought is that the girls, both juniors on the squad, are off somewhere on a lark. Tiffany knows Sarah's parents are out of town and that Jen spent last night at Sarah's house. For a moment, Tiffany imagines her two friends doing something slightly wicked, like joy-riding around Syracuse. "But then I'm like, 'Wait a minute. . . .'"

"Being a cheerleader at Dryden is the closest thing to being a movie star as you can get," says Tiffany's sister Amber. "It's like being a world-class gymnast, movie star, and model all in one. It is fabulous! *Fab-u-lous!* It's so much fun! Because we *rule*."

The Dryden High girls have won their region's cheerleading championships twelve years in a row. The girls' pyramids are such a thrill, the crowd doesn't like it when the cheer ends and the game begins.

"I'm like, 'Hold on, Jen and Sarah would *never* miss a game,'" Tiffany continues. "So the only thing we can do is just wait for them to arrive. And we wait and we wait. And finally, we walk out to the football game and sit down in the bleachers. We don't cheer that day. Well, we may do some sidelines, but we don't do any big cheers because you can't do the big cheers when you're missing girls."

Jen Bolduc is a "base" in the pyramids (meaning she stands on the ground and supports tiers of girls above her), and Sarah Hajney is a "flyer" (meaning she's hurled into the air). At sixteen, Jen is tall and shapely, a strong, pretty, lovable girl with a crazy grin and a powerful mind. She is a varsity track star, a champion baton-twirler, and a volunteer at Cortland Memorial Hospital.

"Jen is a great athlete and a wonderful cheerleader," says Tiffany. "Really strong. And she's so happy! All the time. She's constantly giggling. And she's very creative. When we make Spirit Bags for the football players and fill them up with candy, Jen's Spirit Bags are always the best. And she's silly. Joyful. Goofy. But she's a very determined person."

"Jen is always doing funny things," says Amanda Burdick, a fellow cheerleader, "and she's smart. She helps me do my homework. I never once heard her talk crap about people."

Sarah Hajney is an adorable little version of a Botticelli Venus. She's on varsity track and does volunteer work for children with special needs. "She's a knockout," says former Dryden football player Johnny Lopinto. "I remember being at a pool party, and all the girls, like Tiffany and Sarah, had changed into their bathing suits. And I was walking around, and I just like bumped into Sarah and saw her in a bathing suit, and I was just like, 'Oh my God, Sarah! You're so beautiful!'"

As the football game winds down to a loss, and Sarah does not suddenly, in the fourth quarter, come racing across the field with a hilarious story about how Jen got lost in the Banana Republic in Syracuse, the anxious cheerleaders decide to spend the night at their coach's house. "And we go there, and we begin to wait." says Tiffany. "And we wait and we wait and we wait and we wait."

Before the game is over, a New York state trooper is in Sarah Hajney's house. "I get a phone call on Friday night, October 4, at about—I should say, my *wife* gets a phone call, because I'm taking the kids to a football game and dropping them off," says Major William Foley of the New York State Police.

Major Foley (at the time of the girls' disappearance he is Captain Foley, zone commander of Troop C Barracks, which heads up the hunt) is a trim man in enormous aviators, a purple tie modeled after the sash of the Roman Praetorian guard, and a crisply ironed, slate-gray uniform. The creases in his trousers are so fierce they look like crowbars are sewn into them.

Sitting with Foley in the state trooper headquarters in Sidney, New York, is the young, nattily dressed Lieutenant Eric Janie, a lead investigator on the girls' disappearance. "I know Mr. and Mrs. Bolduc because I lived in Dryden," says Foley. "Ron Bolduc calls me because he's concerned he's not going to get the appropriate response from the state police. A missing sixteen-year-old girl—*this happens all the time*. So I call Mr. Bolduc back and say I will look into it. And what I do is, I ask that a fellow by the name of Investigator Bill Bean be sent. This is unusual for us to send an investigator for a missing girl. We'd normally send a uniformed trooper who'd assess the situation, but in this case [as a favor to Mr. Bolduc], Investigator Bean is the first to arrive at the Hajney residence. And he quickly determines there's cause for concern."

The Hajney house, a snug, one-story dwelling with a big backyard, is outside Dryden, in McLean, a hilly old village settled in 1796. The village houses are done up in pale gray and mauve and preside over lawns so neat and green they look like carpeting. Wishing wells and statues of geese decorate the yards, flags flutter on porches, and there's a farm in the middle of town.

"There are a lot of people, concerned family members, inside the house," says Janie. "And the first obvious fact is: There's a *problem* in the bathroom."

"There are signs of a struggle," says Foley. "The shower curtain has been pulled down: the soap dish is broken off." On the towel rack is Jen's freshly washed purple-and-white cheerleading skirt. Sarah's skirt is discovered twirled over a drying rack in the basement.

"We start treating it as a crime scene," says Janie. "Sarah's parents have gotten the call [they are in Bar Harbor, Maine, for a four-day vacation] and are on their way back."

The first break in the case occurs almost immediately: The Hajneys' Chevy Lumina, which was missing, is found about seven miles from the house in a parking lot of the Cortland Line Company, a well-known maker of fly-fishing equipment. "The trunk is forced open by one of the uniformed sergeants," says Foley, "because we don't know, of course: *Are the girls in the trunk*?"

The trunk reveals that the girls have, in fact, been inside. Investigators tear the car apart and find, among other things, mud, pine needles, charred wood, blood, and diamond-patterned fingerprints suggesting the kidnapper wore gloves, meaning this wasn't some freak accident or a hot-headed crime of passion. This was planned.

Outside the Hajney home, waiting behind the yellow police tape in the cold night, is the other flyer on the cheerleading squad, Katie Savino. Small, with sparkling dark eyes and the merriest laugh, more like a sylph than a human girl, Katie is Sarah's best friend. She watches the troopers go in and out of the house, and waits—full of hope—to speak to an official. What no one knows yet is that Katie could have been the third girl in the trunk. She had made plans to spend the night with Sarah and Jen but, at the last moment, decided to stay home.

Saturday dawns with diaphanous skies. The day is so sunny, so clear, that the natives, accustomed to clouds, find the silver-blue blaze almost disorienting. "It's a *beautiful* day," says Kevin Pristash, a student affairs administrator at State University of New York at Cortland, which is near McLean and Dryden. "And suddenly these posters go up all over town. GIRLS MISSING! It's very eerie. Rumors are rampant. State troopers are everywhere. Helicopters are flying overhead. I go to get gas, and an unmarked car pulls up, and two guys from different police units get out. They're *everywhere*."

Gary Gelinger, an investigator with the state police, is in McLean interviewing the neighbors of the Hajney family. The first kitchen table at which he is invited to sit on Saturday morning belongs to John and Patricia Andrews. Their six-year-old son, Nicholas, attends Dryden Elementary. From an upstairs bedroom, one can look down into the Hajneys' bathroom.

"John Andrews is *not* behaving appropriately," says Janie. "Isn't answering questions appropriately, doesn't seem to be aware of what's going on in the neighborhood. Investigator Gelinger reports back and just says: 'Nah, this isn't good. The next-door neighbor isn't good at all.'"

Back when he attends Dryden High, John Andrews is a bashful boy. The love of his life is cars. His old man has won a Purple Heart during one of his three tours in Vietnam: he's a "USA all the way" kind of religious alcoholic who believes in the belt and is strict about his rules. He beats John and his sisters, Ann and Deborah.

At Dryden, John finds a sweetheart, classmate Patricia McGory. They marry, and John joins the Air Force. At his German base, John allegedly, on two separate occasions, dons a ski mask and gloves and viciously attacks women who are young, attractive, and petite. They have long, fair hair and are his neighbors. He's found guilty of the second assault, dishonorably discharged, and sent to Leavenworth.

When John is released, he and Patricia (who, along with his family, insists on his innocence) buy a house in McLean, and he begins working the third shift as a lathe operator at the same company where his mother is employed, the Pall Trinity Micro Corporation, in Cortland. A year later, in August 1996, the Hajneys purchase the house next door to the Andrews, and John quickly becomes obsessed with their beautiful and dashing daughter.

While the troopers are trying to get ahold of military justice records and follow up leads on other suspects, the massive search has alarmed Tiffany Starr and the cheerleading squad. "We keep hearing different rumors all day Saturday after we go home from the coach's," says Tiffany. "The house where I live is five minutes from the place where Sarah and Jen have been kidnapped. Of course I go wild, thinking they're coming to get me next. We've been imagining that they're after cheerleaders. And Saturday night and Sunday it's just me and my mom at home [her twin sisters, Amber and Amy, are away at college], and everybody knows that. By Sunday, I'm freaking out. And I say, 'Mom, we have to leave now! We have to get out of here!' And my mom says, 'Okay, let's go.' And we throw our stuff in a bag. I can't be in that house another minute. I'm terrified. I'm sure somebody is gonna break in, and we just get in the car and go."

To fully understand Tiffany's dread, we must turn the clock back two years, to 1994, when Tiffany is a sophomore, her sisters are seniors, and their father is the Dryden High football coach. . . .

The Starrs live in a lovely two-story house at the end of a wooded cul-de-sac in the country village of Cortlandville, which, like McLean, feeds into Dryden High. In the backyard is a swimming pool where neighborhood kids scramble and laugh, and on the garage is a basketball hoop, where Stephen Starr shoots baskets with his girls. Coach Starr is admired; his wife, Judy, is clever and good-looking, and his three daughters are the goddesses of Dryden High.

"My family is perfect," says Tiffany. "Besides being the Dryden High School football coach, my dad is the assistant Dryden High girls' track coach, and he is a sixth-grade teacher at Dryden Elementary. With all his jobs, it's years and years before he finishes his master's degree, and I remember the day he comes home; he brings champagne, and he pops it, and my mother and he are so excited! They dream about growing old together and sitting out on our back porch. Mom wants to get one of these swings so they can sit out there while Amy, Amber, and I are at college."

"Dad's so funny," says Amy Starr.

"Dad sitting at dinner—" says Tiffany, laughing.

"The hat backward," says Amy.

"One of those mesh hats," says Tiffany, "backward, kind of sideways backward—"

"He calls me Pinny because I was so skinny," says Amy.

"Amber he calls Amber Bambi," says Tiffany, "and I'm Shrimp or Shrimper."

"And mom's Turtle, and he's Turkey," says Amber.

"Dad loves cookies," says Amy. "You come down to the kitchen, and there he is in the middle of the night, standing with the refrigerator door open. He can eat a whole bag of Oreos or Nutter Butters. He loves peanut butter."

"He dips the peanut butter out of the jar," says Tiffany, "and then dips the spoon into the vanilla ice cream. He's a very happy man."

"So I'm on my way up to bed," says Amber, "and he's on his way downstairs, he has a glass of milk and a plate of cookies, and for some reason this really overwhelming feeling comes over me. And I say, 'Dad! Wait!' And I say, 'Stop! I love you!' And I give him this *really* big hug, and he's like, 'I love you too, kiddo.' And he goes on downstairs. And that's the last time I see him alive."

In the fall of '94, a moody young boy from Truxton, New York, appears on the scene. A sulky rogue with dead-poet good looks, his name is J. P. Merchant and, needless to say, he's irresistible to young women. But romance has a trick of turning ugly when it comes J. P.'s way, and his last high school love affair ended in catastrophe.

Then he meets Amber Starr. She is not like the clingy, docile girls he'd known before. Amber is a Dryden cheerleader and a queen. They start dating. He falls in love; she doesn't. She breaks it off; a hole is burned into his life.

Merchant starts calling. He shows up. He knows Amber's schedule, her whereabouts, her friends. He tells her if they do not get back together he will kill himself. Amber is kind; she speaks with him for hours on the phone, "letting him down gently." In late December, he threatens to kill Amber's new boyfriend. Coach Starr is out of town, playing in a basketball tournament at his old high school, so Tiffany and Judy go to the Cortland County Sheriff on December 27 and file a complaint.

"Merchant is stalking my daughter!" says Judy. She asks for an order of protection. The sheriff arrests Merchant. Merchant's family posts bail: $500. Upon his release, he calls Amber and threatens her. Again, Tiffany and Judy go to the sheriff's department, this time with Amber. It is December 28. Judy begs the sheriff's department for help and protection.

On December 29, a sheriff's officer watches the Starrs' house. The officer goes home when his shift ends. No officer replaces him.

"Our dad raised us to be aggressive, says Tiffany. She lowers her voice in an impression of her father: "'Where's the aggression? *Dive* for the ball! Get in there!'"

"I don't know bow many times I heard *that*!" says Amy.

"'I don't want to hear the word *can't*,'" says Amber, imitating her dad. "'That's not part of our vocabulary in *this* house.'"

Late on December 29, Stephen Starr returns home, eats a plate of cookies, drinks a beer, and goes to bed. Early the next morning, as the family sleeps, J. P. Merchant shoots the locks off the Starrs' back door, climbs the stairs, and is startled to see Tiffany standing in her bedroom doorway.

He aims the Ithaca 20-gauge shotgun at her. "I am ready to die," Tiffany recalls. "I think for sure this is it. But something as simple as shutting my door keeps me alive. He is not after me. He wants Amber. He just isn't going to let anyone get in his way. And I don't try. I shut my door and let him go."

Forever after, Tiffany dreams of stepping into her closet, retrieving her baton, surging up behind him and striking him over the head. But J. P. Merchant moves on quickly—a matter of mere seconds—to Amber's bedroom. As he tells Amber to wake up, her father comes running to protect her.

J. P. shoots Stephen Starr dead with two blasts of the gun.

Somehow the girls and their mother manage to flee the house in their nightclothes. Merchant reloads his shotgun and follows. He fires into the woods at the edge of their house, believing they are hiding there. But the family goes in the opposite direction instead, racing across the yard to a neighbor's. J. P. starts to follow. . . .

Amy Starr suddenly grabs the tape recorder out of my hand and yells into it. "This is reality, people!" she says. "This *really* happened! OK?

We were straight-A students! We had friends. We were cheerleaders. We played sports. We had great lives!"

The Starr sisters are visiting my room at the Best Western Hotel outside Dryden. We have been out for an Italian dinner at the A-1 restaurant, and now the girls are sitting on the huge double-king bed in my room, looking through their high school scrapbooks, doing their best to sort through the painful memories. They've since moved on, entered college (Tiffany is graduating this month from the University of Maryland), and they work every day. "We've not done one thing to mess up," says Amy, who is engaged to marry a "terrific" young man next spring.

But the girls carry scars. They do not talk to strangers now. They do not give out their telephone numbers. They fasten their seat belts to drive one hundred yards across a parking lot. They bolt their bedroom doors. If Russell Crowe appears with a sword, they walk out of the theater. It's six years later, and they still wake in the middle of the night, their hearts beating wildly. But the Starrs are prevailing. Not the growing-up sort of prevailing that most twenty-one-year-olds experience, but the kind of prevailing that comes from being trampled and standing back up.

As for J. P. Merchant, he leaves the cul-de-sac by the Starr home and drives to the grave of his high school sweetheart, Shari Fitts. Shari had committed suicide three years earlier, while she was dating Merchant. There, he puts the gun to his head, pulls the trigger, and kills himself.

"The biggest mistake I made was not cutting off contact with J. P.," says Amber, who is dating now and seems quite happy. She takes the tape recorder out of Amy's hand and starts looking for the volume control. "Now I know, and I can tell other people." She finds the control, turns it up as high as possible, and yells: "*Cut off contact and get professional help*!"

There is silence for a moment. The girls are huddled together over the recorder, surrounded by pictures of themselves in their purple and white track uniforms, basketball uniforms, and cheerleading outfits, their long *Alice in Wonderland* hair tied up in white ribbons. But one picture, from early 1997, is different. It is of Tiffany's cheerleading squad. On each of their uniforms, the ribbons are black.

So is it any wonder Tiffany and Judy pack their bags and drive all the way to Tiffany's grandparents' house in Pennsylvania when Jen and Sarah disappear? As they're driving, the police are narrowing the suspects down to four—the Hajneys' neighbor, John Andrews, and three others. The hour is now approaching 10 p.m. on Sunday. A call comes in . . . like hundreds of other calls. It's a woman in her early thirties named Ann Erxleben, and she holds the key that will solve the case.

Ann is a pleasant brunette, a former class officer, yearbook editor, and member of the softball team at Dryden High. "I'm working at the hospital with Cheryl Bolduc, who is a nurse," says Ann. "And when I hear about the girls missing, I can't even *begin* to imagine the pain Mrs. Bolduc's going through. Then something strange happens.

"My fiancé, Bruno Couture, and I own a hunting camp out in Otselic. [In this part of the country, the word *camp* is used to describe a cabin or lodge on rustic acreage.] A friend of ours, Marcus Hutcheon, has gone up to stay there Friday night. And when he walks in, the place is dark, but he notices a puddle on the floor. A friend of his comes in and shines a flashlight on it and says it looks like blood.

"So I say, 'I think we need to go up there and check it out.' So we get a hold of Marcus, and we drive up to the camp. It's a small place—a basic hunting camp, one room, a loft, a wood stove. Marcus shows us the spot on the floor. It looks like somebody—" Ann's voice falter. "There's been a puddle, a dried puddle, and I'm scared.

"So we drive to the troopers' barracks in Norwich. There isn't anybody there, so we have to call somebody to come. I'm the one who calls. I say, 'Look, we've found blood in our camp.' I feel suddenly guilty. Call it instinct.

"So a trooper arrives, and we drive back up to the camp. The trooper goes inside. He's very nonchalant. He comes out and asks, 'Do you know any people from McLean?' Well, obviously, Bruno has been raised there, and I grew up around there. And he asks us if anybody from McLean has been up there. And I answer 'friends and family.' And the trooper says, 'Well, I've called the barracks in Cortland, and we need to wait for them to come.'

"The Cortland troopers come. It's very dark now. They take a look in the camp and start interviewing Marcus. Then they interview Bruno. Then they turn to me and ask me who I am. I say I'm Bruno's fiancée. And one of the troopers asks if any of my family and friends live near the girls.

"Both Bruno and Marcus look at me. They're waiting for me to make the call as to what to say. I've decided beforehand—it's the only way I can live with my conscience—that I will volunteer no information unless they ask me *directly*. And I look at the trooper and I say, 'Yes, my brother.' And the trooper says, 'Has anybody you know that lives near the girls been up to this camp?' And I say, 'Yes, my brother.' And he says, 'Who is your brother?' And I say, 'John Andrews.'

"And the trooper flies by me so quickly he almost knocks me down. He runs into the camp and starts screaming for the senior investigator. And at that point I just want to vomit. Because my gut instinct is right. I love him, but the kidnapper is my brother, John."

"Ann's done the right thing," says Major Foley from behind his oak desk in the state trooper headquarters. "When the sun comes up at the camp, of course, it's obvious. Because we start to find. . . ."

He stops.

"Parts of the girls," says Lieutenant Janie. "Body parts."

Foley adjusts himself in his chair and tilts his head away with a rush of emotion. "Well, I will tell you what," he says, quietly. "Here is something we will never go into. The details of the torture of those two lovely girls."

Silence.

"We arrested John Andrews," concludes Janie, "Monday at work."

Three days earlier, the day the girls never show up to the football game, John Benjamin Andrews, wearing a dark T-shirt and jeans, ducks under the Hajneys' garage door. He cuts the phone wires. Over his thinning dark hair and fleshy cheeks, he pulls a brown ski mask. He knows there is going to be a mess, so he puts on yellow rubber gloves, the kind people wear to wash dishes. The door to the kitchen is unlocked. He enters, turns, and creeps down the steps to Sarah's room.

What does this grotesque, greasy-eyed nightmare carrying a bag holding duct tape, extra yellow gloves, and six knife blades look like to her? He weighs close to 250 pounds. His bulk must overpower the small, vibrant girl. He binds the little flyer with black plastic ties and seals her mouth with duct tape.

Is he surprised to hear the shower running? Does he realize two girls are in the house? Does he know that Jen Bolduc—whose might and muscle have tossed entire squads of cheerleaders in the air—does he know that courageous Jen will stand and fight? He must be amazed when he lurches into the bathroom and Jen claws him, kicks him, and, who knows, slams him in the face with the shower caddy. John Andrews is out of shape, but he has many knives; she is naked and outweighed by well over a hundred pounds. Sarah and Jennifer are soon trapped in the trunk of the Lumina.

Going the speed limit, the trip to the Otselic camp takes an hour. It is a curvy, up-and-down road. One of Sarah's greatest pleasures in life is to lie down full-length in the back of her brother's pickup, gaze up at the stars, and, as he drives round and round, guess where she is. Now they are passing June's Country Store in Otselic. Now they are turning up Reit Road. It is bumpy. They are passing a farm. The farmer's dog must be barking. The girls are disciplined athletes, trained to think under pressure. Are they planning an escape? Are they making a pact? They are folded together like fawns, and no matter what, as Tiffany and the cheerleading squad say, "These two girls are *there* for each other."

The cabin and its pond are about a thousand yards off Reit Road in Otselic, on the edge of Muller Hill State Forest. At some point John Andrews builds a bonfire. At some point he tortures the girls. He cuts Jen and Sarah into small pieces. He drives back down Reit Road, throwing bloody body parts out the window. He heads toward a state game land and disposes of more. He sloshes motor oil over himself, the front seat, and the dash to conceal clues and leaves the car at Cortland Line Company. He tosses the yellow gloves in a trash can.

"Well, what can I tell you?" says Major Foley. "There's a driving force. A lust. A desire. Mr. Andrews was *going* to attack those girls. Whether he knew Jennifer was there, we'll never know. But he was *going* to commit this crime. What drove him to do it? The easiest answer is a three-letter word: Sin. People do things that are wrong because they *want* to. That's all."

"What makes us do things?" says Ann Erxleben. "What makes us *not* do things? What pushed my brother over the edge? The police tell us it was some kind of woman-hate crime. Because of the way the bodies were mutilated. But John *idolized* my mother."

In 1985, John Andrews's father, Jack, was accused of sexually abusing young girls. He killed himself three years later with a 12-gauge shotgun. Did the son blame the girls? Was he so ashamed and angry that he took revenge against young women for his father's suicide?

Looking for answers about her brother and father has not been easy for Ann. But she is not grim, not somber. She smiles and says what doesn't kill her makes her stronger. She has baked delicious blueberry muffins for me to eat during this interview. She is relatively happy now, the mother of four comely young daughters—a toddler, twins who are athletes, and her oldest daughter, now in college, who was a cheerleader. "It's a little scary for me to think that, in a lot of ways, we both were caring, giving people," Ann says of her brother. "We both were raised the same way; we both were taught the same values, we both were told to do unto others as you would have them do unto you. I said it's scary because I don't know what would make him do what he did."

When word comes on Monday, October 7, Dryden High decides to send notes to the classrooms. "Each teacher has to read to the students that Sarah and Jen have been found and that they are definitely dead," says Tiffany. "When the teachers read the notes to the classes, people jump out of their seats and run down the hallways, screaming. Everybody gathers in the gym and just screams and just cries and cries. And then people speed out to the parking lots, and they just, like . . . *leave*."

Superintendent of Schools Donald Trombley is quoted in the *Ithaca Journal*: "It is unbelievable hysteria."

"I'll never get over it," says Tiffany. "As a female, it's the most terrifying thing to imagine happening to you. Sixteen! They are sixteen! Young women are so protective of their bodies, about being touched . . . and then the way they're killed is so bad. And the question we keep asking is: *Why does it keep happening to us, our town, our group of people?*"

Before the school makes the announcement to the students, Katie Savino, Sarah's best friend, the raven-haired, high-bouncing flyer, the *third girl*, is taken out of class and told privately. On hearing the news, she runs toward Sarah's locker and collapses.

On Saturday, November 2, one day after being indicted on twenty-six counts of murder, kidnapping, aggravated sexual abuse, auto theft, burglary, and criminal possession of a weapon, John Andrews hangs himself in his jail cell with his shoelaces.

Scott and Tiffany's class graduates in 1997. Sarah and Jen's class graduates in 1998. In June 1999, Gary Cassell, the young Dryden High athletic director and the man who became a surrogate father to the Starr sisters, dies of a sudden heart attack. Three days later, Judy comes home from work and softly knocks on Tiffany's bedroom door. She asks Tiffany to get Amy and to come out to the living room. One glance at her mom's pale, twisted face, and Tiffany is terrified.

"And we come out in the living room and we sit down. And mom just says . . . 'Katie Savino.'"

Only two prisoners are receiving visitors today at the Tioga County Jail in Oswego, New York. One prisoner is a young curly-haired woman who is accused of killing her three-year-old child. The other is Cheryl Thayer, who has pleaded guilty to killing Katie Elizabeth Savino.

Katie graduated from Dryden and went on to the State University of New York at Oswego. When news of her death roared across the Finger Lakes region on the morning of June 11, 1999, the home of the Purple Lions was forced to shut down completely. Students simply could not believe Katie was dead.

"We felt like we're living in the Village of the Damned," says a student who described Katie as "the most popular girl who ever lived." "We were mad," says Tiffany. After standing strong through her father, Billy, and Scotty, this one was "just *way* too much"—she became physically ill upon hearing the news. "We're like, '*When is this going to stop?*'"

Twenty-three hundred people attended the memorial service for the cheerleader who pulled a whole school back to something like normality after Jen's and Sarah's deaths. "She really believed Sarah and Jen were with her," says her mother, Liz Savino. "She was always smiling. I mean, she always *glowed*. Katie didn't make friends; she took hostages. She never left a room without a hug and a 'Bye, I love you!' I miss her terribly. I miss her horribly."

"Before Jen and Sarah died, Katie was so innocent," says Tiffany. "I don't think she'd kissed a boy until she was a senior in high school. *If* then. She was very smart, did really well in school, and she was friends with *everybody*. Then when Sarah died, Katie took a lot of her clothes and wore them. She wore Sarah's belt every day. I think it really terrified her that she was supposed to have been [at Sarah's house the night of the kidnapping]. And then on top of it, she lost her best friend in the most painful way that you could possibly imagine."

Katie's killer is tall and slender with lovely, dark, deep-set eyes, black eyebrows, and dark hair pulled high in a ponytail. Long wisps fall across her forehead as she sits very straight on her stool, her narrow shoulder blades drawn back elegantly. She is nineteen and pretty enough that, even in her orange prison pants and top, she looks like she stepped out of a Tommy Hilfiger ad.

"Katie was my best friend," Cheryl says, and immediately a large tear fills the comer of her eye. "I was leaving for California the next day, so Katie stayed and partied with me at a place in Cortland that serves kids drinks."

The tear falls against the side of her nose and begins to roll down—not down the type of burly, pockmarked face one sees in prison movies, but the face of a young girl with her hair pulled up in a scrunchy. It is disconcerting. "Katie and I were refused service because of our age." Cheryl says. "So we both just drank out of our friends' drinks. We left around two o'clock in the morning. When we got to the car. I could feel alcohol in my system, so I called shotgun. And Katie would *never* drive if she's even had one sip of a drink.

"I told the three guys we were taking home that one of *them* should drive," she continues. "But the guys all said they were too wasted. So that's how I ended up behind the wheel, even though I'm from Ithaca and I didn't know the roads. Also the seating arrangement was weird. Katie was sitting in the seat behind me. The guy in the middle was huge. Normally, Katie would have been in the middle.

"I was driving her home first. She told me to take the back roads because they were quicker. I had no idea where we were going." It was so dark, Cheryl had the creepy feeling that if she stuck her arm out the window she would never see it again. Curves appeared suddenly, but even worse were the hills. She missed a turn. Katie laughed and made her stop the car and turn around. Cheryl lost all sense of direction but dutifully took the road Katie told her to take. A minute later. . . .

"I didn't see the stop sign," Cheryl says, "and we got hit by the truck. It was so *dark*!" It's half a cry, and it strikes terror in my heart to hear it. "I didn't know the roads! I didn't see the sign! It's two-thirty in the morning. The roads are deserted. And here comes this *truck* out of nowhere! We were dragged a couple hundred yards under the truck and the car caught on fire. As soon as the truck got stopped, the three guys climbed out. There were flames. My door was wedged closed. The truck driver pulled me out. The moment I was taken out of the car, it exploded."

"Cheryl," I say, "people in Dryden are saying Katie's screams could be heard as the flames shot through the car."

"No," Cheryl says. She waves her hand in vigorous denial. A yellow plastic ID band circles her thin, girlish wrist. Burns are still visible on her slender arms.

"I know Katie didn't die afraid," says Liz Savino. "But I have many, many nightmares about whether she was awake at the end. If she was, that would have been horrific. Absolutely horrific."

"Was Katie conscious at the end, Cheryl?"

Her upper lip trembles, but she speaks with certainty. "I think she was killed the moment the truck hit us. Katie was my best friend. I loved Katie. Everybody loved Katie. Katie was always laughing or shouting. We would have heard her if she were alive."

Liz, a small, personable woman, says she does not want to punish Cheryl Thayer. She remembers that when Katie was applying to colleges, one of her essays talked about sitting at Scott Pace's funeral and holding Jen and Sarah's hands. Liz Savino would like to think "that Katie's life was not in vain," and she believes that if Cheryl is given a chance, she will "teach others a lesson": Don't get in a car with someone who's been drinking. So Liz and her ex-husband, Jim Savino, working with the Cortland district attorney, have asked that Cheryl be released from prison in six months and begin five years' probation. (She was released last summer and is taking classes at Tompkins-Cortland Community College in Dryden.)

"I tried to do what Katie would have wanted," says Liz. "Katie was a true, loyal friend. My way of handling my daughter's death is to live the legacy she would have wanted . . . to try to open myself up to others and be less judgmental. I'm not certain I'm as successful as she was, but I'm certainly trying. I truly believe she is guiding me."

Visiting hour is over. Cheryl must return to her cell. She stands with reluctance. She squares her slender shoulders and turns to go. There is a half moment to ask one last question: Katie escaped fate the first time by not spending the night at Sarah's. . . .

"But fate made *sure* it met Katie," says Cheryl.

Three months after attending Katie's memorial service, her good friend Mike Vogt, the class clown and Dryden High's IAC Division All Star middle linebacker, walks out to a cabin in the woods. Mike is red-haired, big-muscled, fast, born to play football. He's funny, a musician, and absolutely notorious in Dryden for his pranks. Mike drinks real beer onstage in a school play. Mike takes Chris Fox's car, parks it at the school's archery center, and covers it with condoms he steals out of the nurse's office. Mike loves "mudding" and buries all kinds of vehicles up to their axles in the big open fields around Dryden.

"Mikey's my best friend since first grade," says Johnny Lopinto, who played football with him. "I never remember doing *anything* without him. We could be in the shittiest place in the world, and we would hate to be there, but as long as we were together, it was like everything was a big show and we were the only ones watching it. But Mikey was complicated," Johnny adds.

Mike was depressed by Katie's death and probably never got over the loss of his Dryden teammate Scott Pace three years earlier. "Maybe he wanted to protect us from his pain." says Johnny. "The morning after my twenty-first birthday, he walked out to the woods to the cabin that we built when we were younger, and he put a 12-gauge to his head."

"Jill [Yaeger, Tiffany's best friend and fellow Dryden cheerleader] called me at school," says Tiffany. "She was hysterically crying. She was like, 'I'm gonna tell you straight out: Mike killed himself.' It was the *last* thing I thought I was ever going to hear. I *never* prepared myself to have one of my friends kill themselves." She sighs. "When I think about Mike," she says with a sad chuckle, "I can't think about anything but his red hair."

That is the end of the story.

The last Dryden High class that really knew Billy, Scott, Sarah, Jen, Katie, and Mike is graduating this year. And the town? "It's weird, but young death almost seems to be the norm here," says the mother of a Dryden Elementary School student. The town's dead boys and girls live on in legend now. How mythic, how beloved they've become is seen at the graves of the three cheerleaders. They are buried together high on a hill outside McLean.

The graves are simple, but they're laden with a blanket of every kind of memento the townspeople can carry up to the cemetery—stuffed bears, angels, flowers, lighted candles, crosses, butterflies, letters wrapped in see-through sandwich bags, photographs, lip balms [Katie was known for wearing three or four different flavors at a time], poems, ribbons, purple lions, megaphones, sparkle nail polish, and on and on.

On a cold, gray day, Tiffany and Jill agree to take me on a drive. As we go, Tiffany and Jill stare dejectedly out the windows.

"It's gloomy here," says Tiffany.

"It has to do with the elevation or something," says Jill.

"It's usually overcast," says Tiffany.

"Too many corn fields," says Jill.

"Tiffany," I say, "when you get married, do you want to live here?"

"No!" says Tiffany. She smacks the steering wheel lightly.

"Jill, do you want to live here when you—"

"*Absolutely not!*" says Jill.

Indeed, when Tiffany pictures the future—she's a 4.0 student with several job offers—the town of Dryden doesn't even enter into it. She can't afford to buy a car at present, but her "biggest freedom thought," she says, is this:

"I see myself flying down some highway in my new Mustang convertible with the Verve's 'Bitter Sweet Symphony' blasting. I can just see myself flying down the highway, far away, with my hair blowing and just being happy and free! That will be the day that I take this cleansing breath. And life will have been good for a while. And it will be forever."

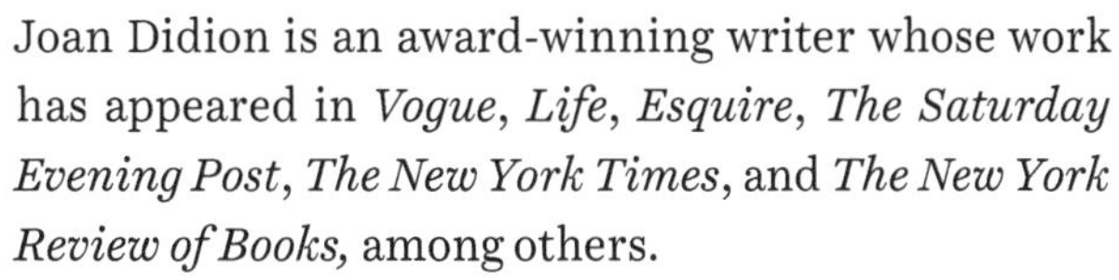

Joan Didion

Joan Didion is an award-winning writer whose work has appeared in *Vogue*, *Life*, *Esquire*, *The Saturday Evening Post*, *The New York Times*, and *The New York Review of Books,* among others.

Didion is the author of a dozen nonfiction books, including *Slouching Towards Bethlehem*, *Political Fictions*, and *Where I Was From*. Her 2005 memoir, *The Year of Magical Thinking*, which chronicles the year following the death of her husband John Gregory Dunne, received a number of awards, including the 2005 National Book Award for Nonfiction. It was also a finalist for the Pulitzer Prize for biography/autobiography. She adapted the book into a play, which ran for twenty-four weeks in New York and was performed around the world.

In addition to her memoirs, Didion is the author of six screenplays and five works of fiction. She holds honorary Doctor of Letters degrees from both Harvard University and Yale University.

Didion was born and raised in Sacramento, California, where she lived for a good deal of her life. She attended University of California, Berkeley, and graduated with a bachelor of arts degree in English. She currently resides in New York.

Some Dreamers of the Golden Dream

In this New Journalism classic, a suburban California woman is convicted of burning her husband to death in their family Volkswagen.

This is a story about love and death in the golden land, and begins with the country. The San Bernardino Valley lies only an hour east of Los Angeles by way of the San Bernardino Freeway but is in certain ways an alien place: not the coastal the California of subtropical twilights and the soft westerlies off the Pacific but a harsher California, haunted by the Mohave just beyond the mountains, devastated by the hot dry Santa Ana wind that comes down through the passes at one hundred miles an hour and whines through the eucalyptus windbreaks and works on the nerves. October is the bad month for the wind, the month when breathing is difficult and the hills blaze up spontaneously. There has been no rain since April. Every voice seems a scream. It is the season of suicide and divorce and prickly dread, wherever the wind blows.

The Mormons settled this ominous country, and then they abandoned it, but by the time they left the first orange tree had been planted and for the next hundred years the San Bernardino Valley would draw a kind of people who imagined they might live among the talismanic fruit and prosper in the dry air, people who brought with them Midwestern ways of building and cooking and praying and who tried to graft those ways upon the land. The graft took in curious ways. This is the California where it is possible to live and die without ever eating an artichoke, without ever meeting a Catholic or a Jew. This is the California where it is easy to Dial-A-Devotion, but hard to buy a book. This is the country in which a belief in the literal interpretation of Genesis has slipped imperceptibly into a belief in the literal interpretation of *Double Indemnity*, the country of the teased hair and the Capris and the girls for whom all life's promise comes down to a waltz-length white wedding dress and the birth of a Kimberly or a Sherry or a Debbi and a Tijuana divorce and return to hairdressers' school. "We were just crazy kids," they say without regret, and look to the future. The future always looks good in the golden land, because no one remembers the past. Here is where the hot wind blows and the old ways do not seem relevant, where the divorce rate is double the national average and where one person in every thirty-eight lives in a trailer. Here is the last stop for all those who come from somewhere else, for all those who drifted away from the cold and the past and the old ways. Here is where they are trying to find a new life style, trying to find it in the only places they know to look: the movies and the newspapers. The case of Lucille Marie Maxwell Miller is a tabloid monument to that new life style.

Imagine Banyan Street first, because Banyan is where it happened. The way to Banyan is to drive west from San Bernardino out Foothill Boulevard, Route 66: past the Santa Fe switching yards, the Forty Winks Motel. Past the motel that is nineteen stucco tepees: "SLEEP IN A WIGWAM—GET MORE FOR YOUR WAMPUM." Past Fontana Drag City and the Fontana Church of the Nazarene and the Pit Stop A Go-Go; past Kaiser Steel, through Cucamonga, out to the Kapu Kai Restaurant-Bar and Coffee Shop, at the corner of Route 66 and Carnelian Avenue. Up Carnelian Avenue from the Kapu Kai, which means "Forbidden Seas," the subdivision flags whip in the harsh wind. "HALF-ACRE RANCHES! SNACK BARS! TRAVERTINE ENTRIES! $95 DOWN." It is the trail of an intention gone haywire, the flotsam of the New California. But after a while the signs thin out on Carnelian Avenue, and the houses are no longer the bright pastels of the Springtime Home owners but the faded bungalows of the people who grow a few grapes and keep a few chickens out here, and then the hill gets steeper and the road climbs and even the bungalows are few, and here—desolate, roughly surfaced, lined with eucalyptus and lemon groves—is Banyan Street.

Like so much of this country, Banyan suggests something curious and unnatural. The lemon groves are sunken, down a three- or four-foot retaining wall, so that one looks directly into their dense foliage, too lush, unsettlingly glossy, the greenery of nightmare; the fallen eucalyptus bark is too dusty, a place for snakes to breed. The stones look not like natural stones but like the rubble of some unmentioned upheaval. There are smudge pots, and a closed cistern. To one side of Banyan there is the flat valley, and to the other the San Bernardino Mountains, a dark mass looming too high, too fast, nine, ten, eleven thousand feet, right there above the lemon groves. At midnight on Banyan Street there is no light at all, and no sound except the wind in the eucalyptus and a muffled barking of dogs. There may be a kennel somewhere, or the dogs may be coyotes.

Banyan Street was the route Lucille Miller took home from the twenty-four-hour Mayfair Market on the night of October 7, 1969, a night when the moon was dark and the wind was blowing and she was out of milk, and Banyan Street was where, at about 12:30 a.m., her 1964 Volkswagen came to a sudden stop, caught fire, and began to burn. For an hour and fifteen minutes Lucille Miller ran up and down Banyan calling for help, but no cars passed and no help came. At three o'clock that morning, when the fire had been put out and the California Highway Patrol officers were completing their report, Lucille Miller was still sobbing and incoherent, for her husband had been asleep in the Volkswagen. "What will I tell the children, when there's nothing left, nothing left in the casket," she cried to the friend called to comfort her. "How can I tell them there's nothing left?"

In fact there was something left, and a week later it lay in the Draper Mortuary Chapel in a closed bronze coffin blanketed with pink carnations. Some two hundred mourners heard Elder Robert E. Denton of the Seventh-Day Adventist Church of Ontario speak of "the temper of fury that has broken out among us." For Gordon Miller, he said, there would be "no more death, no more heartache, and no more misunderstandings." Elder Ansel Bristol mentioned the "peculiar" grief of the hour. Elder Fred Jensen asked "what shall it profit a man, if he shall gain the whole world, and lose his own soul?" A light rain fell, a blessing in a dry season, and a female vocalist sang "Safe in the Arms of Jesus." A tape recording of the service was made for the widow, who was being held without bail in the San Bernardino County jail on a charge of first-degree murder.

Of course she came from somewhere else, came off the prairie, in search of something she had seen in a movie or heard on the radio, for this is a Southern California story. She was born on January 17, 1930, in Winnipeg, Manitoba, the only child of Gordon and Lily Maxwell, both schoolteachers and both dedicated to the Seventh-Day Adventist Church whose members observe the Sabbath on Saturday, believe in an apocalyptic Second Coming, have a strong missionary tendency, and, if they are strict, do not smoke, drink, eat meat, use makeup, or wear jewelry, including wedding rings. By the time Lucille Maxwell enrolled at Walla Walla College in College Place, Washington, the Adventist school where her parents then taught, she was an eighteen-year-old possessed of unremarkable good looks and remarkable high spirits. "Lucille wanted to see the world," her father would say in retrospect, "and I guess she found out."

The high spirits did not seem to lend themselves to an extended course of study at Walla Walla College, and in the spring of 1949 Lucille Maxwell met and married Gordon ("Cork") Miller, a twenty-four-year-old graduate of Walla Walla and of the University of Oregon dental school, then stationed at Fort Lewis as a medical officer. "Maybe you could say it was love at first sight," Mr. Maxwell recalls. "Before they were ever formally introduced, he sent Lucille a dozen and a half roses with a card that said even if she didn't come out on a date with him, he hoped she'd find the roses pretty anyway." The Maxwells remember their daughter as a "radiant" bride.

Unhappy marriages so resemble one another that we do not need to know too much about the course of this one. There may or may not have been trouble on Guam, where Cork and Lucille Miller lived while he finished his Army duty. There may or may not have been problems in the small Oregon town where he first set up private practice. There appears to have been some disappointment about their move to California: Cork Miller had told friends that he wanted to become a doctor, that he was unhappy as a dentist and planned to enter the Seventh-Day Adventist College of Medical Evangelists at Loma Linda, a few miles south of San Bernardino. Instead he bought a dental practice in the west end of San Bernardino County, and the family settled there, in a modest house on the kind of street where there are always tricycles and revolving credit and dreams about bigger houses, better streets. That was 1957. By the summer of 1964 they had achieved the bigger house on the better street and the familiar accouterments of a family on its way up: the $30,000 a year, the three children for the Christmas card, the picture window, the family room, the newspaper photographs that showed "Mrs. Gordon Miller, Ontario Heart Fund Chairman. . . ." They were paying the familiar price for it. And they had reached the familiar season of divorce.

It might have been anyone's bad summer, anyone's siege of heat and nerves and migraine and money worries, but this one began particularly early and particularly badly. On April 24 an old friend, Elaine Hayton, died suddenly; Lucille Miller had seen her only the night before. During the month of May, Cork Miller was hospitalized briefly with a bleeding ulcer, and his usual reserve deepened into depression. He told his accountant that he was "sick of looking at open mouths" and threatened suicide. By July 8, the conventional tensions of love and money had reached the conventional impasse in the new house on the acre lot at 8488 Bella Vista, and Lucille Miller filed for divorce. Within a month, however, the Millers seemed reconciled. They saw a marriage counselor. They talked about a fourth child. It seemed that the marriage had reached the traditional truce, the point at which so many resign themselves to cutting both their losses and their hopes.

But the Millers' season of trouble was not to end that easily. October 7 began as a commonplace enough day, one of those days that sets the teeth on edge with its tedium, its small frustrations. The temperature reached 102 degrees in San Bernardino that afternoon, and the Miller children were home from school because of Teachers' Institute. There was ironing to be dropped off. There was a trip to pick up a prescription for Nembutal, a trip to a self-service dry cleaner. In the early evening, an unpleasant accident with the Volkswagen: Cork Miller hit and killed a German shepherd, and afterward said that his head felt "like it had a Mack truck on it." It was something he often said. As of that evening Cork Miller was $63,479 in debt, including the $29,637 mortgage on the new house, a debt load which seemed oppressive to him. He was a man who wore his responsibilities uneasily, and complained of migraine headaches almost constantly.

He ate alone that night, from a TV tray in the living room. Later the Millers watched John Forsythe and Senta Berger in *See How They Run*, and when the movie ended, about eleven, Cork Miller suggested that they go out for milk. He wanted some hot chocolate. He took a blanket and pillow from the couch and climbed into the passenger seat of the Volkswagen. Lucille

Miller remembers reaching over to lock his door as she backed down the driveway. By the time she left the Mayfair Market, and long before they reached Banyan Street, Cork Miller appeared to be asleep.

There is some confusion in Lucille Miller's mind about what happened between 12:30 a.m.., when the fire broke out, and 1:50 a.m., when it was reported. She says that she was driving east on Banyan Street at about 35 m.p.h. when she felt the Volkswagen pull sharply to the right. The next thing she knew the car was on the embankment, quite near the edge of the retaining wall, and flames were shooting up behind her. She does not remember jumping out. She does remember prying up a stone with which she broke the window next to her husband, and then scrambling down the retaining wall to try to find a stick. "I don't know how I was going to push him out," she says. "I just thought if I had a stick, I'd push him out." She could not, and after a while she ran to the intersection of Banyan and Carnelian Avenue. There are no houses at that corner, and almost no traffic. After one car had passed without stopping, Lucille Miller ran back down Banyan toward the burning Volkswagen. She did not stop, but she slowed down, and in the flames she could see her husband. He was, she said, "just black."

At the first house up Sapphire Avenue, half a mile from the Volkswagen, Lucille Miller finally found help. There Mrs. Robert Swenson called the sheriff, and then, at Lucille Miller's request, she called Harold Lance, the Millers' lawyer and their close friend. When Harold Lance arrived he took Lucille Miller home to his wife, Joan. Twice Harold Lance and Lucille Miller returned to Banyan Street and talked to the Highway Patrol officers. A third time Harold Lance returned alone, and when he came back he said to Lucille Miller, "O.K. . . . you don't talk any more."

When Lucille Miller was arrested the next afternoon, Sandy Slagle was with her. Sandy Slagle was the intense, relentlessly loyal medical student who used to babysit for the Millers, and had been living as a member of the family since she graduated from high school in 1959. The Millers took her away from a difficult home situation, and she thinks of Lucille Miller not only as "more or less a mother or a sister" but as "the most wonderful character" she has ever known. On the night of the accident, Sandy Slagle was in her dormitory at Loma Linda University, but Lucille Miller called her early in the morning and asked her to come home. The doctor was there when Sandy Slagle arrived, giving Lucille Miller an injection of Nembutal. "She was crying as she was going under," Sandy Slagle recalls.

"Over and over she'd say, 'Sandy, all the hours I spent trying to save him and now what are they trying to *do* to me?'"

At 1:30 that afternoon, Sergeant William Paterson and Detectives Charles Callahan and Joseph Karr of the Central Homicide Division arrived at 8488 Bella Vista. "One of them appeared at the bedroom door," Sandy Slagle remembers, "and said to Lucille, 'You've got ten minutes to get dressed or we'll take you as you are.' She was in her nightgown, you know, so I tried to get her dressed."

Sandy Slagle tells the story now as if by rote and her eyes do not waver. "So I had her panties and bra on her and they opened the door again, so I got some Capris on her, you know, and a scarf." Her voice drops. "And then they just took her."

The arrest took place just twelve hours after the first report that there had been an accident on Banyan Street, a rapidity which would later prompt Lucille Miller's attorney to say that the entire case was an instance of trying to justify a reckless arrest. Actually what first caused the detectives who arrived on Banyan Street toward dawn that morning to give the accident more than routine attention were certain apparent physical inconsistencies. While Lucille Miller had said that she was driving about 35 m.p.h. when the car swerved to a stop, an examination of the cooling Volkswagen showed that it was in low gear, and that the parking rather than the driving lights were on. The front wheels, moreover, did not seem to be in exactly the position that Lucille Miller's description of the accident would suggest, and the right rear wheel was dug in deep, as if it had been spun in place. It seemed curious to the detectives, too, that a sudden stop from 35 m.p.h.—the same jolt which was presumed to have knocked over a gasoline can in the back seat and somehow started the fire—should have left two milk cartons upright on the back floorboard, and the remains of a Polaroid camera box lying apparently undisturbed on the back seat.

No one, however, could be expected to give a precise account of what did and did not happen in a moment of terror, and none of these inconsistencies seemed in themselves incontrovertible evidence of criminal intent. But they did interest the Sheriff's Office, as did Gordon Miller's apparent unconsciousness at the time of the accident, and the length of time it had taken Lucille Miller to get help. Something, moreover, struck the investigators as wrong about Harold Lance's attitude when he came back to Banyan Street the third time and found the investigation by no means over. "The way Lance was acting," the prosecuting attorney said later, "they thought maybe they'd hit a nerve."

And so it was that on the morning of October 8, even before the doctor had come to give Lucille Miller an injection to calm her, the San Bernardino County Sheriff's Office was trying to construct another version of what might have happened between 12:30 and 1:50 a.m. The hypothesis they would eventually present was based on the somewhat tortuous premise that Lucille Miller had undertaken a plan which failed: a plan to stop the car on the lonely road, spread gasoline over her presumably drugged husband, and, with a stick on the accelerator, gently "walk" the Volkswagen over the embankment, where it would tumble four feet down the retaining wall into the lemon grove and almost certainly explode. If this happened, Lucille Miller might then have somehow negotiated the two miles up Carnelian to Bella Vista in time to be home when the accident was discovered. This plan went awry, according to the Sheriff's Office hypothesis, when the car would not go over the rise of the embankment. Lucille Miller might have panicked then—after she had killed the engine the third or fourth time, say, out there on the dark road with the gasoline already spread and the dogs baying and the wind blowing and the unspeakable apprehension that a pair of headlights would suddenly light up Banyan Street and expose her there—and set the fire herself.

Although this version accounted for some of the physical evidence—the car in low because it had been started from a dead stop, the parking lights on because she could not do what needed doing without some light, a rear wheel spun in repeated attempts to get the car over the embankment, the milk cartons upright because there had been no sudden stop—it did not seem on its own any more or less credible than Lucille Miller's own story. Moreover, some of the physical evidence did seem to support her story: a nail in a front tire, a nine-pound rock found in the car, presumably the one with which she had broken the window in an attempt to save her husband. Within a few days an autopsy had established that Gordon Miller was alive when he burned, which did not particularly help the State's case, and that he had enough Nembutal and Sandoptal in his blood to put the average person to sleep, which did: on the other hand Gordon Miller habitually took both Nembutal and Fiorinal (a common headache prescription which contains Sandoptal), and had been ill besides.

It was a spotty case, and to make it work at all the State was going to have to find a motive. These was talk of unhappiness, talk of another man. That kind of motive, during the next few weeks, was what they set out to establish. They set out to find it in accountants' ledgers and double-indemnity clauses and motel registers, set out to determine what might move a woman who believed in all the promises of the middle class—a woman who had been chairman of the Heart Fund and who always knew a reasonable little dressmaker and who had come out of the bleak wild of prairie fundamentalism to find what she imagined to be the good life—what would drive such a woman to sit on street called Bella Vista and look out her new picture window into the empty California sun and calculate how to burn her husband alive in a Volkswagen. They found the wedge they wanted closer at hand than they might have at first expected, for, as testimony would reveal later at the trial, it seemed that in December of 1963 Lucille Miller had begun an affair with the husband of one of her friends, a man whose daughter called her "Auntie Lucille," a man who might have seemed to have the gift for people and money and the good life that Cork Miller so noticeably lacked. The man was Arthwell Hayton, a well-known San Bernardino attorney and at one time a member of the district attorney's staff.

In some ways it was the conventional clandestine affair in a place like San Bernardino, a place where little is bright or graceful, where it is routine to misplace the future and easy to start looking for it in bed. Over the seven weeks that it would take to try Lucille Miller for murder, Assistant District Attorney Don A. Turner and defense attorney Edward P. Foley would between them unfold a curiously predictable story. There were the falsified motel registrations. There were the lunch dates, the afternoon drives in Arthwell Hayton's red Cadillac convertible. There were the interminable discussions of the wronged partners. There were the confidantes ("I knew everything," Sandy Slagle would insist fiercely later. "I knew every time, places, everything") and there were the words remembered from bad magazine stories ("Don't kiss me, it will trigger things," Lucille Miller remembered telling Arthwell Hayton in the parking lot of Harold's Club in Fontana after lunch one day) and there were the notes, the sweet exchanges: "Hi Sweetie Pie! You are my cup of tea!! Happy Birthday—you don't look a day over twenty-nine!! Your baby, Arthwell."

And, toward the end, there was the acrimony. It was April 24, 1964, when Arthwell Hayton's wife, Elaine, died suddenly, and nothing good happened after that. Arthwell Hayton had taken his cruiser, *Captain's Lady*, over to Catalina that weekend; he called home at nine o'clock Friday night, but did not talk to his wife because Lucille Miller answered the telephone and said that Elaine was showering. The next morning the Haytons' daughter found her mother in bed, dead. The newspapers reported the death as accidental, perhaps the result of an allergy to hair spray. When Arthwell Hayton flew home from Catalina that weekend, Lucille Miller met him at the airport, but the finish had already been written.

It was in the breakup that the affair ceased to be in the conventional mode and began to resemble instead the novels of James M. Cain, the movies of the late 1930s, all the dreams in which violence and threats and blackmail are made to seem commonplaces of middle-class life. What was most startling about the case the State of California was preparing against Lucille Miller was something that had nothing to do with law at all, something that never appeared in the eight-column afternoon headlines but was always there between them: the revelation that the dream was teaching the dreamers how to live. Here is Lucille Miller talking to her lover sometime in the early summer of 1964, after he had indicated that, on the advice of his minister, he did not intend to see her any more: "First, I'm going to go to that dear pastor of yours and tell him a few things. . . . When I do tell him that, you won't be in the Redlands Church any more. . . . Look, Sonny Boy, if you think your reputation is going to be ruined, your life won't be worth two cents." Here is Arthwell Hayton, to Lucille Miller: "I'll go to Sheriff Frank Bland and tell him some things that I know about you until you'll wish you'd never heard of Arthwell Hayton." For an affair between a Seventh-Day Adventist dentist's wife and a Seventh-Day Adventist personal-injury lawyer, it seems a curious kind of dialogue.

"Boy, I could get that little boy coming and going," Lucille Miller later confided to Erwin Sprengle, a Riverside contractor who was a business partner of Arthwell Hayton's and a friend to both the lovers. (Friend or no, on this occasion he happened to have an induction coil attached to his telephone in order to tape Lucille Miller's call.) "And he hasn't got one thing on me that he can prove. I mean, I've got concrete—he has nothing concrete." In the same taped conversation with Erwin Sprengle, Lucille Miller mentioned a tape that she herself had surreptitiously made, months before, in Arthwell Hayton's car.

"I said to him, I said 'Arthwell, I just feel like I'm being used!'. . . He started sucking his thumb and he said 'I love you. . . . This isn't something that happened yesterday. I'd marry you tomorrow if I could. I don't love Elaine.' He'd love to hear that played back, wouldn't he?"

"Yeah," drawled Sprengle's voice on the tape. "That would be just a little incriminating, wouldn't it?"

"Just a *little* incriminating," Lucille Miller agreed. "It really *is*."

Later on the tape, Sprengle asked where Cork Miller was.

"He took the children down to the church."

"You didn't go?"

"No."

"You're naughty."

It was all, moreover, in the name of "love"; everyone involved placed a magical faith in the efficacy of the very word. There was the significance that Lucille Miller saw in Arthwell's saying that he "loved" her, that he did not "love" Elaine. There was Arthwell insisting, later, at the trial, that he had never said it, that he may have "whispered sweet nothings in her ear" (as her defense hinted that he had whispered in many ears), but he did not remember bestowing upon her the special seal, saying the word, declaring "love." There was the summer evening when Lucille Miller and Sandy Slagle followed Arthwell Hayton down to his new boat in its mooring at Newport Beach and untied the lines with Arthwell aboard, Arthwell and a girl with whom he later testified he was drinking hot chocolate and watching television. "I did that on purpose," Lucille Miller told Erwin Sprengle later, "to save myself from letting my heart do something crazy."

January 11, 1965, was a bright warm day in Southern California, the kind of day when Catalina floats on the Pacific horizon and the air smells of orange blossoms and it is a long way from the bleak and difficult East, a long way from the cold, a long way from the past. A woman in Hollywood staged an all-night sit-in on the hood of her car to prevent repossession by a finance company. A seventy-year-old pensioner drove his station wagon at five miles an hour past three Gardena poker parlors and emptied three pistols and a twelve-gauge shotgun through their windows, wounding twenty-nine people. "Many young women become prostitutes just to have enough money to play cards," he explained in a note. Mrs. Nick Adams said that she was "not surprised" to hear her husband announce his divorce plans on the Les Crane Show, and, farther north, a sixteen-year-old jumped off the Golden Gate Bridge and lived.

And, in the San Bernardino County Courthouse, the Miller trial opened. The crowds were so bad that the glass courtroom doors were shattered in the crush, and from then on identification disks were issued to the first forty-three spectators in line. The line began forming at 6 a.m., and college girls camped at the courthouse all night, with stores of graham crackers and No-Cal.

All they were doing was picking a jury, those first few days, but the sensational nature of the case had already suggested itself. Early in December there had been an abortive first trial, a trial at which no evidence was ever presented because on the day the jury was seated the San Bernardino *Sun-Telegram* ran an "inside" story quoting Assistant District Attorney Don Turner, the prosecutor, as saying, "We are looking into the circumstances of Mrs. Hayton's death. In view of the current trial concerning the death of Dr. Miller, I do not feel I should comment on Mrs. Hayton's death." It seemed that there had been barbiturates in Elaine Hayton's blood, and there had seemed some irregularity about the way she was dressed on that morning when she was found under the covers, dead. Any doubts about the death at the time, however, had never gotten as far as the Sheriff's Office. "I guess somebody didn't want to rock the boat," Turner said later. 'These were prominent people."

Although all of that had not been in the *Sun-Telegram's* story, an immediate mistrial had been declared. Almost as immediately, there had been another development: Arthwell Hayton had asked newspapermen to an 11 a.m. Sunday morning press conference in his office. There had been television cameras, and flash bulbs popping. "As you gentlemen may know," Hayton had said, striking a note of stiff bonhomie, "there are very often women who become amorous toward their doctor or lawyer. This does not mean on the physician's or lawyer's part that there is any romance toward the patient or client."

"Would you deny that you were having an affair with Mrs. Miller?" a reporter had asked.

"I would deny that there was any romance on my part whatsoever."

It was a distinction he would maintain through all the wearing weeks to come.

So they had come to see Arthwell, these crowds who now milled beneath the dusty palms outside the courthouse, and they had also come to see Lucille, who appeared as a slight, intermittently pretty woman, already pale from lack of sun, a woman who would turn thirty-five before the trial was over and whose tendency toward haggardness was beginning to show, a meticulous woman who insisted against her lawyer's advice, on coming to court with her hair piled high and lacquered. "I would've been happy if she'd come in with it hanging loose, but Lucille wouldn't do that," her lawyer said. He was Edward P. Foley, a small, emotional Irish Catholic who several times wept in the courtroom. "She has a great honesty, this woman," he added, "but this honesty about her appearance always worked against her."

By the time the trial opened, Lucille Miller's appearance included maternity clothes, for an official examination on December 18 had revealed that she was then three and a half months pregnant, a fact which made picking a jury even more difficult than usual, for Turner was asking the death penalty. "It's unfortunate but there it is," he would say of the pregnancy to each juror in turn, and finally twelve were seated, seven of them women, the youngest forty-one, an assembly of the very peers—housewives, a machinist, a truck driver, a grocery-store manager, a filing clerk—above whom Lucille Miller had wanted so badly to rise.

That was the sin, more than the adultery, which tended to reinforce the one for which she was being tried. It was implicit in both the defense and the prosecution that Lucille Miller was an erring woman, a woman who perhaps wanted too much. But to the prosecution she was not merely a woman who would want a new house and want to go to parties and run up high telephone bills ($1,152 in two months), but a woman who would go so far as to murder her husband for his $80,000 in insurance, making it appear an accident in order to collect another $40,000 in double indemnity and straight accident policies. To Turner she was a woman who did not want simply her freedom and a reasonable alimony (she could have had that, the defense contended, by going through with her divorce suit), but wanted everything, a woman motivated by "love and greed." She was a "manipulator." She was a "user of people."

To Edward Foley, on the other hand, she was an impulsive woman who "couldn't control her foolish little heart." Where Turner skirted the pregnancy, Foley dwelt upon it, even calling the dead man's mother down from Washington to testify that her son had told her they were going to have another baby because Lucille felt that it would "do much to weld our home again in the pleasant relations that we used to have." Where the prosecution saw a "calculator," the defense saw a "blabbermouth," and in fact Lucille Miller did emerge as an ingenuous conversationalist. Just as, before her husband's death, she had confided in her friends about her love affair, so she chatted about it after his death, with the arresting sergeant. "Of course Cork lived with it for years, you know," her voice was heard to tell Sergeant Paterson on a tape made the morning after her arrest." After Elaine died, he pushed the panic button one night and just asked me right out, and that, I think, was when he really—the first time he really faced it." When the sergeant asked why she had agreed to talk to him, against the specific instructions of her lawyers, Lucille Miller said airily, "Oh, I've always been basically quite an honest person. . . . I mean I can put a hat in the cupboard and say it cost ten dollars less, but basically I've always kind of just lived my life the way I wanted to, and if you don't like it you can take off."

The prosecution hinted at men other than Arthwell, and even, over Foley's objections, managed to name one. The defense called Miller suicidal. The prosecution produced experts who said that the Volkswagen fire could not have been accidental. Foley produced witnesses who said that it could have been. Lucille's father, now a junior-high-school teacher in Oregon, quoted Isaiah to reporters: *"Every tongue that shall rise against thee in judgment thou shalt condemn."* "Lucille did wrong, her affair," her mother said judiciously. "With her it was love. But with some I guess it's just passion." There was Debbie, the Millers' fourteen-year-old, testifying in a steady voice about how she and her mother had gone to a supermarket to buy the gasoline can the week before the accident. There was Sandy Slagle, in the courtroom every day, declaring that on at least one occasion Lucille Miller had prevented her husband not only from committing suicide but from committing suicide in such a way that it would appear an accident and ensure the double-indemnity payment. There was Wenche Berg, the pretty twenty-seven-year-old Norwegian governess to Arthwell Hayton's children, testifying that Arthwell had instructed her not to allow Lucille Miller to see or talk to the children.

Two months dragged by, and the headlines never stopped. Southern California's crime reporters were headquartered in San Bernardino for the duration: Howard Hertel from the *Times*, Jim Bennett and Eddy Jo Bernal from the *Herald-Examiner*. Two months in which the Miller trial was pushed off the *Examiner* front page only by the Academy Award nominations and Stan Laurel's death. And finally, on March 2, after Turner had reiterated that it was a case of "love and greed," and Foley had protested that his client was being tried for adultery, the case went to the jury.

They brought in the verdict, guilty of murder in the first degree, at 4:50 p.m. on March 5. "She didn't *do* it," Debbie Miller cried, jumping up from the spectators' section. "She didn't do it." Sandy Slagle collapsed in her seat and began to scream. "Sandy, for God's sake please *don't*," Lucille Miller said in a voice that carried across the courtroom, and Sandy Slagle was momentarily subdued. But as the jurors left the courtroom she screamed again: "You're murderers. . . . Every last one of you is a *murderer*." Sheriff's deputies moved in then, each wearing a string tie that read "1965 SHERIFF'S RODEO," and Lucille Miller's father, that sad-faced junior-high-school teacher who believed in the word of Christ and the dangers of wanting to see the world, blew her a kiss off his fingertips.

The California Institution for Women at Frontera, where Lucille Miller is now, lies down where Euclid Avenue turns into country road, not too many miles from where she once lived and shopped and organized the Heart Fund Ball. Cattle graze across the road, and Rainbirds sprinkle the alfalfa. Frontera has a softball field and tennis courts, and looks as if it might be a California junior college, except that the trees are not yet high enough to conceal the concertina wire around the top of the Cyclone fence. On visitors' day there are big cars in the parking area, big Buicks and Pontiacs that belong to grandparents and sisters and fathers (not many of them belong to husbands), and some of them have bumper stickers that say "SUPPORT YOUR LOCAL POLICE."

A lot of California murderesses live here, a lot of girls who somehow misunderstood the promise. Don Turner put Sandra Garner here (and her husband in the gas chamber at San Quentin) after the 1959 desert killings known to crime reporters as "the soda-pop murders." Carole Tregoff is here, and has been ever since she was convicted of conspiring to murder Dr. Finch's wife in West Covina, which is not too far from San Bernardino. Carole Tregoff is in fact a nurse's aide in the prison hospital, and might have attended Lucille Miller had her baby been born at Frontera; Lucille

Miller chose instead to have it outside, and paid for the guard who stood outside the delivery room in St. Bernadine's Hospital. Debbie Miller came to take the baby home from the hospital, in a white dress with pink ribbons, and Debbie was allowed to choose a name. She named the baby Kimi Kai. The children live with Harold and Joan Lance now, because Lucille Miller will probably spend ten years at Frontera. Don Turner waived his original request for the death penalty (it was generally agreed that he had demanded it only, in Edward Foley's words, "to get anybody with the slightest trace of human kindness in their veins off the jury"), and settled for life imprisonment with the possibility of parole. Lucille Miller does not like it at Frontera, and has had trouble adjusting. "She's going to have to learn humility," Turner says. "She's going to have to use her ability to charm, to manipulate."

The new house is empty now, the house on the street with the sign that says

PRIVATE ROAD
BELLA VISTA
DEAD END

The Millers never did get it landscaped, and weeds grow up around the fieldstone siding. The television aerial has toppled on the roof, and a trash can is stuffed with the debris of family life: a cheap suitcase, a child's game called "Lie Detector." There is a sign on what would have been the lawn, and the sign reads "ESTATE SALE." Edward Foley is trying to get Lucille Miller's case appealed, but there have been delays. "A trial always comes down to a matter of sympathy," Foley says wearily now. "I couldn't create sympathy for her." Everyone is a little weary now, weary and resigned, everyone except Sandy Slagle, whose bitterness is still raw. She lives in an apartment near the medical school in Loma Linda, and studies reports of the case in *True Police Cases* and *Official Detective Stories*. "I'd much rather we not talk about the Hayton business too much,"' she tells visitors, and she keeps a tape recorder running. "I'd rather talk about Lucille and what a wonderful person she is and how her rights were violated." Harold Lance does not talk to visitors at all. "We don't want to give away what we can sell," he explains pleasantly; an attempt was made to sell Lucille Miller's personal story to *Life*, but *Life* did not want to buy it. In the district attorney's offices they are prosecuting other murders now, and do not see why the Miller trial attracted so much attention. “It wasn’t a very interesting murder as murders go,” Don Turner says laconically. Elaine Hayton’s death is no longer under investigation. “We know everything we want to know,” Turner says.

Arthwell Hayton’s office is directly below Edward Foley’s. Some people around San Bernardino say that Arthwell Hayton suffered; others say that he did not suffer at all. Perhaps he did not, for time past is not believed to have any bearing upon time present or future, out in the golden land where every day the world is born anew. In any case, on October 17, 1965, Arthwell Hayton married again, married his children’s pretty governess, Wenche Berg, at a service in the Chapel of the Roses at a retirement village near Riverside. Later the newlyweds were feted at a reception for seventy-five in the dining room of Rose Garden Village. The bridegroom was in black tie, with a white carnation in his buttonhole. The bride wore a long white *peau de soie* dress and carried a shower bouquet of sweetheart roses with stephanotis streamers. A coronet of seed pearls held her illusion veil.

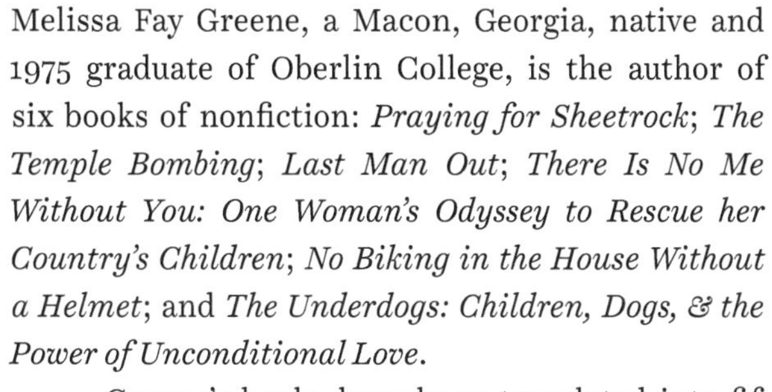

Melissa Fay Greene

Melissa Fay Greene, a Macon, Georgia, native and 1975 graduate of Oberlin College, is the author of six books of nonfiction: *Praying for Sheetrock*; *The Temple Bombing*; *Last Man Out*; *There Is No Me Without You: One Woman's Odyssey to Rescue her Country's Children*; *No Biking in the House Without a Helmet*; and *The Underdogs: Children, Dogs, & the Power of Unconditional Love*.

Greene's books have been translated into fifteen languages and have been honored with two National Book Award nominations, a National Book Critics Circle Award nomination, the Robert F. Kennedy Book Award, the Southern Book Critics Circle Award, the Salon Book Prize, the ACLU Civil Liberties Award, and the Hadassah Myrtle Wreath Award. She holds an honorary doctorate from Emory University, was a 2011 Georgia Writers Hall of Fame inductee, and was a 2015–2016 Guggenheim Fellow.

In 1999, *Praying for Sheetrock* was named one of the one hundred best works of English-language journalism of the twentieth century by the faculty of New York University. *Entertainment Tonight* named it one of the "New Classics: The Best One Hundred Books of the Last Twenty-Five Years."

Greene has also written for *The New Yorker, The New York Times Magazine, The Atlantic, Newsweek, The Washington Post, The Boston Globe, LIFE, Elle, Reader's Digest, Good Housekeeping,* and other periodicals, and she has been a frequent guest on CNN, National Public Radio, and NPR-affiliate stations.

Greene and her husband, defense attorney Don Samuel, live in Atlanta. They are the parents of nine children.

Wonder Dog

How a family struggling with a child's serious cognitive and behavioral disabilities finds peace and reassurance with an assistance dog.

In May 1999, Donnie Kanter Winokur, forty-three, a writer and multimedia producer, and her husband, Rabbi Harvey Winokur, forty-nine, beheld the son of their dreams, the child infertility denied them. Andrey, a pale dark-eyed one-year-old in a cotton onesie, held in a standing position by a caregiver, appeared in a short videotape recorded in a Russian orphanage. If the couple liked the little boy, they could begin the legal process of adopting him. They liked the little boy very much.

Four months later, the Winokurs flew to Russia from their home in Atlanta to adopt Andrey, whom they renamed Iyal, and to adopt an unrelated little girl two days younger, whom they named Morasha. All four appear in another orphanage video: the beaming new parents on the happiest day of their lives, the toddlers passive in the arms of the strangers cradling and kissing them. In August 1999, the family arrived home to congratulations, gifts, and helium balloons.

"Sometime after their third birthdays, our wonderful fairy tale of adopting two Russian babies began to show cracks," said Donnie Winokur, who is now fifty-five. She is pert and trim, with cropped brown hair and a pursed-lips, lemony expression softened by wearying experience. Unlike bright and cheery Morasha, Iyal grew oppositional and explosive. He was a sturdy, big-hearted boy with a wide and open face, shiny black hair in a bowl cut, and a winning giggle. But, triggered by the sight of a cartoon image on a plastic cup, or an encounter with Morasha's Barbie dolls, he threw tantrums that shook the house. He stuffed himself at mealtimes with an inexplicable urgency. In a fast-moving car, he unfastened his seat belt and tried to jump out. He awoke every night in a rage. "I had panic attacks in the night when I heard him coming," she said. "I assumed everything was my fault, that I was not a good-enough mother." In preschool, Iyal plowed his tricycle into other children without remorse, or maybe without awareness. He tried to kiss strangers, or feel their toes. Friends and congregants (Harvey Winokur is the founding rabbi of Temple Kehillat Chaim in Roswell, Georgia) who had assured the Winokurs, "He's all boy!" or "Mine was the same way!" began to fall silent, out of shared concern.

The rabbi wears a carefully trimmed brown beard, wire-rim glasses and a commiserative expression. "Iyal's disabilities began to define our family's existence," he told me.

We sat in their high-ceilinged kitchen in a suburb of Atlanta on a summer Sunday morning; sliding glass doors opened onto a redwood deck filled with flowers and bird feeders. Morasha, thirteen, cute and sporty, packed her pool bag for an outing with friends; Iyal, thirteen, played a video game alone in the den but checked in frequently, anxiously, to know when his mother's crumb cake would come out of the oven. Earlier that day, Morasha played the video game with her brother. In a realm in which they searched side by side for hidden treasure, there was peace between them. "Iyal, push the green button!" she ordered. "The green button! Iyal, steer the canoe!" He obeyed. But outside this virtual kingdom, he doesn't listen to her, especially when she begs him to leave her alone or to get out of her room. It's stressful for a young teenage girl to navigate middle school with a large inept brother lumbering through the same hallways, the target of gibes and ridicule.

For more than a year after Iyal's third birthday, child psychiatrists, pediatricians, and specialists examined him without reaching consensus. Finally he was seen by Alan G. Weintraub, a developmental pediatrician, who noted his small head, the small and widely spaced eye openings, the extra skin folds close to the nose, and the way the middle area of his face appeared flattened. When the little boy became anxious during the exam, he began making animal noises and tried to escape. He detected scary themes in benign pictures. The doctor's conclusion was a blow the Winokurs had not seen coming: Iyal's brain and central nervous system had been severely, irreversibly damaged in utero by the teratogen of alcohol, resulting in an incurable birth defect. Though alcohol consumption by Iyal's birth mother could not be documented, the available evidence pointed to fetal alcohol syndrome, F.A.S., the most extensive form of the range of effects known as fetal alcohol spectrum disorders, or F.A.S.D.

It is well known that maternal drinking can lead to neurobehavioral and growth impairments in a fetus, as well as malformations in the face, palate, joints, kidneys, genitals, heart, brain, and nervous system. There is no known safe window during pregnancy for alcohol consumption of any kind or quantity, according to Dr. Jacquelyn Bertrand of the National Center on Birth Defects and Developmental Disabilities of the Centers for Disease Control and Prevention. The U. S. surgeon general calls for total abstinence. C.D.C. estimates of the prevalence of F.A.S. in America range from 0.2 to 1.5 children per thousand live births, but this data may represent chiefly those children whose facial dysmorphia render them recognizable; the rest may appear physically typical while contending with hidden neurological damage.

It's possible that as many as one in one hundred children are born with some exposure to fetal alcohol. A.D.H.D., learning disability, or mental illness are just a few of the accompanying disorders that may be diagnosed instead. Adults who presented symptoms before the syndrome's description in the U.S. medical literature in the 1970s may never have been given an accurate diagnosis.

Iyal Winokur was intellectually impaired and at high risk for a range of secondary disabilities, including poor judgment, impulsive behavior, social isolation, limited academic achievement, unemployment, drug and alcohol abuse, imprisonment, mental-health problems including suicidal ideation, inability to live independently, and inappropriate sexual behavior. Few medications or therapies could be recommended as truly effective.

At seven, eight, and nine years of age, Iyal often babbled a nonstop stream of senseless chatter and baby talk. He required a full-time aide at school and his mother's undivided attention in the house. Donnie put aside her production career. Harvey juggled the needs of hundreds of congregants while facing escalating mayhem at home. But if their friends wondered what their lives would have been like if they hadn't adopted Iyal, the Winokurs would have reacted with horror. "It's unbearable to imagine our child growing up without us," Donnie says. "We never considered dissolving the adoption! We fell in love with our son." Still, she admits: "Staying in love with him has been trickier. People with brain injuries aren't able to reciprocate love in the ways you expect. You're struggling with this cluster of emotions toward your child—love, but also anger, bewilderment, resentment, frustration, and yearning."

As Donnie found her footing in the parallel universe of special-needs families, she discovered that a nonprofit service-dog agency in rural Ohio placed autism assistance dogs with children. Could a service dog help Iyal? "Are you kidding me?" cried her husband. "We don't need a dog!" He felt that one more howl raised under their roof, one more living creature whining for attention, one more source of strife between the children would push him beyond endurance. "No, Donnie. It's too much. I couldn't take it."

"This could be the help we need," she persisted.

"A dog?" Harvey said. "Forget about it, please. It's me or a dog."

Karen Shirk operates a dog-training school in Xenia, Ohio, a charming antebellum village flattened twice by tornadoes. Dressed in baggy jeans and a man's white T-shirt, swaying deeply as she walked, breathing through the metal button of a tracheotomy tube, she led me into her office at the far end of a brick building that once served as the local V.F.W. Hall. We waded into a crowd of bouncing ecstatic Papillons—toy dogs whose wide, silky ears inspired the breed's name, the French word for "butterfly." Though she stepped away only a moment earlier, the dozen little dogs rejoiced as if they'd feared never seeing her again: some spun in excitement, others leapt onto her desk, and one tap-danced along the computer keyboard. They raised their pointed little faces and emitted high-pitched yips of hallelujah. When Shirk, who is forty-nine, reached her desk chair, they settled on the floor at her feet, folded up their ears like kites and watched her. When she laughed, they took out their ears and waved them around.

As a young woman, Shirk pursued a master's degree in social work and held a full-time job with cognitively impaired adults. She felt, she says, "carefree," until the day she collapsed in respiratory distress and was rushed to an emergency room. Hospitalized for months, she received the grim diagnosis, at age twenty-four, of myasthenia gravis, a rare neuromuscular disease. She left the hospital only to become a respirator-dependent patient in need of constant care.

"Why don't you get a service dog?" a new nurse asked Shirk, six years into her illness. Supine in front of the TV, Shirk seemed unaware of the hour, day, or month. A dog could offer mobility assistance, the nurse said, like opening a drawer and bringing clean socks. She seemed also to suspect that a dog might jump-start the life of this sad and lonely patient.

"How could I take care of a dog?" Shirk rasped. "I can't even take care of myself."

"You could take care of a dog," the nurse said.

Beginning in 1992, Shirk applied by mail to service-dog agencies around the country. Every program rejected her. "They're not going to give a dog to a respirator-dependent individual who will never lead a productive life," she told the nurse. Finally she won a spot at the bottom of a waiting list. In 1994, a trainer visited to prepare for the placement of a golden retriever. Shirk began to feel strangely hopeful. But then the agency sent a letter instead of a dog: "Our guidelines prohibit the placement of service animals with people on ventilators."

"I didn't care if I lived or died after that," she told me, placing a fingertip over the metal knob in her throat to enable speech, in a voice that is winningly husky. "All I could see ahead of me was a long, slow death. I started stockpiling morphine."

"Karen," the nurse said, "get out of this bed, and let's go get you a puppy."

Feebly, she dressed herself in bed and crumpled forward into a wheelchair. The nurse drove her to see a litter of black German shepherd pups, the breed of Shirk's childhood dog, and there she found Ben. "I didn't leap back into life with Ben so much as inch back into it," she said. The puppy had to be taken outside, and to obedience classes. Wherever he frolicked, strangers greeted the tubed-up woman in the motorized wheelchair, as they did not when she was alone. It was a lesson Shirk wouldn't forget.

When year-old Ben graduated from puppy classes, he was a gorgeous animal with a shiny coal-black pelt, orange-flecked brown eyes, and a feathery tail. He wasn't a complex thinker or problem-solver. But he was smart, and she loved him.

She acquired a wheelchair-adapted van and commuted to a dog-training school in Columbus, where Jeremy Dulebohn, a crew-cut man from rural Ohio, taught Ben the basics of mobility work: to open and close doors and drawers; to hand Shirk's wallet to retailers and return it with change to her lap; to brace her for balance as she moved from bed to wheelchair and back; and to remove her shoes, socks, and jeans at bedtime. "When I asked for water, Ben opened the refrigerator and brought me a bottle," she told me. "When I asked for laundry, he pulled my clean clothes out of the dryer, put them in a basket and dragged them over."

Dogs evolved over at least fifteen thousand years to know and like humankind as well as, or better than, we know and like ourselves. Like many German shepherds, Ben was a one-person dog. He seemed to watch Shirk closely when she returned to her apartment following open-heart surgery. "I had a daytime nurse but was alone at night," she says. "I was on a morphine pump and—though I didn't realize it—a deadly combination of drugs. I slipped into unconsciousness." When the phone rang, Ben waited—as he'd been trained to do—for Shirk's command to answer it rather than to let it ring into the answering machine. But that night, with his owner failing, Ben picked up the receiver without her command, dropped it on the bed and barked and barked. It was Shirk's father. Realizing something was wrong, her father hung up and called 911. The rescue team told Shirk she wouldn't have lived through the night.

With Ben at her side, Shirk became manager of a day care facility for cognitively impaired adults. Gaining in strength and confidence, with new medications allowing her to come off the ventilator during the day, she wondered how many other people were being told they were "too disabled" to get a dog. "I could start my own agency," she thought. "I could place four or five dogs a year with people rejected by the big agencies." She mentioned the idea to coworkers and almost instantly heard from a couple seeking a mobility dog for their twelve-year-old daughter, who'd been paralyzed by a spinal stroke. Their impression was that no service-dog agency worked with children.

Shirk studied the Americans With Disabilities Act governing service animals and found no legal impediment to placing a dog with a child if a parent served as cohandler. In October 1998, she assembled a board and founded 4 Paws for Ability, a nonprofit corporation. She rescued Butler, a German shepherd mix, from a shelter; hired a trainer to prepare him for mobility work with the twelve-year-old; and became a pioneer among service-dog agencies. "People started calling from all over to ask, Am I too young? Am I too old? Am I too disabled? Am I disabled enough?" she says. "I said, 'If your life can be improved by a dog, and if you and your family can take good care of a dog, we're going to give you a dog.'"

A couple with a ten-year-old son on the autism spectrum called 4 Paws. This was new ground. Placing dogs with adults with "invisible disabilities" like post-traumatic stress disorder or seizure disorder was the cutting edge of service-dog work; it hadn't been widely tried with children. Patches, a rescue-hound mix, became one of the world's first dogs trained for autism assistance for a child.

In 2001, Dulebohn joined 4 Paws full time as training director. Today he oversees an expanding staff of trainers, vets, groomers, and dog-walkers. The dogs are a mix of shelter dogs, donated dogs, and puppies bred in-house, and every one gets five hundred hours of training, well beyond the 120-hour industry standard. "Any breed can become a service dog," says Dulebohn, who is thirty-seven, "but, over time, we found that roughly 70 percent of Labradors, golden retrievers and German shepherds graduated from our program, while only about 2 percent of other breeds made the cut." It costs $22,000 to train a 4 Paws dog; clients are asked to contribute $13,000 to the organization, with the difference made up through charitable donations and grants. To date, 4 Paws has placed more than six hundred dogs.

For socialization, Dulebohn places foster puppies with local families, and for basic obedience training he places them with specially chosen inmates in regional prisons. "Convicted murderers cry when it's time to give back their dogs," Shirk says. "But we give them another one." Since most 4 Paws dogs go to children—and children want playmates more than they want therapists and trackers—Dulebohn asks the prisoners to teach their pups tricks, including "Roll over," "Speak," "Gimme five," and "Play dead."

"I learned with Ben that a dog helps you make friends," Shirk says. "We place dogs with kids in wheelchairs, kids on ventilators, kids with autism, kids with dwarfism, kids with seizure disorder and cognitive impairments; but if your dog does tricks, other kids want to meet you. Kids will ignore your disability if you've got a cool dog."

One prisoner with a sense of humor returned a dog who—upon hearing the command "Play dead"—lurched, as if shot, staggered across the floor, knelt, got up, buckled, whined piteously, and then dramatically collapsed.

Cool dog. Lucky kid.

In 2007, a phone call came into 4 Paws from an Atlanta mother of a boy with special needs. Iyal Winokur's doctors had tried twenty different medications without lasting success. Iyal was nine; his I.Q. was eighty and falling; his language was primitive. He got hooked on bizarre thoughts and repeated them endlessly. He still suffered from night terrors and bed-wetting. Sometimes Iyal touched his mother's shirt, sniffed his fingers, and tried to wipe off the smell. Aware that a majority of individuals living with fetal alcohol syndrome also fight mental illness, his parents feared impending schizophrenia or psychosis.

"Do you place dogs with children who have fetal alcohol syndrome?" the mother asked Shirk.

"Never heard of it."

Donnie Winokur, who had by then founded the Georgia affiliate of the National Organization on Fetal Alcohol Syndrome, explained with rapid and precise diction.

"Is your son likely to verbally abuse a dog?" Shirk asked.

"Well, yes," Donnie had to admit, at a reduced speed.

"Is he likely to try to physically abuse a dog?"

"It's not impossible," she said, now certain of rejection.

"O.K.," Shirk said. "We'll need a doctor's prescription and we'll need video. We want to see your son every day, everywhere—getting up in the morning, eating breakfast, getting in a car, at school, at bedtime. We need to hear his noises and see his tantrums."

"You'll give us a dog?" Donnie gasped.

That night at home, Harvey gasped, too. "Thousands of dollars for a dog?" he cried. "Instead of for a nanny, or respite care, or a private school? Does that make sense? A dog's not going to mean anything to Iyal."

"It might."

"You're talking about a dog with a vest like a seeing-eye dog? It will be embarrassing to go into public like that!"

"It's already embarrassing to go into public with Iyal, especially for Morasha."

"But a dog in a vest will make him seem so disabled."

"A dog in a vest will tell people that he acts like this because he's living with a disability."

She wore him down. He loved her, trusted her judgment, and knew she wasn't going to give up.

In January 2008, Donnie, her father, her first cousin, and her children drove to Xenia for a ten-day class with other special-needs families and their new dogs. In the parking lot at 4 Paws, parents carried, coaxed, dragged, pushed, chased, and wheeled their children toward the front door. A circle of threadbare sofas, sunken love seats, and canvas sports chairs surrounded a training area in the former V.F.W. social hall. In an inner room, pet crates and pens held dogs of all ages and sizes—two hundred dogs are in training at all times—while dog-walkers, vets, and groomers came and went through the side door. The building smelled fragrantly of dog, with undertones of ammonia.

For children with autism or behavior disorders, dogs were trained in "behavior disruption." For children with seizure disorder or diabetes or respiratory issues, dogs were trained to alert the parents at the onset of an episode, and there have been a few able to predict the medical incidents six to twenty-four hours in advance. (How they do this is something of a mystery.)

"The dogs are nonjudgmental," Dulebohn tells each class. "You've got a kid who's picking his nose? The dog isn't thinking, That is gross. He's thinking, Save one for me! Or your child has disappeared and you say: 'Find Jeffrey.' The dog isn't thinking, Jeffrey's in danger! The dog thinks: *Game on*!"

About 10 percent of 4 Paws placements fail. "Some fail because parents weren't prepared for how much extra work a dog would be," Shirk says. "They can barely get themselves and their special-needs child out the door; adding a dog feels overwhelming." Others fail because it's not a good match. A family's video may not have reflected the severity of behavior. "A child looks gentle on his video, so we place a soft dog," Shirk says. "Then the child's violent meltdowns scare the dog, and he starts avoiding the child." Dulebohn and Shirk try to discourage clients from engaging in "the Lassie syndrome": the belief that a devoted, sensitive, and brilliant dog will gallop into their lives and make everyone feel better.

And yet, sometimes, that's what families get.

Dulebohn matched Iyal with Chancer, a big, good-humored golden retriever with "high self-esteem" who wouldn't be hurt or insulted by the boy. Chancer was originally purchased as a puppy from Mervar Kennel in Youngstown by a family that lost interest in him; he was returned, after a year, overweight, matted, undisciplined, and lonely. Knowing that 4 Paws successfully placed Mervar dogs in the past, Judy Mervar donated Chancer. Like all 4 Paws dogs, he was shown kindness and affection in the course of his training, but he was not offered a long-term close human friendship. "Once dogs have been matched with families, we pet them and love them, but we don't give them that intense, 'I love you so much, you're my baby' kind of one-on-one attention," Shirk says. "We don't take them home with us at night. Every one of our dogs wants that closeness, is primed for that closeness; but we want them to find it with their families, not with our staff." Chancer didn't know what he was missing. But his trainers knew. "Chancer," Dulebohn says, "really needed a boy."

The dog's deeply encoded desire to attach to humans came alive when he was introduced to the Winokurs. A shaggy, tawny giant, he panted and wagged with pleasure. Something similar, on the human side, was sparked, too. Morasha dropped to her knees and embraced Chancer's big neck. Donnie felt like doing the same. "Hi, hi, hi good boy," she cooed, stroking his broad handsome head. Iyal was briefly interested but then wandered off.

They were in a hard stretch with Iyal. He was throwing tremendous rages daily, and instantly did it here. "I'm so sorry," Donnie said, mortified, unable to budge the explosive boy from the dog-training circle on the very first morning. But she was among friends; special-needs parents all, they patiently waited for Iyal's tantrum to die down. Unfortunately, on a lunch break in town, Iyal lost control again and threw a fit in the drive-through lane at Wendy's. He crossed his arms, sat down hard and bawled. The backed-up drivers looked at Donnie with less empathy than had the 4 Paws parents. Shirk says, "Iyal really needed a dog."

At the conclusion of the second day's class, the families were invited to keep their dogs overnight for the first time. At the hotel, Donnie's cousin took Chancer outside for a walk while Donnie supervised Iyal and Morasha in a hot tub in the indoor pool area. "When they came back from their walk," she says, "Chancer looked around, and then broke away! I thought: Oh, my God, he's escaping. We're going to lose him. He streaked past everybody in the solarium and took a flying leap into the hot tub. He was saving Iyal!"

Chancer had not been trained to do water rescue. Why he leapt unnecessarily into a hot tub is hard to know. Shirk thinks that after thirty-six hours, Chancer had bonded to Iyal. The reverse, though, may not have been true yet. Part of the havoc wreaked by alcohol on a child's brain is to scramble the emotional pathways. The routes to friendship, fun, intimacy, and love are underdeveloped or buried under cognitive roadblocks. But Iyal's burst of laughter when the big yellow dog came sailing through the air and clumsily exploded into the hot tub was the greatest sound his mother had heard out of him in a long time.

The morning after Chancer's first night in the house outside Atlanta, the Winokurs woke up after a full night's sleep for almost the first time since 1999. They looked at each other in semihorror: was Iyal still alive? They found him snoozing beside the big yellow dog, the latter hogging the mattress. Since Chancer's arrival in the house, they've rarely been disturbed in the night. Iyal may still wake up, but he's evidently reassured by the dog's presence and returns to sleep.

"The moment he walked in the house with Chancer, I knew something had changed," Harvey says. "I could feel it instantly, the magnetism between Iyal and the dog. . . . Chancer was an emotional and physical anchor for a kid who was pretty lost in the world."

When Iyal is distressed, Chancer is distressed. Unlike Iyal, Chancer knows what to do about it. Iyal rages by crossing his arms, sitting down hard on the floor, and screaming and kicking. Chancer unknots the crossed arms by inserting his wide muzzle through the locked arms from below, opening them up and nuzzling toward Iyal's face, licking and slobbering, until the boy's screams turn to tears of remorse or to laughter.

Chancer sometimes heads off tantrums before they start. If a tutor or a therapist has worked with Iyal in the dining room a bit too long, Chancer moves between the visitor and the boy, clearly relaying: We're done for today. From two floors away, he will alert, flicking his ears, tuning in. Sensing that Iyal is nearing a breaking point, he gallops up or down the stairs to find him, playfully head-butts and pushes him down to the floor, gets on top of him, stretches out and relaxes with a satisfied groan. Helplessly pinned under Chancer, Iyal resists, squawks, and then relaxes, too. The big dog lies on top of the boy he loves, and seals him off from the dizzying and incomprehensible world for a while.

When I ask Dulebohn about Chancer's preternatural sensitivity, he says: "We trained Chancer to disrupt tantrums. Being able to prevent tantrums is coming from subtle training within the family. He may be reading Donnie's body language or facial expressions, or he may be smelling some chemical changes in Iyal or hearing some noises from him that predict a tantrum. He feels rewarded when Iyal stabilizes."

Donnie says: "Lately, and this is the best yet: if Iyal gets distressed, he goes to find Chancer, and he curls up next to him. He picks up Chancer's big paw and gets under it." It's the closest the boy has come to mood self-regulation.

Two weeks after Chancer's arrival, Iyal startled his parents by using multisyllabic words. He was suddenly possessed of opinions, judgments, and important questions, and he expressed them.

"B.C., Before Chancer," Donnie says, "which is how we refer to our life then, Iyal echoed Morasha word for word. It drove her nuts. Every morning I asked, 'Do you want to take your lunch today or eat lunch at school?' and every morning Iyal parroted whatever Morasha said. If she said, 'School,' he said, 'School.' With his frontal-lobe damage, decision-making like that was difficult for him. One morning, A.C., when I asked about lunch, Morasha said, 'School,' and Iyal said, 'I'd rather have lunch from home than a school lunch.' It was a more sophisticated expression of his thoughts than we'd ever heard.

"B.C., driving in the car with Iyal, if I turned down an unfamiliar route, he might say, 'What happened?' A.C., sensing I'd taken a wrong turn, Iyal asked: 'Were you distracted by Chancer and that's why you made a bad turn?' That showed an understanding of cause and effect, and a high-level word choice.

"B.C., Iyal never mentioned his disability, although we have educated him about it. A.C., he suddenly started asking things like, 'Did Chancer's birth mother drink alcohol?' and 'Does Chancer have a boo-boo on his brain?' and 'Why did my birth mother drink alcohol?'"

Before Chancer, Iyal didn't seem to possess "theory of mind," the insight, usually achieved by age four, that other people have points of view different from your own. But Chancer has inspired him to think about what

Chancer likes and what Chancer wants and what Chancer thinks. Only since the dog's arrival has Iyal shown sheepishness or regret following a tantrum, signaling a new awareness that his outbursts may affect others. "Is Chancer mad at me?" he asks his parents. "Mommy, tell Chancer I love him, O.K.?"

"The sad flip side of 'theory of mind,'" Donnie says, "is that Iyal is deathly afraid that if he misbehaves too much, Chancer will want to be someone else's dog. We'll be in a park, and he'll tell me that Chancer is smiling at another kid and wants to be his dog."

The science behind Iyal's cognitive leaps is still in its infancy. Alan M. Beck, the director of the Center for the Human-Animal Bond at Purdue University's College of Veterinary Medicine, is among those intrigued by it. "There is a real bond between children and animals," he told me. "The younger the child, the greater the suspension of disbelief about what an animal understands or doesn't understand." According to Beck, more than 70 percent of children confide in their dogs, and 48 percent of adults do. "The absolutely nonjudgmental responses from animals are especially important to children," he says. "If your child with F.A.S.D. starts to misbehave, your face may show disapproval, but the dog doesn't show disapproval. The performance anxiety this child may feel all the time is absent when he's with his dog. Suddenly he's relaxed, he's with a peer who doesn't criticize him."

The hypothesis is that the sudden drop in Iyal's anxiety level—the sudden decrease in his hypervigilance, the lowering of his cortisol level, and the disarming of the fight-flight physiology—frees up cognitive energy that he can use for thought and speech. "A child with a disability feels freer not to suppress his ideas and behaviors when he's with his dog," Beck says. "There's a level of trust and confidentiality he has with no one else. And it's a good choice: the dog is his true confidant and friend."

Chancer has not cured Iyal.

"From the moment Iyal wakes up in the morning, there's tension in the house," Donnie says. "He has neurological and psychological damage Chancer's paws can't reach. But Chancer mitigates the disability. It's like we have a nanny."

Last fall the Winokur family wrestled with the likelihood that Iyal was being bullied at middle school. "Some boys told me to hump a chair," he reported to his mother and psychiatrist a few days into eighth grade.

"Hump a chair?" Donnie said. "I'm not sure what that means,"

Iyal stood to re-enact it.

"Look at Chancer," murmured the psychiatrist to Donnie. As Iyal engaged provocatively with a chair, Chancer rose, distressed. Whining, he tried to block Iyal's lunges.

On another day, a distraught Iyal told his parents that the boys said: "Go kiss that boy or we'll hang your dog."

"This is the classic setup for people with impaired judgment," Donnie says. "They're at risk of being exploited criminally and sexually. They can become both victim and perpetrator." It may not be classic bullying either. "Iyal may have pursued those boys," Donnie says. "He desperately wants friends. He doesn't understand personal space or social distance. He might have been annoying them, and they reacted."

The school principal was instantly responsive; his staff spoke to the other boys. "But Iyal keeps talking about it," Donnie says. "It's hard for Harvey and me to know if the bullying is still happening or if Iyal has just fixated on the trauma of it. Past, present, and future get confused in his mind."

Chancer doesn't accompany Iyal to school because the boy can't take the reins as Chancer's handler. "He can't even take Chancer for a walk around the block," Donnie says. "He might drop the leash, and Chancer might interpret that release as permission to track a hamburger. Chancer's an amazing service dog, but he is a dog, and he loves meat."

If Iyal ordered Chancer to do a wrong or dangerous thing, or to join him in reckless behavior, would Chancer recognize that they were transgressing? Would Chancer disobey Iyal? "When a dog puts a vest on, it changes his persona," Donnie says. "He knows he's working. In the service-dog world, they call it the halo effect. Guide dogs for the blind are trained in 'intelligent disobedience' for dangerous situations, like traffic. But I don't know if a dog can reason between right and wrong."

With every passing year, the challenges to Iyal's safety, and to the well-being of those around him, multiply. Iyal's attempts to touch his mother inappropriately are escalating; the Winokurs fear that soon the principal's office will be calling them, rather than vice versa. "Harvey and I feel like we're sitting on a volcano," Donnie says. "Iyal is a thirteen-year-old who functions cognitively, emotionally and socially like an eight-year-old. That gap will widen. He will never catch up to his chronological age. And few outsiders perceive the difference between 'neurological noncompetence' and 'behavioral noncompliance,' in other words, that Iyal's doing the best he can."

Iyal will never drive. He will never hold a regular job. He doesn't understand money or time. Experts say that the transition from adolescence to adulthood is particularly difficult for individuals with F.A.S.D. And Chancer won't be around forever. For as long as they live, the Winokurs hope to make sure there is a 4 Paws dog at Iyal's side; for now, they cannot conceive of a life without Chancer.

Chancer doesn't know that Iyal is cognitively impaired. What he knows is that Iyal is his boy. Chancer loves Iyal in a perfect way, with an unconditional love beyond what even the family can offer him. Chancer never feels disappointed in Iyal or embarrassed by Iyal. Beyond cognitive ability or disability, beyond predictions of a bright future or a dismal one, on a field of grass and hard-packed dirt, between the playground and the baseball diamond, you can see them sometimes, the two of them, running, laughing their heads off, sharing a moment of enormous happiness, just a boy and his dog.

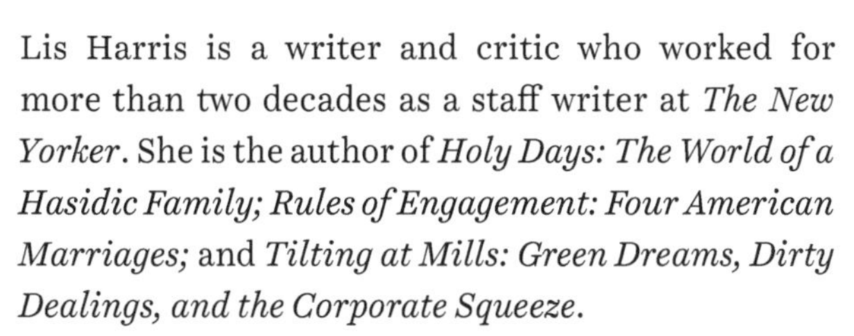

Lis Harris

Lis Harris is a writer and critic who worked for more than two decades as a staff writer at *The New Yorker*. She is the author of *Holy Days: The World of a Hasidic Family; Rules of Engagement: Four American Marriages;* and *Tilting at Mills: Green Dreams, Dirty Dealings, and the Corporate Squeeze.*

Her writing has also appeared in publications such as *The New York Times*, *World Policy Journal*, *Guernica*, *Du*, and *The Wilson Quarterly*.

Harris is a two-time Woodrow Wilson Lila Acheson Wallace Fellowship recipient, and was awarded grants from the J. M. Kaplan Fund, the Fund for the City of New York, the Rockefeller Fund and the German Marshall Fund. Harris is a graduate of Bennington College and has lectured at Yale University, Cornell University, Dartmouth College, New York University, and Wesleyan University, among others.

Holy Days is one of her best-known works. In his *New York Times* review of the book, Christopher Lehmann-Haupt wrote: "What is special about Miss Harris is her combination of openness and skepticism toward her subject. These qualities in various combinations enable her to ask the hard questions without putting off the people who had taken her into their lives."

Harris is a full-time writing professor at Columbia University's School of the Arts. Her forthcoming book is titled *Dream-Land: Three Generations of a Palestinian Family and an Israeli Family in Jerusalem*. She lives with her husband, the painter Martin Washburn, in New York City, where she was born and raised.

Holy Days

A rare glimpse inside the Hasidic Jewish community of Brooklyn, New York—how an ancient and traditional culture is adapting to life the modern age.

EDITOR'S NOTE: "Holy Days" was first published by The New Yorker *in three installments. The following is an excerpt from the second installment.*

Some time after my visit to the new *mikvah* with Sheina, and after the birth of my second child, I return to pay a visit by myself. It is about a forty-five-minute subway ride from lower Manhattan, where I live, to the Kingston Avenue I.R.T. stop. After Park Slope, mine is the only white face in the subway car. It is sundown, the prescribed time for taking a *mikvah,* when I surface, and, as usual, there is a large group of bearded, black-hatted, sombrely dressed men in front of 770, which is just across the street from the subway exit. The neighborhood still seems as dreamlike as it did on my first visit, but the faces above the beards have begun to look more individualized to me; the perceptual trick seems to be to "read" them from the nose up.

As I walk down Union Street toward the *mikvah,* I find myself trailing a black teen-age boy who is bopping along the sidewalk with an enormous radio blasting out reggae music. Formalizing the occasion, I imagine that the music is a kind of fanfare for the ritual I am about to experience for the first time, and that the boy and I form a procession. The farther we get from Kingston Avenue, the more deserted and run-down the street becomes. Across from the tan brickface *mikvah,* which glows faintly in the fading light, is a large, deserted apartment house with broken windows. There are no windows at all in the new *mikvah* building. A fancy brown canvas canopy arches above the entranceway, giving the place the appearance of an elegant salon. I am buzzed in, ascend a flight of stairs, and give eight dollars to a Slavic-looking attendant, who tells me that she can't remember ever seeing me before. Many women both shower and bathe at the *mikvah* in preparation for the ritual immersion. I explain to the attendant that I have already bathed at home, so she leads me to a dressing room with only a shower in it. The shower has a sliding frosted-glass door. There is burgundy-white-and-gold Art Deco paper on the walls, and a bevelled diamond-shaped mirror over a Formica dressing table. There is also a wig stand, a bright-red Clairol Son of a Gun fourteen-hundred-watt hair dryer, a long cream-colored terry-cloth bathrobe, and a pair of multi-colored rubber sandals. The attendant shows me a tan intercom and tells me to pick it up when my preparations are completed, and let the *mikvah* lady know that I am ready.

As I close the door, I notice several women flitting down the corridor. The *mikvah* is considered an extremely private ritual, and there is no socializing here—none of the affectionate banter so prevalent in feminine Hasidic society. Women generally go to the *mikvah* alone, and even Sheina, who has always been eager to act as my cicerone on visits to landmarks of Jewish Orthodoxy, did not offer to accompany me to this one. The lower half of the dressing room is covered with gleaming off-white tile. I had always imagined *mikvahs* to be rather Oriental—vaporous, dim places, chaste seraglios. Nothing could be farther from my preconception than this sleek Swiss spa.

The toilette one makes in preparation for the *mikvah* is elaborate. Having read about (and followed) the complicated instructions before I came, I am not surprised to see a small tray holding Q-tips, cotton balls, tissues, shampoo, baby oil, toothpicks, bleach, alcohol, soap, and Adwe New Fluoride Formula Kosher toothpaste. It is considered extremely important that the waters of the *mikvah* touch every part of a woman's body. Any particle of matter, however minute, that prevents this from happening makes the immersion invalid. The kinds of matter that might—literally—gum things up have been spelled out in excruciating detail by rabbinical authorities; for example, "A splinter which protrudes from the skin, or even if it does not protrude from the skin but nevertheless is on the same level with the outer skin, *must* be removed." Even bits of food that get caught in one's teeth are considered impurities, so a box of dental floss is provided. But, then again, the floss might get stuck, so taped to the little plastic box is the typed message "Don't floss if your teeth are tight together." Most of the people who come to the *mikvah* already know everything there is to know about preparing for it. As a precaution, however, a lengthy checklist has been taped to the wall. Among other things, it suggests that "rabbinic advice should be sought for temporary fillings, root-canal work or capping in progress, nits in the hair, stitches, casts . . . unremovable scabs, unusual skin eruptions." It is further suggested that one ask oneself, "Have I cut finger and toe nails and removed dirt in crevices (bleach helps)? Removed all foreign bodies: false teeth, contact lenses, paint and makeup, nail polish, artificial nails, Band-Aids, bobby pins . . . ?" The list goes on, and suffice it to say that no crevice or orifice of the body is neglected. Scrubbing myself in the shower, I remember a woman who, when I told her of my visits to Crown Heights, commented on the "dirtiness" of the Hasidim, and I laugh out loud. The last words on the checklist are "Now you are ready for the great *mitzvah* of *Tevilah* [immersion]." A French version of the list has been taped below the English one (many French-speaking Jews have been visiting the community recently), and, with characteristic Gallic grace, the French version adds a little coda to this: Now, it says, you are ready to perform the great *mitzvah* of *Tevilah "avec joie el assurance."* I pick up the intercom and call the *mikvah* matron. I do not feel *"joie et assurance."* I feel nervous. I find myself wishing my mother were here. Then one of the kindest, most benign faces I have ever seen appears smiling at the door, and my worries evaporate. The woman, who is middle-aged and wears a dark wig, tells me as she leads me through the climate-controlled corridor that her name is Brachah. *Brachah,* of course, means "blessing." These Lubavitchers really know how to do things. I tell Brachah, as we enter a small, ivory-tiled, antiseptic-looking room, that I've never taken a *mikvah* before. She folds her hands over her stomach and beams. "Well, then, we'll treat you like a *kallah* [a bride]," she says, and proceeds to explain some of the basics of the ritual to me. Then she asks, enumerating the various items on the checklist, if I've remembered to do all of them. I haven't. I've forgotten to comb my wet hair, and I've forgotten my nose, which I now blow, rather showily. Then, after blotting my eyes with a linen cloth to make sure no mascara lingers on my lashes, Brachah leads me over to the *mikvah.* I take off the robe and stand expectantly in the chest-deep warm green water. Brachah tells me to keep my eyes and lips closed but not too tightly and to keep my feet and arms apart, so that the water will touch my whole body. When I go underwater, I curl naturally into the fetal position. When I come up, Brachah places a linen cloth over my head, and I repeat the *mikvah* blessing after her. Then, the cloth having been removed, I go down two more times. The second time down, I see a little speeded-up movie of all the religious people I know performing this ritual. I think of all the generations of people I haven't known who have considered the impurities of the world dissolvable. My grandmother floats by, curled up, like me, like a little pink shrimp. I see her as she was in her very old age, senile and mute, curled up in the same position on her bed. The third time down, I think of my boys suspended inside me, waiting to join the world. I look up and see Brachah's smiling face through the water. I feel good. As I am climbing out, Brachah tells me that some people prefer to immerse themselves with their bodies in a horizontal position, and asks me if I'd like to try it that way. I try it, but find it less satisfactory. It's too much like going for a swim.

When I finish dressing, I find Brachah and the other attendant huddled together at the reception desk. I've told Brachah that I live in Manhattan and came over by subway. "We don't think you should go home on the subway," Brachah says. "It's really not safe to walk alone out there now." It's only a little after eight, but I take their word for it and call Black Pearl, a local car service. (No city radio cabs will come to Crown Heights. No yellow cabs cruise the neighborhood streets.) Five minutes later, a blue Chevrolet station wagon pulls up. I thank the women for their help, say goodbye, and climb into the car. The driver is a garrulous, handsome Haitian. Loud, monotonous music blasts out of the radio. Hanging from his rearview mirror is an air deodorizer, which fills the car with an overpowering sickly-sweet smell. Competing with the air deodorizer is the sharp scent of his after-shave, which he keeps in a kit on the front seat. At a long red light, he splashes a little extra on. My ablutions have made me feel tender, almost porous, and the harsh smells are overwhelming. Is this how Moshe and Sheina feel when they traffic with the outside world? The driver tells me that his company is often called upon to pick up women at that spot, which he seems to believe is a kind of shrine.

"You're Jewish, right?" he says, shouting to be heard over the music. "You have a lot of rules you have to follow?"

I hesitate. I am not up to any discussion.

"Yes, I'm Jewish," I say, as I roll the window down and point my nose toward the fresh air.

That evening, the Lubavitchers were having one of their *farbrengens,* or gatherings, at the synagogue, and Sheina was eager for me to attend. The Rebbe is the only speaker at the *farbrengens,* and he talks extemporaneously and for many hours. Some of these gatherings have been known to last all night. Sometimes they are announced days in advance; sometimes only a few hours' notice is given. When the word gets out that a *farbrengen* is going to be held, everybody telephones somebody else, and in an astonishingly short time the whole community knows about it. I looked forward to the *farbrengen,* which was to begin at nine o'clock. It would be my first chance to see and hear the Rebbe, and also to see the Lubavitcher community assembled in one place. The Rebbe spoke in Yiddish, I had been told, but in deference to the many visitors who came to hear him a simultaneous English translation was provided, and little transistor radios with earphones would be available at the door.

Walking along Eastern Parkway toward the synagogue, Sheina and I encountered Moshe's two sons, Mendel and Shmuel, who were both bachelors in their early twenties. Before we arrived on the scene, they had been having an animated conversation, which our presence somehow stifled. We all walked along together for a while, but in the absence of their father, who had gone on earlier, they seemed uneasy in Sheina's company and downright uncomfortable in mine, and when we arrived at the synagogue they bounded toward the men's entrance like puppies let off the leash.

All Orthodox synagogues have separate women's and men's sections—a practice that was initiated in ancient times by the priests of the Temple, some say, because they thought that otherwise the congregants would be distracted from the religious ceremonies. Whether the priests' plan proved to be effective then I cannot say, but the women's gallery of the Lubavitcher synagogue, which is upstairs, would surely have given them some second thoughts. About four thousand people were crammed into the synagogue—a space that, by a generous estimate, could have comfortably sheltered two thousand. About a third of those present were women, but the area consigned to them seemed hardly large enough to contain half their number. To enter the women's gallery—two adjoining windowless, airless balconies screened off from the men's section, downstairs, by black Plexiglas panels—one simply allowed oneself to be swept forward by a tidal wave of female Lubavitchers of all sizes, shapes, and ages flowing through the women's entrance. Once inside, the lucky found seats, but most either stood in the aisles or scrambled up onto the narrow back ledges of six stepped rows of wobbly wooden pews and teetered this way and that to find a spot that would afford a glimpse of the Rebbe, who had not yet arrived. There was a lot of jockeying for position, some fairly alarming shoving, and sporadic skirmishes inspired—it seemed—by territorial disputes. It was a scene that suggested equally the paintings of Hieronymus Bosch and the Times Square I.R.T. station at rush hour. Sheina quickly found her accustomed place—a minute stretch of bench in the left front corner of the gallery—and somehow tucked us both into it. From this vantage point, if you craned your neck down toward the four-inch span that separated the Plexiglas and the rim of the balcony you had a clear, bird's-eye view of the dais and, on it, a long table covered with a white cloth, where the Rebbe always spoke. Below, a black sea of male Hasidim swayed back and forth. Above, a tremendous din. Downstairs, little boys raced between the men's legs and around the dais, and little girls drowsed on their fathers' shoulders. Upstairs, innocent-looking teen-age girls and delicately powdered old ladies mingled with plump young mothers and innumerable babies. A large contingent of grandmothers, their arms moving like steam shovels, popped small morsels of food into the mouths of restless toddlers. The smell of sour milk and wet diapers was faint but pervasive. Knowing that the Rebbe's talks usually went on for hours, mothers came forearmed, and plastic bags filled with apple slices, pretzels, granola bars, and peanut-butter sandwiches were much in evidence. Ignoring the confusion, a few gallant souls, eyes tightly shut, attempted to pray. Sheina exchanged hugs and hellos with people nearby, and settled down with a bright-colored needlepoint wall decoration (a Hebrew alphabet) that she was working on.

After about half an hour, a regal white-bearded figure with a brisk, almost military gait and kindly, penetrating blue eyes entered the hall, and, except for the lip-smacking sound of sucking babies, it fell completely silent. The Rebbe. Like most of the other men, he wore a wide-brimmed black fedora, a long black coat, black trousers, and a white shirt. Unlike most of them, he wore a tie, also black. Taking a seat at the table, in front of several rows of whitebeards, he gazed placidly at his followers and began speaking, in the manner of a teacher picking up the threads of an earlier discussion with his students. No audience-grabbing anecdotes, no uplifting chorale. He spoke for more than four hours, in a voice that never wavered. The children dropped off one by one, but the rest of his followers listened raptly until the end. I listened carefully, too—to the translated version of his talk—but most of what was said went by me in a billowing gray cloud of words. The Yiddish accent of the translator was so thick, the translation itself so poor, and the nature of the discourse so elusive that the few intelligible statements I caught—"A truly free man is one who studies Torah," "We should dissociate ourselves from idolatry, from things that are foreign to Jews"—were unlinkable. The Rebbe, who is in his early eighties, spoke without notes, pausing for a few minutes every half hour to rest and to hold up a small wine-filled Dixie cup and toast his flock. The men also toasted him, holding paper cups aloft and waiting until the Rebbe looked and nodded in their direction before downing the wine. During these brief breaks, the men sang beautiful Hasidic songs that were thematically related to the Rebbe's discourse. Late in the evening, while scanning the expanse of pale faces downstairs during one such interlude, I happened to catch a glimpse of Moshe—hat pushed back on his head, eyes closed, mouth curved in a slight smile—singing. He looked as if he were crooning a lullaby to a baby.

I have attended many *farbrengens* since then. Often, the Rebbe's talks have been well translated (the translations broadcast on cable television, for example, are models of clarity), the themes broad-ranging and graspable. But one has to learn how to listen to them, and for anyone with a secular background this means acquiring a religious one. Like so many Jewish texts, the Rebbe's talks are not aimed at the uninitiated, nor are they readily accessible to those who have a mere passing familiarity with the subjects touched upon—though his followers insist that the Rebbe can be understood on one level or another by everybody. For a non-Yiddish-speaking layman, the constant references to Talmudic sources, persons, and principles, the Yiddish phrases that no translator—however deft—could even attempt to Anglicize, and the nonsequential, didactic style of discourse can be daunting. During the first two or three *farbrengens* I attended,

I found myself constantly straining, but failing, to make out through the thicket of Hebrew and Yiddish references something more than an occasional "thus," "so," or "obviously." One year and many hours' immersion in Jewish texts later, I came away from the *farbrengens* feeling that I'd understood about half of what the Rebbe was talking about.

Robin Marantz Henig

Robin Marantz Henig is a contributing writer for *The New York Times Magazine* and has written nine books, most recently *Twentysomething: Why Do Young Adults Seem Stuck?*, which she coauthored with her daughter, Samantha Henig. Her previous books include *Pandora's Baby*: *How the First Test Tube Babies Sparked the Reproductive Revolution* and *The Monk in the Garden: The Lost and Found Genius of Gregor Mendel*. She also co-edited *A Field Guide for Science Writers*. Her articles have appeared in *National Geographic, Civilization*, *Discover*, *OnEarth, Scientific American*, *Smithsonian*, and the *Best American Science Writing* anthologies. She writes book reviews and opinion pieces for *The New York Times* and *The Washington Post* and is science editor of *The Virginia Quarterly Review*.

Henig's book *Pandora's Baby* was named Book of the Year in 2005 by the American Society of Journalists and Authors (ASJA) and won NASW's Science in Society Award that same year. *The Monk in the Garden* was a finalist for a National Book Critics Circle Award in 2001. In 2010, she received ASJA's highest honor, its Career Achievement Award, as well as a Guggenheim Fellowship. Her other honors include a fellowship from the Alicia Patterson Foundation, where she now serves on the board of directors; a Sloan Foundation grant; and a fellowship from the Marine Biological Laboratory in Woods Hole, Massachusetts, where she is currently co-director of its Science Journalism Program

Henig lives in New York with her husband, Jeff, a professor at Teachers College, Columbia University.

The Last Day

A compelling profile of prominent psychologist and professor Sandy Bem, who voluntarily ended her life before succumbing to Alzheimer's disease.

Sandy Bem, a Cornell psychology professor one month shy of her sixty-fifth birthday, was alone in her bedroom one night in May 2009, watching an HBO documentary called "The Alzheimer's Project." For two years, she had been experiencing what she called "cognitive oddities": forgetting the names of things or confusing words that sounded similar. She once complained about a "blizzard" on her foot, when she meant a blister; she brought home a bag of plums and, standing in her kitchen, pulled one out and said to a friend: "Is this a plum? I can't quite seem to fully know."

Sandy was a small woman, just four-foot-nine and ninety-four pounds, with an androgynous-pixie look: cropped hair, glasses, and a wardrobe that skewed toward jeans and comfortable sweaters she knit herself in the 1990s. As she watched the documentary, her pulse thrumming in her ears, a woman on screen took a memory test. Sandy decided to take it along with her. Listen to three words, the examiner said, write a sentence of your choice and then try to remember the three words. Sandy heard the three words: "apple," "table," "penny." She wrote a brief sentence: "I was born in Pittsburgh." She said aloud the words she could remember: "apple," "penny." . . . The simplest of memory tests, and she had failed.

The next month, Sandy's husband, Daryl, from whom she had been amicably separated for fifteen years, drove her from Ithaca to the University of Rochester Medical Center for cognitive testing by a neuropsychologist named Mark Mapstone. Mapstone showed Sandy a line drawing and asked her to copy it, and then to draw it from memory ten minutes later. He read her a list of words and had her recall as many as she could. He gave her two numbers and two letters and asked her to rearrange them in a particular order: low letter, high letter, low number, high number. Thank goodness that last one wasn't timed, she thought to herself, as she focused all her mental energy on the task. She felt as gleeful as a kid who had earned a gold star when Mapstone said, "Yes, that's right."

After three hours, Mapstone gave a preliminary diagnosis: amnestic mild cognitive impairment. At first Sandy was relieved—he had said mild, hadn't he?—but then she caught the look on his face. This is not a good thing, Mapstone told her gently; most cases of amnestic M.C.I. progress to full-blown Alzheimer's disease within ten years.

When Sandy went back to the waiting room to meet Daryl, she was weeping uncontrollably. Between sobs, she explained the diagnosis and the inevitable decline on the horizon. She felt terror at the prospect of becoming a hollowed-out person with no memory, mind, or sense of identity, as well as fury that she was powerless to do anything but endure it. With Alzheimer's disease, she would write, it is "extraordinarily difficult for one's body to die in tandem with the death of one's self." That day at Mapstone's office, she vowed that she would figure out a way to take her own life before the disease took it from her.

Later that month, Sandy sat down in her upstairs study—painted a rich burgundy, as the rest of the house was, to make the sprawling old place feel cozy—and looked at her Mac desktop computer screen. She had some trepidation about her plan to keep a journal of her own deterioration. But she opened a new document, gave it a file name—"Memoir"—and began to type. She tried to describe the maddening capriciousness of "a mind that could be so alive one moment with thought and feeling building toward a next step and then someone erases the blackboard. It's all gone and I can't even reconstruct what the topic was. It's just gone. And I sit with the dark, the blank."

The prospect of mental decay was particularly painful for Sandy, whose idea of herself was intimately entwined with her ability to think deeply and originally. She was a pioneer in the field of gender studies: She created the Bem Sex Role Inventory in 1974, which assesses a person's traits along a traditional gender continuum; led Cornell's fledgling women's studies program from 1978 to 1985; wrote a groundbreaking book, *The Lenses of Gender*, in 1993; published a memoir, *An Unconventional Family*, in 1998; became a licensed psychotherapist in 2000; and returned for a second term as the director of Cornell's renamed feminist, gender, and sexuality studies program in 2001. Friends and colleagues knew Sandy to be intensely observant, a person who spoke her mind with a bluntness that could be off-putting. Her best friend, Karen Gilovich, a psychotherapist who lived around the corner, said that one of Sandy's favorite conversational openers was: "I find myself thinking. . . ." You never knew what would follow. She once wondered aloud, for instance, where the line was between acceptable and unacceptable behavior between parents and their children. Would it automatically be wrong for a waitress who comes home exhausted to ask her young son to rub her feet? Massage her back? Cuddle her? "She was the most clear thinker I have ever seen," Karen said, "with the ability to cut to the core of any messy issue."

On June 22, her sixty-fifth birthday, Sandy returned to the University of Rochester for another three-hour consultation. This time it was with a senior neurologist, Charles Duffy, to evaluate not only her cognitive abilities but also her mood and functional status. At one point, Sandy told Duffy she didn't intend to live out her life with dementia. "I want to live only for as long as I continue to be myself," she said.

To her surprise, Duffy began to reminisce about his own life. His mother had had Alzheimer's, he said, and his time nurturing her through her decline profoundly shaped him as a physician, as a researcher, and as a man. He said that Sandy—who had spent her career examining and describing her own life with frank insight and clarity—might have a lot to contribute to the world just by experiencing her disease and giving others a glimpse of how it felt to have it.

Sandy was touched by Duffy's empathy and by his willingness to reveal the private details of his life. Others had stories like his, about people who watch their loved ones slip away, or people who go through that slipping away themselves, and are surprised to find a kind of grace in it: the Zen-like existence in an eternal now, the softening of hard edges, the glorification of simple pleasures. But Sandy knew that wasn't right for her. Not for a moment was she swayed by Duffy's arguments.

Over the next several weeks, Sandy told those closest to her about her diagnosis and her plan to end her life before she became incapable of doing so. She told her two adult children, Emily and Jeremy, both in their thirties, and a handful of others: Karen; Daryl's sister, Robyn Bem; and Sandy's sister, Bev Lipsitz, who lived in Oregon. No one in that inner circle tried to talk her out of suicide; they knew how fierce she could be once her mind was made up. All they asked was that she promise not to choose a method that would be particularly disturbing—using a gun or jumping off a bridge into one of Ithaca's famously beautiful gorges. Sandy had contemplated both of those options, but she didn't want that sort of death either. "What I want," she typed in her journal in an emphatic boldface font, "is to die on my own timetable and in my own nonviolent way."

But when would that be? Sandy knew that the Alzheimer's decline itself was predictable—it usually moves from mild (misplacing things, repeating questions) to moderate (being unable to learn something new, getting lost, failing to recognize loved ones) to severe (losing the ability to speak, swallow or remain continent; needing help with every function of day-to-day life). In the immediate aftermath of a diagnosis of amnestic M.C.I., however, she couldn't know how long each stage might last. She wanted to squeeze in as much intellectual and emotional joy as she could before she died, but she wanted to make sure she didn't wait too long. She needed to be engaged enough in her life to be able to end it.

In early July, Daryl drove Sandy back to Rochester to see Duffy. The doctor suggested that she start on Namenda, one of the few drugs approved by the F.D.A. to treat Alzheimer's. Namenda works by increasing the level of glutamate in the brain and is thought to interfere with cell death. Researchers say that by the time someone exhibits mild cognitive impairment, the brain has been degenerating for years, and the drugs, even if they can slow the decline, are too little too late. But doctors and patients hope that starting a drug soon after diagnosis might make a slight but tangible difference—slowing memory loss enough to forestall total dependence. Sandy quickly agreed, which surprised Daryl, because she usually avoided medication, other than a low dose of Prozac that she had been taking for years for depression.

That summer, Daryl began taking her to most of her doctors' appointments. Sandy could have done the driving herself, but it was good to have Daryl along, so he could recount each visit's details on the ride home as Sandy took painstaking notes. Besides, she was enjoying Daryl's company. Something about her diagnosis had opened up an emotional vein in him.

"Who is this wondrous Daryl?" she wrote in her journal that month, after a drive in which Daryl talked with unexpected empathy about Sandy's early years with a harsh and mercurial mother. She loved the tender, attentive husband who seemed to have emerged from the ruins of her diagnosis. "If some devil had asked whether I would be willing to buy Daryl's deeper self at the cost of my developing dementia," she wrote, "I would say NO without hesitation. But if it comes free with my unstoppable decline into hell, I'm thankful for the gift."

It was a bit like the earliest days of their relationship, back in 1965, when they met at Carnegie Tech in Pittsburgh. She was a senior psychology major; he was a new assistant professor of psychology. Just four months after being introduced by Sandy's roommate, they married.

They vowed at the time to share everything fifty-fifty: the housework, the child-rearing, the inevitable career compromises. For a while, this worked well. So well, in fact, that in 1972 they were featured in the inaugural issue of Ms. magazine, in an article titled "A Marriage of Equals."

The Bems were both psychology professors, at Stanford and then Cornell, and they traveled around the country giving tandem talks about society's creation of sex-role stereotypes. They were a slightly odd couple. Sandy was petite and not the least interested in fashion. Daryl was bigger, dapper, six years older and already a bit stooped, with a scholar's pallor, a kind face, and a courtly manner cultivated over his years of performing as a magician. (He would also come to be known, later in his career, for some controversial experiments involving ESP.)

They turned their politics into a way of life, raising their two children, Emily, born in 1974, and Jeremy, born two years later, in what they described as a gender-neutral way. "Many other feminist couples have experimented with egalitarian relationships and feminist child-rearing," Sandy wrote in *An Unconventional Family*. But few "have shared the details of their daily lives as exuberantly as Daryl and I." She talked about everything, in print and on the lecture circuit: letting Jeremy wear pink barrettes to kindergarten; driving Emily past the same construction site every day because a woman was on the crew; hanging a chart on a kitchen cabinet to let the children know which parent was "on duty" that week.

Despite their good intentions, though, the marriage grew strained. As their children went through adolescence, Sandy complained that she felt like a single parent, with Daryl not fully engaging with the family's needs. They both saw the paradox in their supposedly egalitarian marriage floundering in such a gender-stereotypical way. In 1994, when the children were nineteen and seventeen, the Bems separated.

After the split, Daryl acted on his attraction to men, a part of his sexuality that he never hid from Sandy. He liked to joke that on their first date, he told her there were three things she should know about him—"I'm a stage magician, I'm from Colorado and I'm primarily homoerotic"—and that she calmly replied that she had never met anyone from Colorado.

About a year after the separation, Daryl began a long-term relationship with a communications professor at Ithaca College. Yet he and Sandy never divorced, and he remained a frequent visitor to the big house in Cornell Heights where they raised their children. He ate dinner there a few times a week and stayed involved in the lives of Emily and Jeremy—even more involved, in a way, than when he lived with them. He also remained one of Sandy's best friends and one of her few close confidants. (She had a short-lived relationship with a woman soon after Daryl moved out and remained single after that.) Daryl wrote in the epilogue to *An Unconventional Family*, which was published four years after they separated, "Sandy and I are still kin."

On a quiet Friday morning in November 2010, Sandy sat down with a mug of honey-ginger tea to read two books that Daryl had brought her. By this point, a year and a half after her amnestic M.C.I. diagnosis, she had progressed to what Duffy said was Alzheimer's disease. She had retired from Cornell, but she was doing well. She could still travel alone to familiar destinations, including Austin, Texas, where Emily was living. Jeremy had temporarily moved back home to be with her. She could read novels, even difficult ones like Cormac McCarthy's *The Road*. She played tennis, gardened, and went for walks around Ithaca with a handful of friends, most of them former colleagues from Cornell. She saw a few psychotherapy patients. One would later say that even though Sandy was having some trouble remembering words, "it didn't really matter. In a therapy relationship you're talking more about emotions—and in that regard, she didn't miss a beat."

The first book on her table that Friday morning was *Final Exit*. Sandy read it in the early 1990s when it was published; even then she was intrigued by the argument of the author, Derek Humphry, in favor of self-directed "death with dignity" for people who were terminally ill. The second was a newer book by the Australian right-to-die advocate Philip Nitschke called *The Peaceful Pill Handbook*. The pill in the title (though not literally a pill; it comes in liquid form) was Nembutal, a brand name for pentobarbital, a barbiturate that is used by veterinarians to euthanize animals and that is also used in state-sanctioned physician-assisted suicides. After reading about it, Sandy thought pentobarbital was what she was looking for. It was reliable, fast-acting, and—most important to her—a gentle way to die. It causes swift but not sudden unconsciousness and then a gradual slowing of the heart.

There could be complications, of course, like vomiting; Nitschke and his coauthor, Fiona Stewart, recommended taking an antinausea drug a few hours before taking the fatal dose to minimize that risk. They warned that pentobarbital is detectable in a person's body after death—but that didn't matter to Sandy. In fact, she preferred having people know that she died by her own hand.

One morning during one of Sandy's frequent phone calls to her sister in Oregon, she told her about the decision to use pentobarbital. Sandy had a special relationship with Bev, who was six years younger. When Sandy married Daryl, Bev was fourteen, and Sandy invited her sister to live with them rather than with their parents, whose unhappy marriage made it feel, as Sandy put it in her memoir, as if "chaos could erupt at any moment."

A year before Sandy received her diagnosis, Bev was found to have Stage 4 ovarian cancer. The sisters had discussed the fact that Oregon law allows people with terminal illnesses to take their own lives. Sandy now envied Bev's situation. "I don't think I have ever been as jealous about anything in my life as I am about this," she wrote in her journal shortly after she saw Mapstone. It was weeks before she could get past that jealousy and take Bev into her confidence.

But even if Sandy had lived in Oregon, her Alzheimer's disease would have precluded her from getting help in taking her own life. States that allow for assisted dying require two doctors to certify that the person has a prognosis of less than six months to live, and most people with Alzheimer's have no such prognosis. They also require that the person be declared "of sound mind," a difficult hurdle for someone whose brain is deteriorating.

On the phone that day, Sandy told Bev that pentobarbital was a controlled substance in the United States. She would have to write to one of the foreign suppliers listed in the book and hope for the best. Bev suggested an alternative: When the time came, she could request the drug from her own doctors in Oregon and then give it to Sandy. She didn't think she would need it herself—her cancer seemed to be in remission, and all she really cared about was eventually dying without pain. Like almost everyone else in Sandy's inner circle, Bev was devastated by the prospect of her sister's decline and death, but she tried to tune out her own anticipatory grief so she could focus on helping Sandy die the way she wanted to.

On Dec. 9, 2012, Sandy's daughter, Emily, and her partner, Julius Viksne, had a baby boy, whom they named Felix. Sandy went down to Austin, still able to make the familiar trip on her own. During the previous two years, her life had become more limited, but she continued to enjoy it. She spent time during Ithaca's abbreviated growing season gardening in her backyard, either alone or in the company of Karen or Daryl's sister, Robyn. Although she had abandoned writing in her journal, she could still read novels on her iPad, but nothing quite as complex as *The Road* anymore. She managed her day-to-day needs in part because she was such a creature of habit. She ate almost the same thing every day: a bagel for breakfast, a sandwich for lunch, a piece of salmon for dinner, mugs and mugs of tea throughout the day. Her freezer was always stuffed with ten-pound bags of almonds, so she could roast them by the handful and sprinkle a few onto chocolate frozen yogurt for her nightly treat. By then, she was also taking a second F.D.A.-approved drug, Aricept, which inhibits the chemicals that break down acetylcholine, a neurotransmitter linked to short-term memory; people with Alzheimer's often have lower concentrations of acetylcholine in their brains. Daryl wasn't sure that either drug was making a difference. It was impossible to tell without knowing what Sandy would have been like without them.

Becoming a grandmother was never something Sandy had cared much about. But when Felix was born, she was thrilled. He was in the neonatal intensive-care unit when she arrived in Austin; doctors had detected a bacterial infection in his urine and were administering antibiotics. Sandy sat in a rocking chair alongside the bassinet, and Emily handed the infant to her, naked except for his diaper, the IV port in his tiny hand capped off until the next infusion. She gazed down at her grandson, placid and perfect. She cooed and babbled. For weeks afterward, she talked about those first moments holding Felix. "I don't know what I was saying or what I was doing," she would say. "But he just looked into my eyes."

Emily was surprised to see her mother so at ease in the traditional role of Felix's *bubbe* (Yiddish for "grandmother"). As a parent in the 1970s, Sandy turned every interaction with her children into a political act. During story time, she would go through their picture books with a bottle of Wite-Out and a Magic Marker, changing a hero's name from male to female, revising plot lines, adding long hair or breasts to some of the drawings. Story time was a different experience with Felix. Sandy would cuddle with the baby and turn pages. If she couldn't remember the word for "zebra" or "lion," she wouldn't fuss about it. "Oh, it's some animal," she would say.

She told Emily that her "new brain" might actually make her better suited to being a grandmother than her focused, hyperanalytical "old brain." She seemed to have found a way of being that she liked, content to sing silly songs and make nonsense sounds for hours on end.

Emily liked her mother this way, too. It had sometimes been difficult to be Sandy's daughter. As a child, Emily wanted to wear her hair long and take ballet lessons; Sandy, ever vigilant about gender stereotypes, nudged her to cut her hair and play soccer instead. But now Sandy didn't seem to care about such things. Emily thought that her mother was taking pleasure in life in a way that the old Sandy could not have anticipated—and she found herself hoping that the joy her mother took in Felix might make her reconsider her intention to end her life quite so soon.

The others in Sandy's inner circle saw her relationship with Felix and wondered what it would mean for her original plan. The old Sandy, who valued her rationality and her agency, had been clear that she would be unwilling to keep living when she could no longer articulate coherent thoughts. But this newer Sandy didn't seem unhappy living her life in this compromised way. Ultimately, who should make the decision to die, the old Sandy or the new one?

Ronald Dworkin, an influential legal scholar and the author of *Life's Dominion: An Argument About Abortion, Euthanasia and Individual Freedom,* wrote about a kind of hierarchy of needs for people in Sandy's situation, who want their autonomy to be respected even as disease changes the essence of who they are and what autonomy means. He differentiated between "critical interests" (personal goals and desires that make life worth living) and "experiential interests" (enjoying listening to music, for instance, or eating chocolate ice cream). Sandy was appreciating her experiential interests—playing with Felix and working in her garden—but her critical interests were far more sophisticated and were moving out of her reach. Critical interests should take priority when making end-of-life choices on behalf of someone whose changed state renders her less capable of deciding on her own, Dworkin wrote, because critical interests reflect your true identity. The new Sandy seemed to love being a grandmother, but it was important to take into account what the old Sandy would have wanted.

Granting priority to critical interests is difficult even in a society that tries to do so. In the Netherlands, the Termination of Life on Request and Assisted Suicide Act makes it possible for a doctor to end a person's life when she is not cognitively able to do it herself, as long as she laid out her intention while she was still competent. According to the 2002 law, if someone with Alzheimer's disease has an advance directive declaring her wish to die when her dementia reaches a point she considers intolerable—when she has to be spoon-fed, for example, or put in diapers—that document is sufficient to allow a doctor to perform euthanasia. Nevertheless, it is rare for a doctor in the Netherlands to actually euthanize a patient who has dementia. In fact, one recent survey of 110 Dutch physicians treating dementia patients with advance directives asking to be euthanized found not a single one who had carried out the request. And of the 4,829 people who died in 2013 under the Dutch euthanasia act, just 97 of them, or 2 percent, had dementia.

"You know I plan to kill myself," Sandy said all through 2013, whenever the thought occurred to her. She seemed to say it partly for the sake of others, so they could get used to the idea and steel themselves against pain and grief when the time came. But it seemed that it was also for her own sake, to keep her plan at the forefront of her disintegrating mind. Emily and Felix were living with Sandy at the time, so that Sandy could help with child care while Julius attended nursing school in Colorado. (Jeremy had recently moved out. He was going through a rocky time and was not communicating with the family, though he supported his mother's plans.) It drove Emily crazy to hear her mother continually bring up suicide. "Stop saying that!" she would tell her.

One night in August 2013, when Sandy was home alone, she pulled out a yellow legal pad and sat down at the tile-topped table in her big, oak-trimmed kitchen, where she had eaten thousands of dinners. She had just heard of two experimental treatments for Alzheimer's that she hoped might, in addition to the Namenda and Aricept, keep her functioning so that she could help care for Felix until August 2014, when Julius was scheduled to finish his nursing program and move back home. But the drugs were prohibitively expensive, and she would have to pay for them out-of-pocket, because her insurance wouldn't cover the cost. On the pad, she started to make calculations. The treatment—a combination of IVIG (intravenous immunoglobulin), a drug approved for other neurodegenerative diseases, and repetitive TMS (transcranial magnetic stimulation), which was usually prescribed for depression—cost $6,000 every two weeks at the New York Memory and Healthy Aging Services. What if she could persuade the center to charge less, because at her size she would need less medication? And what if she received the treatment less frequently, maybe every three weeks? It was still a lot of money, but she had never touched her I.R.A., and she was already sixty-nine and was clearly not going to live much longer. She calculated that her savings could cover about $4,000 every three weeks until Julius graduated in a year. At the bottom of the page filled with numbers, she wrote to remind herself not to fret too much over the staggering dollar amount. "Expensive: but now money is *not* an issue (because of imily)." The previously meticulous scholar had misspelled her daughter's name.

Over the next months, Sandy and Daryl boarded a bus early in the morning every few weeks and rode down to Manhattan for the treatments. "I still feel as though I'm me," she told him on one ride. "Do you agree?" He did, sort of. In fact, he was surprised by how much herself Sandy could still be, even as she became less and less the formidable thinker he had always known. He was surprised too to discover that it didn't matter to him. "I realized how little of the fact that she was an intellectual played into my feelings for her," he said. "They were feelings for *her*, not her intelligence. And they were still all there."

Daryl proved himself steadfast, and as her more casual friends fell away, either because Sandy shut them out or because they were unwilling to witness her decline, he became more central to her life. He and Karen were the ones who saw her frequently, and they were the ones she kept checking in with to be sure her suicide window was not about to close.

In October, Sandy wrote to an address in Mexico listed on the website of *The Peaceful Pill Handbook*. Weeks passed, and she fretted that her order had been confiscated at the border. But at last it arrived: a cardboard box, no bigger than a softball, wrapped in brown paper. Sandy eagerly took scissors to the packaging and retrieved two one hundred-milliliter bottles of pentobarbital—she had bought an extra one just in case, even though she believed that one bottle would be enough for a person her size. The drug needed to be kept in a cool place, so she took the bottles down to the basement. For the time being, she could leave the pentobarbital on a shelf, comforted by the knowledge that it was there.

Now that the matter of "How?" was taken care of, the Bems turned back to the elusive question of "When?" They still generally agreed that Sandy would probably be alive until the end of 2014. But even with the treatments in Manhattan, her cognitive deficits were becoming more pronounced. When Bev came from Oregon to visit, Sandy couldn't understand how Bev and she could possibly have had the same parents. She didn't recognize Robyn's name in conversation, and when Emily tried to explain that Robyn was "Dad's sister," Sandy asked who, exactly, was Dad?

Daryl noticed something else disheartening. He had been following Sandy's progress as she took up the piano again. The Bems had always had one in their home, though it was mostly for Daryl, who played and accompanied Emily, whose clear, resonant singing voice carried her through student productions and into a career in musical theater. Sandy had worked her way slowly and steadily through the lesson book, moving from the simplest "Twinkle, Twinkle" tunes to études that were slightly more complex.

Late in 2013, Daryl began to see that Sandy could teach herself to play up to a certain point in a piece, but the next time she sat down at the piano she had to flip back several pages and work her way up all over again.

A few months later, whenever she sat down and flipped back several pages, she could make it only part of the way to where she had been the last time she played. And a few months after that, she would sit down at the piano, flip back to the beginning and get stuck at "Twinkle, Twinkle."

Even that was O.K., Daryl thought. She seemed to be enjoying whatever it was she *could* play. And then one day, she didn't even have that. Even the easiest pieces had become too difficult. Almost simultaneously, she was no longer able to read novels on her iPad or follow movie plots with complex flashbacks. Eventually there were only two movies she enjoyed: *Mary Poppins* and *Funny Girl*.

Right around Christmas, Julius dropped out of nursing school and rejoined his family. Sandy no longer felt it made sense to spend thousands of dollars in the hope of staying a little more functional a bit longer for Felix's sake. She told Daryl she wanted to stop the treatments. Shortly afterward, over dinner in her kitchen, she told him something else: She wanted to talk about when might be a good date to die.

O.K., Daryl said mildly, trying to stay focused on the task at hand, pre-emptively shutting down thoughts about what it would really mean to lose her. How about June? He knew how much Sandy would want to get back to her garden when the dreary Ithaca winter finally ended, and he hoped this would be a way to make her last few months happy ones. She agreed that June sounded right.

At the time, Emily, who was splitting time between her mother's house and her own home, was back in Austin. She and Julius were planning to buy a house a few miles beyond the Ithaca city limits, and she was preparing for the move. One day in April, Emily returned to Ithaca and was driving home from a bank with her father, who was helping her secure a mortgage. She was at the wheel of Sandy's car.

Should we change the car registration and put it in your name? Daryl asked. Emily started talking about wanting to wait until late summer, when she would be in her new house and would need to change the address only once. Maybe in July she could ask Sandy to sign over the car to her.

"Oh, she'll be dead by June," Daryl said.

Emily struggled to keep the car on the road. "What did you just say?"

Daryl looked at her, surprised by her surprise. He assumed Sandy had talked to Emily. But she hadn't, and Emily thought June was much too soon. She was looking forward to the summer with her mother and her son—Felix running around his *bubbe*'s backyard in the late afternoon light while Sandy puttered in the garden, digging a hole here, moving a rose bush there, pulling up weeds around the lilacs.

Emily was angry at her father for speaking so pragmatically about her mother's death. She was angry too at her mother for choosing a date that was so soon, and at her mother's inner circle for allowing all of it to happen. That night, she sat with her parents and Robyn while they discussed the situation. Emily felt as though she was defending her mother's life against everyone who wanted her to end it.

"You're just doing the math," she told Daryl. "It's like you're just calculating: Judging by the rate of decline of X amount, you can predict that by time Y this will be the case. But you can't!"

"O.K., so maybe not June," Daryl said, backing off. He had spent his life avoiding conflict. "We just thought that with your mother turning seventy-seven on June 22, that might be a good time."

"Well, that's nuts," Emily said. "How can you just pick a month like that?"

"What month did we say, again?" Sandy asked.

"June," Daryl said.

"Why don't you just say August?" Emily said. "It could just as easily be August as June."

"What month did we say, again?" Sandy asked.

"June," Daryl said.

"August, June—you can't just draw an equation," Emily said.

"What month did we say, again?" Sandy asked.

Emily turned to her mother. "You slogged through the winter," Emily told her. "By late May, it will be gorgeous around here." She wanted Sandy to hold out for one more summer. She wanted Sandy to *want* to hold out.

"I'm sure it would be nice," Sandy agreed. But her voice was flat; the prospect of one more summer, even with Emily, even with Felix, even with her garden, no longer seemed to be enough.

The nagging sense that there might be more time, that there should be more time, is inevitable for those close to a person with dementia who wants to end her life. At an annual conference in Chicago last summer of the World Federation of Right to Die Societies, a collection of fifty-one member organizations that push for right-to-die laws in twenty-three countries, the problem of timing was a running theme. When someone has dementia, said Rodney Syme, an Australian right-to-die advocate, "if you want to have personal control over what's happening, it means that you need to show considerable courage and considerable maturity." And it means, he said, that a person in a position like Sandy's might have to give up some period of time in which she might still be able to take some small pleasures in her life, just to be certain of ending it while she still could.

One night in April when Daryl was over for dinner, Sandy said to him out of the blue, "You're so smart."

"Is that it, or is it that as you get dumber, I feel smarter to you?" Daryl asked with a smile, taking a risk that Sandy still retained her puckish sense of humor.

She laughed. "I guess that's it," she said.

But she told him that she could feel herself slipping and that the day of her death would need to be "sooner rather than later." Daryl pulled the 2014 calendar down from the kitchen wall. He chose a date. How about Tuesday, May 20?

Sandy agreed, and Daryl wrote it down. She told Karen, Bev, and Robyn what she had decided. She planned to tell Emily but wanted to do it in person when her daughter returned from Austin. Emily and Felix arrived in Ithaca on May 13, and her parents told her that Sandy would die the following Tuesday. Emily was appalled. Just one week from today? She was sure it was much too soon.

That evening, she sat with her parents on the big L-shaped white couch in Sandy's oversize living room, the site of many serious family conversations over the years. Bev, Karen, and Robyn were there as well. Emily had no problem with the general idea of Sandy's ending her life soon, she said angrily, but now? *Now?* Karen and Robyn tried to explain how deeply changed Sandy was: She rarely laughed and seemed to find little joy in people or experiences. Emily thought everyone was thinking too narrowly. They assumed that her mother's joylessness was a result of the encroaching disease. Emily saw it as depression. The neurologist had recently taken Sandy off Prozac and started her on Zyprexa, an antipsychotic. Maybe her dose should be adjusted. Or the doctor should prescribe a different drug. Emily felt that they all needed more time to sort out what was causing Sandy's change of mood.

As the weekend approached, there was another discussion on the big white couch. Karen and Robyn wanted to make it clear to Emily how much Sandy had declined in the month she was away. "You didn't see this moment, Em," Robyn said, "when your mom was standing in the kitchen. She looked a bit lost and turned to me and said: 'I'm hungry. What do I do when I'm hungry?'"

And just the other day, Robyn went on, Emily had been chatting in the kitchen with her mother and Bev. After Emily walked out, Sandy turned to Bev and asked, "Who is that person's mother?"

"You are," Bev said, trying not to cry.

"I thought so," Sandy said. "I thought it might be me."

Emily now understood that Sandy was deteriorating rapidly. Karen organized a small gathering on Sunday, May 18, to celebrate Sandy's life. It was very intimate, just Sandy, Daryl, Emily, Karen, Bev, and Robyn. (Jeremy had moved out West and still wasn't in contact with his family, though Sandy and Daryl left a voice mail message to let him know when Sandy would die.)

At the gathering, Daryl talked about a lawsuit that the Equal Employment Opportunity Commission filed in 1972 against AT&T for sex discrimination in its recruitment practices, in which he and Sandy took the stand together to testify as a team.

"Did I really do that?" Sandy asked, pleased.

He talked about her expert testimony in another lawsuit, filed by the National Organization for Women against The Pittsburgh Press, that went all the way to the Supreme Court in 1973 and made it illegal to categorize classified job listings by gender.

"Did I really do that?" Sandy asked again.

Karen talked about how, relatively late in life, Sandy decided to go back to school at Rutgers and get a doctor of psychology degree while still teaching part time at Cornell. In 2000, at fifty-six, she opened a psychotherapy practice, turning the den in her house into an office that she made comfortable with big pillows. Emily said her mother had always been fearless and had raised her and her brother to always think for themselves.

The next day was warm and sunny, so a small family entourage went to Stewart Park, on the shores of Cayuga Lake, for what they all knew would be a final outing. Julius pushed Felix in a stroller, with Bev and her partner alongside them; Emily walked behind, holding her mother's hand—something she hadn't done since she was a child. When they all stopped at the playground to let Felix run around, Emily pulled Sandy over to sit with her on a bench nearby.

Emily said she understood why her mother felt she needed to take her life now. She spoke admiringly of Sandy's ability to find exactly the right moment—not too early, not too late. "I think you nailed it," she said. Sandy was quiet while Emily spoke, looking into her eyes. Her relief was deep and obvious, but all she said before they hugged was, "I'm so glad."

On her last day, five years after she first went to see Mapstone, Sandy set about creating a tidy paper trail to make sure no one else would be held responsible for her death. She found the printout of an email, with the subject line "ENDING," that she sent to Daryl nine months earlier, stating why she wanted to die and saying that no one—not her physician, not her attorney, not anyone—had offered help or advice. In the email, she had written that she would add the date of her death, "and perhaps other thoughts," when the time came, another way to make it plain that her death was her decision alone.

When the time did come, there were really no other thoughts. All the ideas Sandy might have wanted to express in writing—the sophisticated musings, the incisive arguments, the upending of conventional thinking—were already beyond her. Sandy sat down with the printout of the "ENDING" email and in longhand wrote out the date, May 20, 2014, the one she had been repeating to herself ever since Daryl wrote it on the calendar. She followed it with a simple declaration: "The time has come to end my life. I love you, Daryl." She signed it, formally, Sandra L. Bem. Then she and Daryl went for a walk in the Fall Creek Gorge, a ruggedly beautiful spot, 110 stone steps down from the noise of Stewart Avenue.

When they got back, Sandy and Daryl watched *Mary Poppins*. Emily, Bev, and their partners had assembled at Karen's house. Karen wanted Sandy to feel as if "a loving net was around her" as she prepared to die—though it had to be love at a distance, because Sandy wanted no one but Daryl in the room.

Around 5:30 p.m., Sandy took antinausea medicine and poured herself a glass of wine; she had read that drinking alcohol after taking the pentobarbital would mask its bitter taste and speed its action. With Daryl accompanying her, she carried the glass of wine upstairs to her bedroom and set it on the nightstand. Next she had to trim the foil off the collar of the 100milliliter vial of pentobarbital using manicure scissors and remove the small rubber stopper. Daryl held his breath, unsure whether Sandy could manage all these maneuvers on her own. She did. She poured the pentobarbital into a glass and set it next to the wineglass.

"Now what?" she asked. Daryl didn't know what to say. They had expected the preparations to take an hour or so, yet just fifteen minutes had passed.

"Have you decided what to wear?" he asked. She said she was happy with what she already had on. She got into bed and looked at the two glasses on the nightstand. She asked which was the drug and which was the wine.

"The drug is clear, and the wine is red," Daryl said.

Sandy nodded and looked around the room and then at the two glasses again. She asked which was the drug and which was the wine. Daryl told her again.

"Can I sip some of the drug and then drink some of the wine?" Sandy asked. "That's not a good idea," Daryl said. "You don't want to fall asleep before you've drunk it all."

"O.K., I'll drink the whole thing," she said, and she did. He asked if it tasted terrible. "No," she said. "It's intense, but it's not bitter. I'm not having any problem with it."

She put the glass down. "How much wine am I supposed to drink?" she asked. Daryl told her she could have as much as she wanted. She took a sip.

"I have to go pee," she said.

"You can't go pee," Daryl said. "I'm afraid you'll fall asleep."

"Can you come with me?" she asked.

So Daryl and Sandy walked to the bathroom together, and Daryl sat outside the door while his dying wife sat on the toilet.

He helped Sandy back into bed, and within five minutes she was unconscious. Daryl watched her for a while, not quite feeling anything. Still to come were the calls to 911 and the coroner and the undertaker, and the writing up of the death notice, highlighting the reasons for Sandy's decision. Still to come, too, was the brutal reality of what it would feel like for Sandy to be completely gone from his life. "How powerful a presence is her absence," Daryl would say at a memorial service that summer, quoting from a poem by Fred Chappell. "The rooms were quiet when she was resident./Now they lie silent. That is different."

For now, though, Daryl simply gazed at his unconscious wife. Around 8:30, he telephoned Bev at Karen's house around the corner. Bev came over to sit with him at Sandy's bedside. They were quiet, watching the sheet go up and down with each breath. Over the next hour, the sheet's rise and fall began to slow. Then it stopped.

Gerri Hirshey

Gerri Hirshey has worked as a features writer, columnist, reporter, and essayist for more than thirty years at publications including *The Washington Post*, *The New York Times Magazine*, *Vanity Fair*, *GQ*, *Esquire*, and *New York*. In the 1980s, she was the first female contributing editor at *Rolling Stone*, writing celebrity profiles of entertainers, including B.B. King, Michael Jackson, Jodie Foster, and James Brown.

Her work has also appeared in *O: The Oprah Magazine*, *More*, *The Nation*, *Food & Wine*, *Ladies' Home Journal*, and *Parade.*

Hirshey is the author of several books, including *Nowhere to Run: The Story of Soul Music*, now in its seventh reprinting, and *We Gotta Get Outta This Place: The True, Tough Story of Women in Rock*. Her most recent book is *Not Pretty Enough: The Unlikely Triumph of Helen Gurley Brown*, a biography of the longtime editor of Cosmopolitan.

Hirshey lives in New York City with her husband, Mark Zwonitzer, a writer and documentary filmmaker. They have two young adult children.

On the Bus with B.B. King

On the road with the great blues man and his beloved guitar, Lucille. Classic music journalism by *Rolling Stone*'s first female contributing editor.

The trucker is squinting hard through the downpour of a sudden tempest, steering his load of appliances along the slick Connecticut four-lane. He's nattering on the CB radio as the mammoth motor coach pulls alongside. The lights are on in the bus's private lounge, and despite the rain, the windows have been pushed open. Looking out at the trucker is a seventyish black man popping a Diet Coke and a smile. *Bwwaaaaaaaaaa*. The trucker leans on his horn in a delighted blast of recognition. There's an American vision sweeping past, and the driver is hollering the news into his mouthpiece: *It's B.B. King!*

B.B. grins at the honking salute. Even when he was in his early twenties, plying the rural juke joints and eye-blink towns outside Memphis, he says, he loved to hear his imminent arrival announced on local radio, to have excitable women trill the news as he sauntered past with his guitar: *B.B. King's in town!*

At seventy-three, he is King of the Blues Worldwide, according to the custom tour jacket tossed on the seat; a national treasure by virtue of his Presidential Medal of the Arts—and a real gone daddy if you count his fifteen children by as many women. Shanghaied by a fatal attraction to one Gibson guitar, now speeding headlong into his fiftieth year on the road, B.B. King has to be the hardiest, the most mythic, the almighty rollingest stone.

Tonight, ours is a procession befitting the elder statesman of blues highways. Our "chase" vehicle is B.B.'s band bus, with his name and the likeness of his guitar, Lucille, painted on the side. B.B. leads the way in his private Fortress of Solitude, a custom-configured, Belgian-built VanHool motor coach rigged with a 120-channel satellite dish, a kitchen, a shower, six TVs and a 500-horse engine smart enough to diagnose its own ailments via computer printout. "This is home," says B.B., waving at the stacks of his beloved electronic gizmos, the milk crate full of videocassettes, the sound system playing Dexter Gordon.

He leans back into the buttery leather of the horseshoe-shape banquette, looking relaxed in his traveling clothes. As usual, B.B.'s cool will frost your eyeballs: burgundy silk shirt, knife-pleated black slacks and soft, boaty loafers with woven black-and-burgundy leather insets. He's conjuring road stories, shaking his head as he recalls some of the wheezy highway schooners that brought him so far: "We were in Louisiana one morning. I had a big bus, my name on it. We broke down in this small town . . . . "

B.B. is off, reaching into his bottomless sack of anecdotes and B'isms. Painted from life with the broad strokes of a Mississippi Delta impressionist, these are the twelve-bar picture stories that have made his blues believable for so long:

He's trudging down a dusty two-lane, a lone, worried black man in too-fine clothes. Dawn is breaking as he comes to a whites-only cafe and walks around, instinctively, to the back door. The owner is just opening up when B.B. identifies himself and explains his problem: a breakdown, a busload of hungry musicians. Sure would help if they could come in and sit down. The man says OK and sets up a table. As the band wolfs biscuits and gravy, the jumpy owner stands at the front door, greeting his white regulars. To each he blurts apologetically: "That's B.B. King and his band. The bus broke down and . . . . "

B.B. laughs at the vision of the nervous but kindly man who dared serve him a square meal beneath the menacing wings of Jim Crow. "I'm glad that's changed," he says. "Thank God for the change."

We're bumping over a dark, grassy area on a rain-swept peninsula in southern Connecticut, toward an outdoor gig made possible by a last-minute letup in the rain. Summer is almost gone, but the B.B. King

Blues Festival, barnstorming tents and amphitheaters from Toronto to Tulsa, still has another month to go. For the headliner, that's the briefest moment in time.

"Fifty years—really?" a fan is squeaking.

B.B. is doing his ritual meet-and-greet after the show. Tonight's dressing room is a cramped RV behind the tented stage. Outside, the fitful strobe of heat lightning reveals a line of autograph seekers about a hundred feet long.

"Feels like I just got here sometimes," B.B. says. "But, yeah, I got serious about things in '48."

He was twenty-three then and had been doing farm work since he was six. B.B. has great recall for the significant numbers in his life. He likes to roll them off:

$22.50: his salary driving a tractor on a Mississippi plantation six days a week, in 1946;

Twelve percent: the alcohol content of the Pep-Ti-Kon "family" tonic that sponsored his first ten-minute spots on Memphis' legendary black radio station, WDIA, in 1948;

A penny a pound: The '48 rate for picking cotton across the river in Arkansas every afternoon after B.B.'s Pep-Ti-Kon gig (this, he notes, was triple the rate in his native Indianola, Mississippi);

$12: the cash a certain Miss Annie gave him for his first paying gig, a couple of hours at her West Memphis juke joint. She'd happily turn off the box, she told B.B., "'cause the ladies like to dance to a live man."

Which Miss Annie saw he was.

"So you go ahead and do the math," B.B. says by way of explaining his career choice. But even he falters trying to calculate his lifetime one-nighters. The miles traveled between them would bankrupt any latter-day frequent-flier program. Riley B. King, billed as the Beale Street Blues Boy in post–World War II Memphis, then Blues Boy King, then Bee Bee, then B.B. (and now, to his nearest and dearest, just B), has carried his blues to eighty-eight countries. Most years he averaged 340 shows until recently, when he "cut back" to 250. He has released seventy-six albums (the latest, *Blues on the Bayou*, came out in October).

Volumes have been written limning B.B.'s legend. But it takes a serious road trip—submersion in B.B.'s diesel-scented, day-for-night existence—to appreciate his astonishing lust for the Life. B.B.'s story is the road, as American as Woody Guthrie's in its tuneful observations, hipper than Kerouac's in its outsider wisdom. And in a nation known for producing wanderers of distinction, no one—save perhaps Lewis and Clark—can match B.B. for sheer endurance.

Having held the floor for maybe fifteen thousand-plus smoky, hip-twitching nights, he has allowed himself a total of three months' scheduled vacation time. In half a century, he says, he's missed only eighteen gigs. Most of them, he points out, were promoter mix-ups or "acts of God—you know, the weather and such."

Though he is in most ways a modest man, B.B. is very proud of his golden anniversary. Traveling with him through New England, Manhattan, Maryland, Texas, and Oklahoma, I've seen him celebrate it on-stage every night, fists raised, eyes closed, with a mighty bellow: "You've kept me out here for FIFTY YEARS! THANKYEW!"

In quieter moments, B.B. admits he's been married more to the road than to the two fine women who tried to be his wife—and to the many others who bore his children. He'll tell you that Lucille, his darkly gorgeous Gibson guitar, has always been the home-wrecker, that only one woman has ever come close to bringing him out of himself the way Lucille can every night. Named for the vixen who ignited a brawl and a roaring house fire at one of B.B.'s early gigs, the current Lucille (the sixteenth) is waiting for him now in the bus. She drew her own applause as she was escorted back there, gently, via golf cart. Watching Lucille's stately departure, some boys just stared, slack-jawed and silent, as the lightning flashed Excalibur-like off her gleaming gold frets and pickups.

The kids always come around: lanky Hanson look-a-likes, dreadlocked tenth-graders in surfer jams—the "guitar kids," B.B. calls them. They understand that whatever fills arenas nowadays can be traced directly to the big flat fingers now curled around an autograph pen. Theirs is a global tribe; they show up in Moscow, Kyoto, Rio. B.B.'s kids are virtually all male, downylipped dreamers who lie in their childhood beds and practice the most urgent fingerings in the dark. Tonight, once they reach his plastic-slipcovered inner sanctum, they stare unabashedly at his hands. Across the blasé "whatever" faces of the Info Age's first spawn, I detect the refreshing bloom of awe.

"I have this one really important question—OK?"

A female voice cuts through the basso murmur. She says her name is Ann. She looks eighteen or so; there is a feisty DiFranco cut to her jib: frizzy hair flying from a leather clip, baggy shorts, and sandals. She says she's a singer-songwriter.

"Do you ever get tired of singing and playing?"

"No. Never."

Ann isn't buying it. "Look, even I get tired, because it's so emotionally draining," she says. "So painful sometimes. I put so much of me in my songs, things that really hurt me. And to do it over and over . . . . "

For the first time tonight, B.B.'s smile has vanished. He is almost stern as he leans across the table and tells her: "Don't think about the hurt. Don't think people are responding to the hurt when you play to them. *Don't . . . do . . . that*. It's about the music. You don't know what they find in it—some connection. Who knows? Leave it at that. Don't think of being *hurt* . . . . "

Morning is breaking civilly enough on the Connecticut shoreline as we settle into the private lounge of B.B.'s bus to talk en route to Baltimore. He slips off his shoes, which he always buys at Rochester Big and Tall in New York for his "big old weird feet." Reflexively, he shuts down the throat-killing AC vents and slides the windows open to a powerful highway racket.

Traveling with B.B. is not for the fainthearted. The company is genial, but the pace is brutal by any standards. After every show, B.B. spends up to two hours talking to those who clamor to see him up close. At 2 a.m., with six hundred miles to be covered for the next gig, even when B.B.'s diabetes is working its sneaky hoodoo on his blood sugar, no one is turned away. The band is often abed or winding down in some hotel lounge before the boss finishes work. Lately, B.B. has been suffering from insomnia—the damned diabetes, he thinks—so he sits in his room, clicking at his laptop computer, answering letters, playing solitaire or his beloved cybergame, Freespace, past dawn.

Creep down to the hotel coffee shop after a couple of hours sleep, and that sound—the low, impatient diesel rumble—is always right outside. B.B. owns the band bus, but his private leased coach is a recent indulgence. "There's two other things I thought I owed myself the last five or six years," he says. "A suite—not a huge one, but a parlor and a bedroom. And a first-class ticket on the airplane."

The object of all these splurges: privacy. He says he's such a creature of group travel that he catches himself closing his bedroom door behind him during the rare times he's at home—alone—in his Las Vegas town house. Having the coach to himself gives him a great deal more solitude. On a full tank it has a cruising range of more than twelve hundred miles. "You need that to keep up with the man," says today's driver, Hap Arnold.

The remarkable engine that is B.B. has been sputtering a bit lately, owing to a flare-up of the diabetes that was diagnosed several years ago. He has been wondering if it's the same thing that might have blinded and then killed his mother when he was just nine and she was in her late twenties. With great effort, he pared more than thirty pounds off his ample self. His pockets rattle with Ziploc bags of prescribed medications. He does not drink alcohol or eat meat. B.B. carries no masseurs or personal trainers on tour, just a small space heater to ward off air conditioning in his dressing rooms. This morning he's salting the first of a few stabilizing light meals—a couple of hard-boiled eggs. He pops open a wake-up Diet Coke.

"I've been thinking about that girl last night," he says, meaning Ann. Hers wasn't a new question, but it nettled. Why do folks always fixate on the pain? B.B. just hates it when people come up to him and confess how they held fast to his music when their lives and loves fell apart. He is always polite, but the truth is, he'd like to pound a wall.

"People say, 'Oh, me and my girl broke up last week and, boy, I've been playing you ever since.' It's not really flattering. Any way I can get them to listen to me, I guess I should be happy. I shouldn't be surprised that they reach out to the *hurt* in it. But don't play it simply because you lost someone or you *hurt*. I'd still like very much to know that I'm a pretty good musician. And you can hear it even if you haven't been hurt."

Pain is hardly a taboo subject for B.B. It keeps cropping up in conversation as it does in life, as natural and persistent as crabgrass. He'll finish an anecdote: It hurt me. You don't know how that hurt. B.B. even speaks the word with the same upward-sliding glissando that makes his guitar licks instantly recognizable. In hours of conversation, he demonstrates great intimacy with all kinds of hurt: romantic, racial, professional. He admits that his own hurts have compelled and propelled him. He's played them, shouted, stomped, and roared them. He's autopsied and orchestrated them.

I've been downhearted, baby . . . .
Have you ever been mistreated?
How blue can one man get?

Growing up poor and motherless in the segregated South, B.B. says, he has lived some very deep blues. And he has no problem with people thinking that pain may have pushed and shaped his art. But he would like this understood: B.B. King also owns the copyrights. All this time and mileage he has put in are not about the triumph of misery as much as its subjugation. His favorite blues are about survival, not submission. He says he's tickled at the way audiences are reacting now when he powers through a song from his new CD called "I'll Survive." Night after night, they rise to their feet when he brings it home with those two words. Respected, well paid, draped with honorary degrees and awards, he relishes his role as the poet laureate of Enlightened Complaint.

"Can you imagine," he asks me, "how a seventy-three-year-old guy has all these young people coming out nightly? Just to see me? How lucky can you be?" He's just as ready to admit that, yes, every day he also has the blues, if only for a moment. That's life. We haven't been talking five minutes when B.B. mentions what he calls his education hang-up.

"By coming out of school in the tenth grade, I've never caught up," he says. "I'm always trying to learn what everybody else knows. For example, if I'm with somebody and they say, 'Yeah, when I was going to college, I learned so and so . . . . ' Well, I feel a little inferior at the time. I have that little complex. I always feel that I'm the one that has to learn."

Press him about his honorary degrees from the likes of mighty Yale and tiny Tougaloo College, the Kennedy Center Honors, his 1987 induction into the Rock & Roll Hall of Fame; remind him of the seminars he gives at universities like Northwestern to demonstrate his philosophy of funk and technique, and he'll finally acknowledge: "I feel I have a reasonable degree in art, in what I'm doing now. I started feeling this way not awful long ago. People praise you—I love it. But they don't know my limits as I do. I know my limitations *very* well."

Not that he is one to rest easy with them. He classifies himself as "very aggressive" in trying to learn things. To illustrate his point, B.B. hands me a zippered case full of CD-ROM disks with the invitation, "Go on, check it out." I find Success Builder disks for Algebra 2. Geometry. Elementary

Spanish and French. Reptiles of the World. Architecture. What else is in B.B. King's Compaq laptop? Letters, compositions in progress.

All this talk of sophisticated communications leads him to remember a very basic message sent to him one night in Chicago. It came when he felt like a big deal—recording star, lady's man, King of Saturday night—until this blues blindsided him and he came undone:

B.B.'s got a band, paying it pretty good, too. They're playing a joint called Roberts, and B.B. is strong, loose, and juiced with the promise of a new release. He tells the crowd he's got a new ah-blum out. "Ah-blum." After the show there's the rasp of a note sliding under his dressing-room door. It says, "The word is 'al-bum,' not 'ah-blum.' "Walking by the band room, he hears the guys saying "ah-blum." They're laughing . . . .

"That hurt me deeply," B.B. says. "One of the guys that was doing it I thought was a friend. To be a friend, he should have told me, straightened me out."

Suddenly he brightens with a coda to the story. About a decade later, in St. Louis, someone sent a note backstage asking whether he remembered the ah-blum message, which was meant kindly. Then the writer stood revealed: "It was a beautiful lady." B.B.'s smile bespeaks a happy ending to that blues.

"As a tractor driver, sex was always on my mind. It didn't take much to get me going. If I drove past a girl picking cotton, I'd notice the way she bent down. The way her buttocks outlined the back of her dress could fire me up for hours. On a scorching summer day, the sight of beads of perspiration on a soft feminine neck would arouse my imagination."

In his 1996 autobiography, *Blues All Around Me*, B.B. often admits to his runaway lusts, complete with a description of his senior-citizen circumcision ("and my penis, thank you very much, has been in good working condition ever since"). There have been so very many women to bounce him headlong between desperation and divine inspiration. "It took me a long time to realize that you can't have *all* of the women," he says now. "I've *always* loved the girls."

B.B. pronounces the word more like *gulls*. And by grammar school, he had figured out how to get to them. He was shy. He stuttered. He was no Romeo. So: "I played my harmonica. And the girl that I was crazy about she was crazy about one of my cousins. But when I would play the harmonica, she would listen, seem to soften up a little bit. Others would say, 'Oh, Riley can really play, can't he?' Well, that's like you pat a little dog on the head if he bring you the paper. He's ready to go back and get you another one."

Petting—the female kind—was what B.B. figures he was after. Losing at an early age the only people who loved him truly and unconditionally (his mother, then his grandmother) might have marked young Riley as a needy young man. His parents divorced when he was five, and his father would not find him for some years. An aunt and uncle would have taken him in, but he was steadfast in his intent to live alone at ten.

"Everybody cared about me," he says. "But how much? The house where we lived—my room, my grandmother and I—I wanted to stay there. I felt that it was nobody but me. I just felt it was me against the world. So there was something about the place—the way they left it. And I can have that now. This is mine. If nothing else."

He says he still craves the comforts of some imagined domestic hearth. Despite his two divorces, he insists that "the times I was married were the happiest times of my life." He likes the idea of a woman waiting for him at the end of the day, looking down the road for him. And when he was a teenager, the beauty of that vision threw him full force at Miss Martha Lee. She was the most enticing of the women he noticed as he jounced along high above the cotton rows, one of nine big-shot tractor drivers on Mr. Johnson Barnett's mammoth plantation. Theirs was a spare, quiet Delta wedding of seventeen-year-olds, in 1942.

"I guess I was looking for love, because I'd never had anybody I believed truly loved me," he says. "More than to tolerate and put up with me—to truly love me. So when I did get married, young, I was crazy about the girl. It seemed to me that I finally had love."

Things were fine for a few years. Lucille wasn't in the picture; B.B. had a series of raggedy, cheap guitars and a nettlesome little itch: "For some reason, my mind was not settled at being a husband like a husband should be. Now I wanted to play an instrument. Now I'm thinking that there's something out there for me. I don't know what to do, but I'm seeking. I'm looking for it. She'd fight me on it."

He remembers the night he saw the end coming.

The house supper sounds common enough by Delta standards—hamburgers in the kitchen, bed taken out for dancing, some live music courtesy of Riley B. King. B.B. doesn't know the people or the place. It could be rough, but Martha is hardheaded about coming along: "It don't make no difference.

You go and I go." But he sneaks off alone. He's at the house supper an hour when the woman, a stranger, starts to flirt, sits in his lap, just talking. Now, a man can't be ungentlemanly and toss the girl off . . . boom! The door opens. Martha.

"I swear to you, I didn't know the lady," B.B. says now. "And that's when my wife looked at me differently. We lived together four or five more years, and she never believed I was telling the truth."

After their divorce, he was on the road nearly a decade and saw that look plenty of times. "I kept searching, searching. Seemed to be me alone. I'd run into ladies, thought we had a thing going real good. Then we'd start to talk about my music." His voice rises to the descant timbre of Female Complaint: *"Get another job."* Then, one night in a club back home, Sue Hall hit him like a wrecking ball. She was lovely, he says, bright enough to go to business college and to help manage his affairs, light-skinned enough to get arrested in Ocala, Florida, for being with a man as dark as B.B.

In 1958, Sue married him on the condition that she could come with him, at least part of the time. They tried it, but after nearly a decade they came apart, too. And it's clear when he talks about his second wife that she is his great regret. He says she was the one who came closest to giving him what Lucille is so generous with: release. He figures he's still looking for the feeling: "Since my early childhood, I have had a problem trying to open up. *Please* open me up. Look inside! 'Cause I can't. I don't know how to."

It's no surprise, then, that B.B. is such an accomplished poet of Yearning. Longing and regret pepper his lyrics like birdshot. "The Thrill Is Gone," his signature piece, was written in the wake of his divorce from Sue. The melody, like the woman, confounded him for eight years. "I think I understand women better than a lot of men do," he says. "But no man, I believe—even King David—really understands ladies. And maybe that's the way it should be. Because ladies are *verrrrry* mysterious as far as I'm concerned."

These days, he says, he's getting to appreciate his conversations with women. In fact, he'd rather talk or go to a movie. For so many years, talk—if it came at all—was but a dinner mint after the real feast. "I haven't been no angel," he says. "Haven't had a halo around my head. I've always liked girls. I don't throw 'em out in the street, I don't treat them badly. I do see a person, and I'd like to be married again. But I'm not ready. I can't even open up to her, not like I would like to. I think I'm starting to see the problem."

"When I was five and my daddy was coming to Gainesville, my mother dressed me in this beautiful crinoline dress. She would allow me to stand in front of the big picture window. And I would wait and wait. And then I would hear the bus coming. And I would get so excited, my little heart would just pound. He'd come maybe four or five times a year, whenever he was performing in the area."

Patty Elizabeth King, born forty-one years ago to B.B. and Essie Williams, who owned the Blue Note in Gainesville, Florida, gave this interview to People magazine in 1993 from a prison in that city. She was serving time for cocaine trafficking, and B.B.'s bus was arriving again, to play his sixty-ninth prison show. Patty cried when he left.

"My father was always in my life," Patty King says now. "He supported us. We've always been able to get in touch with him. If there was ever a problem, he was trying to solve it. I've called him in the middle of the night with problems, or just needing to talk to someone, and he's always there."

Released from prison and reunited with her four children, she now works with an elder-care organization in Gainesville to support the two young sons still at home. She is writing a memoir: *Blues Baby*. And, if anything, it will be a love song to her father. She says she's made it a point to reassure B.B. that papa's rolling-stone lifestyle was not an issue: "I tell him that he's done well by us. I don't want him to think that things that have happened to me in the past had any kind of bearing on him. He's just a great dad. He's my father, and he's my friend."

B.B. says that most of his children are doing well. They are spread out all along the road, from California to New York. Among the four sons and eleven daughters are a preacher, a blues singer, homemakers. He has helped support all of them, sent those who wanted to college, and is sending their children now—seven at present. They come out to see him as he passes nearby, generally on his dime, and fuss over him in hotel suites, cooking fish and greens, bringing along grandchildren to spoil. "I haven't been there all the time," B.B. says. "I've been the loner; I've run here, ran there. But I've always kept a place where they could get in touch with me, and they do."

His youngest, Riley B. King Jr., wrote from a prison in Huntsville, Texas. B.B. says he drew eighteen years for drug-related thefts. Once he had served five years, B.B. set his attorneys to pressing for an early release. "He's my son, and I love him," he says of the boy who used to come out on the road with him. But Riley's early letters from prison were angry and accusatory. "He seemed to think that his mother and me didn't do everything we could have done," B.B. says. He tried tough love—*don't bother writing back if that's all you have to say*. They settled things; the lawyers went to work. Once or twice a year, B.B. drove through the prison gates to visit his namesake. (On November 3rd, Riley B. King Jr. was paroled; B.B. got the news on the road.)

"I wasn't much of a father," B.B. says. We spend a good deal of time discussing B.B.'s will, which is a source of pride and comfort to him. His blues will provide a substantial legacy. The education fund he started for his descendants is close to $2 million. "This is my way of trying to show them that Dad did love them," he says. "For those days that I wasn't there to hold their hands when they needed me."

He feels he's changed a lot—for the better—in the last ten years: "I think I'm a better father. My kids say, 'You're all right.' Some of them are very outspoken. They wouldn't say it if they didn't think so."

It took him years to make peace with his own father. Albert Lee King was also a traveling man, since his work as a tractor driver kept him away from home all week. "My dad never told me that he loved me," B.B. says. "Never. But when he was pleased with me, he called me Jack. I could always tell when my dad loved me. That's when my little heart would bust."

The ladies still like to dance to a live man. I watch them nightly from a gloriously loud spot behind the horn section. Dancing women always ring the front, jostling moony guitar kids. As one female security guard at a harborside Baltimore venue explains: "Lucille *understands*. Lucille is a girlfriend." And all the churning hips are sassing back: teen queens in twin-scoop halter tops, bifocaled soccer moms, a hard-rockin' grandma who's rumbling up the center aisle, fists pumping: *Do it, pretty baby. Rock me hard!*

It's hard to sit still with B.B.'s fine, tight eight-piece band at full throttle, with the huge beat of two drum sets, a bass rumble that walks right up your pant legs, a rhythm guitar courtesy of "The Fabulous" Leon Warren that is anything but utility. The cables and curtain pulls vibrate; flecks of abused drumstick fly up toward the lights. Bandleader and trumpet player James "Boogaloo" Bolden must weigh three hundred pounds, but he never stops dancing, a syncopated Frigidaire with his COOL setting on permafrost.

Live! is the key to B.B. King's longevity. He noticed long ago that record sales always went up in towns he had played. Crowds got bigger every time he went back, which is probably why, wherever we go, people holler at B.B., "See you next year!" It's a marker as reliable as an equinox: *B.B. King's in town!*

Throughout this string of one-night stands, I make sure to claim my lookout in time to see B.B. walk into the noise and light. There is always a chair in the wings for him to wait for the moment. As he sits there, profiled in the half light, his festival-casual silk shirt falling over his tux pants, there is something calm and Mandela-like about him. The usually expressive face is inscrutable as he surveys the pandemonium of his own making, then steps out to face its consequence as saxman Melvin Jackson hollers:

"Mr. Beeee Beeeeee *King*!"

They're on their feet before he's played a note. It happens nearly every night. And this is where the long road leads, to pangenerational crowds, solid ticket sales, and a robust stock portfolio—B.B. favors blue-chips. At this level, the road becomes its own destination. It affords a nightly renewal that keeps Bob Dylan plying the gyms of backwater academe, propels the rich-as-Croesus Stones, grandfathers now, gigging uproariously toward the millennium.

"You say you want *more*?"

In the glow of an hour's unconditional love, B.B. forgets how much his damned feet hurt, and Lucille sounds forever young. She sails, seduces, stings when the left fingers slip into the trademark perpendicular slide that stamps a B.B. King note. Sitting down casually with his bass and rhythm guitarists, he belts "Rock Me" with enough body language and hormonal glee to make the jaded drink vendors scream here on the Baltimore harbor.

"Domestic disturbance in Aisle Three," crackles a security walkie-talkie. "Man gettin' b'lligerent with his lady, all units . . . . "

Unaware of the wee squall of mace that results, B.B. leans back and roars into the lights.

"Rock me, baby . . . like my back ain't got no bone."

It's tough to get B.B. to own up to his own eloquence. Bulldog him with it, as I'm trying to this muggy Chesapeake morning, and he puts all his achievements at the foot of an entrenched Inferiority Thing. "Stupid fingers"—not

agile or fast enough—is the explanation he has long given for the development of his signature style: “I always liked the steel guitar. I also love the guys that play the bottleneck. Just love the sound of it. But I could never do it; I never made it do what I want. So every time I would pick up the guitar, I’d shake my hand and trill it a bit. For some strange reason my ears would say to me that that sounds similar to what those guys were doing. I can’t pick up the guitar now without doing it. So that’s how I got into making my sound. It was nothing pretty. Just trying to please myself. I heard that sound . . . . ”

B.B.’s signature vibrato is the stringed equivalent of the best soul singer’s melisma—the art of drawing out a note, pulling it like taffy, releasing it a scant heartbeat before the ear can say, “Yes, *now*!” It satisfies like the perfect, unpredictable logic of Miss Ella’s scat. In its fiercer moments, the kind that upend the hairs on your neck, such art does nothing less than make a fragmented world whole.

He has said that money was his first muse, the one that freed him from plantation work. I ask him when the music itself began to shape the life, and he says that it was pretty early on: “I was starting to hear the sound. It was more like a little itch—yeah. Any time I played, I enjoyed playing. The music was soothing to me. Just the notes from a guitar sounded like somebody bringing a kid candy. It was good for me.”

After five decades and millions of permutations on six strings, is he satisfied with his own music?

“It wasn’t what I wanted it to be. I still every so often would search for it. When I’m practicing now, I’m really chasing that sound.” B.B. is dead certain that a perfect sound exists in his universe, though he can’t possibly describe it: “I’ve got close to it, but I haven’t heard it yet.” Ask him whether he’s OK with the idea that he might never hear it, and his ferocity is startling: “No! No, I’m not. As long as you’re alive, there’s a chance. As long as you study and try, there’s a better chance. So I still study, I still practice.”

B.B. is cracking another breakfast egg; we’ve left the dark of the harbor tunnel, and the shipyards of Baltimore shimmer in a morning haze. A big tanker horn blasts farewell. B.B. says he knows this East Coast corridor well. Baltimore had the Royal Theater, part of the Grand Slam in the restless and sophisticated black music market. Playing there, as well as the Apollo in Harlem, the Howard in Washington, DC, and Chicago’s

Regal, certified you as a "made" act. Provided you survived. It was right here in Baltimore that B.B. endured the greatest public hurt that he has ever suffered.

The pretty men are all on the bill, Sixties soul singers so handsome, so clean in soft alpaca and vented sharkskin: Sam Cooke, Jackie Wilson, the Drifters. B.B.'s capable band backs them all; from backstage, he hears the screeching—the kind of uncontrolled, love-me-thrill-me-take-me female wailing that a man only dreams of. Finally, the blues singer is introduced, and those pretty little things are booing. B.B. dresses sharp, but he does not look pretty when he plays, and Lucille makes him grimace, wince, and go all guppy-mouthed. Louder comes their cruel descant: Booooooooo. Tears are rolling down his cheeks as he sings "Sweet Sixteen." He cries hardest when he reaches this line: "Treat me mean, but I'll keep on loving you just the same . . . . One of these days you'll give a lot of money to hear someone call my name . . . . "

"They got quiet then," B.B. says. "I guess they saw the tears. And they applauded me. But that one time, I was hurt like never before. I've felt it many times, been cut down to size for being a blues singer."

He has taken it from the other side, too, for not being blue enough. B.B.'s 1970 "crossover" hit, "The Thrill Is Gone," raised hackles with some blues purists for its gusting studio strings. The very eclecticism that has made his blues popular music—the covers of Ellington classics like "Don't Get Around Much Anymore," the duets with the likes of George Jones and Joe Cocker, the bits of comic onstage shtick that have roots in Ma Rainey's black vaudeville—can set some root-blues aficionados to fanning themselves with a Blind Lemon Jefferson album sleeve.

"Blues purists have never cared for me anyway," B.B. says a bit crossly. "I don't worry about it. I think of it this way: When I made 'Three O'Clock Blues' [his first hit on the R&B charts, in 1951], they were not there. They were not. The people out there made the tune. And blues purists just wrote about it. The people is who I'm trying to satisfy."

Likewise, he has no patience for the self-styled ethnologists who seem to think that a guy who started singing on a Delta street corner shouldn't cover a swank Sinatra tune. B.B. can still sing his uncle's stentorian field hollers, loosed at the end of the workday:

If I feel like this tomorrow . . . .
Feel like I'm gonna make my getaway . . . .

B.B. honors the memory, but he's not going to drag that out on *The Tonight Show*.

"For God's sake, why Vegas?"

This is the question that B.B.'s manager, Sid Seidenberg, fairly shrieked when B.B. decided to make that neon Gomorrah his putative home, in 1975. On the surface it made some sense—Elvis was wowing capacity crowds at the Hilton's showroom, and B.B. rocked those high rollers at the hotel's big lounge hard enough to secure a five-year contract. But at the time, B.B. also had a big IRS debt and an alarming weakness: "I used to gamble like mad. Keno is the thing that got me hooked." There's still a glint in his eye as B.B. describes his biggest score: "They paid me $50,000 in crisp $100 bills!"

Seidenberg, a CPA turned manager who has been with B.B. for more than thirty years now, has guided his sole client into ambitious "five-year plans," hammered out the corporate endorsements that long eluded bluesmen and heckled record companies into respectful box sets, "superstar" duet projects and the like. Seidenberg also suggested a gambling cure to B.B.: Don't draw your salary in Vegas—have them bank it. And don't take casino credit—write checks. Write them out with all those scary zeros and you'll realize how much you're spending. "I did that," says B.B., "and when I noticed how big some of those checks were, that cured my gambling. I go home now; I don't want to go to the casinos."

He prefers to stay at home, in the town house that two secretaries watch over during his long absences. B.B. admits it's more like a warehouse, chockablock with souvenirs, electronic gadgets, and the largest collection of hats this side of Elton John's closet. One of his secretaries, Laverne Toney, has instructions to leave all of B.B.'s toys where they lie when she goes in to empty the six VCRs of his favorite soap-opera tapes (*The Bold and the Beautiful* and *The Young and the Restless*); she ships them out wherever he is. The boss's other secret vice is really kinky: The man can't stop buying office supplies—pens, computer disks. Toney giggles when she conjures the image: big bad old bluesman cruising Staples for a deal on double-A batteries. . . .

"Home? Can you believe that? I'm going home. Gonna stay in my pajamas till I have to get on the next plane. Just sit there . . ."

B.B. is fantasizing about his imminent three-day stopover in Las Vegas. Having rejoined the tour in Dallas after a couple of weeks' absence, I find B.B. looking tired, a bit gray and worrying aloud. "I've always had confidence," he says as he waits to mount the outdoor stage amid a cloud of Texas-size crickets. "I've never thought of going onstage and passing out or anything, just going out trying to make people happy and having fun myself. But it started two months ago, when my diabetes got really out of whack—I started not having the confidence I've had. Each night is like, 'God, can I make it? Can I make it?' So if I can make it tonight and tomorrow . . . . "

We have two nights left out here. And B.B. says he knows he could not make it—anywhere, any time—if not for his cadre of men. Their loyalty and honor have sustained him on the road. Despite our sue-me, sue-you times, B.B. says, their working arrangements are simple. "Just this," he says, extending a big hand and shaking it in the air. Bandleader James Bolden has made that handshake last more than twenty years; few have been with B.B. less than a decade.

B.B. calls it a family: bass player, rhythm guitarist, keyboard player, two trumpets, one saxman, a pair of drummers, roadies, assistants, drivers, security men, and Sherman Darby, the calm, durable tour manager given to watching Truffaut movies—in French—while he does paperwork on the bus. And Norman.

Every busy statesman must have his attendant, and for close to forty-five years, on and off, B.B. has been aided, annoyed, and abetted by one Norman Matthews, a fellow Mississippian and one of his very oldest and truest friends. They met on Norman's birthday in April 1947. They have dodged whining bullets in boardinghouses together, drowned happily in the company of willing women and—before the days when B could command a nightly plate of smoked salmon backstage—shared the last of the tinned sardines and pork and beans.

"You don't think that's good, young lady, you try it when you're hungry," Norman says. He still has a photo taken on a day they were "just plain starvin'" somewhere in the Carolinas. A desperate B.B. went fishing—and ended up in the creek, drenched and still hungry. Norman says he could always finesse a little something. "I dealt a little three-card monte, picked up some change . . . . "

Now that B.B. is mainly vegetarian, and in need of many small meals, Norman is ever at his elbow with a Diet Coke, a sandwich, a Tupperware container rolling with hard-boiled eggs. Norman accompanies B.B. on his yearly tune-up at the Pritikin Longevity Center, in Santa Monica, and absorbs the directives of its dietitians and doctors. Norman cooks a mean plate of butter beans; he knows the names and locations of all B.B.'s lady friends, children, and grandchildren who show up along the road. The two don't have to talk much. Hand signals, shrugs, the semaphore of a raised eyebrow do the job. "I have one brother that's as close as he is," B.B. says. "Norman knows everything. And he tells me *everything*—whether I want to hear it or not."

The loyal bodyman is an honored tradition in soulful circuits: In the Sixties the self-styled King of Rock & Soul, Solomon Burke, employed a midget—Little Sammy—to boogaloo beneath the fifteen-foot ermine-trimmed train of his cape and keep it snapping neatly behind him. Ship out with James "Butane" Brown and you'd better know how to handle a hysterical woman and a hot comb.

The key to a bodyman's strength and longevity is in his very transparency. Much of the time, Norman is onstage but unseen. "Nobody knows who Norman Matthews is, and ain't nobody about to find out," Norman tells me. Even when B.B. and the band are in summer casuals (tuxedo pants and silk print shirts), Norman tucks himself into a fly tuxedo studded with B.B. King lapel pins and American-flag pins. You can always tell where Norman has been sitting by the small heaps of souvenir guitar picks and Lucille-shaped pins that trickle from his pockets.

Toward the end of every show, Norman walks onstage during the final ovation and gives the boss a cup of cold water and handfuls of the giveaways to toss out. Willie King, B.B.'s son, wraps a snowy towel around his father's wet neck and helps him into a warm tour jacket for the final bow. Norman wields a flashlight to get the boss safely backstage. They make a slow, stately procession, two elderly men stepping cautiously out of the bright clamor and into the darkened wings.

One more show to go—Tulsa, Oklahoma—and B.B. is down. He hasn't slept at all. Didn't yesterday, either. As we load up to leave Dallas, a fretful Norman says the boss isn't even eating. Almost before the city limits, B.B. is finally out, slumbering past the newly carved condo buttes, the grazing cattle, the highway that narrows as we hit Oklahoma and becomes a two-lane bordered by trailer parks and ammo shops. He dreams past Okmulgee, where leathery dudes in pickups hoot, honk, and raise arms ringed with tattoos of barbed wire as they recognize the bus with Lucille's likeness. Tulsa is announced by the hiss of brakes. B.B. moves slowly through the front lounge; pillow marks still crease his cheek as he follows Lucille into the hotel lobby. "Gonna sleep some more," he mumbles. "Feel like hell."

Yet four hours later, B.B. is transformed: jaunty Kangol cap, big grin, a wicked cackle as he light-fingers a forbidden bag of chips from the bus kitchenette. He's well enough to talk, strong enough in the hour we sit outside the riverside venue to accept the wild embrace of bluesman Buddy Guy, who has bounded onto the bus after his set in crisp white overalls, bandanna, and glistening Jheri curls. "Where is my King?" Guy is yelling. "I have come to honor my King!"

Along with tour stalwart Dr. John and muscular newcomer Susan Tedeschi, Guy has put the crowd gathered here on the banks of the Arkansas River in a party mood. This being big-oil/cheap-gas country, rackety five-dollar helicopter rides departing from the festival grounds compete with B.B.'s set, which is full, strong, and celebratory. "FIFTY YEARS!" I hear again over the chopper's thwuck thwuck. "THANKYEWWWWW!"

As the eternal flame—Norman's flashlight—guides him back down to the grass, I hear B.B. say to his old friend, "Guess we made it, man."

He is ravenous after the show, chomping on a plate of broccoli, beets, baby corn, carrots. Between bites, he's talking about tonight's walk into the light: "Even when I'm sick, it makes me feel better. I swear to God, it's like therapy for me when they say, 'Here's B.B. King.' And if I'm able to get to that microphone, I feel better. I don't want to stop. Never. I'll retire five or ten years after I'm dead."

He says he will slow down enough to do the things he enjoys. He will spend more time at home in Las Vegas. He plans to fix up the fifty acres he has bought near Indianola, so he can kick back there with the three generations he has begat. And he will keep practicing, straining to hear that sound he hasn't heard yet, coming from himself. If he and Lucille can agree to see a bit less of each other, maybe he'll even get married, provided that his current flame waits. B.B. has a hope chest—nearly $1 million set aside so that any surviving spouse won't have to tussle with that huge crowd of kin when he's gone.

Whenever he gets the chance, when anything crowds him—the business, the women, the kids—he says he will grab a set of keys and do his very favorite, soulsoothing thing. B.B.'s final picture story is not a blues but an American reverie—a rippling mirage, perhaps, since it must take place in the Nevada desert some miles from his town house.

It is hot—hotter than ever it got in Mississippi cottonfields—but blessedly free of the weepy humidity that darkened work clothes half an hour into the day. The dead quiet is broken by the growing roar of an engine powering up the desert road. The motor was built in 1984, the last year that Chevy made its low-riding half-car/half-pickup, the El Camino. This one has been overhauled and painted a baby blue that vibrates against the parched ochers and reds. An elderly black man in soft, expensive clothes is driving; his only air conditioning is the masterful cool of Mitt Jackson's vibraphone floating from the dashboard. Painted on the truck's side are two small musical notes that announce to the rattlesnakes, the roadrunners, the sleepy buzzards:

B.B. King's in town!

Elizabeth Kaye

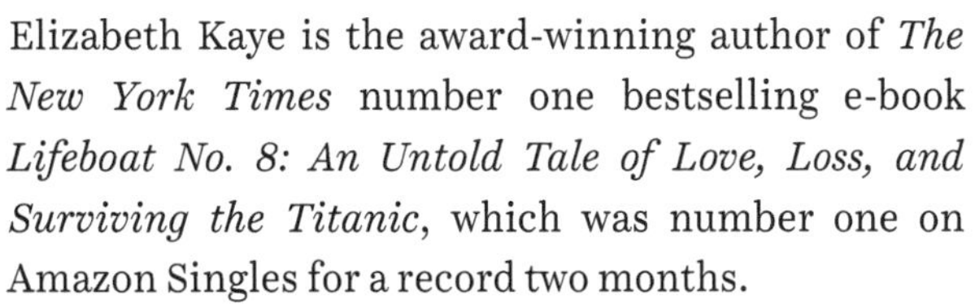

Elizabeth Kaye is the award-winning author of *The New York Times* number one bestselling e-book *Lifeboat No. 8: An Untold Tale of Love, Loss, and Surviving the Titanic*, which was number one on Amazon Singles for a record two months.

A recipient of the Alicia Patterson Fellowship, she has been a contributing editor to *Esquire*, *Rolling Stone*, *Elle*, *Harper's Bazaar*, and John F. Kennedy Jr.'s *George* magazine, and a frequent contributor to the Arts pages of *The New York Times*.

She is the author of six books whose subjects range from American Ballet Theatre to the Los Angeles Lakers. The recent collection of her extensive magazine writing about men, *Men: What They Do, What They Think, and Why,* features profiles of iconic figures ranging from Kobe Bryant and Phil Jackson to Sen. Edward Kennedy and Anthony Hopkins. Other books by Kaye include the memoirs *Mid-Life: Notes From the Halfway Mark* and *Seven Men*.

She lives at the beach in Los Angeles with her man and their cat.

Nureyev Dancing in His Own Shadow

Celebrated and famously volatile ballet dancer Rudolf Nureyev, captured intimately at the end of a glorious career.

What would he seem to be if you did not know what he once was? He never was like the others, and he is not like others now. Long ago, Balanchine told him, "Go and dance the princes out of your head." It may be that he tried. Yet in all the ways that matter most, he was those princes and noblemen: He was Albrecht, compelled to dance himself to death; he was Siegfried, stunned and beckoned by a private, exquisite vision.

There have been times when he felt like the Chosen One, and times when he wondered whether being chosen was a blessing or a curse. Either way, he was indentured by his gift. Ordinary men have careers; Rudolf Nureyev had a destiny. He is aware that dancers often say you cannot be born to dance. "I say you can," he says. "Witness with my life."

He was six years old when he discovered dance. Even now, he can summon every detail of that evening: the tasseled velvet curtain, the stage lights of orange and blue and green. And he remembers the deliberate way the curtain rose, and that the stage was huge and deep, and the way a fresh breeze wafted from it and glazed his cheek. "And then," he recalls, "the gods came dancing."

At that moment he knew that he would be a dancer. He aspired to be bold and unfettered, to inhabit the air. Whether he aspired to be a god was of scant importance. In every city of the world, audiences gathered to receive him as one. And they were not simply responding to a great dancer; they were responding to something infinitely more mystical and uncommon: an artist who was, as Pavlova and Nijinsky had been before him, the living embodiment of the Dance.

He took his bows in a hailstorm of roses. He was courtly, then ardent, as he kissed his partners hand. He acknowledged the shouts of "bravo!" with one uplifted hand, a gesture steeped in majesty and insolence. Then he disappeared behind enfolding curtains, and the houselights went back on. And in taking his leave, he abandoned his audience to the pallid company of other mere mortals.

He was twenty years old when these rites began. He is fifty-two now. And in those intervening years he came to know as much as any man may ever know about what it means to be consumed by a passion.

Rudolf Nureyev opens his eyes. It is eight in the morning. He is tired but cannot fall back to sleep. Last night, after a performance at the Orpheum Theater in San Francisco, he ate dinner, drank a beer and several glasses of wine, returned to his hotel room alone, played piano for an hour, then watched movies on television until 4:30 in the morning. There is nothing unusual in this chain of activity. It was developed over years of traversing the planet on a stateless passport, making his home in the presidential suites of every great and half-forgotten city of the world. Now it is his basic pattern, a proud man's insistence on fashioning a bulwark against loneliness and need.

Nureyev has never liked to be alone. Nighttime visitors to his home have always noted the book-strewn canopied bed, assorted volumes set out like provisions to nourish him through the long night ahead. And though he has come to cherish solitude, he often desires whatever he does not have: Alone, he is apt to crave company; in company he may crave seclusion. And there are no patches of gray; only the irreconcilable tension of black and white.

But even in the years when he could choose from an unending array of women and men, he gave precedence to the adoring strangers who composed his most satisfactory and enduring relationship. "You share so much of yourself onstage," he says, "afterwards you don't want to share. You want to keep yourself to yourself. At fifty-two I don't have a lot of time left to be with me. But if you say that it sounds heavy, *tragique*. It isn't. What it is . . . finally, you marry yourself."

Nureyev enters the kitchen of his hotel suite, padding across the linoleum as silent as a cat. The larder is stocked with his usual fare: packets of instant chicken soup, a five-pound bag of sugar, whole-wheat English muffins, and tea. Years ago his appetites were uniformly voracious, and in a single day he could consume numerous meals, attend half a dozen movies, make love to several people. "We want caviar," he would chant along with Cecil Beaton, "and we want it fresh and we want it now."

At that time, in his twenties, he was bemused by the abstemious habits of the great choreographer Sir Frederick Ashton. In his early fifties, Ashton lunched on boiled eggs. Now, at the age Ashton was then, Nureyev eats boiled eggs, and usually prepares them himself.

"With age you have less desires," Nureyev believes. "You want less and less and less. Eat less. Less love. Less everything."

A few hours later, Nureyev leaves his hotel. He is in a terrible mood. All around him, the air is fragrant and clear. Usually he appreciates fine weather, but now he doesn't notice. There is no special reason for this mood; it seems no more than a foray into the low-grade suffering he tends to enjoy; it has appeared and will depart, as have so many others, with all the meaning of passing clouds. But at this moment his lips are folded into a regal pout, his nostrils are flared, there is steel in his eyes. It is the face of a horse ready to buck, but the body retains its pantherine grace. His walk is deliberate, elegant, contained, his steps long and slow, his hands folded before him, one resting over the other. It is a walk replete with the slightly weary grandeur of a man who would never dream of changing places with anyone, yet has long experienced his own station as a great—and terrible—burden.

Nureyev's Chilean driver opens the door to the San Francisco opera house. Nureyev enters, trailed by his Russian masseur and a sixty-nine-year-old Armenian woman, a friend of many years who rose at six a.m. to make him soup. They proceed to the rehearsal hall, where the American Ballet Theatre company is taking class.

With younger dancers Nureyev will be sly and lascivious and playful, accessible at one moment, at the next, remote. To them, he is a master, a legend, a danseur noble, though most are too young to have seen him when he was, as his mentor Nigel Gosling wrote, "one of those strange haunted creatures that ballet throws up from time to time, through whom some intense, urgent message seems to be passing."

That message was conveyed with such scorching abandon that many critics assumed Nureyev would streak through the ballet world with all the brilliance and longevity of a shooting star. Instead, he stayed on to rouse people who had no serious interest in ballet, forging a vast new ballet audience, while also becoming the first pop icon of the sixties, harbinger of the most blatant and confused sexual era in recent memory. Untamable and defiant, he was part James Dean, part Mick Jagger, part Lord Byron, a blend of fierce sexual authority and the vulnerability of a waif. Later, Baryshnikov's virtuoso performances would athleticize ballet, but it was Nureyev who romanticized it, and without him many of today's young dancers might not be dancing now.

No one, these danseurs say, used the floor as Nureyev did, or had his authority or range of emotions. But lately they also say other things. Why, they ask, does he go on? Why does he dance now that he is no longer the fiery Tatar boy Margot Fonteyn recalls as "a young lion leaping"?

"It's so good to have you in class," a male dancer tells him.

"Because I look so good," asks Nureyev, "or the idea?"

"Well . . . the idea," says the dancer.

Nureyev smiles. "You bitch," he says.

But he pays no attention to what they think. If he paid attention, as he perceives it, he would lose and they would win. The prospect is untenable. He is still fighting his way as he did from the beginning, still embroiled in the furious battle that pitted him first against the father who opposed his ballet training, then against the ballet establishment, critics, and competitors, and finally and most fervently against his own limitations and gravity itself. He was a relentless fighter because he wished so desperately to win. And though he can no longer win in the glorious way that he once did, the battle itself has become a way of life. He can't relinquish it.

Nureyev takes his place at the barre. As he begins his pliés, his expression turns rapt, as if he were lost in some private music. From the outset, he was enchanted by the process of dancing, and class, where that process began, was a respite from the hunger and cold of Ufa, a frigid region dwarfed by snowless mountains, where his family subsisted on baked potatoes. "Class was extraordinary ritual," he recalls. "All unpleasant things vanished."

But today he is too tired to do a good class, and he knows it. And when the young dancers begin their pirouettes, he simply stops and stares. His gaze honed by an uncanny ability to perceive what is wrong in a step, he tells himself, "You could help them create something."

Even in his heyday he was unusually generous in the studio, ready to work endlessly with any dancer who desired his help at any hour of the day or night, his manner typically demanding and uncharacteristically patient. These days he often feels unappreciated. "Nobody's dying to delve into my baggage of knowledge," he will say. In a better mood, he feels differently. "I'm dying to teach somebody," he says with a grin, "but somebody grateful."

And in class, the danseurs practice a la seconde turns, their left legs extended at a 90 degree angle while the pumping motion of their right foot propels them around and around at warp speed. There was a time when Nureyev's execution of this bravura step roused an audience to its well-tended feet, as it did when he and Fonteyn performed *Swan Lake* in Vienna and took eighty-nine curtain calls, still the most ever taken, according to the *Guinness Book of Records*. But now, as he studies the fast-spinning young men, his expression veers from quizzical to interested to contemptuous. Then he tilts his head, shuts his eyes for a millisecond, and arches his neck, a characteristic gesture. It is the gesture of a man who does not give up, who cannot be intimidated by loneliness or frailty or laughter, the gesture of a man who wills himself on, knowing that the nights of eighty-nine curtain calls are far behind him. Watching the young men dance before him, he knows they cannot approach his artistry just as he cannot approach their youth.

"But then suddenly you can do one movement, one gesture," he tells himself, "and you're younger than all of them."

He is a beguiling and difficult figure. His sense of self is as epic as his distrust of others; together, they render him as impenetrable and imperial as he desires to be.

"I used to be so intimidated by you," a younger male dancer tells him.

"But no more?" Nureyev asks.

"Well," says the dancer, "a little."

Nureyev smiles, satisfied. "Just enough," he says, "to be attractive."

Among friends, or after some wine, he will be unguarded and expansive, and as an evening wears on, he will seem youthful and impish. But more often he will be coiled and watchful, ruled by instinct, a cat prepared to pounce. His attitude toward others is ever changing: Warmth cools to indifference, or is supplanted by ice, and these alterations occur with a suddenness that is inexplicable even, at times, to Nureyev himself. Speaking with friends he can be happy, open, engaged. "Yes, sure, of course," he will say, and then he will change. "I don't know," he says abruptly, dismissively, retreating behind a curtain drawn through will or need.

He can be a saint, he can be a devil; it is difficult to ascertain which role he relishes more. "Stage is cathedral," he likes to say, and he means it. Yet onstage, his back to the audience, he works at making other dancers laugh, teasing them with funny faces and dirty names. "The stage is a cathedral for Rudolf," says a ballerina, not unkindly, "when he's facing front."

Because of his early obsession with dancing, he was never really a child; now that same obsession keeps him from seeming middle-aged. Even at fifty-two, and despite a strong attraction to caution and logic, he is rash, elemental, unrepentant. "You swine," he shouts at a recalcitrant dancer as he slaps him across the face. But there are equally sudden bursts of warmth: the enveloping bear hugs, a delighted "aha!" upon seeing an old friend. Outrageously theatrical and unabashedly genuine, his behavior is both an uncensored reflection of his emotions and his longest-running performance.

He loves to shock, to test others' limits. Speaking of the ballet *Blown by a Gentle Wind*, he calls it *Blowjob in the Wind*. At a dinner party, he mentions a Russian public official. "He has large dick," he announces to twelve well-dressed, sedate diners, "which he is eager to share."

A woman leans across the bouillabaisse and crystal. "Mr. Nureyev," she says earnestly, "I've always had such respect for you."

Nureyev laughs. "But no more," he says.

At other times he will be humorless, unreasonable. And though he has ceased to underscore his points by hurling chairs across a stage, his reputation for being temperamental makes hirelings dart gingerly, placating him, anticipating his needs, their anxiety to avoid mistakes making mistakes inevitable. Two hours before he is to dance at the Kennedy Center, an assistant hands Nureyev's tea tray to a new driver. Mr. Nureyev will need this at the theater, he explains, with the subdued urgency that characterizes such instructions. Moments later, Nureyev's white stretch limousine pulls up at the stage door, the tea tray perched on the backseat in solitary splendor. A few minutes later, a dilapidated taxi pulls up behind the limousine and an annoyed Nureyev emerges from it.

Yet it is impossible to predict what will ruffle him: He takes bad news in stride just as often as he is incensed by a trifle. Easily hurt and quick to see slights, he can feel his anger coming, dark and forceful as a locomotive. "Don't speak of this," he will warn, "or I will get angry and then I get ugly." To ignore these warnings is to learn that he means them. But the sway he holds over others is not due to temper, but to a sweetness that emanates from him unexpectedly, like perfume from a thorny rose. When Margot Fonteyn was hospitalized he hastened to her bedside, carrying a bagful of *I Love Lucy* videos and an armful of teddy bears. One night, after an engagement, wealthy guests vied for his attention at a dinner party, but he reserved the seat beside him for a shy and elderly friend. When she demurred, convinced he should sit with someone more prominent, he told her, "I don't need another performance."

Yet he can also be as harsh as Siberian weather. "That Yiddish bitch," he says of a woman whose largely favorable review of his performance mirrored his own analysis.

He exerts a force beyond the obvious pull of his gift and fame, and even those who encounter him in his more virulent moods and vow never to speak with him again keep his photographs displayed on their living-room tables.

His years in the Soviet Union convinced him that no one can be trusted; thirty years as an international celebrity has done little to erase that sense. And this abiding suspicion intensifies his fierce loyalty to the knot of friends he calls "family." Typically his relationships are unusually difficult and unusually sweet. Many of his strongest ties are with women who have the time and inclination to accompany him on the road or to movies and galleries or on shopping expeditions. Often he wants to see two movies and a play in a single day or to organize an elegant dinner for Jacqueline Onassis and Margot Fonteyn on one day's notice. They will exhaust themselves to bring these wishes into being, repaying his affection in ways that border on the pathological. Yet to fully gain his confidence is nearly impossible, and no one gains it in any measure without first passing one of his tests.

"I do not want crusts on my toast," he announced at the first breakfast served to him in the home of Phyllis Wyeth, who was to become a close friend.

"In this house, Rudolf," she told him, "you cut the crusts off yourself."

But the most rigorous tests are reserved for himself, and he plunges into them with the fervor of one who has never doubted the therapeutic value of hardship. He was always arrogant, but years of independence and adversity have made him brave, and he insists on bravery in others. "Is good for you to have to struggle," he commented when his manager, who speaks no Russian, was attempting to navigate Leningrad. Years ago, arriving at La Scala to mount *The Nutcracker*, he informed Italy's prima ballerina, Carla Fracci, that he intended to rechoreograph all of their pas de deux. There were only five days until the first performance. "It is quite impossible," said Fracci. Nureyev turned to the rehearsal pianist.

"*Maestro*," he said.

They worked hard for four days, and at the performance, during the final pas de deux, the audience began to applaud, and rose to its feet, shouting "bravo!" During the curtain call Nureyev beamed, knowing as Fracci also knew, that the evening was one of her most successful. Taking her hand, as he brought her forward for yet another bow, he turned to her and said, "You see what it is to have courage."

Even in the classics he was an intensely personal dancer. All that he was and never could be was manifested in his art. It may be that no successful man was ever more primitive or more extraordinarily refined. He was brutal and tender, spiritual and carnal; in the span of a few minutes, he could evoke Christ on the cross and Mephistopheles.

As a poor child trapped in a remote province, he dreamed of Leningrad, home of the Kirov Ballet, spawning ground for Pavlova, Balanchine, and Nijinsky. He was seventeen when he finally auditioned for the academy where Kirov dancers train, seeking to begin serious training at an age when it is customarily completed. His compact muscles were wrong for ballet; the late start presented serious problems. "Young man," a Kirov teacher told him, "you'll either become a brilliant dancer or a total failure. And more likely you'll be a failure."

Three years later, a young French writer attended one of his early performances. "I think I just saw the world's greatest dancer," she cabled her editors. "Master your emotions," read the reply. But soon came countless echoes of her assessment. "There is something of the genius in him," the great teacher Vera Volkova told Fonteyn, "He has the nostrils."

Yet dancing would never come easily to him. Even in his prime, his technique could be ragged, and though it lent his performances an intriguing edge absent from more consistent performers, it frustrated Nureyev beyond endurance. Rehearsing *La Bayadére*, he practiced until his legs wore out, trying to perfect double assemblés. Performing them, he lost control; mortified, he fled the stage. The next day, he was at work again, applying himself with all the focused intent of Sisyphus pushing the stone uphill. "Everything that Rudy had," says Carla Fracci, "he really obtained with his will."

"Surely he ought to save somewhere," Margot Fonteyn thought when she first saw him dance, certain that the effort he expended on each motion would preclude finishing his solo. She was not yet acquainted with Nureyev's strength or his desperate drive to match the ideal that possessed him. Termed a perfectionist, he disliked the word. "Perfection is sterile," he says. "My ideal is not everybody's perfection."

His strivings to reach that ideal were more intense because he knew he would usually fail to achieve it. "You sense expectation of the audience," he recalls, "and you expect from yourself something extraordinary, you have to astonish yourself, you expect a miracle and you're not sure it's going to be there."

His own severest critic, he plunged into black moods, unsettling members of the Royal Ballet, his adopted company. "He's angry with himself," Margot Fonteyn would tell them, "and with nobody else."

But then, often when he was tired, his muscles would simply go his way. And later, attempting to describe those moments, he would speak of exultation and transcendence. But at the time there was only the leaping and the soaring and the inner voice that told him, *I am.*

And for all the work invested in technique, no work was required to convey his love of dance. Nor did he labor on the passionate urgency that animated every step he took onstage. "That passion is already embedded in me, you know," he says. "I don't have to work on it."

Rudolf Nureyev returned to Leningrad in November 1989. He was fifty-one years old. He had come to dance one final time with the Kirov Company before it was too late. In the considered opinion of many, too late had come and gone. "What variation of the variations will he do?" his former Kirov ballerina's wondered.

Nureyev still worshiped the Kirov, still viewed the company as the most lyrical and sublime. And he still revered the Kirov's former prima ballerina, Natalia Dudinskaya, who had been forty-eight years old when she honored the twenty-year-old Nureyev with an invitation to make his debut with her.

Dudinskaya understood the way that magic is created onstage, and from her Nureyev absorbed what cannot be taught. Speaking of her, he would always extol her power "to sparkle, to make performance," qualities he would revere and revel in for the rest of his life. And in all that she taught him about dancing, she was steeping him in an ideal. This was the nineteenth-century ideal of classicism, one Nureyev could mold himself to readily, for it was the absolute expression of what he had always been. "I am a romantic dancer," he used to say, and it was a precise description.

But then, in the silence after a performance, he would remove his makeup and costume and slip back into a Soviet world he instinctively opposed, where his refusal to join the communist party or go to indoctrinations or sit on the company bus singing Soviet songs made clear that he had no stomach for living in the expected manner. "Like amoeba," as he describes it now.

He defected in June 1961, a twenty-three-year-old with thirty-six francs in his pocket, ignorant of Western ways, commencing a life that would be forever haunted by nightmares in which he made desperate runs for the border. And now, returned to the Kirov, he was pleased at the prospect of dancing once more on its stage.

"It will be good for you," he told himself, "cleansing experience."

But for twenty years he had driven his body through as many as 250 performances a year, a feat just this side of masochism. And though his artistry was still matchless enough to cause the young Kirov ballerina he partnered to marvel, even Nureyev had long admitted his feet were shot and that his jump and elasticity were gone. But then artistry outlasts facility; that is the way things are. And thirty-two years had passed since the night of Nureyev's dazzling Kirov debut, and now he was forced to stop rehearsal in order to rest, and Dudinskaya walked with a cane.

Nureyev's Kirov engagement underscored that he had delayed the reckoning for as long as he could. "I have outlived my time," he would say a few weeks later, and it was true, of course, as it always becomes true for dancers. The process is swift and punishing, though considerably more so for some than for others. It had not been easy for Erik Bruhn, the brilliant Danish dancer who was the love of Nureyev's life. "You panic," Bruhn said, looking back at when he began to lose his powers. "Whether you talk about it or not it is with you day and night."

For Nureyev, it was no better, and likely far worse. Unlike Bruhn, or Baryshnikov, for whom performing was often painful, Nureyev was one of those theatrical creatures who found onstage a universe far stronger and more appealing than life.

"What you have onstage may be untrue," he often said, "but maybe it's more true than the other."

Over the years, knowing he needed to dance less, he had attempted other ventures, only to be disappointed. Lukewarm reviews greeted his brief foray into movies; faint praise or none was bestowed on most of his original choreography. Most recently, after an agonizing seven-year tenure, he resigned his prestigious post as artistic director of the Paris Opéra Ballet, a position widely viewed as ideal for him. And though his directorship breathed life back into that moribund company, he had been so determined to keep dancing that he dedicated six months a year to performing in any far-flung cranny with a stage. And his protracted absences from Paris—in violation of his contract—angered the company and the management. "Paris Opéra Ballet does not give sabbaticals," the board's president said.

And now he was touring the United States in a stage revival of *The King and I*. His drawing power was still phenomenal, and in nine months on the road, the production would make $11 million, but his reviews were poor and sometimes downright insulting, and in any case, he would rather have been dancing.

Years before, he told Bruhn that unless he danced incessantly he would lose belief in himself. Now, dancing much less, he had become more easily hurt and needful of reassurance, maladies apt to worsen as time passed.

For inexorably, his life as a dancer was ebbing away. It was, he would explain, a "gradual descent," the demand for him diminishing, fewer engagements. In the spring of 1990, his dance troupe, Nureyev and Friends, would play a dozen cities in Mexico, Canada, and the United States, and the tour, he assumed, would be his last. "There's a natural kind of death," he tells his manager. There are times when he is fatalistic about this and times when he isn't.

He has always dreaded this moment, steadfastly contriving to postpone or ignore it. Turning thirty-nine, he was scared and depressed. Never again, he told Bruhn, would he dance Siegfried in *Swan Lake*. But he continued for ten more years, until critics who had lavishly praised him began beseeching him in print to find another outlet for a talent that was still formidable, but utterly changed.

"You want me to stop? No, I'd die," he said to Clive Barnes eight years ago.

"I don't know. Maybe I will die," he says now, "God knows."

For Rudolf Nureyev, reaching middle age was bound to be uniquely traumatic, not only for him, but for his audience, who did not wish to age any more than he did. He had been beautiful, of course, but there was more to it than mere aesthetics. As Nijinsky had before him, Nureyev had come to represent human possibility. That was at the heart of his legend. His own youth had burned so intensely that it could ignite the forty-two-year-old Margot Fonteyn, who was about to retire when she met him, having danced her first *Swan Lake* when Nureyev was three months old. And because he had embodied youth and seemed to bestow it, it was no wonder that dancers and audiences presumed that Nureyev would never grow old.

One night, preparing for the tour he assumes will be his last, he does a barre backstage. "This is the crux of my training," he says, executing a slow turn that requires utmost control. Then he stops, his face pensive. "Crux . . . crux . . . is that like crucifixion?" he asks.

Fourteen years ago, seeing the end of his career encroaching, the great Russian danseur Yuri Soloviev committed suicide. "You have to be a dancer to understand," Nureyev had said upon hearing of it. Every dancer could recite a grim litany of that single theme. And one night a Russian-speaking man comes backstage and tells Nureyev of a retired Kirov dancer who currently does wardrobe for college productions. Listening, Nureyev tightens his lips and shakes his head, as if trying to ward off what he is hearing. Later, repeating the story to a friend, a shudder goes through his body. "It is grotesque," he says. And now, at fifty-three, he is no longer being invited to dance leading parts. "So when I went to Kirov," he says one evening, suddenly sad, as if the truth were dawning on him at that very moment, "when I went to Kirov . . . that was last time."

"But I can still pull it off, no?" he asks. "Have to do longer classes and practice in nice warm weather in good climate. But I can pull it off. It would be no problem."

Curtain time for *The King and I* is 8:30. At that time precisely, twenty minutes before his first entrance, Nureyev strides through the stage door. In the old days, to feel an adrenaline rush before a performance, he worked himself into a rage and became verbally abusive. "I always thought it was funny," recalls Margot Fonteyn. "But you could take it personally."

These days, the reason for his last-minute arrival is a source of speculation among crew and cast. "He does it to get that rush," says a stage manager.

"He does it," says an actor, "because he can."

Backstage, Nureyev is unfailingly sweet with the dozen youngsters who play his children. A few months into the tour, they wrote a newspaper and proudly showed it to him. "Is it good?" they asked.

"Is very good," he told them, "but you need gossip."

When he is not onstage, he retreats to his dressing room and plays the piano. Convinced he learns best from what is most difficult, he has been teaching himself Bach's *Das Wohltemperierte Clavier.* He plays haltingly, but prettily. "Is probably absurd," he tells a friend, "but it gives me thrill."

Since arriving in the West, he has talked of becoming a conductor, a career with the advantage of enduring past middle age. Recently, his manager investigated the possibility of his enrolling at Juilliard, and he has been encouraged by two European conductors. "I need third blessing," he told Leonard Bernstein a year ago.

And now, as he plays, a worn Neiman Marcus terry-cloth robe is draped over his shoulders, obscuring his bright silk costume. His feet, brutalized from the years of dancing, are covered by heavy gold clogs. On the dressing table, Lancôme mascaras and a sienna lip pencil are tossed beside bottles of back- and chest-pain remedies, and a pile of half-read fan letters filled with long-familiar phrases: *Thank you for all the joy . . . your genius will remain with us . . . I will never forget how brilliant you were . . . forever etched in my memory. . . .*

Hearing his cue, Nureyev hurries toward the stage, the robe still over his shoulders, like a boxer about to enter the ring. His dresser follows, carrying a Thermos filled with heavily sugared tea. Waiting in the wings, Nureyev sips the tea, winks at chorus boys, or pinches them, and calls the cutest ones Poopsie. Stepping out of the clogs, he steps onto the stage, and his dresser turns the shoes around so he can slip back into them easily.

Dancing, he loses himself in the thrill of movement. Acting, he watches and criticizes himself. "Is like a sports commentator," he tells a friend. "I am always thinking. Now he runs, now he turns."

"Your king enjoys being king," a fan tells him backstage.

"Why be king," he asks, "if you can't enjoy it?"

Nureyev is preparing to leave the theater. There is just the barest chill in the California night air. But he is always cold, and now he dresses in a wool sweater, buttons a heavy Missoni sweater over it, dons his large tweed coat, a multicolored Kenzo cape, and his beret.

Years ago, leaving a stage door, he required police protection. Rudimania was in full force then, that pre-Beatles orgy of mass hysteria, complete with wild-eyed fans straining against barricades. Now wherever he goes, a small group of fans still waits, and sometimes this pleases him, and sometimes it reminds him of how much things have changed. "You're ten years too late," he once told an autograph seeker. On this night, a dozen men and women stand at the stage door.

"Mr. Nureyev," a man calls to him, "I'd just like to tell you how wonderful you are."

Nureyev smiles. "Don't restrain yourself," he says.

He signs the programs, then bids the fans good night, moving swiftly to his waiting car. He gathers his heavy coat around him and glances up disapprovingly at the dark, starry sky. He pulls the coat still tighter. "I'm afraid of the cold," he says.

He does not look back. He never did. "Look back," he used to say, "and you fall downstairs." Still, at rare moments, it pleases him to recall his past.

"Nothing was extraordinary in a way," he says of the years following his defection. "I went to Paris Opera—I danced there already in my mind. I went to La Scala, to Covent Garden—I already danced in my mind everywhere."

Once, attending a play, he had somehow known the entire plot. He couldn't understand why. "Then it dawned on me," he says, "that a few years before, they gave me the script to read. In a way, coming to the West was like that. I already read that script, I wrote it myself, and now it is happening according to that."

As a young Kirov dancer, he dreamed of dancing with Fonteyn, though prior to meeting her in 1961, Nureyev knew neither what she looked like nor her age. "But name," he says, "was magic."

Their partnership was to be an inspired union of the world's most elegant ballerina and its most explosive danseur. And their eighteen-year age difference and the disparity in their backgrounds and training were subsumed by a shared aesthetic that permitted their onstage melding to be seamless and sublime. For fourteen years they were in such demand that when the Royal Ballet performed abroad, they danced every performance, while a generation of the Royal's ballerinas languished in the wings, and most of the company's danseurs, knowing their day would never come, disintegrated into alcoholics.

But for Nureyev and Fonteyn, those years were an enchantment intensified by knowing it could not last. "If I'm sensible," Fonteyn thought after their first few performances, "I would retire now on this high note." But she went on, as enthralled with him as he was with her, neither of them wanting it to end, and Nureyev dreading it particularly.

"When my time comes," she once asked him, "will you push me off the stage?"

And he had answered, "Never."

But in 1980 Fonteyn was sixty years old. Nureyev was forty-two and still dancing Romeo, while she had forsaken Juliet for Lady Capulet. She often spoke of retiring.

"Why don't you just keep going," he would say.

"I've done that," she finally told him. "I've kept going for a long time."

Then she was gone, and he found himself wishing that Gelsey Kirkland could provide for him the igniting force he had provided for Fonteyn. But that did not happen, of course. The glory of their years together was never to be replicated. And though many fine things came to Nureyev after Fonteyn stepped aside, nothing would ever be quite the same.

Like anyone, he has good nights and bad nights, and the bad nights can be bad indeed. Those are nights when it seems that no one is more alone than a man who owns six extraordinary dwellings but has forsaken his homeland.

Information was always his one real possession, his means to satiate curiosity and fill the void. "I want to be pupil," he always insisted to choreographers.

His passion for learning was obvious, and noted by anyone who saw him fixate on Balanchine or Ashton during rehearsals, or watched him navigate a museum, magnifying glass in hand, or observed his excitement upon being given the complete works of Shakespeare, or knew of the intent way he read all of Byron before choreographing *Manfred*. But for Nureyev, knowledge is like sex: It soothes and tantalizes but does not save, and on bad nights he is apt to dismiss his assiduously gathered information as "haphazard," and sink into his resident sadness.

In the beginning, there were countless distractions from that sorrow. "I was in love with three people," he recalls. "I was in love with Margot, in love with Erik Bruhn, in love with Ashton." And wherever he went, men and women desired him. "To know what it is to make love as a man and as a woman," he says now, "is special knowledge."

But within this libidinous mélange, Erik Bruhn was an exception: The only person perceived by Nureyev as a peer, he was also the only person who could wield power over him.

The West's leading danseur, Bruhn was an exquisite Dane mired in all the psychic baggage his nationality implies, a perfectionist who could give an impeccable performance and come offstage feeling suicidal. Nureyev was a nineteen-year-old student when he saw a film of Bruhn dancing the *Black Swan* pas de deux, and was transported by a reserve and simplicity so counter to his own flamboyance.

"Bruhn is cold," a student commented.

"He's so cold he's like ice," Nureyev answered. "Touch it and it burns you."

And from the moment he saw Bruhn dance, his defection was assured. "Whether as friend, lover, or enemy," he told himself, "I have to go to that camp and learn it all." Within a year, he was in Copenhagen studying with Bruhn's teacher, and he had become Bruhn's lover.

Nureyev was twenty-three then, young and very raw, still developing his technique, while the thirty-three-year-old Bruhn was polishing what critics uniformly hailed as technical and artistic perfection. But Nureyev was hungry, while Bruhn, having always lacked the stimulus of competition, had long sensed himself at a dead end. And now he found a tonic in Nureyev's dancing, and inspiration in the unabashed romanticism he had never had. At the same time, he found a threat, and he was not alone in that.

"Some people," Bruhn said later, "said that Rudik came out of Russia for the express purpose of killing me." He never believed that himself, but his mood often turned morbid and dark. And he accused Nureyev of trying to unseat him.

"How can you be so evil?" Nureyev answered, and burst into tears.

Still, ambivalent as he must have been, Bruhn helped Nureyev in every possible way and even coached him for his first *Giselle* with Fonteyn, an event swamped in such endless hype that it was destined to either break Nureyev or make his career in the West. But afterward, when the audience response turned to pandemonium, and Nureyev, overcome by the triumph of the moment, knelt and kissed Fonteyn's hand, Bruhn fled the theater. "And I was running after him and fans were running after me," Nureyev recalls. "It was a mess."

And when Nureyev came to be perceived as the West's leading danseur, they were pitted against each other. "I mean, the press saw us together," Bruhn said, "and they watched us like hawks, and it was as if they had placed bets on which of us was going to survive."

Their romance was too tempestuous to last, though their working relationship continued, always strangely diabolical, as if each existed to be a challenge to the other, and to fill the other with despair. "After seeing your Albrecht," Nureyev once told Bruhn despondently, "I don't think I can ever dance it again." Yet, their professional alliance remained productive for a quarter of a century.

Erik Bruhn was fifty-eight when he was diagnosed with lung cancer. After that, there was not much time. Nureyev hastened to the hospital. Bruhn had always hoped he would not die in one of his depressions because, "Then, everything would seem meaningless," he once explained. But now, in a Canadian hospital, the two men spent the day together, and afterward it was said that it had been one of their very good days. The next morning, Nureyev returned to the hospital. Bruhn was in a coma.

Later, Nureyev's bedside visit was related to Carla Fracci, Bruhn's primary partner and one who knew of their hold on each other. "Erik waited for Rudy," said Fracci, "before he would let himself die."

It is almost two in the morning. Nureyev sips wine in the hotel bar. Gradually the night turns into one of those occasions when each conversation takes a dark turn and all triumphs attenuate into sorrow.

There is the Royal Ballet's misuse of him after Fonteyn retired, the Boston Ballet's failure to credit him for his production of *Don Quixote*, which assured the company's survival. "Very ungrateful of Boston Ballet," he says. "However. What other cheerful matters?"

Lately he has been preoccupied by his replacement at the Paris Opéra Ballet by the thirty-one-year-old Patrick Dupond. "He's very nice boy," Nureyev says. "He's charming at the dinner. But he doesn't know classical dance."

Not all that Nureyev did as the Paris Opéra Ballet's artistic director was successful but it was all the product of an original and intriguing mind: a Cinderella set in the Hollywood of the 1930s; a production of Henry James's *Washington Square* set to music by Charles Ives; the commissioning of works from all the great modern choreographers, from Martha Graham to Paul Taylor to Merce Cunningham to Glen Tetley.

"It isn't nothing," he says. "It isn't shit. They *know* it. But they won't say it."

A ragged woman enters the lobby. She approaches Nureyev, asking him for money in thickly accented English.

"You are from where?" he asks.

"From France," she says.

Nureyev pulls nine crumpled dollar bills from his pocket, slowly smoothing each one against his leg. He hands the bills to the woman. As she walks away, he shakes his head. "Why I help the French?" he wonders.

He finishes his glass of wine. He is silent for a moment. "Nobody remembers me," he says finally. All evening, people have asked for his autograph, but the attention did not register. In the distance he hears Elvis singing "Suspicious Minds." "What happened to Elvis?" he asks.

And suddenly he seems bereaved, and the glamour of his past seems very long ago. Once, there were trips with Bobby Kennedy and Margot Fonteyn on Onassis's yacht. And there was the night Montgomery Clift cooked him a steak, and the evening Princess Margaret refused to stand up because her sable coat was shorter than his, and there were the dinners he gave for Maria Callas at his villa in Monte Carlo. Now, so many years later, his New York City living room is dominated by two mustard-colored velvet couches purchased from the Callas estate.

Nureyev raises himself up from the banquette. As he slowly crosses the empty lobby, his loneliness seems grim and basic and unassuageable. He rings for the elevator, and once inside, moves into the corner, holding on to the brass rail as if it were a ballet barre. Then the elevator door closes and he ascends to his vast suite, a solitary traveler in a world without memory.

In February, Nureyev is in San Francisco and no longer certain that his ballet troupe will go on tour.

"It's off, it's on," he tells a friend. "Every day there is big question if it's happening or not happening." He doesn't bother going to class. Without incentive, he sees no point in subjecting himself to the strain. "After three days off, I'd faint," he said nearly twenty years ago. Now he stays away for a week.

"How can you?" a dancer asks.

"With pleasure," he says.

Then the tour is set, and each day he calls the presenters to complain about the scheduled program. "Is too thin," he keeps saying. He wants to add Flemming Flindt's *The Lesson* but is told it is too expensive. "Then I just will not go to any official receptions," he replies. "You don't respect my choice, I don't respect your effort." A week later, he gets what he wants.

At month's end, American Ballet Theatre comes to San Francisco for a fiftieth-anniversary gala and two weeks of engagements. The company's new executive director, Jane Hermann, has long been a friend of Nureyev's, briefly fueling speculation that she would ask him to take over the company as artistic director when Baryshnikov quit. Then it is rumored that she would invite him to take part in the gala, but she doesn't. In private, he speaks bitterly of ballet politics and of feeling passed over; in public he maintains his diva-like exterior. The evening of the gala, his chauffeur drives him to the restaurant where he is to join the stars who took part in the event at a celebratory dinner given by Hermann. The chauffeur circles the block of the restaurant, unable to find a place to park. "There's no parking till midnight," he explains to Nureyev.

"It's midnight in Paris," Nureyev says.

Having arrived before the other guests, he drinks a beer in the bar. He hates to wait but does so now with equanimity. Soon people in evening clothes trickle in, among them the columnist Herb Caen, who often saw Nureyev dance in San Francisco. Now he tells Nureyev about the gala. "Best performance I've ever seen," says Caen.

Nureyev's mouth tightens. "Good," he says.

And as Caen describes the evening's program, which included a brief film clip of Nureyev dancing *Raymonda*, Nureyev listens politely, his proud face upturned as if posing for Scavullo. In a few days his frustration will boil over in a nasty public scene with Jane Hermann, but for now, a man who has known Nureyev since the early days watches him from a corner, "How gracious Rudolf is," he thinks, "about his star having fallen."

The Rudolf Nureyev Farewell Tour opened in Querétaro, Mexico, in March 1990. Nureyev arrived in Mexico feeling ill, shuffling as he walked, and calling his condition pneumonia.

"How will he ever recover in time?" the dancers asked one another.

This is the second year that Nureyev will dance only character parts, having scaled down a repertoire that previously included Balanchine's *Apollo*. Recently the Balanchine estate refused to give him permission to dance it, one more sign that it is time to accept what has long been obvious. On opening night, while Nureyev dances, two of the company's ballerinas watch him from the wings. Among themselves, they describe his movements as "poetic . . . profound . . . distilled," and as the tour continues they watch him every night, and sometimes they weep, moved by how much he loves the process of dance.

Long ago Nureyev said, "The only voice you listen to is that of your talent." Now he says, "The only critic is a full house," and as he travels to a succession of what one dancer calls "suburbs and outskirts," the houses are full consistently.

As the tour reaches its end, presenters call Nureyev's manager, requesting Nureyev and Friends for 1991. The offers are from Grand Rapids, Philadelphia, Athens, Ohio—hardly the world's great venues. But to Nureyev, all that matters is that there is still a demand for him.

All that he had ever done implied that the end would come with a bang, but it is not working out that way. And maybe that is just as well, for a whimper might be kinder. And maybe the reckoning can be staved off a little more, and in the time newly bought maybe the inevitable would seem more tolerable.

And if he is not the most cautious custodian of his legend, perhaps he has come to believe what Erik Bruhn said several years before: "If we go on beyond the age when things become difficult, it doesn't really matter, because even if we lose face our achievements have already been recorded in history."

One night, standing backstage, he watches his protégé Charles Jude, a French-Vietnamese dancer with a distinct resemblance to the young Nureyev. "After you," Nureyev once told Fonteyn, "he's my favorite partner."

Jude is dancing *The Sleeping Beauty* grand pas de deux, which Nureyev used to dance in a manner as thrilling as it was exquisite. And as Jude completes a series of grand jetés, the audience begins to cheer. Nureyev smiles. "Fireworks are for youth," he says.

Moments later, it is time for him to perform Othello in *The Moor's Pavane*. When he is finished, the ovation begins, as it has each night. The audience is fervent. And it is not merely a performance they applaud. They are applauding a life given over to the Dance. Nureyev stands before them, regal as he was as a youth. Still they applaud him. He bows once more. The slight smile he allows himself is incandescent.

Rudolf Hametovitch Nureyev, contract player who never cancels, enters yet another airport. It is eight in the morning, and he is headed from Washington, DC, to Thunder Bay, Ontario. He has just learned there will be a layover in upstate New York. He is not pleased. "Fucking Buffalo," he says.

He sits and reads the paper. Visible behind him, through a window, there are huge jets like those he emulated in the days when he could leap and soar. "Is very impressive when jumbo jet moves on the runway," he says, "and goes more to the ground before it goes up, and then—this extraordinary thing—it takes off and flies."

But now Nureyev walks deliberately onto the airplane. He regrets nothing. He wants only to go on, to move forward as he has since he was born, fifty-three years ago, on a train speeding through the Ural Mountains.

No figure in dance is more admired by Nureyev than the American choreographer Paul Taylor. A year ago, outside Cairo, Taylor found a tiny beetle pushing on Cheop's pyramid, as if trying to scale a structure that has become synonymous with the human spirit. Taylor brought the beetle home and placed it in a cricket cage. Like all beetles, this one makes a ball of grass and twigs and then rolls it. "But they don't just roll it the easy way," says Taylor, "they roll it uphill. And they're programmed to do that. It's not that they decide. Every day the beetle rolls that ball. And every day it tries to reach the top of the cage. It can't. It's impossible. But that doesn't stop him from trying."

With love, and without irony, he named the beetle Rudolf.

Jeanne Marie Laskas

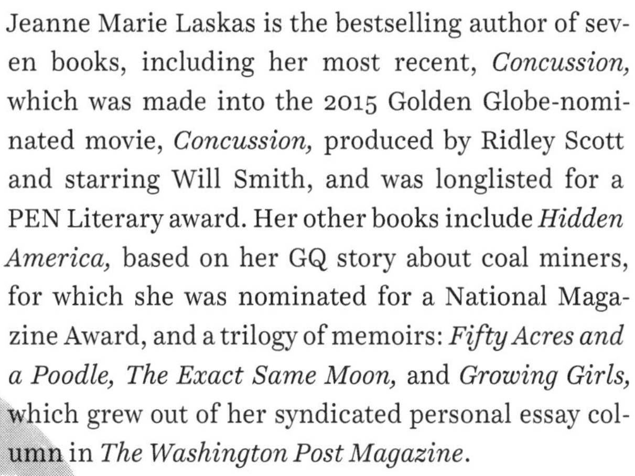

Jeanne Marie Laskas is the bestselling author of seven books, including her most recent, *Concussion,* which was made into the 2015 Golden Globe-nominated movie, *Concussion,* produced by Ridley Scott and starring Will Smith, and was longlisted for a PEN Literary award. Her other books include *Hidden America,* based on her GQ story about coal miners, for which she was nominated for a National Magazine Award, and a trilogy of memoirs: *Fifty Acres and a Poodle, The Exact Same Moon,* and *Growing Girls,* which grew out of her syndicated personal essay column in *The Washington Post Magazine*.

Laskas writes regularly for *The New York Times Magazine, The New Yorker,* and *GQ* about subjects ranging from migrant workers and fake hit men, to cowboys, airships, mules, and the White House. Her work has appeared in *Esquire, Smithsonian,* and numerous other magazines and anthologies including many in the *Best American* series. She has won more than a dozen Gold Quill awards for Excellence in Journalism.

A professor at the University of Pittsburgh, where she teaches and directs The Writing Program, Laskas is the founding director of the university's Center for Creativity. She lives on a horse farm with her husband and two daughters in Scenery Hill, Pennsylvania.

The New Face of Richard Norris

Richard Norris undergoes complex transplant surgery, giving him a new face and a new life, but leaving him with many of the same problems.

Before we bring him in, maybe we can open the floor to some questions. This will be your first time meeting him. He's very comfortable with people evaluating him. Because right now he's being looked at almost as an experiment. Which he is. He's a human-subjects experiment.

Richard Norris was twenty-two when he shot himself in the face. This was back in 1997. He doesn't remember how or why it happened, but his mom, who was three feet away, said it was an accident. She remembers pieces of Richard's face showering her body. This was in the living room. The gunshot had blown off his nose, cheekbones, lips, tongue, teeth, jaw, and chin, leaving just his wide brown eyes and a swirl of nameless twisted flesh.

The miracle that would come to define Richard's life begins with these tragic details. Like most miracles, with each retelling, the edges of the story sharpen, the colors become more vibrant, and the shadows disappear. Ashamed of his appearance, Richard became a hermit, living for nearly a decade on a foggy mountaintop in rural Virginia with his parents. They covered the mirrors in the house so Richard wouldn't have to look at his hideous face. He stayed in his room even to eat, wore a black mask on the rare occasions he came out. According to legend, one time the cops stopped him at gunpoint, mistaking him for a robber.

Then one day, searching on the Internet, his mom found Eduardo Rodriguez, a Baltimore reconstructive facial surgeon. He promised Richard he would make him normal. Over the next few years, Rodriguez performed dozens of surgeries using Richard's own flesh, fashioning a nose-shaped appendage out of tissue from his forearm and a small chin out of flesh from his legs, but these crude approximations failed to make Richard normal. Meantime, Rodriguez had a grander idea in mind. He was driven to achieve perfection. He had been practicing face transplants on cadavers. What he envisioned for Richard was the most extensive transplant any surgeon had ever attempted: He would give Richard a whole new face.

"It's showtime," Rodriguez said one day.

"You're my godsend," Richard's mom said.

"Let's do this thing," Richard said.

The surgery started at dawn on March 19, 2012. The face of a recently deceased twenty-one-year-old man came off as one solid flap, skin, muscle, bone, nerves, blood vessels, tongue—everything as one piece. Rodriguez removed what was left of Richard's disfigured face, dissected down to the skull. He attached the new face midway back on Richard's scalp. He stabilized it with screws, tapped the jaw together, and finally draped the skin and sewed it down like a patch on a coat or a pair of jeans.

You can see the junction; the incision actually goes here in the coronal, extends in front of the ear, and goes posteriorly all the way down, uh, to the neck.

Rodriguez and his team worked nonstop for thirty-six hours, and when they were finished, Richard's mom looked at her son and felt like he was somehow resurrected. "We have Richard back!" she said on the phone to Richard's dad, who had not had much of anything to say for many years.

With his new face, Richard, now thirty-nine, became a media sensation for a time, the story of the miracle told many times over until it hardened even in Richard's mind into a kind of precious jewel.

Maybe we can scroll through some of the clinical photographs while we're talking. I feel very happy about the bony union here. That's the donor palate.

And that's the donor floor mouth. The donor hair, it's a little darker than his. His is a little bit more salt-and-pepper.

Most of the thirty or so people gathered in the conference room are wearing white coats or lanyards or both, and they sit visibly captivated by the photographs Rodriguez is describing. The mood is electric, scrambled, like a show on opening night. The pictures show Richard, who's waiting in an adjacent room for his cue to enter. The expectation lends an extra edge of drama to the presentation. He's flown up here to New York from the foggy mountaintop where he still lives, so that the assembled doctors and other clinicians at NYU Langone Medical Center can meet him.

Rodriguez is an imposing figure, tall and broad, with a big dimple on his giant chin, wide pinstripes, cuff links, and unbuckled galoshes affecting a disheveled nonchalance. In the wake of his world-famous work on Richard, he was just named NYU's chair of plastic surgery, a substantial professional promotion ("like I've just been handed the keys to the starship *Enterprise*," he told me). In part, he's been hired to get NYU into the face-transplant business, and today, as the hospital begins the process for its first one, he's brought his star patient before his new colleagues.

One of the things you'll notice is he has a couple of these scratches. He tends to pick and scratch a bit.

Since the first face transplant, in 2005, only three American hospitals have performed the procedure. Many of the twenty-eight transplants were partial, sections of the face transplanted from deceased donors. Richard's transplant was a full face and is said to be the most ambitious ever. Rodriguez likens the medically complex procedure to the Apollo moon landing.

Surgical difficulty aside, the fact that Richard didn't need a new face to survive raised an ethically grim question: Is a "life-enhancing" surgery worth the risk? There was a good chance he'd die—either on the operating table or later, if his body rejected the face. Of course, for people disfigured like Richard, the breakthrough represents something far beyond a mere enhancement. Here was new hope for millions of people disfigured by trauma, burns, disease, or birth defects. Wounded warriors suffering ballistic facial injuries would now have a surgical option that would go light-years beyond the currently available treatments. No more Band-Aid cosmetic surgeries. No more skin grafts that might only complicate your appearance. Now you could get rid of that face and replace it whole. "We've gone beyond the boundary of what we thought was even possible," Rodriguez tells me.

One by one, some of the specialists in the conference room who had a chance to evaluate Richard earlier today stand up to speak of their findings. Concerns emerge, principally about Richard's state of mind. Has he become too emotionally attached to Rodriguez, the medical attention, the fame? What will happen to him now that Rodriguez has moved on to a new hospital, new face transplants, new miracles?

We were both struck by how good he looks and the really excellent aesthetic result.

He reported to me no chewing or swallowing problems.

I was having trouble understanding him.

I asked: Do people understand you? Are you mostly intelligible?

He hasn't done any exercises.

He said he just wants to move on, do his own thing.

I think he's maybe overwhelmed, like you said.

He is not in any kind of psychotherapy.

He seems to have somewhat habituated to all the media attention.

He's sort of had this Mick Jagger status.

He feels there's a sense of abandonment.

I did not get the sense that he was open to therapy at this time.

In terms of any concerns about suicidality or low mood, severe depression, I would say that he denies it. I don't know fully if that's exactly accurate. I would want to speak with him again.

When Rodriguez gives the nod, the door flies open and Richard saunters in, dressed in a bright purple Baltimore Ravens hat and jacket. He's been living with his new face for two years now, and he's undeniably attractive—clean-shaven, youthful, the kind of guy you would hire to run the front office. He takes a seat facing the crowd, arms splayed out, cool as Justin Bieber on a late-night talk show. Everyone stares at him, and some cock their heads. He's used to this; sometimes people applaud. Is he smiling? His new face doesn't move a lot. Does it move at all? He might be smiling, or it might just be the will of the room. His eyes, the one part of his original face still intact, dart like anyone's eyes, and I find myself chasing them, the only reliable clue as to what might really be going on in there.

One of the things I wanted to know when I first reached out to Richard was how he felt about the miracle. What was it like to walk around with someone else's face? I thought it might be kind of unsettling, or confusing. You're chewing with another man's teeth? When I wrote to him to ask, he told me he had an agent. Cal Ripken's agent, he pointed out. He said everything about his new face was great. He has received thousands of letters from fans. One of the fans is now his girlfriend. She lives in New Orleans. He said he was planning to go meet her in person. He said he was in college now, wanted to focus on school, on being normal. Then he invited me to the foggy mountaintop. The fog was famous, he said, had recently made national news when it caused seventeen pileups involving ninety-five vehicles in one night.

When I get there, the sun has already burned the fog off the morning, which is oddly disappointing. Richard's house isn't actually at the top of the mountain. There's a street carved about midway up with a dozen or so homes, and his is a small yellow double-wide with red trim, a carport, and a for sale sign out front. The storm door has a bear etched into the glass. Richard opens it and welcomes me inside. He's wearing a black Under Armour shirt and cargo pants and he's thin, old-man thin. His posture has curved into a slump from years of hanging his head low, from years spent feeling he was hideous to look at, so now he has to make a conscious effort to stand up straight.

He seems nervous. His hands tremble, bringing constant sips of water to his mouth. His lips can't quite grip the bottle, so each sip is more a little pour. He fights a constant drool with the help of a towel. His new face is a marvel nonetheless. *It's a new face.* Wide and open, the cheekbones of an Irishman and the wrinkle-free complexion of a college kid. It's difficult to reconcile the youthful face with the body of a man nearly forty. I am trying not to stare. I am trying to stop looking for the seams, where the new connects to the old, the eyelids, the neck, the scar in front of his ears. I am trying to stop thinking about his beard, which isn't really *his* beard, except now it is, and it grows. I'm distracted by a thousand little thoughts like these. Coupled with his lack of facial expression—a solid, largely unmoving veneer—in all these ways the barrier to getting to know Richard feels to me immediately and appreciably steep. Microexpressions, split-second movements of the face, are said to communicate wide arrays of meaning. Even infants who are blind are said to use facial cues to tell their parents how they feel. You don't recognize how true these theories likely are until you are with someone with a face frozen in place.

"Here you go," Richard says, picking up a DVD. It's a copy of the hour-long TV special Ann Curry did about him. He takes a Sharpie from his pocket, signs his name on the DVD, hands it to me.

It's a little bit awkward. I don't know where to begin. A face is a surprisingly intimate and complex subject. Part personal, part public. Partly a thing, partly an idea. Part physiology, part psychology.

I spin the Ann Curry DVD on my finger.

Richard leads me through the living room past his mother, who is on a recliner, staring into a laptop. She does not look up. He shows me his room. It's neat as a hotel. No clutter. Just pictures on the walls, every newspaper and magazine article ever written about him, each of them framed. "They even did me on *Ripley's Believe It or Not!*," he says, pointing to one of his clippings. "In Japan I got rated in the top fifty miracles."

I ask him about school, how it's going, how it feels to interact with students. Do they know he has a new face?

"I don't have any classes right now," he says. His voice is muffled, like it's coming from the same place his eyes are, somewhere deep inside. New lips, new mouth, new tongue—it's remarkable he can form words at all. He says he's between classes. At the moment. Well, he isn't actually in school. He's taken some online courses. A lot of what Richard presents to the world is vague. The girlfriend. He says they're soul mates, but so far she's still just a Facebook profile. He says they text all the time. He can't wait to meet her in person.

He leads me back into the living room, where his mom is poking her keyboard angrily. He leaves me here. Two dachshunds sniff at my feet.

"So you like my two little wieners, huh?" his mom says to me, closing her laptop. She has a round face surrounded by gray curls, a soft neck, wide arms. "That one is Raven and that one is Mark—after the race-car driver. She's spoiled rotten. Mark is, too. He's got cancer."

Raven climbs a set of doggie steps up to the couch, digs intently at a blanket, around and around, until she has made herself a cocoon fully covering her body, with just her little nose popping out.

I compliment Richard's mom on the house, the homey feeling, the beautiful views off the back deck.

"You want to buy it?" she asks. It was a mistake moving up here, she says. She never liked it, and neither did Richard. The old house, they gave it to Richard's sister, because she was having trouble making rent. "We're below poverty line," she says. She invites me to sit down on an adjacent recliner. "I have fibromyalgia," she says. "That's why I have these heated blankets."

Richard comes back, carrying pill bottles. "This is what I take every day," he says. "These are my pills." It's a five-pill maintenance regimen he'll need to keep up for the rest of his life; his body will always regard his new face as a foreign object, prompting his immune system to constantly attack it. The drugs trick the immune system by kicking it into its lowest possible gear. This leaves Richard vulnerable to every conceivable health problem down the line. Cancer, diabetes—all the majors.

"He's not supposed to smoke," his mom says. He can't get sunburn. He can't get a cold. He can't drink. He can't fall and risk injury. He can't afford to tax his immune system at all. Even a cut could trigger rejection. It starts as a blotchy rash; it means his body is winning the fight to reject the transplant, and Richard has to be flown to the hospital to receive rounds of emergency drugs intravenously. Uncontrollable rejection would mean an almost certain death; the only things left of Richard's old face are his eyes and the back of his throat. Everything else is now gone for good. "I have to keep watch that his face doesn't go yellow," his mom says. "He's had two rejections so far."

"I'll leave you two talking," Richard says, and he heads outside for a smoke.

His mom motions toward the mantel on the fireplace, where two framed photographs stand side by side. One is Richard's high school portrait. The other is Josh, the twenty-one-year-old donor, who used to have the face Richard now has.

"Isn't that amazing?" she says of the resemblance.

It really is. I don't know which is which, who is which, or what. Pronoun problems emerge. I didn't know Richard as a young man, and now the young face of one is attached to the aged body of the other.

"The likeness?" she says. "It's *Richard*." She tells me she met Josh's mom, visited her at her home. "Real down-to-earth person. I said, 'I really like your kitchen.' That was the kitchen I wanted. Island in the middle of it. Her cabinets had glass in them. I said, 'I'm gonna have to get Eddie to make me a kitchen like that.'"

Eddie is Richard's dad. He used to be a long-haul trucker, but he had to quit when he started needing insulin. He was not in favor of the idea of Richard getting a face transplant. "I like your regular face," he said at the time. Richard's mom told him to back off. "It's Richard's choice," she said. Rodriguez told Richard and his parents that the surgery would be extremely risky—it would take a day and a half—and that Richard would have only a 50 percent chance of surviving it. "And he told us that if the face transplant didn't take, Richard would die because there would be nothing of his old face left," his mother tells me. "But it worked out great."

I ask her if she thinks Richard has changed since his surgery. Does she see a big difference in his personality?

"Yeah, he gets out a little more than what he did," she says. Which still isn't a whole lot. He can't drive, because he could have seizures. She can't drive on account of her fibromyalgia. So the two of them are mostly stuck here, dependent on Eddie.

I lean up in the recliner, stretch my legs out straight. Right now this story is not screaming: miracle.

"What Richard is, he's a lab rat," she says. "He gets to be a brat sometimes. Gets on my nerves so bad. I've always told my kids I don't care if I'm ninety-five years old, if you do something I don't think you should, I'll climb up on a chair and I'll slap you good."

I ask her what she means by "lab rat," and she says exactly that: an animal people do experiments on. "Lab rat," she says. "I don't think he'll ever be able to work like in a normal life. He spends his time in hospitals, everybody poking and prodding, studying him. A boss don't want somebody that's gonna be absent 99 percent of the time."

She says Richard doesn't complain about being a lab rat. He'll do anything for Rodriguez, and so will she.

"Did you meet Dr. Rodriguez?" she asks me. "Me and the nurses, we said, 'Yeah, he sure is good candy-looking stuff.'"

Rodriguez, forty-seven, didn't start out wanting to be great. Or not this great. He was in dental school. His parents had emigrated from Cuba. A Miami drill, fill, and bill dentist—that was his destination.

He speaks in the present tense when he talks about his past. "It's this pursuit of understanding," he tells me, sucking on a peppermint. "Pursuit of knowledge." He tells me about medical school after dental school. General surgery. Plastic surgery. Microsurgery. "Pursuit of being better. Aim for excellence. I think humility is an important factor." He discovered in himself all the components of a star surgeon, and he could not quiet his urge to learn: "Like being in a library and you keep looking, and it leads you to another thing and you keep going." Soon he's in surgery heaven, in Taipei, Taiwan, Chang Gung Memorial Hospital, a mecca for craniofacial and microsurgery, ninety-nine operating rooms, reattaching fingers, attaching toes to hands, round-the-clock microsurgery, free flaps—taking tissue from one part of a person's body and attaching it to another—*a hundred free flaps every single month*. "Crank it up," Rodriguez tells me, bouncing his head with the memory. "Push and push and push."

Eventually he comes home, accepts a post in Baltimore at the University of Maryland Shock Trauma Center. "Now I'm treating soldiers. Gunshot wounds. Explosions," he tells me. He's fixing faces. A guy needs a nose; Rodriguez takes flesh from his leg and makes him a nose, a chin, a cheek. "Everything is, like, happening now. These patients start coming out of the woodwork. 'There's this crazy guy in Baltimore; I think he might help you.' It's like Doctor Dolittle. People just come from everywhere."

But there are limitations, sculpture-wise, when it comes to making a nose. It would be so much better to put a real nose on someone. People had of course been doing organ transplants for years. But a face is a whole new ball game.

A face isn't an organ, like a liver or a heart. A face is muscles, nerves, bones, and skin. A face is more like a hand or a foot. These kinds of transplants, composite-tissue transplants, sparked a fiery ethical debate from the beginning, back in 1998, when the first successful hand transplant occurred. This sort of surgery was, after all, elective surgery. Would it be worth the risk that a lifetime of immunosuppressant drugs would present? Composite-tissue transplantation became a reality when Clint Hallam, a forty-eight-year-old man from New Zealand, got a new hand that was bigger and pinker than his other hand. *But it was a hand*. If they could do a hand, what about a face? Should they?

Hallam's own experience was not particularly encouraging. The new hand freaked him out. One hand his, one hand somebody else's. He couldn't handle it. "Take it off," he said to his doctors. They refused. He persisted. They refused. So he stopped taking his meds, hid the hand from view so no one could tell what was happening to it. Doctors ended up having to amputate what was left. A mess. *How stupid can you get?* Hallam, they said, was a psychopath. Physical rejection may be a conundrum, but psychological rejection was the stuff of madmen.

In 2003, the Royal College of Surgeons of England, and a year later, a national ethics committee in France, said that face transplantation would be going too far. The risk of complication would far outweigh the benefits. A new hand might be a reversible decision. But a new face? Once you take your old face off, you're committed. You live your whole life like that, taking medications to keep your new face on so you don't die. All this, for elective surgery?

Nevertheless, the first face transplant was performed in France in 2005. It caught the surgical world by surprise. It was a partial, a triangle. The nose and lips from a deceased donor were removed and sewn onto a woman whose face had been bitten off by a dog. Everyone had thought the first face transplant would be done in the United States. Just a year earlier, the Cleveland Clinic had gotten ethical approval and had started testing prospective patients. But then France did it first, and the worldwide race to do something bigger, better, was on.

Meanwhile, Rodriguez—with all the cowboys in his field now talking face transplants—is imagining something bolder than what's been tried. He's practicing on cadavers, taking the face off one and putting it on another, not just the triangle but the whole face. He isn't sure about the procedure. Could he do it? Like a fighter pilot on a flight simulator, he practices the surgery on his computer. He's got all his training behind him, and all the technology before him, and he's looking at Richard. He's looking at two or three other people who might be good candidates. "But I'm not totally convinced yet," he tells me, still engrossed in the unfolding dramatization of his life. "I'm apprehensive about it. I think it's a big deal. Taking someone's face off." There is no turning back once you do something like that. The old face is mangled and useless; you can't put it back on. "I'm thinking about it very systematically."

He tells me about going to Paris, having lunch with Pascal Coler, a thirty-year-old man who got a new face in 2008. Coler had lived with big tumors all over his face. A terrible life. "And I have a very good steak tartare," Rodriguez says. "And next to me is Pascal, chowing down the biggest porterhouse. As normal as can be. No one looks at him. He has a job, a potential girlfriend. I'm like, holy mackerel, this is huge. We've gone beyond clinical; now we can change someone's life."

I want to ask Rodriguez how one patient who seemed reasonably content during one meal is enough to quiet an entire internal moral crisis, but he's on fast-forward, the adventure playing out like an action movie.

"Let's go!" he tells me. "It's on!"

So in Baltimore, a team of five surgeons is mobilized—two to work on the donor, three on Richard—and the operating rooms are readied. "I go, 'Richard, if you want to pull the plug right now, do it,'" says Rodriguez. "'I don't want you to feel any pressure; there's a lot going on here, and I just need you to tell me right now if you're ready, and if you aren't, we just walk away and it's all good.'"

The surgery, which started with incisions from Richard's scalp to his neck, began at dawn on March 19, 2012, and continued nonstop for the next thirty-six hours. Richard's old face was removed to expose his skull, eye sockets, and throat and neck muscles. The donor face was applied in one solid piece that included the jaw, tongue, muscles, skin, nose, teeth, and eyelids. Hammers and saws were used to shape Richard's new jaw. Metal plates stabilized the donor face and allowed doctors to attach it to Richard's skull with screws.

"He said, 'Let's go. We're doing it.' That's it. You get yourself in your mental game. It's fourth and goal, and we are going into the end zone. We're going to win the Super Bowl. This is the moment of no return. Complete silence in the room; like, holy mackerel. Tough moment. No failure. This is it. We're going to make this thing. The face is one unit. I'm picking it up. I'm laying it on him. I've got to get everything centered, it can't be off-kilter, the nose has gotta be straight, everything's gotta land perfectly.

"Now, this organ is not receiving blood. It needs to receive blood. The longer it takes to receive blood increases the chance for acute rejection. We gotta get this thing drinking.

"Connecting the artery, then the vein, and then we release, and it really is like a miracle. Impressive. You see the blood just coming from the neck, crossing the lips. Seeing the nose—it's white and it turns pink, like normal flesh. It takes seconds. And now we're thinking, Okay, I can take a little breather, but we still have to push ahead, I have to get Richard out of the operating room. We still have to connect the nerves, a lot of nerves. We have to suture the inside of his mouth and tongue; everything has to be sutured. And fix the rest of the bones. Line up the soft tissue. Line up his hairline. Line up his eyebrows. Get the eyelids. So all that needs to happen.

"We're at about eighteen to twenty hours. We've still got a lot to go. I predicted twenty-four to thirty-six hours. I think the unique thing about this face transplant is that it was so extensive and comprehensive. I say this very humble, up to that point, nothing of that level had been performed."

Doubt, when it comes to miracles, is like steam on a mirror. You have to wipe it off if you want to see anything. And what choice do you have? You've already moved forward. You've given a guy a new face. You've gotten a new face. Your kid has a new face. There is no turning back.

One day on the foggy mountaintop, Richard and I get bored sitting around his house, so we decide to take a drive. He is a man of hard-earned platitudes. "Sometimes God will put you on your back to make you look up. Sometimes you need that nudge." He's grateful for his new face. He's grateful to Josh, the donor. Five other people are now living with organs from Josh. "It helps you understand . . . I'm not going to say the afterlife, but what you do here on earth and what you leave here on earth—it's totally two different things." He tells me about his efforts to raise awareness for organ donation; he's become something of a national spokesman for the cause.

In the car, we talk about all the fun things we'll do on our drive. His sister lives about an hour away, in the house Richard grew up in, the house where this whole mess started fifteen years ago, when he shot himself in the face. We haven't talked much about the accident. He doesn't remember anything. Morning or night, nothing. "It's just a cobweb." He suggests we stop at a beautiful lookout place, too. First, though, he asks me to stop at a store. "Something for my throat," he says. He comes out of the store carrying a brown bag. We continue our journey, go up into the voluminous mountains rolling every which way you look.

We talk about cracked iPhones. He's going to start a business fixing cracked iPhones. We talk about his girlfriend. "Melanie," he says, pulling up a picture of her as if to offer proof. "She's real." He can't wait to meet her in person. We talk about being a lab rat. On this matter he says he's honored. In a way, his whole life has been volunteering. When he was in high school, he was a volunteer firefighter. Now, with his new face, doctors are learning so much about how to treat soldiers suffering ballistic facial injuries. He likes helping people. He likes giving people hope. "A drop of hope can create an ocean," he says. "But a bucket of faith can create an entire world."

"That's true," I say.

"My throat," he says. We're getting higher, and my ears have popped. He's stretched out, relaxed. He reaches into the brown bag, pulls out a bottle of Wild Turkey.

"For my throat," he says. He can't take over-the-counter medications, he says. Too risky with his meds. There's a backpack at his feet. He opens it, pulls out some tubing and a wide syringe, about a half-inch across, the kind you use to give medicine to horses.

"I don't like the taste," he says.

He hooks the syringe to the tubing, lifts up his shirt. I think I'm supposed to pretend this is not happening. I'm driving. There's a port under his shirt, connected to his stomach. I was not aware of that. He hooks the tubing to the port, so now the fat syringe is standing straight up.

He opens the Wild Turkey and starts pouring.

"Richard, I don't think Dr. Rodriguez would want you doing this—"

All this talk of risk, all the meds, no smoking, no drinking, no falling. A lab rat. Everything measured and quantified and documented.

The Wild Turkey isn't going down. It's clogged. He jiggles the syringe. Nothing is happening.

"Can you pull over?" he asks. "This isn't working right."

I pull over. There are no cars anywhere. We are deep into the mountain range.

He gets out, flips the syringe, emptying it. He gets back in and examines all the tubing, pinches this and that, allowing some stomach juices to squirt out.

"So that's how you eat?" I ask. "You use the tube?"

"No," he says. He used to. He doesn't need it anymore.

He reconnects everything, pours again. The whiskey goes quickly inside him, like water down a drain.

He looks at me. "This is how it's supposed to work."

"This is for your *throat*?"

“I can’t take over-the-counter medication,” he says again.

Everything about him is vague. Except this isn’t vague. He refills the syringe, lets another round drain into him, and another. I don’t know how much. It seems like a lot. I wonder what it will be like to be with a drunk Richard. I imagine his sister, the beautiful lookout place. It doesn’t happen. Within five minutes he folds, like a shot animal folds, over himself, folded, eyes open, his body deflated, the tube hanging out, dignity depleted.

“Richard?” I say. “Richard?” I shove his shoulder and nothing happens. He is dead. He is on my watch and he is dead. I hear gurgling. Breathing. He’s on my watch and he is not dead.

My watch?

The breathing is going in his mouth and out his nose. I am studying his face to make sure air is moving. In his mouth. Out his nose. This didn’t used to be his mouth or his nose. He can smell with that nose. He can chew food with a dead man’s jaw and teeth. There is no denying how fantastic that is.

I don’t know where to go. I don’t know one foggy mountaintop from another. I can’t wake him up.

I have his address in my GPS. I hit “previous destination.” When we get to his house, I drag him out of the car, exactly the way you drag a drunk out of a car, one arm over my shoulder, little steps. I kick the etched bear on the storm door to open it.

“Hello? Hello?” I deposit him in his mom’s recliner, wait for someone to come home, or for him to wake up.

One day I ask Rodriguez how he picked Richard over the other candidates he had for his epic heroic story. “I had developed a relationship with Richard, so I knew the kind of person he is,” he tells me. “This is an individual that I can trust as someone that can really care for this gift. Keep in mind, someone had to die for him to receive this face. So there’s a certain sense of responsibility and burden that I need to make sure that this is not going to be wasted. This has to be a responsible person that will share the precious gift and take this gift and make something with it, and of it.”

“A lot of responsibility,” I say.

“A lot,” he says.

I ask him if he thinks people can get overly invested in the happily-ever-after in his line of work.

"Of course," he says. "Of course."

A recent article by Rodriguez in the medical journal *The Lancet* features before-and-after pictures of Richard. Side by side, the change is stunning, from a man with a mangled swirl of a face to regular guy. The more I look at the picture of Richard's disfigured face, the more I wish I knew it. His eyes are bigger, rounder, provide a wider window. His eyebrows are all mid up, one curved sharply, the other a gentle swoop, thick scars in between. His lower face is cartoonish, like a drawing of an old guy who took his dentures out. There is so much to find in this face, so many avenues of inquiry.

Patient selection, Rodriguez writes in *The Lancet*, is the key to success when it comes to face transplantation. "Patient selection by a thorough screening process . . . serves as the best safeguard against ethical challenges," he writes. "Rigorous preoperative psychiatric and psychological selection of patients deemed to be stable, motivated, and compliant by a multidisciplinary team is a crucial determinant of a safe and rapid recovery."

The article looks back at all twenty-eight face transplants that have occurred and represents Rodriguez's full circle from doubt to certainty. Three people have died from complications. Everyone else is said to be doing great.

NYU hospital issued a press release when the article was published, extolling Rodriguez's call for a "moral imperative" to offer face transplants, the "Mount Everest" of medical-surgical treatments.

And yet while the debate about the ethics of face transplantation has shifted dramatically since the early days of harsh warnings against the procedure, researchers in a recent academic survey of the "successful" transplants note a distinct paucity of data on the psychological outcomes for these patients, who, they point out, often suffer from PTSD, alcohol abuse, and opiate dependence as a result of the trauma leading to their initial disfigurement.

Another journal article, in *Anthropology Today*, considered the topic under the heading "Ethical slippage and quiet death," with Richard's picture occupying an entire page.

I try to tell Richard's mom about the Wild Turkey, but this is a difficult conversation, and I'm not sure it's the right thing to do. She's in her recliner, and she has a migraine hangover. The medicine leaves her woozy. Eddie is over there feeding Slim Jims to Mark and Raven. Richard is in his room.

"Richard isn't supposed to smoke," I start.

"Oh, I know," she says. "And you know, sometimes he drinks until he passes out."

I'm relieved, but not.

She talks about God. She talks about Rodriguez. Everything comes back to Rodriguez: "My godsend." That's a lot of pressure on a savior. I wonder what exactly happened back in 1997 when Richard shot himself in the face. In an e-book version of the story, Richard says he was blindingly drunk, had come home and become verbally abusive with his mom, who sent him to his room to sleep it off. That part appears to be true, according to a police report filed in the Henry County Sheriff's Office. But the rest of the story—that a shotgun happened to be tilted in a gun case and, upon coming out of his room, Richard was asked by his mom to straighten it, causing it to fire accidentally—appears to be apocryphal. According to the report: "Mrs. Norris was standing in the doorway of Richard's bedroom; fussing at Richard about him wanting to go out again. Richard took a shotgun from his gun cabinet and told Mrs. Norris that he would just shoot himself. When Richard racked a shell into the shotgun's chamber, the gun fired.... There was what appeared to be human flesh, bone, and teeth on all four walls in Richard's bedroom." Mrs. Norris told police, "Richard's face exploded."

It would take fifteen years to fix what had gone wrong that night—or at least to try to.

"The really weird thing is, me and Richard's girlfriend found Dr. Rodriguez at the same time," his mom tells me. She pulls her blankets up. I'm sitting on the couch with Raven. Richard has joined us, is seated in the other recliner.

"Girlfriend?" I ask. Richard had a girlfriend before the transplant?

"She was looking online for doctors to help Richard same time I was," his mom says. "She found him same time as I did."

"Wait, who is this?"

"His girlfriend," she says. "Me and her could not get along."

"Girlfriend?" I say, looking over at Richard.

"An old one," he says. "Old, *old*. She was going to college to be a nurse."

I need a time-out. What year are we in? The accident happened in 1997. The new face didn't come until 2012.

"You had a girlfriend when you were disfigured?" I ask Richard.

"I lived with her," he says. "For two years."

"When you were disfigured?"

"Yeah."

"But I thought you were a hermit," I say. What about the foggy mountaintop? The covered mirrors and the black mask?

"This was during the whole stage of my disfigurement when I was working for race teams," Richard says. "When I was at the racetrack, it was like nobody didn't care. They didn't care what I looked like. Only thing they cared about was how good I could set that race car up."

"You had a job? And a girlfriend? And an apartment? You were living a whole life?"

"Yeah."

So why did he need a new face? Why had he endured the complications involved in freeing him from disfigurement? The thirty-six-hour operation, a 50 percent chance of dying on the table, a life of antirejection medications. No sunburn. No falling. Watch out for yellow. Two rejections so far.

"I didn't like the girl," his mom says. "She tried to cut me out of everything."

There was a fight. At their apartment. Richard was convalescing after a surgery, and his mom came by. "She wouldn't let me in to see Richard," she says. "So I went through her. And she told me, get out of her house, the doctor said nobody could see Richard. I said, 'I ain't just nobody, I'm his mother. I'm gonna see him.' I whopped her. And I had her on the floor. I just told her, I said, 'You don't take my son away from me. Nobody takes my son.' And she said, 'I'm gonna call the law.' I said, *'Well, just call the law.'*"

"I got rid of her," Richard says.

"Then we moved up here in 2005, away from everybody," his mom says.

Which is right about the time they found Rodriguez.

"We don't like it here," his mom says.

"It's the most boringest place on earth," Richard says.

Being famous is better. One of Japan's top fifty miracles. And he was willing to go through with getting a new face. And there was all that salvation his mom needed. And the wounded warriors needed him. And humanity needed him. And having a new face is better than some old disfigured one. You can't argue with that.

Richard wishes Rodriguez had stayed in Baltimore. He doesn't like New York. But wherever in the world Rodriguez needs him, he'll be there. And yes, as to smoking, he shouldn't. And yes, the incident in the car? "Uh-huh," he says. There's a certain amount of self-medication, he says. "But that's just self-medication." We're at NYU again, and he's not exactly sure what today's event is. Some kind of fund-raiser, he thinks. We're in the waiting room. He looks great in his suit. "I'm sure they'll be very nice people," he says. He likes people. He likes visiting patients. People come to talk to Rodriguez, or the team back in Baltimore, and Richard joins them. They want face transplants. They want to know what it's like. He tells them what it's like. He knows exactly how they feel. It's something positive he can do with his life. A face. "This is what I am," he tells me. "There is nothing more important than a face."

He brings up Hallam, the guy with the hand. "He couldn't take it, so he had to cut it off," he says. "So now they say, 'Is the face transplant going to have that identity crisis, too?' Well, if he does, *we're screwed.*"

A woman with curly dark hair peeks into the waiting room. "We're ready!" she says. We head down the hall. Richard takes two steps into the conference room, and the people burst into spontaneous applause.

"Hi, Richard!"

"Hello, Richard!"

Rodriguez sits at the head of the table. Pretty little cookies are laid out. "This institute was made possible by these incredible people," he says to Richard.

"It's our pleasure, Richard."

"God bless you."

"You're very brave."

"You're a real ambassador."

Richard thanks them on behalf of all the people in the future who might be helped. "A drop of hope can create an entire ocean," he says. "A little speck of faith can create a world. You give that speck of faith to them."

"He never really thought about himself in all of this," Rodriguez says. "He's always thought about helping the wounded warriors and the other people, and providing hope. He's a remarkable man."

"And they can do research on me as well," Richard says.

And that about wraps it up?

A woman has a question. She has wide shoulders, blond hair.

"What about your family?" she says. "Do they have therapeutic resources available to them to support you?"

"Actually, the support I get mainly is from therapists," Richard says. "They send me home with homework, give me exercises to practice, to help with my speech, my swallowing, you know. Physical therapy helps a whole lot, played a huge role in my recovery."

The woman tries again.

"Emotionally, did you feel you got the support you needed?"

"Emotionally I can get lab work done no matter where I am, if I'm home, if I'm in Baltimore. If I'm here, I get it done here. That way the lab work is always current."

I want to jump in here. I want to tell the woman with the questions about Wild Turkey, the poverty line, lab rats and wiener dogs, illness and violence.

Rodriguez jumps in. "The answer is yes and no," he says. "This is a new field. Every transplant has to be well thought out. One thing that you can appreciate with Richard is there was not a step missed in this rehearsal and this practice. And now Richard is our ambassador, and he can help us."

"You are one of the greatest people I've ever met," one in the crowd says to Richard.

"Terrific. So handsome."

"Thank you," Richard says, reaching for Rodriguez. "It comes from his hands. His hands."

Richard calls me shortly before he heads to New Orleans to meet Melanie, the new girlfriend. I wish him well. I feel nervous for him, want her to be real. For all his guile, he's a trusting soul. And he needs a girlfriend or some companion to assist him through life. If there's a future for him, it is almost assuredly off the foggy mountaintop. But under whose watch? Who will drive him around? He's a science experiment. He's a lab rat. He's not a normal sort of boyfriend.

One day Melanie appears on my Skype screen. She's real. She's lovely. Richard is sitting next to her, waving to me. He wipes constant drool with the help of a towel. She just came home from work and put a pot roast in the oven. Richard folded the laundry. She wants to care for him. She finds a well of kindness in him. She's been burned so many times. She says nothing about his medical-rock-star status, nothing about the drool. "Why does anyone fall in love?" she says with a shrug, when I ask about the relationship. She's the first person I meet who talks about Richard as just a regular person. He's not: a miracle. He's not: a medical circus act. He's not: an ambassador of anything. He's a guy with barely a tick of a functioning immune system, thanks to the inexorable march forward of technology and a worldwide race for surgical glory. But for now, at least, she doesn't need to have that conversation. I get the sense she would have liked Richard with his old face just the same.

In short order she introduces Richard to her kids, her mom; everybody likes everybody. She meets Richard's mom by phone, and so far so good. One day she notices maybe a rash? "What is that?" she asks Richard. "I don't think it's anything," he says. He doesn't want it to be anything. He's finally with her, and he wants to stay. "I'm worried," she says. "It's getting worse." She takes a picture of the rash, insists that Richard send it to the doctors in Baltimore keeping track of his medical care.

"Get here," they say. "Next plane out."

If it's acute rejection and they can't reverse it, he dies.

He's hospitalized for two weeks, pumped full of stuff to get the rejection under control, then sent back to the foggy mountaintop to recover.

"Come back," Melanie tells him. "Please come back. We'll eat crawfish. You'll wear your sunscreen. I'll keep you safe."

Adrian Nicole LeBlanc

Adrian Nicole LeBlanc is a journalist who is best known for her 2003 nonfiction book *Random Family: Love, Drugs, Trouble, and Coming of Age in the Bronx,* which chronicles the struggles of two young women as they deal with love, growing families, and prison time. The book took more than ten years to research and write and has received many awards, among them the Anisfield-Wolf Book Award and the Ron Ridenhour Book Prize. In 2010, it was named one of the Top Ten Works of Journalism of the Decade by the Arthur L. Carter Institute of Journalism at New York University. Before turning to writing full time, LeBlanc was the fiction editor at Seventeen. Her work was also featured on NPR's *All Things Considered* in an audio documentary about her last days with her father.

As a freelancer, LeBlanc has written for many publications including *The Village Voice, Harper's, The New York Times Magazine,* and *The New Yorker.* Grants, fellowships, and residencies have been essential to continuing independent work, including: The Barbara Deming Women's Memorial Fund, the Open Society Institute, the Dorothy and Lewis B. Cullman Center for Scholars and Writers at the New York Public Library, Blue Mountain Center, Cottages at Hedgebrook, and the MacDowell Colony. In 2006, she was a recipient of a MacArthur Fellowship.

LeBlanc was raised in Leominster, Massachusetts, where plastics originated. Her hometown informs everything she writes about. She is currently completing another decade's long project, a nonfiction book about stand-up comedy.

The Troubled Life of Boys: The Outsiders

A look at high school boys as they struggle with the changing perceptions of masculinity in the feminist culture of the 1990s.

The fight takes place in the bright light of adult view—on a weekday afternoon, on a tree-lined residential street, within sight of the police station and a block from the middle school. The smaller boy, about twelve, waits until there is a safe distance between himself and the other boy, about thirteen. Then he sends a curse. It lands. He waits. No response. He follows with a homophobic slur. His opponent—a chubby boy nicknamed Sex Machine—finally turns around.

A freckled friend of Sex Machine's loops around him on his bicycle, lazily doing doughnuts. He prods Sex Machine chirpily: "You gonna take that? He's a punk!" Halfheartedly, Sex Machine blusters back a retort. More friends appear and cajole him, challenging him to at least pretend that he has nerve.

"C'mon, Sex Machine!" one shouts, then whispers to another, alarmed: "Look at him. He keeps backing up!"

Whatever started the fight is irrelevant. The friends clamber up a nearby wire fence to get a good view, hyper spiders clinging to the mesh.

Sex Machine is frightened. Despite his oversize T-shirt, you can see the rise and fall of his heaving chest. A man's voice chimes in and shouts encouragement to the smaller boy from the driveway.

"That's his father!" a boy says. "Can you believe it? He's telling him to fight!"

"That's not right," says a girl.

Borrowing from the man's confidence, the smaller boy rushes forward and swings. Sex Machine stumbles backward as he tries to duck. A woman leans out from the second-floor window of a ranch house and says, "Come in, come in," without sounding as though she means it, a weary Juliet.

Sex Machine looks desperate, flailing his arms frantically, trying to flag down a car. Luckily, one stops. Apparently, it's his mother. All the tension and fear that his body has been holding bursts into punctuated sobs. He storms around the car to the passenger side. His freckled friend, who had been cheering within inches of the action, cycles over and dismounts to say goodbye. With all the fury raging inside him, Sex Machine bellows, "You didn't help me!" then shoves him to the ground.

Antrim, New Hampshire, where the fight took place, is a long way away from Littleton, Colorado, as well as from Conyers, Georgia, where a fifteen-year-old boy shot six classmates at his high school in May. It is one of nine towns whose regional high school, ConVal, sits in Peterborough, New Hampshire, the setting that inspired Thornton Wilder's *Our Town*. But what it shares with those other places, and with countless others across the country, is a brutally enforced teenage social structure.

Boys at the bottom of the pyramid use different strategies to cope—turning inward and outward, sometimes in highly destructive ways. (There has been a fivefold jump in the homicide and suicide rates of boys in the last forty years, a rise some experts attribute to increasing male depression and anger as well as access to guns, among other factors.) Most boys live through it, suffer, survive. But the journey may be especially deadly now because, as the avalanche of new "male identity" literature demonstrates, the old prescriptions for behavior no longer hold, and the new ones are ambivalent. Today's young males may be feminism's children, but no one is comfortable with openhearted or vulnerable boys.

ConVal is in some ways progressive. There are about nine hundred students and an administration that consciously works to minimize the ultramacho sports culture that dominates many schools. Says Bob Marshall, the head of the social studies department, who founded the football program in 1992: "We had to create a football culture. People didn't know when to cheer. We didn't even have a school song."

Even so, the traditional hierarchies operate: the popular kids tend to be wealthier and the boys among them tend to be jocks. The Gap Girls-Tommy Girls-Polo Girls compose the pool of desirable girlfriends, many of whom are athletes as well. Below the popular kids, in a shifting order of relative unimportance, are the druggies (stoners, deadheads, burnouts, hippies, or neo-hippies), trendies or Valley Girls, preppies, skateboarders and skateboarder chicks, nerds and techies, wiggers, rednecks and Goths, better known as freaks. There are troublemakers, losers and floaters—kids who move from group to group. Real losers are invisible.

Bullying, here as elsewhere, is rampant. Even in small-town, supposedly safe environments like Peterborough, a 1994 study found, the vast majority of kids from middle school up are bullied by their peers. The shaming is sex-based, but the taunting is more intense for boys—an average high-school student, according to another study, hears twenty-five antigay slurs a day.

To be an outcast boy is to be a "nonboy," to be feminine, to be weak. Bullies function as a kind of peer police enforcing the social code, and ConVal's freaks are accustomed to the daily onslaught. The revenge-of-the-nerds refrain—which assures unpopular boys that if they only hold on through high school, the roster of winners will change—does not question the hierarchy that puts the outcasts at risk. So boys survive by their stamina, sometimes by their fists, but mainly, if they're lucky, with the help of the family they've created among their friends.

A good day for Andrew, fourteen, occurs when R., a boy who torments him, is absent from school, like when he was suspended for ripping the hearing aid out of another classmate's ear. R., fifteen, weighs more than two hundred pounds. Andrew, a small boy with straight, dirty-blond hair and glasses, takes care to note R.'s better days—say, when Andrew helps him with an assignment, when he's in a good mood or distracted by harassing someone else.

The trouble started long before the appearance of R. "First people harassed me because I was really smart," Andrew says, presenting the sequence as self-evident. "I read all the time. I read through math class."

Back then, in middle school, he had the company of Tom Clancy and a best friend he could talk to about anything. He says things are better now; during school, he hangs out with the freaks. Yet the routine days he describes sound far from improvement—being body-slammed and shoved into chalkboards and dropped into trash cans headfirst. At a school dance, in the presence of chaperones and policemen, R. lifted Andrew and ripped a pocket off his pants. "One day I'll be a 'faggot,' the next day I'll be a 'retard,'" Andrew says. One girl who used to be his friend now sees him approaching and shouts, "Oh, get out of here, nobody wants you!"

Andrew joined the cross-country team but the misery trailed him on the practice runs. He won't rejoin next year although he loves the sport. Recently he and some other boys were suspended for suspected use of drugs. According to Andrew, he used to earn straight As; now he receives mostly Cs and Ds. He does not draw connections between the abuse and the changes in his life.

He also does not expect help from the adults around him. He suspects they have their reasons—some don't care, while others worry only about physical attack. When I point out that he's being physically attacked, he imagines that the teachers think it's horsing around, although he does wonder why the teachers can see the same kid pushing other kids every day and don't just tell the kid to stop. "Maybe have a talk with him or do something," he says. "One little push isn't that much, but when it's every day, it's something." He only wishes that someone had helped in middle school, before the contagion grew. "When it first starts to happen, there's definitely something you can do," he says. "But you can't turn a whole school."

Neither does Andrew tell his parents. He believes they think he is popular. "If I try to explain it to my parents," he says, "they'll say: 'Oh, but you have plenty of friends.' Oh, I don't think so. They don't really get it." His outcast friends, however, do.

One of them is Randy Tuck, a five-foot-four-inch sophomore with a thick head of hair and cheeks bright red with acne. He rescued Andrew from a "swirly" (two boys had him ankle up, and headed for the toilet bowl).

Randy moved from Alaska to New Hampshire almost three years ago. To his frustration, his classmates called him Eskimo Boy. Art is his solace, along with the occasional cigarette. He loves to draw. He used to sketch Ninja Turtles and now, with the help of an art teacher, he's studying anatomy. He associates with the freaks during school mainly because they let him. He says, “They are friendly, but not welcoming.”

Classmates debate with Randy about his atheism, but he refuses to believe a God could arrange a life as unlucky as his. Andrew blames himself. Randy says, “Andrew’s vulnerable and small and weak and R. takes advantage of that.” Randy utilizes ‘”verbal bashing” as a defense, although he admits that its powers don’t prevent physical attack. R. surprised him one day in the hallway. He passed Randy, then turned around and punched him in the spine. But Randy also notes that R. can be funny. “When he’s not in a bad mood, he can be very entertaining.”

Andrew says that the ostracizing “does build up inside. Sometimes you might get really mad at something that doesn’t matter a lot, kinda like the last straw.” He could understand the Columbine killers, Dylan Klebold and Eric Harris, if their misery had shown no signs of ending, but Andrew remains an optimist. After all, there are some people who have no friends. “Things are not going up really fast, but they are getting better,” he says. “I might have a week where they get worse, but overall they are getting better, definitely.”

The quips ricochet around the bedroom like friendly-fire darts. Myles Forrest, sixteen, a sophomore with baby fat and sweet eyes, is one of George Farley’s closer friends. George, also sixteen, is a floater. He has set up camp with ConVal’s freaks for now. George sees weakness everywhere—in women who look for milk cartons with the latest expiration date at the store where he works; in the unemployed drunk who receives an allowance from his working wife; in white girls who think they are cool because they date guys who are black. Softness arouses his contempt. He is no more gentle with himself. The volleying with Myles, who wears his Y2K T-shirt — “01-01-00”— relieves George of the clearly burdensome obligation of having so much edge.

“The end of Myles’s life,” George starts.

“The end of life as we know it,” Myles says. The phone rings. George lifts the receiver. “Myles Forrest, loser,” he announces, and so the afternoon begins.

Myles and George provide sustenance between insults. Myles fiddles with his computer—one of two—as George peers out over the street. “What’s up with the dress?” George asks, spotting an exchange student from ConVal.

"What? He's Hindu," says Myles.

"I said, What's up with the dress?"

"It's like a cult thing," Myles says, somewhat sharply.

"That's a dress," George says, losing steam.

"It's like a cult thing. It's like a kilt."

"You know I'm messing with you, don't go getting all politically correct with me." (Later on, Myles will explain the theory of equal-opportunity hatred: "You ever notice that you can't hate a particular group, but if you generally hate everybody nobody seems to mind?") The sarcasm slows when the Quake competition begins.

It strikes me as I watch them in front of the famously violent video game that it is one way for the boys to enjoy closeness without it being threatening. The violence of the game, the state-of-siege mentality, the technical expertise required, supplant the macho expectations and give the boys a rest from the relentless one-upmanship. Rather than insult each other, they can attack the game. Soon enough, they are allies in the search for snacks, rushing down the stairs. They amble past the locked gun case behind the door leading through the playroom, to the kitchen. George sticks his head in the fridge.

"How about some of these worms?" he asks, holding a baggie of bait. "Fishing is like alcoholism. It's an excuse to drink. Or maybe they're trying to level the playing field. How hard can it be to outsmart a fish?"

"Catching it is kinda fun—" Myles tries.

"Now ice fishing—alcoholism in the extreme," George continues. "Cold, boring, worry about falling through the ice. Hey, my girlfriend dumped me. She dumped my slacker [expletive]."

"I thought you were gonna give her the—" Myles tries.

"Yeah, but she surprised me."

"Irony of ironies. So, technically, you're the loser."

"Shut up," George says, sounding sad.

"To the winner goes all the spoils of war," Myles appeals.

"Shut up," George says, relocating to the sunroom. He lifts Fido, Myles's lizard.

"Watch out, George," Myles says protectively. George presses Fido into the aquarium to make the wood chips fly.

"That's cruel, stop it," Myles says, retrieving his lizard, as George moves on to his lectern, the Stairmaster.

"That cat is wishing for a tail," George says, observing Myles's tailless cat.

"To the victor goes the spoils of war," Myles sighs, mock ruefully.

"Stop defending your tailless cat," says George. "Anyways, so Colleen broke up with me."

"You already told me that," Myles says. He glances at his buddy. "I thought that's what you wanted."

"I did," George says, sounding far from sure. Now that he has been rendered single, what will come of the flirtation he lost his girlfriend for?

The new girl, a computer skateboarder chick, likes to spar. George says, "We're both the same person, but it's hard when you have two sarcastic people making fun of each other, and then they get worse and worse until—"

"Until there's no place you can go," Myles says knowingly.

"Shut up, you slack [expletive]," George says, knowing, too.

Teenagers find heroes among their friends. Tyler Snitko, seventeen, pulls other outcasts in, functioning as a kind of human insulation for the freaks. To each taunt he quips, "Thank you." He booms, "These are my people," opening his arms, his fingernails polished black, to embrace his fellow freaks at lunch time in what has been labeled Mutant Hall. In the presence of someone like Tyler, more vulnerable teenagers are less likely to be picked on, and they intuitively know this.

Tyler's hero is his grandfather. Not only did the old man give him advice that he often quotes ("Sometimes there are going to be rat bastards in life, and you have to deal with them"), but he also backed up the talk with action: he gave Tyler his first set of weights.

Tyler kept his strategy secret, taking long, midnight runs because he did not want to jeopardize his affiliation with the freaks, who were supposed to be "all skinny and pale." He soon discovered that his best friend, Toffer, seventeen, studied jujitsu to control the anger building in himself.

Toffer knew what it was like to be excluded. His isolation began in elementary school, and only in high school, through his friendship with Tyler and with his girlfriend, Anne Baker, did the fog begin to lift. Through the worst of the ostracization, the boys had each other. Says Tyler: "Other people turned me away, like I'd bring the whole house down. He stood by me."

Toffer, whose name is Christopher Eppig, is a senior who looks very much like Jesus. He survived the solitary years by not showing emotion. He shows very little emotion now. "I think it was the fact that I couldn't completely control myself that scared me," he says flatly. "I didn't like myself because I didn't have anything. No athletics, no grades. The only thing that kept me going was that I hated them more than I hated myself.

"Before, all I knew was what people were telling me about myself, and it wasn't a positive image, and I wasn't interested in who I was," he continues. "Jujitsu gave me something else that I was, that was better and more believable."

The friendship with Tyler created elbow room. They joined the wrestling team. They formed a band named Gawd. It helps that Tyler's parents encourage his use of their renovated colonial as a social center, and that his dad quit his job as an executive to stay home full time. His parents call the arrangement a luxury, a decision they made around the time when Tyler's mother was promoted to assistant principal of a middle school. Then Tyler had the great good fortune of several growing spurts, which, at last measure, topped six feet to match the hard-earned bulk.

His upbeat personality may defuse hostility, but his physical presence is a moat. A friend who has known Tyler since childhood, who will only give his online name, Bladerunner, says: "He is just really nice and he sticks up for people."

Bladerunner, seventeen, has had his own troubles. A boy he'd met in the hospital after a suicide attempt wanted to beat him up, and for months, the tranquil New Hampshire town became a minefield for him. Bladerunner stopped visiting the park and dreaded school. The restaurant where he washes dishes was the only place he anticipated with some pleasure because his boss treats him "like a person." Otherwise, he met Tyler at the Incubator, a room where students go when they have a free period. They would get passes to the weight-lifting room.

Bladerunner didn't stick with the weights, but it mattered that Tyler encouraged him. Recently, Tyler invited Bladerunner to be a vocalist for Gawd. "I realized I was walking around people on eggshells, because I'm always afraid of what's going to happen to me, or what people are going to think," Bladerunner says. "I am going to try to take what I am afraid of and look it in the face, as much as it might physically hurt."

Even as it helps in the day-to-day of high school, bodily renovation perpetuates the hierarchy. Bulking up—or being near someone who does—just means the pyramid starts lower down. Tyler sees similarities between

R. and himself: "He gets respected because he throws his weight around. I get respected because I don't have to." He also recognizes how the pressure to prove his masculinity drove him to objectify girls. "I treated my girlfriends really bad," he says. "I admit it. I was like, Oh, there's a pair of boobs, I'll go stand next to it. I think I'll go talk to it."

Of course, trivializing girls is a most likely result of a pecking order in which girls represent "femininity," the perceived threat to conventional masculinity, the mix of which leaves boys so confused these days. The fear of feminizing boys is embedded in the hierarchy of the social cliques: winner-loser, popular-outcast, boy-girl. "This fear of sissifying boys," says Olga Silverstein, author of *The Courage to Raise Good Men*, "I think it's going to be the last prejudice to go."

The danger signs are everywhere, but only if you want to see. Banning trench coats, installing metal detectors and security guards—the quick-fix solutions to the problem of seemingly rampant boy violence—"becomes a weird kind of McCarthyism," says Russell Novotny, a 1999 ConVal graduate. "The only way to get kids not to hurt each other is to get kids not to want to hurt each other," a process he compares to a road. "It's the whole little-step thing. You take a little step and suddenly you are in the woods. How did I get here? We are so far into the woods. For every mile you walk, you have to walk a mile back. You can't look too far ahead or you trip over what's in front of you." Or you look at what's in front of you, a boy like J., and you don't really see him.

J., who doesn't want his name to be used, ranks as a loser. He finds temporary refuge with the burnouts, but his precarious welcome depends upon their mood and whether or not he has weed. His greatest flaw seems to be his willingness to try anything to fit in.

"That kid does whatever you tell him to do," says Josh Guide, a classmate. Past instructions are rumored to include wading knee-high in a running brook, with his sneakers and socks on, fetching sticks. He doesn't fight back when people shake him down for money. He claims to get high when a classmate sells him oregano with chives. He falls off his bicycle when the other boys are done using it and ignores the bleeding, which, during a game of basketball, stains another boy's new Tommy Hilfiger shirt.

"Now I have AIDS," the boy says, disgusted. J.'s distress is so apparent that the boy says, "I'm kidding," but his hostility is clear. This particular afternoon, J., who has ragged black hair and a crumpling smile, opens his mouth as if to speak, but doesn't. He saves his mouth for his teachers.

The week after the shootings in Littleton, Colorado, ConVal High School held an assembly about school safety. J. recounts what happened in his class next period. "I said, 'I wish those kids would come over here and blow away the teachers,'" especially an assistant principal, with whom J. had a long history. J. says, "I am always in trouble, every day, for my attitude."

According to J., the classroom teacher said, "I'm kind of concerned about you."

"Nothing to be concerned about," J. replied. "Everyone hates him anyway."

"Do you want to go to the office?" she asked.

"Hell, no," he said. Then she sent him there.

Ordinarily, J. would have been sent home for cursing. He knew the drill. This time, however, he waited for the Peterborough police, who, he says, searched his knapsack and escorted him to the station, where he was charged in juvenile court with disorderly conduct. (ConVal officials cannot comment on J.'s case because he is a juvenile and because it is pending.)

That night, the police appeared at the homes of members of J.'s family with a search warrant and collected handguns and sporting rifles. The next day, news cameras greeted ConVal students in the parking lot. The print media continued the story, and J. became known as a copycat in a wider world. "It's retarded," he says. "I shouldn't have got in trouble. If it was some good kid that did it, they wouldn't have gotten in trouble." Many students feel that the administration overreacted, less because of Columbine than for the fact that even if he had meant what he said, he was an unlikely candidate to carry out that particular kind of plan. Says one parent, sighing, summing up a typical adult response, "That's just J. being J. again."

Being J., according to J., is as inevitable as his difficulty in school, which he compares to his unhappiness in his family life. He says: "I try not to spend much time at home. It's like I'm a failure. My sister is a straight-A student and everything." He doesn't get along with his stepfather. Right now, his relationship with his mother isn't good. "Whenever I get in trouble, she yells at me for ten minutes, then she stops," J. says. "They yell nonstop, then they forget what they are yelling for. They don't even punish me. It's like a habit with them."

J. spends his days watching television. In the afternoons, he goes to the nearby basketball court. His mother tracks him down. (She declined to comment for this story.) J. says, "Then she yells at me all the way home, then I fall asleep and get up and do it all over again."

More upsetting to J. than his threat to an assistant principal—and more memorable to many ConVal students—was an event for which he was suspended earlier. He stepped into a bathroom to smoke a joint. It wasn't getting high, or even getting high during school, that was so problematic to the other students, but that he had selected a bathroom without ventilation that led directly into the hall where a teacher stood. J. heard the teacher but still kept smoking. "I just finished cuz I knew I was gonna get caught," he says.

"How stupid can you get?" George asks. "He just proved to everyone that he's the [expletive] everyone thinks he is."

Andrew ventures, "Not to be mean to J., but that's plain old stupid."

Even Tyler, who tried to defend what was left of J.'s eroding reputation, admits: "That was the stupidest thing I ever heard of. I don't even know why I tried to protect that kid."

Drugs—at least temporarily—blur the social lines. Boys and girls from different groups get high together; says George: "Polar opposites—they are bound together by drugs." James Key-Wallace, a 1999 graduate, attributes the social leveling to limited distribution: "The drugs come from the same half-dozen sources. You're going to come in contact on grounds that demand respect." Says Hayden Draper, who also just graduated: "Popular kids do drugs. Unpopular kids do drugs. Everyone has their own place to get high." J., however, was all alone.

Since Columbine, the Safe School Committee at ConVal has undergone a renaissance. The Peterborough police have stationed an officer at the entrance. But many of the students believe that a shooting spree like that of Klebold and Harris's could happen anywhere. Says Toffer: "It certainly didn't happen because of the lack of a safe-school committee. Their problem was, they weren't accepted, and they weren't going to be accepted, and that's the way that our society is. There are always people that are going to be cast out and people that are cast in."

Colleen, George's ex, a slim girl with short straight hair and an easy smile, grew up down the street from J. He's generally annoying, she says. He used to sing Christmas carols on the bus in June, but he is not cruel.

Everyone, she says, has their days. What J. hates is people talking down to him, so she takes care not to do that. She feels the same way when people talk down to her because she is a girl. "There are times I can talk to him about things, without it being weird and without him being a pervert," she says. It's all relative. When you are close to the bottom, there's not much room left to fit. She recalls J. at his happiest during a class he described to her, in the high school's on-site preschool, how content he felt playing among the little kids.

Jill Lepore

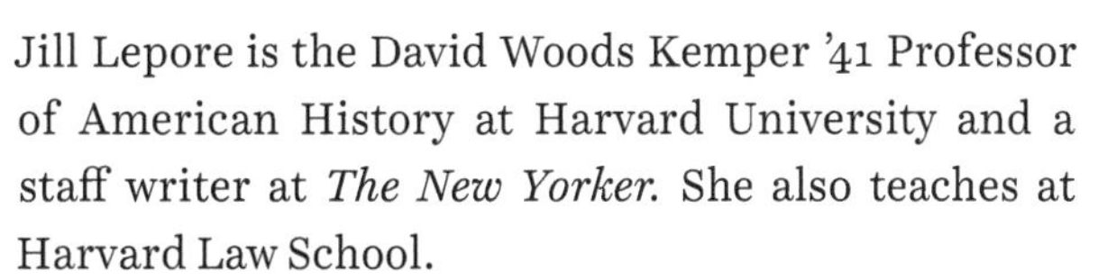

Jill Lepore is the David Woods Kemper '41 Professor of American History at Harvard University and a staff writer at *The New Yorker.* She also teaches at Harvard Law School.

A prize-winning professor, she teaches classes in evidence, historical methods, the humanities, and American political history. Much of Lepore's scholarship explores absences and asymmetries of evidence in the historical record. As an essayist, she writes about American history, law, literature, and politics. Her essays and reviews have been translated into German, Spanish, Italian, Portuguese, Latvian, Swedish, French, Chinese, and Japanese, and have been widely anthologized. Her books include a political history of early America in the form of a trilogy, *The Name of War*, winner of the Bancroft Prize, the Ralph Waldo Emerson Award, and the Berkshire Prize; *New York Burning*, a finalist for the Pulitzer Prize; and *Book of Ages*, a finalist for the 2013 National Book Award for Nonfiction. Her other books include *The Mansion of Happiness*, a finalist for the Carnegie Medal for Excellence in Nonfiction; *The Story of America*, shortlisted for the PEN Literary Award for the Art of the Essay; *Blindspot*, a novel jointly written with Jane Kamensky; and *The Secret History of Wonder Woman*, a *New York Times* bestseller and winner of the 2015 American History Book Prize.

Lepore has been contributing to *The New Yorker* since 2005. A recent series of essays examines the Election of 2016, considering, for instance, the role of polls, facts, parties, and the conventions. She is currently writing a history of the United States.

Prodigal Daughter

A writer researching a book about Ben Franklin's extraordinary sister Jane finds illuminating connections to her own spirited, artistic mother.

In the trunk of her car, my mother used to keep a collapsible easel, a clutch of brushes, a little wooden case stocked with tubes of paint, and, tucked into the spare-tire well, one of my father's old, tobacco-stained shirts, for a smock. She'd be out running errands, see something wonderful, pull over, and pop the trunk. I never knew anyone better prepared to meet with beauty.

"Fingers nimble, brush or thimble," my mother's college yearbook said about her. The cabinets in our kitchen used to be a murky green. One day, I came home from kindergarten to find that my mother had painted every cabinet sunflower yellow. "I was just so sick of that green," she said, washing up, briskly, at the kitchen sink. She stitched quilts; she painted murals. She had one dresser drawer filled with buttons and another with crayons. She once built me a dollhouse out of a stack of shoeboxes. She papered the rooms with scraps of wallpaper and lit them with strings of colored Christmas-tree lights as brightly as she lit my childhood with her trapped passion.

She'd grown up in a small town in Massachusetts, a devout Catholic. After college—a Catholic school in New Rochelle—she'd wanted to go places. It was 1949: the war was over; the world was wide. She got engaged to a man named Winstanley, who had a job with the State Department; she wanted to marry him because he was about to be posted to Berlin. That fell apart. For a while, she worked as a designer for the Milton Bradley Company, in Springfield, but she couldn't stand how, from her apartment, she could hear the keening of the polar bear in the city zoo. ("He had the smallest cage you ever saw," she told me. "All night, he cried.") Then she drove across the country in a jalopy and took a slow boat from San Diego to Honolulu. After that, she became a stewardess, so that she could see Europe. In 1955, she had to quit and come back home, to Massachusetts, to take care of her mother, who was dying. That's when she met my father, a junior-high-school principal: he hired her as an art teacher. Every day, he left a poem in her mailbox in the teachers' room. The filthiest ones are the best. ("Marjorie, Marjorie, let me park my car in your garagery.") He told her he wanted to live in Spain. He was courting; he was lying; no one hated to go anywhere more than my father; he almost never left town. Except for during the war, he had never lived anywhere but his mother's house.

My mother married my father in 1956. She was twenty-eight and he was thirty-one. She loved him with a fierce steadiness borne of loyalty, determination, and an unyielding dignity. On their honeymoon, in a cabin in Maine, for their first breakfast together, she made him blueberry pancakes. Pushing back his plate, he told her he didn't like blueberries. In fifty-five years of marriage, she never again cooked him breakfast.

Before I was born, my parents bought a house on Franklin Street. (My mother promptly planted a blueberry bush in the back yard.) The year I learned the alphabet, the letter "J," the fishing hook, was my favorite, except for "F." "I am four and my mother is forty-four and my father's name is Frank and my house is 44 Franklin Street," I would whisper, when no one was listening: I was the youngest.

The street I grew up on was named for Benjamin Franklin. For a long time, no name was more famous. "There have been as great Souls unknown to fame as any of the most famous," the man himself liked to say, shrugging it off.

Benjamin Franklin was born in Boston in 1706. He was the youngest of his father's ten sons. His sister Jane was born in 1712. She was the youngest of their father's seven daughters. Benny and Jenny, they were called, when they were little.

I never heard of Jane Franklin when I lived on Franklin Street. I only came across her name on a day, much later, when I sat down on the floor of a library to read the first thirty-odd volumes of Benjamin Franklin's published papers. I pulled one volume after another off the shelf, and turned the pages, astonished. She was everywhere, threaded through his life, like a slip stitch.

We "had sildom any contention among us," she wrote him, looking back at their childhood. "All was Harmony."

He remembered it differently. "I think our Family were always subject to being a little Miffy."

She took his hint. "You Introduce your Reproof of my Miffy temper so Politely," she wrote back, slyly, "won cant a Void wishing to have conquered it as you have."

He loved no one longer. She loved no one better. She thought of him as her "Second Self." No two people in their family were more alike. Their lives could hardly have been more different. Boys were taught to read and write, girls to read and stitch. Three in five women in New England couldn't even sign their names, and those who could sign usually couldn't actually write. Signing is mechanical; writing is an art.

Benjamin Franklin taught himself to write with wit and force and style. His sister never learned how to spell. What she did learn, he taught her. It was a little cruel, in its kindness, because when he left the lessons ended.

He ran away in 1723, when he was seventeen and she was eleven. The day he turned twenty-one, he wrote her a letter—she was fourteen—beginning a correspondence that would last until his death. (He wrote more letters to her than he wrote to anyone else.) He became a printer, a philosopher, and a statesman. She became a wife, a mother, and a widow. He signed the Declaration of Independence, the Treaty of Paris, and the Constitution. She strained to form the letters of her name.

He wrote the story of his life, about a boy who runs away from a life of poverty and obscurity in cramped, pious Boston to become an enlightened, independent man of the world: a free man. He meant it as an allegory about America.

"One Half the World does not know how the other Half lives," he once wrote. Jane Franklin was his other half. If his life is an allegory, so is hers.

"Write a book about her!" my mother said, when I told her about Jane Franklin. I thought she was joking. It would be like painting a phantom.

History's written from what can be found; what isn't saved is lost, sunken and rotted, eaten by earth. Jane kept the letters her brother sent her. But half the letters she sent him—three decades' worth—are missing. Most likely, he threw them away. Maybe someone burned them. It hardly matters. A one-sided correspondence is a house without windows, a left shoe, a pair of spectacles, smashed.

My mother liked to command me to do things I found scary. I always wanted to stay home and read. My mother only ever wanted me to get away. She brought me with her wherever she went. She once sent me to live with my aunt in Connecticut. ("Just to see someplace different.") One year, she saved up to send me to a week of Girl Scout camp, the most exotic adventure I had ever heard of. I got homesick, and begged her to let me come home. "Oh, stop," she said. "And don't you dare call me again, either." When I was eleven, she took me to New York City, a place no one else in my family had ever been. It was the weekend of the annual gay-pride parade, on Christopher Street. "Isn't that interesting?" she said. She took a picture of me next to five men dressed in black leather carrying a banner that read "Cocksuckers Unite"—this was 1978—so that I'd remember the existence of a world beyond Franklin Street. No one else in my family left home to go to college. My mother made sure I did. She might as well have written me a letter: "Run away, run away." By then, I didn't need a push.

Jane Franklin never ran away, and never wrote the story of her life. But she did once stitch four sheets of foolscap between two covers to make a little book of sixteen pages. In an archive in Boston, I held it in my hands. I pictured her making it. Her paper was made from rags, soaked and pulped and strained and dried. Her thread was made from flax, combed and spun and dyed and twisted. She dipped the nib of a pen slit from the feather of a bird into a pot of ink boiled of oil mixed with soot and, on the first page, wrote three words: "Book of Ages"—a lavish, calligraphic letter "B," a graceful, slender, artful "A." She would have learned this—an Italian round hand—out of a writing manual, like "The American Instructor: Or, Young Man's Best Companion," a book her brother printed in Philadelphia.

At the top of the next page, in a much smaller and plainer hand, she began her chronicle:

> Jane Franklin Born on March 27-1712
> Edward Mecom Marryed to Jane Franklin the 27th of July 1727.

The Book of Ages: *her* age. Born, March 27, 1712; married, July 27, 1727. Fifteen years four months. She was a child. The legal age for marriage in Massachusetts was sixteen; the average age was twenty-four, which is the age at which her brother Benjamin married and, excepting Jane, the average age at which her sisters were married.

The man she married, Edward Mecom, was twenty-two. He was poor, he was a saddler, and he was a Scot. He wore a wig and a beaver hat. She never once wrote anything about him expressing the least affection.

She added another line:

> Josiah Mecom their first Born on Wednesday June the 4: 1729

She named this child, her first, for her father.

> and Died May the 18-1730.

The child of her childhood died three weeks shy of his first birthday.

"A Dead Child is a sight no more surprizing than a broken Pitcher," Cotton Mather preached, in a sermon called "Right Thoughts in Sad Hours." One in four children died before the age of ten. The dead were wrapped in linen dipped in melted wax while a box made of pine was built and painted black. Puritans banned prayers for the dead: at the grave, there would be no sermon. Nor, ministers warned, ought there to be tears. "A Token for Mourners or, The Advice of Christ to a Distressed Mother, bewailing the Death of her Dear and Only Son" cited Luke 7:13: "Weepe not."

What remains of a life? "Remains" means what remains of the body after death. But remains are also unpublished papers. And descendants are remains, too. The Boston Puritan poet Anne Bradstreet wrote about her children as "my little babes, my dear remains." But Bradstreet's poems were her children, as well: "Thou ill-form'd offspring of my feeble brain." Her words were all that her children would, one day, have left of her. "If chance to thine eyes shall bring this verse," she told them, "kiss this paper."

Jane didn't know how to write a poem. She couldn't have afforded a headstone. Instead, she went home, and wrote a book of remembrance. *Kiss this paper.*

College was something of a bust. It was the nineteen-eighties. On the one hand, Andrea Dworkin; on the other, Jacques Derrida. I took a job as a secretary, on the theory that it would give me more time to read what I wanted. "Is that working out?" my mother wanted to know. I wrote a graduate-school application essay about a short story of Isak Dinesen's called "The Blank Page." Very "A Room of One's Own." Very "The Madwoman in the Attic." ("I write now in my own litle chamber," Jane wrote, when she was sixty-four, "& nobod up in the house near me to Desturb me." She was very happy to have that room, but not having it sooner isn't why she didn't write more or better.) Then, suddenly, I realized that my life plan—bashful daughter of shackled artist reads "The Yellow Wallpaper"—was narrow, hackneyed, daffy.

I was sick of silence, sick of attics and wallpaper, sick of blank pages and miniature rooms, sick of blighted girlhood. I wanted to study war. I wanted to investigate atrocity. I wanted to write about politics. Really, I wanted to write about anything but Jane Franklin.

"What about beauty?" my mother pressed. I kept making excuses. I was pregnant. ("Edward Mecom Born on Munday the 29 March 1731.") I was too busy. ("My mind is keept in a contineual Agitation that I Dont know how to write," Jane once apologized.) I was pregnant again. ("Benjamin Mecom Born on Fryday the 29 of December 1732.") I was so tired. ("My litle wons are Interupting me Every miniut.") I was pregnant again. ("Ebenezer Mecom Born on May the 2 1735.") I felt rebuked, even by Jane herself. ("I was almost Tempted to think you had forgot me but I check those thoughts with the consideration of the dificulties you must labour under.") I hadn't forgotten her. I just couldn't bear to think about her, trapped in that house.

But Benjamin Franklin: I adored him. He was funny and brilliant and generous and fortunate. Every year of his life, his world got bigger. So did mine. When he had something to say, he said it. So did I. My mother and I had got tangled up, like skeins. I wasn't the one who identified with Jane.

The more I thought about Jane, the sadder it got. I tried to picture it. Her belly swelled, and emptied, and swelled again. Her breasts filled, and emptied, and filled again. Her days were days of flesh: the little legs and little arms, the little hands, clutched around her neck, the softness. A baby in her arms, she stared into kettles and tubs, swaying. The days passed to months, the months to years, and, in her Book of Ages, she pressed her children between the pages.

Her husband fell into debt. He may have gone mad. (Two of her sons became violently insane; they had to be locked up.) Jane and her children lived with her parents; she nursed them, in their old age. Josiah Franklin died in 1744. He was eighty-seven. In his will, he had divided his estate among his surviving children. Benjamin Franklin refused his portion: he gave it to Jane.

In 1751, Jane gave birth for the twelfth time. She was thirty-nine. She'd named her first baby for her father; she named this baby, her last, for her mother, Abiah Franklin:

> Abiah mecom born augst 1st 1751.

The month Abiah Mecom was born, Benjamin Franklin took a seat in the Pennsylvania Assembly. His eighty-four-year-old mother wrote him a letter, with her daughter at her side. "I am very weeke and short bretht so that I Cant set to rite much," Abiah Franklin explained. She asked her daughter to write for her. Aside from Jane's Book of Ages, and notes she made in books she read, this is the only writing in her hand to survive, for the first four decades of her life:

> P S Mother says she an't able and so I must tell you my self
> that I rejoyce with you and bles god for you in all your
> prosperity and doubt not but you will be grater blessings
> to the world as he bestows upon you grater honers.
> J M

Mother says she an't able and so I must. They'd got tangled, too.

Jane's baby, Abiah Mecom, died within the year. So did Abiah Franklin:

> my dear Mother Died May 8 1752.

She loved her; she washed her. She buried her. But it was Benjamin Franklin who paid for a gravestone, and wrote an epitaph:

Josiah Franklin
And Abiah his Wife
Lie here interred.

They lived lovingly together in Wedlock
Fifty-five Years.
. . . .
From this Instance, Reader,
Be encouraged to Diligence in thy Calling,
And distrust not Providence.
He was a pious & prudent Man,
She a discreet and virtuous Woman.
Their youngest Son,
In filial Regard to their Memory,
Places this Stone.

This book of remembrance was a monument, not to his parents but to Franklin himself: prodigal son.

"Do the right thing with Spirit," Jane once wrote. It's just the kind of thing my mother liked to say. One of Jane's sons became a printer. He once printed a poem called "The Prodigal Daughter": "She from her Mother in a Passion went, / Filling her aged Heart with Discontent."

My mother's heart began to fail. She had one heart attack, and then another. Surgery, and more surgery. Eventually, she had a defibrillator implanted in her chest. I'd visit her in the hospital; she'd send me away. All I wanted was to be there, with her, but that only made her remember going home to watch her mother die. "See? I'm fine," she'd say. "Now. Please: go. You have things to do."

I decided I had better read whatever of Jane's letters had survived. The first is one she wrote in 1758, when she was forty-five years old, to Franklin's wife, Deborah. This is her voice, gabby, frank, and vexed:

> Dear Sister
> for so I must call you come what will & If I dont Express my self proper you must Excuse it seeing I have not been acostomed to Pay my Complements to Governer & Baronets Ladys I am in the midst of a grate wash & Sarah still sick, & would gladly been Excused writing this Post but my husband says I must write & Give you Joy which we searly Joyn in; I sopose it will not be news to you, but I will tell you how I came by it, Mr Fluker Tould Cousen Williams & he Docter Perkins who Brought it to my Poor Son nedey

> who has a nother Relaps into Raising Blood & has not Done won stroke of work this month but was Just a going to begin when he was again taken Ill pray Pardon my Bad writing & confused composure & acept it as coming from your Ladyships affectionat Sister & most obedent
>
> Humble Servant
> Jane Mecom

She was in the middle of a great wash. One of her lodgers, Sarah, was ailing. Her poor son Edward (Neddy), who was married and a father, was sick again—weak and listless and coughing blood. But she had heard from Neddy, who heard it from her doctor, John Perkins, who heard it from Jonathan Williams, Sr., the husband of Jane's friend Grace, who heard it from a Boston merchant, Thomas Flucker, that Benjamin Franklin had been given a baronetcy. Jane's husband told her she must send her congratulations, "searly"—surely. She was miffed. If this ridiculous rumor was true, why, for heaven's sake, was she the last to know about it?

"Your loving Sister," or "Your affectionate Sister," is how Jane usually signed off—not "your Ladyships affectionat Sister & most obedient Humble Servant." That was a jab. Must she curtsey?

By words on a page, she wanted to be carried away—out of her house, out of Boston, out into the world. The more details the better. "The Sow has Piged," a friend reported from Rhode Island, reminding her, "You told me to write you all." She loved gossip. "Cousen willames Looks soon to Lyin," she told Deborah, "she is so big I tell Her she will have two." She once scolded her niece for writing letters that she found insufficiently chatty. "I want to know a Thousand litle Perticulars about your self yr Husband & the children such as your mother used to write me," Jane commanded, adding, "it would be Next to Seeing the little things to hear some of there Prattle (Speaches If you Pleas) & have you Describe there persons & actions tell me who they Look like." Stories, likenesses, characters: speeches.

My mother wasn't much of a letter writer. If she telephoned, she would yell, "This is your mother calling!" My sisters and my brother and I got her an iPad for her birthday. "If you call here keep talking as it takes us time to get to the phone," she e-mailed me. She had a cell phone, for emergencies; she brought it with her when she had to go to the hospital. Once, she was kept waiting on a gurney, in a hallway, for hours.

"This is your mother calling!"

"I know, Mom. Why haven't they gotten you a room?"

"Oh, I don't mind," she said. "The people here in the hallway are just *fascinating*." She was giggling.

"Mom. Did they give you something for the pain?"

"Oh, yes, it's wonderful."

"The people are interesting?"

"Oh, yes. It's like a soap opera here."

Jane, writing to her brother, worried that she had spelled so badly, and expressed herself so poorly—"my Blundering way of Expresing my self," she called it—that he wouldn't be able to understand what she meant to say. "I know I have wrote and speld this worse than I do sometimes," she wrote him, "but I hope you will find it out."

To "find out" a letter was to decipher it, to turn writing back into speech. Jane knew that letters weren't supposed to be speeches written down; they were supposed to be more formal. Her brother warned her that she was too free with him. "You Long ago convinced me that there is many things Proper to convers with a Friend about that is not Proper to write," she confessed. But, then, he scolded her, too, for not being free enough. "I was allways too Difident," she said he had told her.

"Dont let it mortifie you that such a Scraw came from your Sister," she begged him.

"Is there not a little Affectation in your Apology for the Incorrectness of your Writing?" he teased her. "Perhaps it is rather fishing for Commendation. You write better, in my Opinion, than most American Women."

This was, miserably, true.

It was the diffidence that got to me. Female demurral isn't charming. It's maddening. Half the time, I wanted to throttle her. Could she ever, would she never, express a political opinion?

I read on. And then, in the seventeen-sixties, a decade of riots, protests, and boycotts, something changed. Jane's whole family was sick. Her daughter Sally died; Jane took in Sally's four young children; then two of them died, only to be followed by Jane's husband and, not long after, by

Jane's favorite daughter. "The Lord Giveth & the Lord taketh away," she wrote in her Book of Ages. "Oh may I never be so Rebelious as to Refuse Acquiesing & & saying from my hart Blessed be the Name of the Lord." And then: she put down her pen. She never wrote in her Book of Ages again.

"Realy my Spirits are so much Broken with this Last Hevey Stroak of Provedenc that I am not capeble of Expresing my self," she wrote to her brother. She did not think she could bear it. In the depth of her despair, she began to question Providence. Maybe her sons had failed not for lack of merit but because they were unable to overcome the disadvantage of an unsteadiness inherited from their father. Maybe her daughters and grandchildren had died because they were poor, and lived lives of squalor. Maybe not Providence but men in power—politics—determined the course of human events.

She wrote to her brother. She wanted to read "all the political Pieces" he had ever written. Could he please send them to her?

"I could as easily make a Collection for you of all the past Parings of my Nails," he wrote back. He sent what he could. She read, and I read.

She left home in 1775, after the battles of Lexington and Concord, when the British occupied Boston. For a while, she lived with her brother in Philadelphia. After he left for France, she spent the war as a fugitive. "I am Grown such a Vagrant," she wrote him. When peace came—after he helped negotiate it—he returned to Philadelphia, and she to Boston.

He gave her a house in the North End. She loved it. "I have this Spring been new planking the yard," she one day boasted, and "am Painting the Front of the House to make it look Decent that I may not be Ashamed when any Boddy Inquiers for Dr Franklins Sister."

She knew, for the first time, contentment. Except that she was starved for company. "I Injoy all the Agreable conversation I can come at Properly," she wrote to her brother, "but I find Litle, very Litle, Equal to that I have a Right to by Nature but am deprived of by Provedence."

It was a shocking thing to say: that she had a right to intelligent conversation—a natural right—but that Providence had deprived her of it. Before the war, she had favored independence from Britain. After it, she found her own kind of freedom. Once she started writing down her opinions, she could scarcely stop.

"I can not find in my Hart to be Pleasd at your Accepting the Government of the State and Therefore have not congratulated you on it," she wrote to her brother in 1786, when he accepted yet another political appointment. "I fear it will Fatigue you two much."

"We have all of us Wisdom enough to judge what others ought to do, or not to do in the Management of their Affairs," he wrote back. "Tis possible I might blame you as much if you were to accept the Offer of a young Husband."

She let that pass. "I have two favours to Ask of you," she begged him: "your New Alphabet of the English Language, and the Petition of the Letter Z."

"My new Alphabet is in a printed Book of my Pieces, which I will send you the first Opportunity I have," he answered. "The Petition of Z is enclos'd."

In "The Petition of the Letter Z," a satire about inequality, Z complains "That he is not only plac'd at the Tail of the Alphabet, when he had as much Right as any other to be at the Head but is, by the Injustice of his Enemies totally excluded from the Word WISE, and his Place injuriously filled by a little, hissing, crooked, serpentine, venomous Letter called S." In another essay, Franklin proposed a new alphabet. Jane found it cunning, especially since, as she explained, "I am but won of the Thousands & thousands, that write on to old Age and cant Learn."

"You need not be concern'd in writing to me about your bad Spelling," he wrote back, "for in my Opinion as our Alphabet now Stands, the bad Spelling, or what is call'd so, is generally the best." To illustrate, he told her a story: A gentleman receives a note that reads, "Not finding Brown at hom, I delivered your Meseg to his yf." When both the gentleman and his wife are unable to decipher the note, they consult their chambermaid, Betty. "Why, says she, y. f spells Wife, what else can it spell?"

Jane loved that. "I think Sir & madam were deficient in Sagasity that they could not find out y f as well as Bety," she wrote her brother, "but some times the Betys has the Brightst understanding."

"How's that book about Jane Franklin coming along?" my mother asked, every time I took her out. (We'd go to art museums, mostly. I'd race her around, in a wheelchair.) "Better," I said.

When Jane was seventy-four, she read a book called "Four Dissertations," written by Richard Price, a Welsh clergyman and political radical. The first dissertation was called "On Providence." One objection to the idea that everything in life is fated by Providence, Price wrote, is the failure to thrive: "Many perish in the womb," and even more "are nipped in their bloom." An elm produces three hundred and thirty thousand seeds a year, but very few of those seeds ever grow into trees. A spider lays as many as six hundred eggs, and yet very few grow into spiders. So, too, for humans: "Thousands of Boyles, Clarks and Newtons have probably been lost to the world, and lived and died in ignorance and meanness, merely for want of being placed in favourable situations, and enjoying proper advantages." No one dies for naught, Price believed, but that doesn't mean suffering is fair, or can't be protested.

At her desk, with Price's "Four Dissertations" pressed open, Jane wrote a letter to her brother. "Dr Price thinks Thousand of Boyles Clarks and Newtons have Probably been lost to the world," she wrote. To this, she added an opinion of her own: "very few we know is Able to beat thro all Impedements and Arive to any Grat Degre of superiority in Understanding."

Benjamin Franklin knew, and his sister knew, that very few ever beat through. Three hundred thousand seeds to make one elm. Six hundred eggs to make one spider. Of seventeen children of Josiah Franklin, how many? Very few. Nearly none. Only one. Or, possibly: two.

Benjamin Franklin died in 1790. He was eighty-four. Jane died four years later. She was eighty-three. If she ever had a gravestone, it's long since sunken underground. She believed in one truth, above all: "The most Insignificant creature on Earth may be made some use of in the scale of Beings."

It wasn't until last year, sitting by my father in a room in intensive care in a hospital in the town where he'd been born eighty-seven years before, that I realized I had waited too long to write the only book my mother ever wanted me to write. From this Instance, Reader, Be encouraged to Diligence in thy Calling.

We buried my father. My mother ordered a single gravestone, engraved with both their names. I wrote as fast as I could. Meanwhile, I read my mother letters and told my mother stories. In a museum, I found a mourning ring Jane had owned; I told my mother about how, when no one was looking, I'd tried it on. (I didn't tell her that it didn't fit, and that I'd found this an incredible relief.) In a library not a dozen miles from Franklin Street, I found a long-lost portrait of Jane's favorite granddaughter:

another Jenny, age nine. I brought my mother a photograph. She looked, for a long time, into that little girl's eyes. "She's beautiful," she said. She smiled. "I'm so glad you found her."

"That mother of yours," my father used to say, shaking his head, besotted. He knew he could never live without her. I never knew—never saw, never in the least suspected—that she couldn't live without him, either. But, after his death, she didn't last out the year. She died at home, unexpectedly, and alone. She kept her paintbrushes in glass jars in my old bedroom. She was eighty-five.

I finished the last revisions. Too late for her to read it. I wrote the dedication.

Their youngest daughter. In filial regard. Places this stone.

Suzannah Lessard

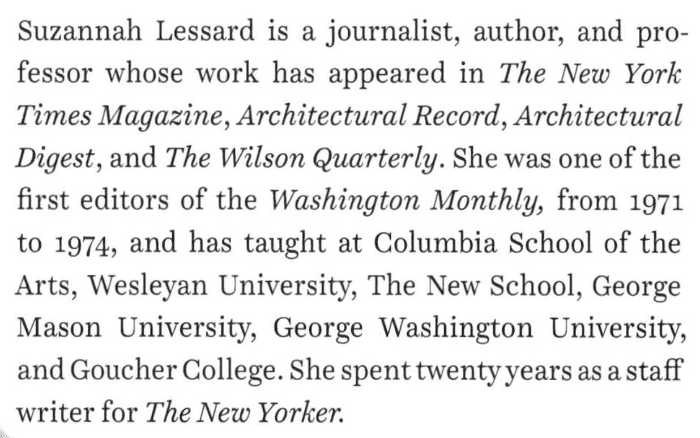

Suzannah Lessard is a journalist, author, and professor whose work has appeared in *The New York Times Magazine*, *Architectural Record*, *Architectural Digest*, and *The Wilson Quarterly*. She was one of the first editors of the *Washington Monthly,* from 1971 to 1974, and has taught at Columbia School of the Arts, Wesleyan University, The New School, George Mason University, George Washington University, and Goucher College. She spent twenty years as a staff writer for *The New Yorker.*

Lessard is a recipient of the 1995 Whiting Award as well as the 2003 Mark Lynton History Prize for *Mapping the New World: An Inquiry into the Meaning of Sprawl.* She also received a 2001 fellowship at the Woodrow Wilson International Center for Scholars in Washington, DC, and a 2002 Jenny McKean Moore Fellowship for creative nonfiction at George Washington University.

One of Lessard's best-known works is her memoir, *The Architect of Desire: Beauty and Danger in the Stanford White Family.* Her next book, *The Crack of Dawn: A Meditation on the American Landscape*, will be published in 2018.

The Split

In Manhattan, the opulent Upper East Side, one of the nation's richest neighborhoods, gives way to Harlem, one of the poorest.

In the middle of Park Avenue, just north of Ninety-Sixth Street in Manhattan, there is a little nowhere of a paved-over spot that is the last in a sequence of otherwise lushly cultivated malls running up the center of the avenue from Forty-Sixth Street. Looking south from that island, one sees the parapets of Park silhouetted against the sky—two phalanxes of Italianate apartment buildings, built in the nineteen-twenties, quoined, rusticated, and corniced, in many instances, and from twelve to fifteen stories high. Facing each other, they stand at attention, chests swelling, the cornices creating the effect of a martial hat with a brim and generally making a statement of high-bourgeois solidarity which brooks no contradiction. This is the Upper East Side.

Turning to the north, one sees a porous hodgepodge of nineteenth-century tenements and high-rise public housing divided by four sets of train tracks which shoot out from under the hill at Ninety-Seventh Street, continuing on a viaduct that cuts a wide swath through the vista. The viaduct bodychecks the two sides of Park Avenue, reducing it to a mingy, shadowed passage not even up to the standard of an ordinary street. This is Harlem. Here at Ninety-Sixth Street, the nation's richest neighborhood collides with one of the poorest so sharply that it is very nearly possible to stand with one foot in each.

The community immediately north of Ninety-Sixth Street is East Harlem, also known as the Barrio, because of the many Puerto Ricans who live there. In 1990, the median family income in the Barrio (somewhat skewed by residences attached to Mount Sinai Hospital and by a thin strip of wealth that continues up Fifth Avenue) was twenty thousand dollars a year; farther north, in the Bradhurst area of Harlem, it was six thousand dollars a year, the lowest in the United States, with the exception of a former leper colony in Hawaii. The neighborhood immediately to the south of Ninety-Sixth and Park is Carnegie Hill, an old-fashioned, traditionally Wasp neighborhood, where the median family income is a modest hundred and twenty-nine thousand a year. Carnegie Hill overlaps with the Upper East Side historic district, which runs from Fifth Avenue to Lexington Avenue and from Seventy-Ninth Street down to Fifty-Ninth. South of Seventy-Second Street there is an eight-block area where the median household income of homeowners is seven hundred and thirty thousand dollars a year. At Ninety-Seventh and Park, unemployed men of varying ages sit on milk crates outside a bodega drinking *cerveza fria.* A few blocks south on Madison, you can buy a little girl's dress for four hundred and seventy dollars.

For New Yorkers, this abrupt juncture of the Upper East Side and Harlem is like a formation of the Ice Age: dramatic, but so familiar that it is barely noticed. The divide reflects a split in American society that is usually blurred by geographic distance, yet even here, where it is abrupt and plainly evident, it is somehow unseen.

Sometimes, as a way of trying to take in more deeply what the split is, and what it is to cross it, I would take the subway to 125th Street and then walk back through East Harlem toward Ninety-Sixth. Or, conversely, I would get off at Fifty-Ninth Street and follow the procession of Park Avenue uptown. In either case, what I found was that, though I was alert and absorbed in the world around me right up to the boundary, at the moment of crossing I would go into a little blackout, a shutting down of awareness, as if at that moment I had stepped into a special chamber designed to equalize the effects of vastly differing pressures.

Katharine Hellman, a young woman who works as a therapist in an elementary school in Harlem, knew what I meant by a disjunction that was almost more than one could absorb. She grew up in a wealthy family on the Upper East Side, assuming, as a girl, that a normal home was a Park Avenue duplex with Magrittes on the wall, as she put it. When she first started working in Harlem, she always felt a tremendous pressure, on returning to her own world, to tell what she knew—to try to convey, for example, that that day she had visited the home of a student where there was no furniture. "I had never conceived of such a thing," she said. "I wanted to bring people from my world to the apartment with no furniture. It seemed like important knowledge. You have to see it—if you haven't seen it, there is something about it you might not get."

The school Hellman works at is on a nearly abandoned street where brownstones with punched-out or blocked-up windows have lost their stoops, so that the pedimented landings hang disconnected in the air. One June Friday after school in that early period of her career, she travelled up to her family's vacation home, a farm in Connecticut, for the weekend, and found herself standing in a lovely field. She thought it was a good thing that it took some time to get there, because "if you went from one place to the other instantly you would go crazy because you couldn't make the shift fast enough,"

The shift can be difficult to absorb in the reverse direction as well. A young woman I will call Manuela, a high-school student who had worked in a crack factory for a time, was taken by a neighborhood program on a day trip to Princeton University. She was enraged that she had been shown this beautiful college world, because she knew that she could never become a part of it. She attends a high school in East Harlem that was founded expressly to prepare students for college, but in actuality most of the kids are nowhere near that level. Manuela says that when she was very small her mother was almost certainly on drugs; she remembers dialing 911 once because she was alone in the apartment in the middle of the night. She was not yet in school when her mother died of AIDS, and she now lives with her grandmother.

Manuela was upset by her visit to Princeton. Yet it is also true that people who live in the inner city know very well how others live: if nothing else, television is a daily reminder. Yolanda Sanchez, who works in a clinic in the Bronx, felt no shift in pressure in the days when she still lived in East Harlem, where she had grown up, and was going to school on the Upper East Side, studying to become a social worker. "I might think, Isn't it amazing that a person would be able to afford to pay another to wash the street in front of their house," she said. Pedro Gomez is an affable young man who lives in the Barrio and works as a doorman at a Park Avenue apartment building that is right on the border. At work, in his uniform and white gloves, he seems to enjoy himself as he chats with the gentlemen leaving for their offices and crouches down to eye level with children on their way to school. Of the boundary that he crosses daily he said to me, "There's no difference—it's just people."

The grid was laid down over the countryside of Manhattan Island in 1811, and ran all the way up to what it designated as 155th Street, although for the most part the city had grown only as far north as Houston Street at that time. It was a neoclassical conception, a rational ideal that was typically nineteenth-century: the whole Midwest was gridded into states, counties, and homesteading lots. In New York, the primary function of the grid was to facilitate real-estate development. The grid-makers were so far ahead of the time, however, that there was nothing for decades after they laid it down but a dreary cross-hatching of muddy tracks in a wasteland of disturbed earth.

Though East Harlem is farther north than the Upper East Side, it was settled earlier, by Irish fugitives from overcrowded immigrant slums downtown. They built shanties along the Harlem River and were called goaters, after their favorite form of livestock. As conditions downtown worsened, the squatter community grew. By the eighteen-sixties, the first urban structures had gone up, and after 1880 most of the tenements were built in the "dumbbell" style—an improvement over downtown models in that the buildings had slight indentations on the sides to let in light and air. With their narrow facades obediently aligned with the gridded street front, the first tenements stood alone in the wasteland, or in twos or threes, accompanied only by occasional goaters' shanties.

The same surreal vistas of urban buildings exposed on the naked grid did not appear on the Upper East Side until 1894, when Caroline Schermerhorn Astor—the wife of William Astor and the cofounder of the society list known as the Four Hundred—built an imitation French chateau in the mud at Fifth Avenue and Sixty-Fifth Street, thereby signaling to Gilded Age society not only that this would be the next fashionable neighborhood but that architectural excess was as acceptable in the city as it had become out of town. East Harlem was at this point a teeming neighborhood, upon which wave after wave of immigrants—Irish, then German, then Jewish—crashed, and it soon rivaled the Lower East Side in horrific health conditions and overcrowding, as well as in a pulsing dynamism. On the Upper East Side, other palazzo builders followed Mrs. Astor, and a costume ball of town houses in a dazzling variety of architectural styles appeared on the side streets off Fifth Avenue.

Park Avenue, known as Fourth Avenue then, remained through all this a seedy neighborhood, because the New York Central Railroad ran up the middle in an open cut, spewing cinders and rattling with noise. Then William Wilgus, the vice-president and chief engineer of the railroad, saw that if the railroad switched from steam to electric power the cut could be covered up and the value of the land along the avenue—land owned by the New York Central and the Vanderbilts—would soar. The avenue was renamed Park, and development there was modeled on the grand nineteenth-century visions of Baron Haussmann, Napoleon III's master planner, who had rebuilt Paris, creating wide boulevards to reflect the imperial status of modern France.

It was not until 1921, however, that the prototypical Park Avenue apartment building went up—the Marguery, a colossus consuming the entire block between Forty-Seventh and Forty-Eighth on the west side of Park, offering seventeen- and eighteen-room apartments and containing several restaurants managed by the Ritz. One or two members of Society succumbed to the lure of luxury and convenience over the hidebound convention of the town house, and then there was a reverse domino effect—a sequential uprising of Marguery-type buildings, creating the consistent architectural panorama that is the Park Avenue we know today, continuing right on up to Ninety-Sixth Street, where it was brought to a halt by the emergence of the tracks from under the hill there, and by the crash of 1929.

By this time, East Harlem had become a predominantly Italian neighborhood, its residents still very poor, but working, and with middle-class people who offered them professional services living in their midst. Beginning in the twenties and thirties and gaining momentum in the fifties, the Italians of East Harlem moved on, yielding to Puerto Ricans. This turnover reflected an established pattern of successive upward mobility, except that Harlem generally was becoming an "inner city": it was more and more isolated from the mainstream economy and was losing its middle-class population as its lower-class population lost jobs, while crime and dissolution separated it further from the mainstream society.

Ordinary things about the Upper East Side became vivid, even astonishing, when I had walked down into the neighborhood from Harlem. I noticed how during the morning rush hour Park Avenue streams with taxis as if with yellow pigment, but the atmosphere is nonetheless serene, for trucks are banned and the lights are not staggered—the traffic is brought to a halt for the entire length of the avenue every few minutes. I was struck by the men in midlife issuing from their buildings with lobbies that looked small and cozy in comparison with the grandeur of the façades. I noted the playfulness in their clothing—a bright-colored cashmere scarf or a ski cap with a tassel. They looked very clean, and I saw in their faces an attractive worldly complexity—the well-being that comes of having one's powers fully engaged. I watched them take time for an easygoing exchange with the doorman, sometimes getting into a cab he had hailed, or into a chauffeured car, or walking on down spacious, uncrowded sidewalks with a light, elegantly shod step.

I became aware for the first time that the Upper East Side is rooted in midtown—one of the highest-priced shopping districts in the world. But in contrast to the shops in midtown those on the Upper East Side have an intimate quality. Some of them might almost be a part of someone's home. (Much on the Upper East Side beckons with a homelike allure while at the same time the way is barred: the lobby is guarded by a doorman; the shop has a buzzer on the door.) Here you can find a store devoted entirely to buttons, or to shaving equipment, or personalized stationery and engraved invitations. The window displays often include a rough, beat-up common object, like an old knocked-together wooden chest, little more than a crate, or an old scale, rusty and chipped—objects that might look shabby elsewhere but look luminously beautiful here because they are placed and lit so perfectly, their textures and irregularities becoming, in that pristine environment, aesthetically pleasurable.

The burnishing effects of care also have a way of disguising common objects, so that the display in a liquor-store window somehow makes it look like a bookstore, and the bookstore looks like an art gallery; and the dressy pumps in the shoe-store window somehow look like vintage brandies, while stylishly decorated eggs clustered in the window of a bakery look like fancy shoes. Inside, the bakery is humbly picturesque, as if it were situated in a remote European village—an effect so studiously managed that entering the store is almost like entering a painting.

Real estate in the Upper East Side historic district is perhaps the most valuable, block by block, in the United States. On the side streets, one is hard put to find even a square inch that is not polished or steamed or embellished by a planter bearing, say, meticulously groomed small evergreens of an exotic variety. There is no improvisation here. Not a sliver of space has been neglected; indeed, there are quite a few buildings that are themselves barely more than slivers—contemporary architects' ingenious designs for the use of lots that would ordinarily be considered too narrow to build on. There is in this a kind of massing that is like a popular social event—an effect of crisp, alert energy, of contained excitement, even of merriment. The town houses crowd each other like jostling children eager for sweets, barely holding a line: their different roofs (dormers, rounded slate, the slanting glass of studios), some peaked and others corniced, making up a playful visual text that streaks back and forth across the architectural vocabulary of Western civilization.

Stopping in at the offices of local political representatives—a member of the community board, a State Assembly person—I heard about recent concerns of the neighborhood: Double-parked cars. Whether to create a private security district. Cleanup around a public school. This is an activist community, highly sensitive to any inroads on quality of life, and it expects its political representatives—who tend to be of a lower socioeconomic class than their constituents—to act quickly and effectively on its complaints. Nevertheless, meetings of Community Board 11 are famously decorous. ("Wasps don't shout, they sue," one representative commented.) The most boisterous meeting in memory had to do with the children's zoo.

In the course of my walks across the split, I became acutely conscious of the purr in the atmosphere along these quiet streets where chores are diligently performed by a vast staff (garbage stacked neatly just before pickup, brass polished, clean clothing delivered), of a pervasive sense of contentment that is profoundly reassuring even for the passerby. A woman walks under trees toward the light-filled open space of Park Avenue, in a coat that is both generously cut and sharply shaped and sways from shoulders to midcalf; she has tidy ankles and trim, close-fitting shoes. It was the delineated wrist and ankle that, in the end, emerged for me as the hallmark of the Upper East Side: somewhat in defiance of fashion and in contrast to the muffled, bundled look of the parkas and sneakers that are ubiquitous in East Harlem and, when they are old and less than clean, can seem to be on a continuum with the pile of rags in a doorway beneath which one can barely discern the shape of a sleeping body.

At Lexington and 124th Street, I know that I am in the Barrio because I see oranges peeled in a decorative way hanging in a string bag from a vender's cart. Spanish crackles around me. Emmaus House, a shelter across the street, which also provides a variety of other services to the homeless, looks worn and trafficked, the walls of the entryway silvered as if by a million hands. Drug addicts nod out, a dealer deals, the vender greets passersby. Though nearly everyone I see, with the exception of some young people, looks battered or injured or in some way physically stressed, the atmosphere is gregarious, at moments rippling with fun.

To the east, activity falls off quickly. Many buildings are boarded up, and the traffic is so light that even on the avenues men can work on cars well away from the curb. Along 120th Street, a stand of housing projects opens up the sky. Shades are drawn. Inside, intercoms and elevators are usually broken, and graffiti-ridden halls smell of urine; they are the domain of drug users, and are unsafe for the families attempting to bring up children. The exterior is banal and bureaucratic, but when I step off the street and into the domain of the projects the hair rises on the back of my neck.

East Harlem has the highest density of public housing in New York, and New York has the highest density in the country. Most of the housing went up in the late fifties and the sixties, driven by powerful visions of urban renewal which ripped out organic neighborhoods and, with them, the generative, socializing life of the street. As architecture, the projects reflect Le Corbusier's dream of the Radiant City, in which people would live in high-rise buildings separated by green expanses, connected by high-speed rail running at about the third-story level—a democratic utopia where architecture would break away from the class-ridden traditions of the past.

In the sixties and seventies, the population of East Harlem, like that of inner cities across the country, declined drastically, and the neighborhood went from being one of the most populated areas in the city to being one of the least populated. For decades, the available housing stock decreased steadily as the city pursued a policy of slum clearance through demolition. Because of this policy, a porous, flattened landscape began to appear, in which little groups of town houses or tenements are left free-standing, surrounded by vacant lots—a landscape eerily similar to that of the goaters' time, when urban buildings, alone or in small packs, first started going up on the empty grid. One even comes across plywood shacks in vacant lots in East Harlem—they are called casitas—which echo the shanties of the previous century. There is in large stretches of East Harlem a marginal, maverick feeling, a faraway mood, a deadness in the air that seems incompatible with the charged, compressed atmosphere of Manhattan. One would not be altogether surprised to see a goat.

These are some of the community concerns in East Harlem: The third highest incidence of AIDS in the city (after Chelsea and the Greenwich Village area). A generation lost to crack and heroin. That generation's children, traumatized in early life, now filling the schools. Teenage pregnancy: Overcrowding. Apartments with no heat. Poor health. High unemployment. Visiting politicians on 116th Street, I came across the idea that the Barrio could become a mecca for tourists—a kind of Latin Quarter that would draw people from south of Ninety-Sixth Street with restaurants and night clubs—and the idea of turning the old Washburn Wire factory, closed in 1982, into a shopping mall, and a rumor that the "smart money" was buying above Ninety-Sixth Street now and soon there would be hard bargains to be driven with developers, who would be refused access to the neighborhood unless they hired residents. The Barrio is an Empowerment Zone, which means that there is federal money to support businesses there, and it is not to deny that good may come of this (though businesses don't generally thrive where people have little money), or that hope itself can be productive, to say that beyond these good things there is an abyss of need that seems to engulf them. The spirit of the age is that all problems can be solved by free enterprise, and this creates an atmosphere of boosterism in which it becomes a kind of betrayal to acknowledge that abyss.

To the west of Park Avenue and a few blocks up there is an area where weeds grow on unused land and a single ailanthus tree leans into two brownstones that cling to each other alone in a desert, their empty window frames on the top floor open to the sky. Following Madison downtown from there, I came upon blocks that are razed completely on either side—the naked grid as it was laid down in 1811. That morning, the wind blew the way it blows in bleak rural places. Shards of brick—remnants of demolished houses—gave the terrain the reddish look of the desert in Utah. The effect of the brick remnants was to blur the distinction between the architecture and its surroundings, as in places like the Moroccan desert, and northern Portugal, where the houses are made out of materials taken from the earth in that very site and so blend with the ground. Garbage had been blown into drifts, especially in the westernmost block, which was surrounded by a chain-link fence. Pieces clustered up against the fence assumed an iconographic intensity, a feeling of trapped souls or fugitive ghosts. Across the reddish shards of the unfenced block I saw, faraway-seeming, tiny, and straining into the wind, a woman pushing a baby in a stroller, to what destination it was hard to imagine.

South of this wasteland I came upon a casita, a rough plywood shelter sitting on cinder blocks in the middle of a vacant lot, also enclosed by chain link. The sides of this casita were open to waist level; it looked like a rustic structure in a remote tropical place near the sea. Hanging from the struts were various objects: a fancy sombrero, a small facsimile of a hot-air balloon with a mouse in the basket, Christmas wreaths. Steps up to the open doorway were guarded by two seated rag dolls, black-faced, in neon-pink hats, and clothes of a paisley material. On the ground around the shelter, other objects—plastic pumpkins, a Superman figure, a plaster version of a terra-cotta Indian head—were placed in a way that made them interesting, like the ritualistic placement of rocks in a Japanese garden. Most arresting of all, however, were three medium-sized reproductions of landscapes in ornate gold frames, covered in clear plastic for protection, hanging on a white-painted brick wall at the back of the lot. One was of a sylvan scene of cows in a French Academic composition; one was of horses with vast mountains in the background, in a style reminiscent of the Hudson River School; and the third, smaller, was of the interior of a redwood forest. A placard affixed to the chain link identified this little world as "Peaceful Valley."

Some casitas are simply shacks, and most of of them are like little clubs—they are places to socialize. I also saw several that looked as if they might be primary dwellings. Almost all are decorated in some way; but some, like Peaceful Valley, can be seen as artistic installations of a kind, in which banal, artificial objects become fascinating because of their context, though to say even this much belies the unself-conscious, spontaneous nature of the casitas. There is no irony in the use of these objects, as there is in the sophisticated art exhibited at the Museo del Barrio, in which one also sees, occasionally, trinkets, religious images, or banal commercial objects—a scavenger aesthetic that is both amusing and arresting.

The Museo, now at Fifth Avenue and 104th Street, sprang up in the heart of the Barrio—it was situated there for a long time and collected and exhibited only Puerto Rican artists. Consequently, it has roots in the community; it sponsors, for example, a Three Kings' Day parade, a popular yearly event in the neighborhood. Yet it also belongs on the Museum Mile that includes the Metropolitan and Guggenheim Museums and the Museum of the City of New York, which is right next to the Museo, at 103rd Street. Having expanded its mandate to include the work of artists from all over Latin America, the Museo fills a gap in the international spectrum of curatorship in the city. In this, as an institution, the Museo truly belongs to both worlds.

Civitas, a citizens' organization based on the Upper East Side, also spans the divide, but from the perspective of planning and zoning—taking on the physical nature of the split. It consistently examines the transition between the neighborhoods, conducting a study of Madison Avenue straight on up to 125th Street, for example, or considering the Ninety-Sixth Street corridor with the needs of both neighborhoods in mind.

Then, there is Central Park, which extends from Fifty-Ninth Street to 110th Street, well into Harlem—literally common ground. Engineered and designed by Frederick Law Olmsted and Calvert Vaux in the mid-nineteenth century, it is both an artifact and a work of art, the creation of a pastoral landscape in the English Romantic tradition—truly a painting into which one can step. For a long time, the Park above Ninety-Sixth Street, and especially in the Hundreds, was deserted, overgrown, and dangerous: the Harlem Meer, a lake at the northern edge, was silted up with garbage—the same shopping cart protruded from the muck for years. Today, because of the work of the Central Park Conservancy, a private charity, the northern part of the Park is of a piece with the rest. The Harlem Meer now looks like a picture out of a storybook, with a bright-painted cottagelike structure on its edge and a flock of ducks that banks perfectly over blue waters in which, on still days, a prison that towers over Central Park North is reflected. Signs prohibit fires: it was once so wild here that people roasted whole pigs—a favorite Puerto Rican dish—over bonfires with impunity.

The government, of course, is the only enterprise that is truly equal to the scale of the divide. But in the last decade the sense that government can and should strive to bring about social and economic justice has lapsed to the point where that aspect of our political imagination has fallen into neglect—into a dreary wilderness akin to that of the Harlem Meer before its restoration. Standing on the island at Park and Ninety-Sixth Street, one cannot contemplate the Harlem vista for long without taking in an atmospheric sadness, the residue of defeated visions—of the failure of good intentions, epitomized eloquently by the stands of public housing.

There is another kind of common ground that I discovered in my travels across the line, however, one that is more important than art, or architecture, or even political institutions, and is the ground on which political life dedicated to equality must be based. This is the commonality of experience. Elsie Aidinoff, née Vanderbilt, who has taught and volunteered in Harlem for three decades but lives on the Upper East Side and finds herself from time to time in the venues of the extremely wealthy, makes the observation that over the years she has come to see the similarities between the worlds rather than the differences—that she has seen extraordinary, inexplicable courage in the face of the hardships that life can bring on both sides of the line, and, equally, spinelessness. She has noticed, too, the deleterious effect that not needing to work has on both the very rich and the welfare-dependent poor, and also the way that she as a mother sometimes feels more closely connected with a mother in Harlem than with a person on the Upper East Side who is not a parent.

Stephen Kurtz, a psychotherapist who practiced for many years both in prosperous venues and in Harlem, told me that, in terms of the interior landscape of people's lives, the divide does not show up. Suffering, he said, is the same on both sides of it, as is his job, which is to be with people in their suffering. He didn't mean that as many people suffer the emotional anguish of dying prematurely from AIDS on the Upper East Side as in East Harlem. What he meant was that the agony of dying young in East Harlem is no different from that of dying young on the Upper East Side, or—more to the point, more subtly—that people respond in a wide variety of ways to the same conditions but that the variety of response seems to have nothing to do with class or economic circumstances.

Kurtz allowed that one difference did show up from his point of view: while middle-class kids have any number of second chances, inner-city kids often have none. One bad mistake and they are lost, as Elsie Aidinoff observed of adults as well: families in poverty live on a brink where one misfortune—the breakup of a marriage, an illness, the loss of a job—sends the family headlong into disaster. "The older couple of kids may have made it, but the others are lost," she says. ("Lost" is a common term among people who work with kids in this territory.) Kurtz's observation fillets the issue in an exact way: it is precisely *because* it is the same for a rich mother to watch her child fail as it is for a poor one that it is intolerable for an Upper East Side child to be given any number of second chances while the Harlem child makes one mistake and ends up in jail—and thence, almost inevitably, on a destructive life course, or dead.

Approaching Ninety-Sixth Street and Park Avenue through Carnegie Hill, I became conscious of a secluded feeling there, a quietness that comes from being at a distance from midtown with little through traffic to and from East Harlem: in a way, the nearby border of East Harlem might be the shore of a sea. There is a sense of older, less aggressive wealth here, and of discretion. Perhaps because it is a neighborhood where there is some social continuity between the generations, in certain midday moments, in a shift in the light, or in the silence created by a pause in traffic, the apartment buildings can seem to sag a little with the emotional weight of all the family life that has taken place within them—more, really, than a building can reasonably be expected to absorb. In that passing moment of candor, of tiredness, the buildings seem childishly dated, their authority thin, the defense they offer against the elemental facts of life that befall us all pitifully penetrable.

Then, beginning around two-thirty in the afternoon, massing herds of children begin to appear outside the numerous private schools in Carnegie Hill. With their teachers standing around the doors, and their mothers and nannies on the outer edges, they seem to be enclosed in a ring of safety and belonging. The mothers and children, or nannies and children, or children alone drift out into the neighborhood, and then one sees that the ring of safety includes all of Carnegie Hill: they buy snacks and eat them as they walk along or, in clement weather, as they sit in chairs set outside stores. Two little boys press their noses against the window of

William Greenberg's, a bakery of the highest order, looking at schnecken—Greenberg's famous cinnamon rolls and an after-school favorite.

In December, Christmas trees decorated with white lights are placed on the malls all the way up Park Avenue from Forty-Ninth Street to Ninety-Sixth Street. This is a New York tradition that is less famous, perhaps, than the tree at Rockefeller Center, yet more resonant in feeling. Certainly it belongs to all New Yorkers, not just residents of the Upper East Side. I learned only recently that the practice was initiated in 1945 by Mrs. Stephen Clark, a resident of Park Avenue, who was married to the heir to the Singer sewing-machine fortune. In that year, Mrs. Clark lost a son in the war; the trees were a memorial to all the men from the City of New York who had died overseas.

The trail of starry firs comes to an end at Ninety-Sixth Street, but no one would think for a moment that because of this they honor a casualty from East Harlem any the less, or that his mother's grief is in any way less than Mrs. Clark's was. Nor could anyone imagine the memorial being conceived in any other than an inclusive way. And yet when it comes to the less heroic kinds of suffering, imposed in larger doses by poverty but common to all, that sense of commonality often fails.

Of course, it is not just suffering that runs across the line like the grid: it is joy and humor; it is all of organic human life with its infinite richness, a richness that so far outdistances the richness that money confers that it, too, confounds the boundary. Although in one sense the Upper East Side is a beautiful neighborhood in contrast to the often raw ugliness of parts of East Harlem, it is even true that beauty, in the sense of the Joycean poetry of the world, travels across the line as obliviously as the grid does. A child emerging in wonder from a shop where plaster statuary is being made, the tiny lights that line the window of a video store blinking wildly in late-afternoon light, a woman in a kerchief sitting on a small, low bench outside a funeral home, almost lost in the pails of flowers around her: Life is life wherever it is, inherently equal in a way that mere social and economic differences could never alter.

The late afternoon is a time that is particularly susceptible to life's magic spells: farther along that day, I saw a brick wall at the back of a casita on which a blue sky with clouds had been painted. On this mural, tall, narrow birdhouses in variegated colors had been placed at slight angles, creating a vertiginous effect. The painted sky was honeyed with real sun, and real birds flew to and from the birdhouses. In a big scruffy lot next door, vacant so long that trees had grown to maturity; a bonfire was reaching the point where a base of red-hot coals had built up, and a small group of men stood around the entrance of the casita smoking, waiting till the moment was right to start roasting a pig.

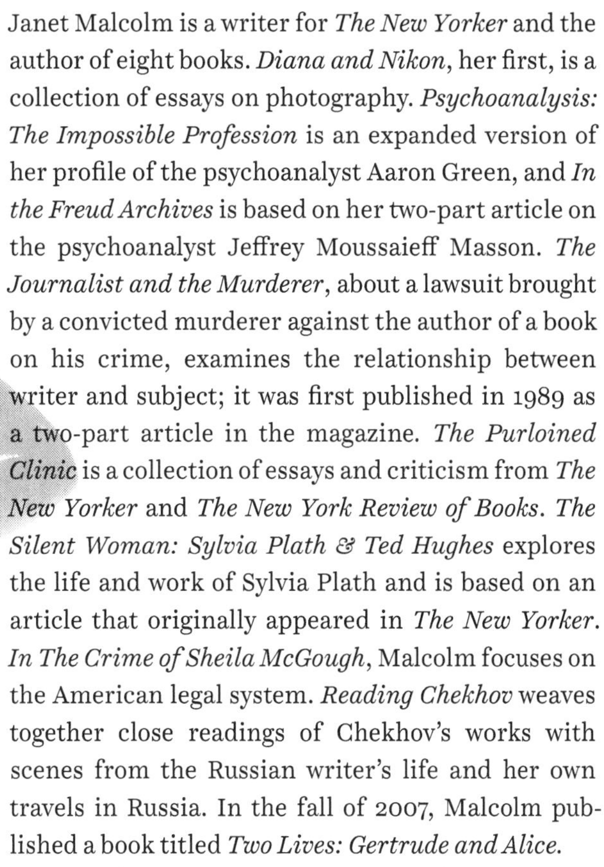

Janet Malcolm

Janet Malcolm is a writer for *The New Yorker* and the author of eight books. *Diana and Nikon*, her first, is a collection of essays on photography. *Psychoanalysis: The Impossible Profession* is an expanded version of her profile of the psychoanalyst Aaron Green, and *In the Freud Archives* is based on her two-part article on the psychoanalyst Jeffrey Moussaieff Masson. *The Journalist and the Murderer*, about a lawsuit brought by a convicted murderer against the author of a book on his crime, examines the relationship between writer and subject; it was first published in 1989 as a two-part article in the magazine. *The Purloined Clinic* is a collection of essays and criticism from *The New Yorker* and *The New York Review of Books*. *The Silent Woman: Sylvia Plath & Ted Hughes* explores the life and work of Sylvia Plath and is based on an article that originally appeared in *The New Yorker*. *In The Crime of Sheila McGough*, Malcolm focuses on the American legal system. *Reading Chekhov* weaves together close readings of Chekhov's works with scenes from the Russian writer's life and her own travels in Russia. In the fall of 2007, Malcolm published a book titled *Two Lives: Gertrude and Alice.*

Malcolm was born in Prague and emigrated to the United States with her family in 1939. She currently lives in New York City.

Yuja Wang and the Art of Performance

The young pianist is known not only for the brilliance of her music, but also for her dramatic, often surprisingly sexy outfits.

What is one to think of the clothes the twenty-nine-year-old pianist Yuja Wang wears when she performs—extremely short and tight dresses that ride up as she plays, so that she has to tug at them when she has a free hand, or clinging backless gowns that give an impression of near-nakedness (accompanied in all cases by four-inch-high stiletto heels)? In 2011, Mark Swed, the music critic of the L.A. *Times*, referring to the short and tight orange dress Yuja wore when she played Rachmaninoff's Third Piano Concerto at the Hollywood Bowl, wrote that "had there been any less of it, the Bowl might have been forced to restrict admission to any music lover under 18 not accompanied by an adult." Two years later, the *New Criterion* critic Jay Nordlinger characterized the "shorter-than-short red dress, barely covering her rear," that Yuja wore for a Carnegie Hall recital as "stripper-wear." Never has the relationship between what we see at a concert and what we hear come under such perplexing scrutiny. Is the seeing part a distraction (Glenn Gould thought it was) or is it—can it be—a heightening of the musical experience?

During the intermission of a recital at Carnegie Hall in May, Yuja changed from the relatively conventional long gold sequinned gown she had worn for the first half, two Brahms Ballades and Schumann's "Kreisleriana," into something more characteristically outré. For the second half, Beethoven's extremely long and difficult Sonata No. 29 in B-Flat, known as the "Hammerklavier," she wore a dress that was neither short nor long but both: a dark-blue-green number, also sequinned, with a long train on one side—the side not facing the audience—and nothing on the other, so that her right thigh and leg were completely exposed.

As she performed, the thigh, splayed by the weight of the torso and the action of the toe working the pedal, looked startlingly large, almost fat, though Yuja is a very slender woman. Her back was bare, thin straps crossing it. She looked like a dominatrix or a lion tamer's assistant. She had come to tame the beast of a piece, this half-naked woman in sadistic high heels. Take that, and that, Beethoven!

A few months before the performance, I asked Yuja why, out of all Beethoven's sonatas, she had selected the "Hammerklavier," and she said that she had done it out of defiance. She wanted to prove that she could play the most difficult of Beethoven's sonatas. I said that I was probably not alone in finding the sonata hard, almost unpleasant, to listen to, and several days later she sent me a link to a video of a lecture about the "Hammerklavier" by the Hungarian-born pianist András Schiff. Schiff speaks in the slow, self-savoring way in which many Eastern European men speak, to let you know how interesting and amusing everything they say is—except in his case it is.

Schiff characterized the work as "the greatest" and "most monumental" of Beethoven's sonatas, "a work that everybody respects and reveres but very few people love." Schiff's object was to communicate his own "deep love for this piece," and he began by talking about Beethoven's metronome markings, which are "incredibly fast" and are ignored by most pianists, who play the piece slowly and ponderously. The piece "is not pretty," but it is not "heavy-handed. . . not made of lead." Schiff mocked the pianists who protract the long third movement to show that "we are very deep and profound. . . . You can have lunch and dinner and breakfast, and we are still sitting here." Schiff went on to say, "If you play this piece at Beethoven's tempi, then it's not ponderous anymore. . . . It is not a piece in marble. . . . It is incredibly human and alive."

At Carnegie, Yuja did not play the piece quite at Beethoven's tempi—these days, few pianists do apart from Schiff—but I found myself responding to it as I had not responded to recordings by the great Maurizio Pollini and Mitsuko Uchida. I had not been able to get past the music's unprettiness. But now I was electrified. The forty- or fifty-minute-long piece (depending on how ponderously or not ponderously you play it) seemed almost too short.

A communication from another audience member, the pianist Shai Wosner, helpfully explained the inexplicable: why a piece that is about struggle and difficulty should have given the pleasure it gave in Yuja's interpretation. "There is hardly any passage in it that is truly comfortable to the hand," he wrote, along with "a certain harmonic tension that runs pretty much throughout the piece between B-flat major and B minor, Beethoven's 'dark, forbidden' key." He went on:

> With all the Beethovenian struggle, this piece is also a very "cleanly" conceived sonata, more faithful to the Classical sonata model than any of Beethoven's other late Sonatas. So what I loved about Yuja's performance was how this other aspect of the piece came across . . . her effortless approach brought out the brilliant, clear structure of Hammerklavier and highlighted it from another angle. Like a great monument that's not made of stone but of light-reflecting glass.

Anthony Tommasini, reviewing the performance in the *Times*, wrote, "Ms. Wang's virtuosity goes well beyond uncanny facility. . . . She wondrously brought out intricate details, inner voices and harmonic colorings. The first movement had élan and daring. The scherzo skipped along with mischievousness and rhythmic bite." Neither Tommasini nor Wosner mentioned Yuja's dress, but I wondered about its impact on their experience. I know that what I saw was intertwined with what I heard. Looking at her in that remarkable getup was part of the musical experience. But what part?

Yuja had played the "Hammerklavier" a week or so earlier in Santa Barbara, and Mark Swed had again not failed to notice what she wore. This time, perhaps not altogether seriously, he attributed her choice of costume to altruism. Six days earlier, Murray Perahia, who is sixty-nine, had played the "Hammerklavier" nearby, in Los Angeles. "Hers is a 40-year age advantage," Swed wrote, so "as if to level the field technically, she came out onto the stage . . . tightly squeezed into a red-orange gown and wearing platform heels so high that she could barely walk." Swed praised both performances. "Perahia's understanding, feeling and urgency produce a 'Hammerklavier' for the ages," while Wang, "with a flick of her dazzling fingers on the keys, sends an electric current through the 'Hammerklavier' that makes it modern music, Beethoven for the 21st century." And, while Perahia "emerged from his ordeal exhausted, hardly able to walk offstage" (in spite of his flat-heeled shoes), Wang "in the manner of the greatest virtuosos of yore . . . made this great effort seem almost effortless and was ready for three amazing encores."

In New York, as it happened, Perahia had once again played the "Hammerklavier" a few days before Yuja did and again had had the starch taken out of him. Tommasini returned to Perahia's performance in his review of Yuja's (he had enthusiastically reviewed the Perahia on May 9th) and held up the older pianist's exhaustion as a sort of necessary tribute to the piece's profundity and monumentality. "This was not a probing or profound Hammerklavier," he said of Yuja's interpretation, as if suddenly remembering himself and wishing that his praise of her had been more grudging. I could hear András Schiff laughing to himself. *We are very deep and profound. . . . You can have lunch and dinner and breakfast, and we are still sitting here.*

Tommasini ended his review by complaining about the five encores that Yuja played, each one making the "Hammerklavier" recede "further from memory." I have to say that I agreed with him. I had heard these encores before. Yuja habitually wheels them out at performances. They include Vladimir Horowitz's amusing high-speed "Carmen" Fantasy and an equally funny arrangement by various hands of the Alla Turca movement of Mozart's Sonata No. 11 in A Major. The audience, as Tommasini felt obliged to report, went mad with delight. When I first heard Yuja play these encores, I went mad with delight, too. But this time I wished she had left us with an unmediated memory of her "Hammerklavier." The roars that went up after the encores were greater than those after the "Hammerklavier." This seemed wrong. But in the split between the concert proper and the encores we may read the split in Yuja herself—her persona as a confident musical genius and as an uncertain young woman making her way through the maze of a treacherous marketplace.

She was born in Beijing to a mother who was a dancer and a father who was a percussionist. She is vague about her emergence as a prodigy. She likes to tell interviewers that her mother wanted her to be a dancer, but that she was lazy and chose the piano because she could sit down. She was performing publicly by the age of six, and entering competitions from which she always emerged with the first prize. When she was nine, her parents enrolled her in the Beijing conservatory, and when she was fourteen they sent her to a conservatory in Calgary, Canada, where she learned English. From there she went to the Curtis Institute, in Philadelphia, whose head, the pianist Gary Graffman, immediately recognized her quality, and took her on as his student, something he did only with the most outstanding talents, such as Lang Lang. Yuja hasn't lived in China since.

About a year ago, I began meeting with Yuja in the Sky Lounge, on the top floor of the building she lives in on Riverside Boulevard, in the West Sixties—a common space with a view of the Hudson River and the New Jersey shoreline, whose privileged-looking armchairs and little tables evoke first- and business-class waiting rooms at airports. When I say "the building she lives in," I am speaking loosely. Yuja tours the world, playing in premier halls, either in solo recitals or with leading orchestras, in London, Paris, St. Petersburg, Edinburgh, Bucharest, Caracas, Tokyo, Kyoto, Beijing, Tel Aviv, Jerusalem, Sydney, Amsterdam, Florence, Barcelona, and San Francisco, among other cities, and spends only a few weeks, between more than a hundred scheduled performances, in the apartment, a studio she bought in 2014.

When you walk into the apartment—which is small and dark—the first thing you see is a royal-blue nylon curtain suspended from the ceiling like a shower curtain and drawn around a lumpish object that turns out to be a Steinway grand piano. The curtain is there to muffle the piano's sound, to accommodate a neighbor for whom the practicing of a world-class pianist is not the thrill it would be for you and me. The rest of the apartment has the atmosphere of a college dormitory room, with its obligatory unpacked suitcase on the floor and haphazard strewings of books and papers and objects. There may be a few stuffed animals on the bed or maybe only a sense of them—I am not sure because I was at the apartment only once. Yuja prefers to see interviewers in the Sky Lounge. When I proposed visiting the apartment again—this time with a notebook—she politely demurred. It was too much of a mess, or the cleaning woman hadn't come.

Yuja speaks in fluent—more than fluent—English, punctuated by laughter that gives one to understand that what she is saying is not to be taken too seriously, and that she is not a pompous or pretentious person. Occasionally, there is the slightest trace of an accent (vaguely French) and a lapse into the present tense.

We talked about her life as a child prodigy. "Oh, yes, I'm a real prodigy," she said. "They still call me wunderkind. I remember when I went to the conservatory for the first time. All the other kids were looking at me like—by then I was already a child star—like I am another species in a zoo. Oh, my God, she's here."

"You seem so unspoiled," I said. "Were you more spoiled then? Or were you unspoiled even then?"

"I think unspoiled came later," Yuja said.

She recalled something I didn't and still don't completely understand about the effect that playing Mozart had on her as a child. She said that performing his Twelve Variations in C Major ("Twinkle, Twinkle, Little Star") permitted her to feel for the first time what it was like to have stagefright. She was eight or nine.

"I was always quiet before a concert, while the other kids were so nervous. They talk, some are very noisy. I don't understand. Why are you nervous? *Until* the first time I played Mozart. I was not nervous until I was onstage. Then I felt I was in a completely different time and space. My fingers just played. And I thought there is a difference between practicing at home and playing onstage."

I asked if she could explain further what had happened to her when she performed the Variations.

"Maybe intuitively I was struck by the beauty, by the symmetry, by how like something inherent in nature it is. Before, I was, Oh, Mozart is so boring."

When I told her of my feeling of awe at the superhuman feat that is a concert performance, she said, "For me that's normal—like talking." She has the erroneous idea that writing a book is a similarly remarkable achievement. She became a serious reader in her teens. Among the books she recently read are Virginia Woolf's *The Waves* and Immanuel Kant's *Critique of Pure Reason*. When I commented on the high-mindedness of her reading, she quickly said, "No, I'm always reading something trashy, too."

I asked about her home life in China. "Did your parents immediately realize that you were different from other children?"

"I don't know. They're very naïve people. Extremely conventional and traditional. Very Communist. If you read Dostoyevsky or Tolstoy, you will understand what kind of people they are. Just simple, extremely kind. My dad was really talented, and my mom also. They are extremely artistic—or autistic," she said, with a peal of laughter. "Their environment never allowed them to develop to their full potential."

"Is this what you mean by 'very Communist'?"

"Yeah. Because you have to go to Party meetings and talk about how to do well for society. Twenty-year plan. Five-year plan. You work for the common welfare rather than for the individual. Working for the individual is almost synonymous with being selfish. Which is not how I feel. I feel lucky that I came out when I was fourteen." Yuja's mother came for her graduation from Curtis and for her Carnegie Hall début; otherwise, Yuja sees her parents only when she performs in Beijing. She speaks of them in an affectionate but veiled way, always stressing their kindness.

When I asked Yuja to elaborate on her sense of the political differences between China and America, she paused before answering. After a while, listening to her, I realized that she was talking about an entirely different subject. I decided to persist. "I asked you about politics, and you have been talking about music," I said.

"You noticed?" she said, laughing.

My visit to Yuja's apartment had taken place after this conversation. It was around four on a hot August afternoon, and Yuja was dressed in denim shorts, very short ones, and a tank top. We had tickets to a five-o'clock concert of advanced contemporary music at Alice Tully Hall, and Yuja was debating whether to change for it. She rummaged through the suitcase on the floor and extracted two garments—strapless black-and-white minidresses made of a stretch fabric, called bandage dresses by their French designer, Hervé Léger, because that's how they fit, and characterized by Yuja as "modern and edgy" as well as practical, because they don't have to be ironed and lie nice and flat in a suitcase—and asked my opinion. Should she wear one of them or stay in the shorts? I asked what the issue was—was she interested in comfort or in how she looked? She stared at me as if I were crazy. What weird world was I living in where comfort could even be thought of? She wiggled into one of the bandage dresses, added her high heels, and we walked the three blocks to Lincoln Center at a brisk clip.

In February of this year, on four successive nights at Geffen Hall, Yuja played Mozart's Piano Concerto No. 9 in E-Flat Major, the "Jeunehomme"—written when Mozart was barely twenty-one and considered his first masterpiece—with the New York Philharmonic, under the Swiss conductor Charles Dutoit. This was a departure for Yuja. Her career has been built on her playing of the Russian Romantics, the "red-blooded" and "hot-blooded" composers, as she calls them, Tchaikovsky, Rachmaninoff, Prokofiev, for whose "passionate, emotional" pieces her short flame-red dresses seem to have been made. For a while, there was a picture of Yuja in front of Carnegie Hall in the flame-red dress she had worn at a recital in May, 2013, her arms raised high in the air in a gesture of culminating abandon. It stopped passersby. Now she was entering a new phase of engagement with Mozart and the nineteenth-century German classical composers. The picture of her in front of Geffen Hall was unremarkable.

A day before the first concert of the series at Geffen, I attended an open rehearsal at the hall. The Mozart concerto was on the first half of the program, to be followed by Respighi's orchestral pieces "Roman Festivals," "Fountains of Rome," and "Pines of Rome." The Respighi pieces were being rehearsed first, and when I arrived at the hall, around noon, much Respighi remained to be played. Yuja was waiting in the small room upstairs where soloists change clothes and receive visitors. She showed me a closet where the three dresses, designed by Roberto Cavalli, she would wear at the concerts were hanging. I took an immediate dislike to one of the garments—a short pink dress with black swirling lines on its gathered skirt and bodice. It was neither ultra-short and tight nor long and clinging. It was a kind of girlish summer dress. I did not like the idea of Yuja wearing it onstage. The two other dresses were a glamorous dark-blue long gown and a short, also concert-worthy dress.

Yuja curled up on a sofa—she was wearing tight-fitting black leather trousers—and laughingly recalled a newspaper headline she had seen during a tour: " 'Twenty-Eight-Year-Old Wunderkind.' Isn't that an oxymoron?" she said. I had arrived early at Lincoln Center, and stopped into a café for a sandwich, though not so early that there was time to eat the whole large overstuffed thing. When I offered Yuja the half sandwich the waiter had wrapped, she accepted. Predictably, she opened the sandwich and ate the chicken, then the tomato, then the lettuce, and then—unpredictably—the bread.

Dutoit, a tall man of seventy-nine, appeared with his fourth wife, Chantal Juillet. After husband and wife hugged Yuja, Dutoit stood back to look with elaborate mock lecherousness at her tight trousers. Dutoit and Yuja go back a long way. The infamous habit of Dutoit's second wife, Martha Argerich, of cancelling concerts at the last minute had given Yuja one of her early breaks. Argerich was one of the stars Yuja replaced while she was still a student at Curtis; Radu Lupu, Yefim Bronfman, Evgeny Kissin, and Murray Perahia were others. ("With Martha it was like, 'I'm tired . . . do you want to play with the Boston Symphony for me?' And I'm like 'Of course!—Wrong question!' " Yuja told an interviewer for the Australian magazine *Limelight.*) Yuja's ability both to learn fast and to turn the disgruntlement of audiences into amazed delight did not go unnoticed. "By the end of the final movement"—of Tchaikovsky's Piano Concerto No. 1—"the audience stood and roared," the *Philadelphia Inquirer* critic David Patrick Stearns wrote in a review of the concert at which Yuja replaced Argerich.

After some cheerful banter, Dutoit left to rehearse the final Respighi, and Yuja excused herself to warm up in a large adjacent room that had a piano. She preferred that I not go into the large room with her but didn't object to my staying in the small room, where I could hear her play phrases over and over and feel that I was uselessly eavesdropping on coded artistic secrets.

At the concert proper, the following night, Yuja wore the glamorous dark-blue gown, and played with delicacy and beauty. She and Dutoit and the orchestra were in elating rapport. The first cadenza produced one of those you-could-hear-a-pin-drop hushes in the sold-out hall. She had gone very quiet, and the audience followed as if mesmerized. No one coughed.

"Who can play Mozart the way she did?" Graffman said afterward. "It was so natural, in such good taste. Not that she was doing anything. That's just the way it came out. Who can do that and also play the Horowitz 'Carmen' Fantasy?" In the *New Criterion*, Nordlinger wrote, "Mozart ends with a rondo—and it should be fast, exuberant, and fun. It was. Wang ripped the notes out of the keyboard, as much as played them. At one point, I almost laughed out loud. That's how funny she was, and how funny Mozart is."

Yuja must have liked reading this. She had once talked about how funny Mozart is: "Mozart is like a party animal. I find I play him better when I am hung over or drunk." At the same time, she saw Mozart's music as "noble, tragic, like a great Greek play. The human emotion is there but with a lot of godliness in it." On the second night, my heart sank when Yuja walked onstage in the pink dress. Was it my imagination or was her playing less inspired than it had been the night before?

Meeting Yuja in the Sky Lounge a few weeks later on a rainy day, I told her of this impression, and she did not contradict it. "Because of that dress, the little pink one, because it's so different from everything I've ever worn, I didn't really feel myself, and maybe that came through. I liked the pink dress because it was different. Sometimes, the difference might become the style of my next season. It could be what's going to come. Or it could be something to discard. You don't know until you try it." She added, "They wanted to put in social media that I was dressed by the designer Roberto Cavalli."

"Were you feeling something related to the dress while playing?"

"No, not while playing. Just when I walked onstage. This was a cute little pink dress, and I thought, It's not me. It's about a young girl. Just the opposite of the nude dress."

In 2014, when an interviewer from the London *Telegraph* asked Yuja about "her fondness for riskily short, clingy dresses," she gave a flippant reply: "I am 26 years old, so I dress for 26. I can dress in long skirts when I am forty." But in fact Yuja's penchant for the riskily short and clingy has less to do with allegiance to the dress code of her generation than with an awareness of her own "super-smallness," as she calls it. She knows that small tight clothes bring out her beauty and large loose garments don't. But she is not just a woman who knows how to dress. She is a woman who is constantly experimenting with how to dress when she is playing on a concert stage. She is keenly aware—as many soloists affect not to be—that she is being looked at as well as listened to. Reviewing the Carnegie Hall recital Yuja played in May, 2013, Zachary Woolfe wrote in the *Times*, "I confess that while perhaps 90 percent of my attention was on her precise yet exuberant playing, a crucial 10 was on her skintight flame-colored dress." Woolfe went on to brilliantly anatomize the experience of simultaneously listening to and looking at Yuja: "Her alluring, surprising clothes don't just echo the allure and surprise of her musicianship, though they certainly do that. More crucial, the tiny dresses and spiky heels draw your focus to how petite Ms. Wang is, how stark the contrast between her body and the forcefulness she achieves at her instrument. That contrast creates drama. It turns a recital into a performance." When Yuja played the "Jeunehomme" in the girlish pink dress, that contrast was absent. The sense of a body set in urgent motion by musical imperatives requires that the body not be distractingly clothed. With her usually bared thighs, chest, and back demurely covered by the black-splotched pink fabric, this sense was lost.

Yuja's customary self-presentation as a kind of stripped-down car is, of course, only one way of appearing onstage to artistic advantage. When Maurizio Pollini plays in some nondescript suit, his body-aliveness is no less present for us. Martha Argerich's widow's-weeds black gowns heighten the beauty and mystery of her playing. Plainness is never a mistake on a concert stage. For the two remaining Mozart performances, Yuja, realizing her misstep, returned to the designer she regularly uses.

The "nude dress" was a long gown (in recent years, long gowns have been admitted into Yuja's concert-clothes closet, but they have to be slinky) made of body-stocking fabric with sparkling encrustations at bosom and stomach and a long swishing skirt. Yuja wore this fabulously gorgeous costume at the third concert—which had the electricity of the first one—and felt comfortable and happy in its defiant sexiness and her feeling of nakedness.

I looked out the window of the Sky Lounge and saw the New Jersey shoreline disappearing in a gray mist. Yuja herself was in a dark mood. She had recently returned from a European tour and was exhausted and dispirited. In Munich and Paris, she had played the Mozart piano concerto with Valery Gergiev and the Vienna Philharmonic, and the reception had been only O.K. A blog about the Paris concert saying, "Yuja Wang disappoints," had stayed with her. She paraphrased its words: " 'She didn't have emotion. She's not yet mature enough to play Mozart.' " She went on, "With Rachmaninoff, Prokofiev, Tchaikovsky I can blow them away. 'So amazing, so impressive!' But I went for the surprise, for the unexpected. I ask myself, Am I playing for the applauding, for the standing up, or am I playing because I really like something in the music and I just want to play?"

She talked in the same dark vein about her personal life. She spoke of the "too many people" she meets on tour: "Who are your real friends?

I naturally give my love and friendship, but once the tour is over are they really your friends? What's always there, of course, is music. The other things come and go—except maybe your parents." She laughed. "And Gary."

Gary Graffman, who is eighty-seven and now retired as the head of Curtis, and his wife, Naomi, who is eighty-eight, are Yuja's best friends in New York and perhaps in the world. Graffman, you may recall, is the distinguished pianist whose career was disrupted in the late nineteen-seventies, when he lost the use of his right hand. When I visited the Graffmans in their apartment at the Osborne, on West Fifty-Seventh Street, they spoke of Yuja as of a beloved granddaughter of whom they are so proud they can hardly stand it. When I asked Graffman how she compared with the other prodigies at Curtis, he said, "She was remarkable among remarkable students. She didn't play like a prodigy. She played like a finished artist." Naomi recalled that when Yuja first arrived at Curtis, Gary asked her to take the new student to lunch, and she dutifully did so. "By the time lunch was over, I thought she has to be at least thirty-five or forty," Naomi said. "She was speaking so intelligently about so many things." Yuja was fifteen and a half.

As Yuja had been a musical wunderkind at six, at twenty-nine she is a kind of existential prodigy, already undergoing the crisis that ordinary people undergo in midlife. "I've been doing this for twenty-nine years. Do I want to go on doing it, or is there something else waiting for me?" She spoke of her sense of alienation from people who don't have to constantly and relentlessly study music and practice, of feeling like an outsider, sometimes even "I don't like to say but almost like a prisoner. I haven't ever enjoyed my free time. It's always like I am challenging myself. I must be a little masochistic." She would see people walking in the park on a beautiful day and long to join them. But by the time she had untied herself from the mast of her art it was midnight, and there was no one to join her in a walk in the park.

At the "millennials' parties" she had attended on the last two nights of the Mozart concerts (their purpose was to encourage young people to go to concerts), she had wearily answered questions from a stage. "I would have enjoyed these parties five years ago," she said. "I still enjoyed them. They were fun. Nice people. I had lots of drinks. But I get the same questions again and again. It's like water goes into the same spot. And then I become a little unpleasant. And then I feel guilty that I was unpleasant. They ask me things like"—she began speaking in a mocking singsong voice—"'Are you single?' 'How do you memorize your pieces?' 'How do you pedal with your heels?' 'Who do you buy your dresses from?' 'Why do you wear short dresses?' 'Why do you wear long dresses?' 'Why do you have short hair?' 'Do you like travelling?' 'Why don't you play more Prokofiev?' 'Why do you play Mozart?' "

The room had darkened, and everything on the river was disappearing. When I drew Yuja's attention to the apparition of the sublime in the window, she was looking at her phone. "I'm just checking," she said. "I'm not being impolite." Yuja treats her phone the way almost every young (and not so young) person today treats it—as a transitional object. She and I have corresponded by e-mail (largely about chocolate), and the messages from her phone are filled with emoticons and LOL-like abbreviations. In deference to my age, she does not text me.

When I commented on her melancholy, she denied—and then acknowledged—it: "It's a very depressing thought. Just touring and playing—the same things or different things. But in society people don't allow you to be sad or depressed. It's like a bad thing. It's why I'm antisocial. I feel this negative energy. 'She just complains a lot.' Excuse me, that's part of what I do. You feel all these things. As a musician, you probably feel them more intensely. But society wants me to be happy. My parents. They are the most unintrusive parents. 'I don't care what you do—just be happy.' " She made an *urrrgghh* sound and laughed.

Yuja has made changes in her professional life that she is not sure have solved the problems of doubt and restlessness by which they were impelled. Last year, she abruptly left her manager, Earl Blackburn, of the large Opus 3 Artists agency, with whom she had been since she was sixteen, and joined Mark Newbanks, whose London-based agency, Fidelio Arts, has only three other clients—but what clients!—the conductors Gustavo Dudamel, Lionel Bringuier, and Esa-Pekka Salonen. Although Yuja doesn't speak of it in such terms, the change of managers has the atmosphere of the dissolution of a marriage: a young wife leaves the dull, older husband for an exciting younger man. Naomi Graffman spoke of Blackburn's extraordinary devotion to Yuja: "He coddled her as no one had ever been coddled before. Every little thing she wanted or needed, he did it for her. He would brush her teeth for her if she wanted." The younger man is different. He does not take Yuja's clothes to the cleaners; recently, he did not offer to pick up a Russian visa for her, as Blackburn would have done. "She was furious," Gary said. "Never having had experience with anybody else, she thought that was what managers did." I happened to have heard about the Russian visa from Yuja. She had not mentioned Newbanks, just the fact of this and other annoying little errands she had to run, followed by the playful question "Shall I hire a boyfriend or an assistant?"

I proposed a boyfriend/assistant. Earlier, she had spoken of the obstacle her touring schedule put in the way of lasting romance. The boyfriend/assistant—i.e., a muse—would always be in the next seat on the plane. "No," she said, "guys won't do that. It's O.K. for a woman to do that. It's harder for guys to get rid of their egos, to be even a little bit subservient." She added, "Of course, I want guys who are successful. Which means that they have their own work, that they're busy—and that I am the one who visits them."

I asked if her romances were with artists of her calibre.

"Not of my calibre," she said without hesitation (and the obligatory peal of laughter). "I never meet people of my calibre who are available."

She talked of the older and old people with whom she feels happy and comfortable (the conductor Michael Tilson Thomas is a kind of runner-up to Gary Graffman in the lovable-mentor sweepstakes): "people who have their whole life behind them"—as opposed to the young with their oppressive burden of futurity. Another older friend, Emanuel Ax, invited her for Thanksgiving last year, and she accepted, but in the end did not go, preferring to "be home and snuggle up and watch Netflix."

She spoke of leaving Earl Blackburn not regretfully, exactly, but with a kind of cold wisdom about the possible pointlessness of the gesture that people three times her age don't often achieve. "There was nothing wrong with the old manager. He really built my career. He was really caring. But I was, like, if I don't make a change, I'll never make a change. I'm bad at confrontation. So I just did it out of the blue. But nothing much has changed. It's a little better here and there. But it's still the same circus."

When I met for coffee with Newbanks—a suave, slender, elegantly dressed man of forty-eight, a former cellist—he told me that his aim as Yuja's manager was to cut back on her engagements and "put air" in her schedule. "She had three days free when I met her—that's impossible." Another goal was to steer her toward experimentation with repertoire, and one of these experiments has already taken place—in March, Yuja played for three nights with the New York Philharmonic in Messiaen's "Turangalîla-Symphonie," conducted by Salonen. "Turangalîla" is a thrilling, mad, loud piece that features two solo instruments, the piano and the ondes martenot, an early electronic instrument that makes unearthly wavering sounds not easy to hear over the orchestral pandemonium. Yuja's playing was brilliantly audible. She played from a score, and on the night I attended did her own page turning, which lent a certain suspense to the proceedings. The pages flew at a rate of about one every thirty seconds. Would they lie flat? Page turners usually give a little firm pat to the page they have just turned to make sure it will stay in place. Later, Yuja told me that she had put adhesive on the pages to insure that they would stay in place.

Newbanks told me that it is customary for management to take twenty percent of a soloist's fee and fifteen percent of a conductor's fee. I asked him, as I had asked Yuja, what her fee was, and, like her, he wouldn't tell me. "No one in the business talks about it," he said. The business evidently exacts a vow of omertà from its members. Newbanks laughingly (perhaps a little nervously) said that Yuja had alerted him to my unseemly interest in money. When I put the futile question to her, she had answered, "I don't usually like to talk about fees," and added, with uncharacteristic humorlessness, "I feel it is degrading to art to measure it with money."

As patches of blue and orange appeared in the sky of the Sky Lounge, Yuja's internal bad weather seemed to lift as well. She recalled her time in Europe with Gergiev: "He is amazing. This is the first time I am playing Mozart with him, and I was curious how he would do it. I did Russian stuff with him before—the energy for the Russian stuff was unbelievable. And he had the same energy for Mozart, which is scary, because it's overwhelming for Mozart. But it put us into a good place. He has that. Claudio"—the conductor Claudio Abbado—"had that. Claudio is like intense listening. It makes you feel so scrutinizingly uncomfortable. And that place of uncomfortableness is exactly where you want to be every time you are onstage. Because that makes you play better, and that is when you are growing. Feeling comfortable is always like O.K., I'll do the thing again. Been there done that."

Yuja reveres Abbado, who died in 2014. When, in the interview for *Limelight*, she was asked what it was like to play under Abbado, she spoke of how "obscure and mysterious" the experience was. During rehearsals, "he didn't say a word—to me at least. And then in the concert, everything just came out. You don't really know what happens with the gestures or the energy field. . . . He made everyone play his or her best . . . without any words."

She spoke of her new repertoire: "It makes me happy playing 'Hammerklavier' rather than playing Rach 3 another twenty times. I used to only play pieces I was comfortable with and good at, Rachmaninoff, Prokofiev, Tchaikovsky. Now I propose music I won't be comfortable with. This is the only way to get out of my skin, out of myself, and to learn." She added, laughing, "But once in a while I crave those Russians. My heart is crying, *Where are they?*"

A week or so after Yuja's "Hammerklavier" concert, the photograph that accompanies this piece was taken at the new Steinway piano showroom, on Sixth Avenue at Forty-third Street. When I arrived at the showroom, around noon, Yuja, wearing one of her bandage dresses, was sitting on a table, facing a mirror, as a hair-and-makeup man from Paris applied mascara to her eyelashes. She was patient and compliant and practiced. She had done this before. There are many beautiful portraits of Yuja floating around the print and Internet worlds. After greeting me, she began lighting into Tommasini for his comment about her encores. "If instead of feeling exhausted I feel exhilarated, and want to make people happy by giving them a gift, why not do it?" she said. "It feels like home to play those familiar pieces. People play encores after much more sublime pieces. Why can't you do it after climbing Mt. Everest? Stupid conservative doctrine."

We were on a below-street-level floor, filled with pianos. The photographer, Pari Dukovic, and his three assistants were placing lights and screens around one of them. They had been there since eight-thirty in the morning (catering and hair and makeup had followed at eleven-thirty). Several of Yuja's concert dresses were strewn around an alcove serving as a dressing room, among them the blue-green dominatrix gown she had worn to play the "Hammerklavier." This was the dress finally chosen for the portrait. The hair-and-makeup man, with whom Yuja had established laughing rapport, revised something in her hairdo at her request. "My cheeks are too fat," she said as she looked in the mirror. She ate a few forkfuls from a plate of salad that her friend Carlos Avila, a pianist who teaches at Juilliard, brought her from the catering table. Then she slipped into the blue-green dress and stepped into stiletto heels, and the photo shoot began. Yuja went to the designated piano, and Dukovic—a handsome young man, with a warm and charming manner—began circling around it, snapping pictures with a handheld camera, as she played bits and pieces of repertoire. At first, she played tentatively and quietly, starting a piece and trailing off—and then she worked her way into a horrible and wonderful pastiche of Rachmaninoff, Chopin, Beethoven, Mozart, Gershwin, Horowitz, Tchaikovsky, all mushed together, playing louder and louder and faster and faster, banging with mischievous demonic force, as Dukovic continued his circling and snapping, like the photographer in the famous orgasmic scene in "Blowup." Yuja ended with a parodic crescendo as Dukovic shouted, "I love you!" and she burst into laughter.

The arresting photograph that was chosen out of the hundreds, possibly thousands, of pictures Dukovic took of Yuja at the piano and, later, in the first-floor showroom, posed full figure in front of a piano with its lid up, represents her as no concertgoer has ever seen her. The wild disorder of the hair has never been seen in a concert hall. (Yuja's hair tends to stay in place throughout the most rousing of her performances.) And the foreshortened, oversized hand is an obvious deviation from the consensus we call reality. Will Yuja cringe when she looks at the photograph? Or will she see it as expressive of her impudent, defiant nature and find in it, almost hear in it, an echo of her incomparable musicality?

Susan Orlean

Susan Orlean is the bestselling author of eight books, including *The Bullfighter Checks Her Makeup*, *My Kind of Place*, *Saturday Night*, and *Lazy Little Loafers*. In 1999, she published *The Orchid Thief*, a narrative about orchid poachers in Florida, which was made into the Academy Award-winning film, *Adaptation*. Her 2011 book, *Rin Tin Tin: The Life and the Legend*, was a *New York Times* bestseller and a *New York Times* Notable Book.

Orlean has been a staff writer for *The New Yorker* since 1992. Her subjects have included umbrella inventors, origami artists, skater Tonya Harding, and gospel choirs. Her work has also appeared in *Esquire, Rolling Stone, Outside, Smithsonian*, and *The New York Times*.

Orlean graduated with honors from the University of Michigan and was a Nieman Fellow at Harvard University in 2003. In 2012 she received an honorary Doctor of Humane Letters from the University of Michigan. In 2014, she was awarded a Guggenheim Fellowship in Creative Arts/Nonfiction. In 2016, she was selected as the Bernardine Kielty Scherman Fellow at the MacDowell Colony. She has lectured at Yale University, New York University , University of California, Berkeley, University of Michigan, Kenyon College, the Bread Loaf Writers Conference, Goucher College, and Harvard University, among others, and has been awarded residencies at the MacDowell Colony and at Yaddo.

She is currently writing a book about the Los Angeles Public Library.

La Matadora Revisa Su Maquillaje (The Bullfighter Checks Her Makeup)

Every time Cristina Sanchez kills a bull, she presents an unforgettable tableau—a self-possessed young woman elegantly and lethally playing out an ancient masculine ritual.

I went to Spain not long ago to watch Cristina Sanchez fight bulls, but she had gotten tossed by one during a performance in the village of Ejea de los Caballeros and was convalescing when I arrived. Getting tossed sounds sort of merry, but I saw a matador tossed once, and he looked like a saggy bale of hay flung by a pitchfork, and when he landed on his back he looked busted and terrified. Cristina got tossed by accidentally hooking a horn with her elbow during a paa with the cape, and the joint was wrenched so hard that her doctor said it would need at least three or four days to heal. It probably hurt like hell, and the timing was terrible. She had fights scheduled each of the nights she was supposed to rest and every night until October—every night, with no breaks in between. It had been like this for her since May, when she was elevated from the status of a novice to a full *matador de toros*. The title is conferred in a formal ceremony called "taking the *alternativa*," and it implies that you are experienced and talented and that other matadors have recognized you as a top-drawer bullfighter. You will now fight the biggest, toughest bulls and will probably be hired to fight often and in the most prestigious arenas. Bullfighting becomes your whole life, your everyday life—so routine that "sometimes after you've fought and killed the bull you feel as if you hadn't done a thing all day," as Cristina once told me.

When Cristina Sanchez took her alternativa, it caused a sensation. Other women before her have fought bulls in Spain. Many have only fought little bulls, but some did advance to big animals and become accomplished and famous, and a few of the best have been declared full matadors de toros. Juanita Cruz became a matador in 1940, and Morenita del Quindio did in 1968, and Raquel Martinez and Maribel Atienzar did in the eighties, but they all took their alternativas in Mexico, where the standards are a little less exacting. Cristina is the first woman to have taken her alternativa in Europe and made her debut as a matador in Spain.

There was a fight program of three matadors—a corrida—scheduled for the Madrid bullring the day after I got to Spain, and I decided to go so I could see some other toreadors while Cristina was laid up with her bad arm. One of the three scheduled to perform was the bastard son of El Cordobes. El Cordobes had been a matador superstar in the sixties and a breeder of several illegitimate children and a prideful man who was so possessive of his nickname that he had once sued this kid—the one I was going to see—because the kid wanted to fight bulls under the name El Cordobes, too. In the end, the judge let each and every El Cordobes continue to be known professionally as El Cordobes.

The kid El Cordobes is a scrubbed, cute blonde with a crinkly smile. Outside the rings where he is fighting, vendors sell fan photos of him alongside postcards and little bags of sunflower seeds and stuffed-bull souvenirs. In the photos, El Cordobes is dressed in a plaid camp shirt and acid-washed blue jeans and is hugging a good-looking white horse. In the ring, he does some flashy moves on his knees in front of the bull, including a frog-hop that he times to make it look like he's going to get skewered. These tricks, plus the renown of his name, have gotten him a lot of attention, but El Cordobes is just one of many cute young male matadors working these days. If his knees give out, he might have nothing.

On the other hand, there is just one Cristina, and everyone in Spain knows her and is following her rise. She has gotten attention far outside of Spain and on television and in newspapers and even in fashion magazines; other matadors, even very good ones, fuse in the collective mind as man-against-bull, but every time Cristina kills a bull she forms part of a singular and unforgettable tableau—that of an attractive, self-possessed young woman elegantly slaying a large animal in a somber and ancient masculine ritual—and regardless of gender she is a really good matador, and she is being painstakingly managed and promoted, so there is no saying where her celebrity will stop. This is only her first season as a full matador, but it has been a big event. Lately El Cordobes or his publicist or his accountant has been igniting and fanning the rumor that he and Cristina Sanchez are madly in love, with the hope that her fame will rub off on him. She will probably be more and more acclaimed in the four or so years she plans to fight, and she will probably be credited with many more putative love affairs before her career is through.

Before the fight in Madrid, I walked around to the back of the bullring and through the *patio de caballos*, the dirt-floored courtyard and stable where the picadors' horses and the donkeys that drag away the dead bull after the fight relax in their stalls and get their hair combed and get fed and get saddled. I was on my way to the bullfighting museum—the Museo Taurino—which is in a gallery next to the stalls. It was a brilliant day with just a whiff of wind. In the courtyard, muscle men were towing equipment back and forth and unloading a horse trailer. Another twenty or so men were idling in the courtyard in the few pockets of shade or near the locked door of the matadors' chapel, which is opened before the fight so the matadors can stop in and pray. The idlers were older men with bellies that began at their chins and trousers hiked up to their nipples, and they were hanging around just so they could take a look at the bulls for tonight's fight and see how they were going to be divvied up among the three matadors. Really, there isn't a crumb of any piece of bullfighting that goes unexamined by aficionados like these men. I lingered for a minute and then went into the museum. I wandered past the oil portraits of Manolete and Joselito and of dozens of other revered bullfighters, and past six stuffed and mounted heads of bulls whose names were Paisano, Landejo, Mediaonza, Jocinero, Hermano, and Perdigon—they were chosen for the museum because they had been particularly mean or unusual-looking or because they had killed someone famous. Then I stopped at a glass display case that had in it a picture of the matador Juanita Cruz. The picture was an eight-by-ten and looked like it had been shot in a studio. Juanita Cruz's pearly face and her wedge of a chin and her pitch-black hair with its tiny standing waves were blurred along the edges, movie-star style. She looked solemn, and her eyes were focused on middle space. In the case next to the picture were her pink matador knee socks and her mouse-eared matador hat and one of her bullfighter suits. These are called *traje de luces*, "suit of lights," and all toreadors wear them and like to change them often; Cristina has half a dozen, and Juanita Cruz probably owned twenty or so in the course of her bullfighting career. This one was blush-pink with beautiful gold piping and sparkly black sequins. It had the classic short, stiff, big-shouldered, box-shaped toreador jacket but not the capri trousers that all matadors wear, because Juanita Cruz fought in a skirt. There is no such thing as a matador skirt anymore—Cristina, of course, wears trousers. I looked at the skirt for a while and decided that even though it looked unwieldy it might actually have been an advantage—in a skirt, you can bend and stretch and lunge with a sword unconstrained. On the other hand, a skirt would have exposed so much fabric to the bull that in a fight it would have gotten awfully splashed and smeared with blood. Every matador has an assistant who is assigned to clean his suit with soap and a toothbrush after every fight. Juanita Cruz was popular and well accepted even though she was an anomaly, but late at night, as her assistant was scrubbing her big bloody skirt, I bet he cursed the fact that she had been wearing so much fabric while sticking swords into bulls.

I went to visit Cristina at home the morning before she was going to be fighting in a corrida in a town called Mostoles. It was now a week since her injury, and her elbow apparently had healed. Two days earlier, she had tested it in a fight in Cordobes and another the following day in Jaen, and a friend of mine who reads Madrid's bullfight newspaper told me Cristina had gotten very good reviews. It turns out that I was lucky to catch her at home, because she is hardly there during the bullfighting season—usually she keeps a rock star schedule, leaving whatever town she's in with her crew right after she fights, driving all night to the next place on her schedule, checking into a hotel, sleeping until noon, eating lunch, watching some television, suiting up, fighting, and then leaving again. She was going to be at home this particular morning because Mostoles is only a few miles from Parla, the town where she and her parents and sisters live. She had come home the night before, after the fight in Jaen, and was planning to spend the day in Parla doing errands. The corrida in Mostoles would start at six. The assistant who helps her dress—he is called the sword boy, because he also takes care of all her cutlery—was going to come to the apartment at five so she could get prepared and then just drive over to the bullring already dressed and ready to go in her suit of lights. Parla is an unglamorous place about forty minutes south of Madrid; it is a kernel of an old village that had been alone on the wide open plains but is now hemmed in by incredibly ugly high-rise apartment buildings put up in the midsixties for workers overflowing the available housing in Madrid. The Sanchez apartment is in a slightly less ugly and somewhat shorter brick building on a busy street, on a block with a driving school, a bra shop, and a bank. There is no name on the doorbell, but Cristina's father's initials are barely scratched into a metal plate beside it. These days it is next to impossible to find Cristina. The nearly unmarked doorbell is the least of it. Cristina has a magician press agent who can make himself disappear and a very powerful and self-confident manager—a former French bullfighter named Simon Casas—who is credited with having gotten her into the biggest bullrings and the best corridas in the country but is also impossible to find and even if he were findable he would tell you that his answer to your request to speak to Cristina is no. He is especially watchful of her international exposure. Simon Casas didn't know I was coming to see Cristina in Parla and he might have disapproved simply to be disapproving, and after I saw him later that afternoon in Mostoles, prowling the perimeter of the bullring like an irritable wild animal, I was that much gladder I'd stayed out of his way.

Anyway, Cristina wasn't even home when I got there. I had driven to Parla with my translator, Muriel, and her bullfighter husband, Pedro, who both know Cristina and Cristina's father, Antonio, who himself used to be a bullfighter—if it sounds like just about everyone I encountered in Spain was or is a bullfighter, it's true. We needed to see Cristina for my interview and then get right back, because Pedro had a bullfight that night in a town on the other side of Madrid. No one answered the doorbell at the apartment. Cristina's car wasn't around, so it looked like she really was gone. A car is the first thing matadors seem to buy themselves when they start making big money—that is, when they start getting sometimes as much as tens of thousands of dollars for a major fight. The bullfighter car of choice is a Mercedes, but Cristina bought herself a bright red Ford Probe, which is much sportier. She also bought her mother a small business, a gift store. We decided to wait a bit longer. Pedro killed time by making some bullfight business calls on his cellular phone. Just as we were debating whether to go looking for Cristina at her mother's store, Mrs. Sanchez came around the corner, carrying a load of groceries; she said Cristina was at the bank and that in the meantime we could come upstairs. We climbed a few flights. The apartment was tidy and fresh-looking and furnished with modern things in pastel tones, and in the living room there were a life-size oil painting of Cristina looking beautiful in her suit of lights, two huge photographs of Cristina in bullfights, one of her as a civilian, a large photograph of the older Sanchez daughter getting married, and a big-screen TV. On almost every horizontal surface there was a bronze or brass or pewter statuette of a bull, usually bucking, its withers bristling with three or four barbed harpoons called *banderillas*, which are stuck in to aggravate him before he is killed. These were all trophies from different corridas and from Cristina's stint as a star pupil at the Madrid bullfighting school. Lots of Cristina's stuff was lying around the room. On the dining table were stacks of fresh laundry, mostly white dress shirts and white T-shirts and pink socks. On the floor were a four-foot-long leather sword case, three hatboxes, and a piece of luggage that looked like a giant bowling-ball bag, which is a specially designed case for a matador's $20,000 suit jacket. Also, there was a small black Kipling backpack of Cristina's, which cracked me up because it was the exact same backpack that I was carrying.

Mrs. Sanchez was clattering around in the kitchen, making Cristina's lunch. A few minutes later, I heard the front door scrape open, and then Cristina stepped into the room, out of breath and flustered about being late. She is twenty-five years old, and has chemically assisted blond hair, long eyelashes, high cheekbones, and a tiny nose. She looks really pretty when she smiles and almost regal when she doesn't, but she's not so beautiful that she's scary. This day, she was wearing blue jeans, a denim shirt with some flower embroidery, and white slip-on shoes with chunky heels, and her hair was held in a ponytail by a sunflower barrette. She is not unusually big or small. Her shoulders are square and her legs are sturdy, and she's solid and athletic-looking, like a forward on a field hockey team. Her strength is a matter of public debate in Spain. The weakest part of her performance is the very end of the fight, when she's supposed to kill the bull with one perfect jam of her sword, but she often doesn't go deep enough or in the right place. It is said in certain quarters that she simply isn't strong enough, but the fact is that most matadors mess up with the sword. Later, when we were talking, I brought it up, and she shook her head and said, "People who don't understand the bullfighting world think you have to be extremely strong, but that's not the case. What is important is technique and experience. You have to be in good shape, but you don't have to match a man's strength. Besides, your real opponent is the bull, and you can never match it in strength."

Her mother came in and out of the room a few times. When she was out, Cristina said in a low voice, "I'm very happy with my family, but the time comes when you have to be independent." The tabloids have reported that she has just bought a castle on millions of enchanted acres. "I bought a small piece of property right near here," she said, rolling her eyes. "I'm having a house built. I think when I come back from my winter tour in South America I'll be able to move in."

What I really wanted to know was why in the world she decided to become a bullfighter. I knew she'd grown up watching her father fight, so it had always been a profession that seemed normal to her, even though at the ring she didn't see many girls. Plus she doesn't like to sit still. Before she started training to be a matador, she had worked in a beauty parlor and then as a typist at a fire-extinguisher factory, and both jobs drove her crazy. She is a very girly girl—she wears makeup, she wants children, she has boyfriends—but she says she could only imagine doing jobs which would keep her on her feet, and coincidentally those were jobs that were mostly filled by men. If she hadn't become a matador, she thinks she would have become a trainer at a gym, or a police officer, or perhaps a firefighter, which used to be her father's backup job when he was a bullfighter, in the years before he started advising her and became a full-time part of her six-person crew. She didn't become a woman matador to be shocking or make a feminist point, although along the way she has been shunned by some of her male colleagues and there are still a few who refuse to appear in a corrida with her. Once, in protest, she went to Toledo and instead of having a corrida in which three matadors each killed two bulls, she took on all six bulls herself, one by one. She said she wants to be known as a great matador and not an oddity or anecdote in the history of bullfighting. She simply loves the art and craft of fighting bulls. Later that day, when I saw her in the ring, I also realized that besides loving the bullfight itself she is that sort of person who is illuminated by the attention of a crowd. I asked her what she'll do after she retires from the ring in three or four years. "I want to have earned a lot of money and invested it wisely," she said. "And then I want to do something in the movies or on TV."

She mentioned that she was eating early today because she had a stomachache. With a fight every night for months, I suppose there would be nights when she felt crummy or wasn't in the mood. Cristina laughed and said, "Yeah, sometimes you do feel like, oh God, I don't have the slightest desire to face a bull this afternoon!" Personally, I'm not a huge coward, but the phrase "desire to face a bull" will never be part of my life, any afternoon, ever. I figured that nothing must scare her. She shook her head and said, "Failure. My greatest fear is failure. I'm a woman who is a fighter and I always think about trying to surpass myself, so what I most fear is to fail."

Just then, Mrs. Sanchez came into the room and said the sandwiches were ready, so Cristina started to get up. She paused for a moment and said, "You know, people think that because I kill bulls I have to be really brave, but I'm not. I'm a sensitive person, and I can get super-terrified. I'm afraid of staying home by myself, and I get hysterical if I see a spider." I asked if bulls ever haunted her dreams, and she said, "I don't dream much at all, but a few times I've dreamed that a bull was pursuing me in the ring, up into the stands. And the night before my debut in Madrid, I did dream of bulls with huge, twisted horns."

I had seen the first bullfight of my life a few days earlier, on that night in Madrid, and it was a profound education. I learned that I should not eat for several hours beforehand and to start looking away the minute the picadors ride in on their stoic-looking blindfolded horses, because their arrival signaled that the blood and torment would begin. At first, in Madrid, I had been excited because the Plaza de Toros is so dramatic and beautiful, and also the pageantry that began the corrida was very nice, and when the first bull galloped in, I liked watching it bolt around the ring and chase the matador and his assistants until they retreated behind the small fences around the ring that are there for their protection. The small fences had targets—bull's-eyes, actually—painted on them. The bull would ram into them with its horns and the fence would rock. The more furious bulls would ram again and again, until the matador teased them away with a flourish of his cape. The bulls were homely, with little heads and huge briskets and tapered hips, and they cornered like school buses and sometimes skidded to their knees, but they had fantastic energy and single-mindedness and thick muscles that flickered under their skin and faces that didn't look vicious at all and were interesting to watch. Some of the fight was wonderful. The matador's flourishes with the shocking pink and bright yellow big cape and his elegance with the small triangular red one; the sound of thousands of people gasping when the bull got very close to the cape; the plain thrilling danger of it and the fascination of watching a bull be slowly hypnotized; the bravery of the picadors' horses, which stood stock-still as the bull pounded them broadside, the flags along the rim of the ring flashing in the late-afternoon light; the resplendence of the matador's suit in that angling light, especially when the matador inched one foot forward and squared his hips and arched his back so that he was a bright new moon against a sky of sand with the black cloud of a bull racing by. I loved the ancientness and majesty and excitement of it, the way bullfighting could be at once precious and refined yet absolutely primal and raw. But beyond that I was lost and nauseous and knew I didn't understand how so many people, a whole nation of people, weren't shaken by the gore and the idea of watching a ballet that always, absolutely, unfailingly ends with a gradual and deliberate death. I didn't understand it then, and I doubt I ever will.

In the little brick bullring in Mostoles, Cristina killed two bulls well but not exceptionally—for the first kill the judge awarded her one of the bull's ears, but for the second she got no award at all. A once-in-a-lifetime sort of performance would have earned two ears, a tail, and a hoof. After that second fight Cristina looked a little disgusted with herself, and she hung back and talked for several minutes with her father, who was standing in the crew area, before she came out and took the traditional victory walk around the ring. She was clearly the crowd favorite. People wave white handkerchiefs at bullfights to indicate their support; in Mostoles it looked like it was snowing. As she circled the ring, men and women and little kids yelled, "Matadora! Matadora!" and "Olé, Cristina!" and tossed congratulatory sweaters and flowers and shoes and blazers and sandwiches and a Levi's jacket and a crutch and a cane, and then a representative of a social club in Mostoles stepped into the ring and presented her with an enormous watermelon.

After the fight, Cristina left immediately for Zaragoza, where she would have her next fight. I went back to Madrid to have dinner with Muriel and Pedro. Pedro had just finished his fight, and he looked very relaxed and his face was pink and bright. The restaurant, Vina P, was practically wallpapered with old and new fight posters and photographs of bullfighters and some mounted bulls' heads. Its specialty was slabs of beef—since the animals killed in bullfights are butchered and are highly sought after for dining, the specialty of the house might occasionally be straight from the bullring. Pedro said Vina P was a bullfighters' restaurant, which means it is the rough equivalent of a sports bar frequented by real athletes in the United States. Before I got to Spain I imagined that bullfighting was an old and colorful tradition that was preserved but isolated, a fragile antique. Cristina Sanchez would be honored, but she would be in the margins—it would be as if she were the very best square dancer in America. Instead, she looms, and bullfighting looms. There are tons of restaurants in every city that are bullfighter- and bullfight-aficionado hangouts, and there are pictures and posters of bullfights even in the restaurants that aren't, and there is the bullfight newspaper and regular television coverage, and every time I turned around I was in front of the headquarters of some bullfight association. At a gas station in a nowhere place called Otero de Herreros the only bit of decoration I saw was a poster for an upcoming fight; it happened to have a picture of Cristina on it. The biggest billboards in Madrid were ads for Pepe Jeans, modeled by Francisco Rivera Ordonez, Matador de Toros. Mostly because of Cristina, bullfight attendance is up and applications to the Madrid bullfighting school are up, especially with girls. The Spanish tabloids are fat with bullfighter gossip, and they are really keen on Cristina. That night while we were eating dinner, Pedro noticed a gorgeous young man at another table and whispered that he was a Mexican pop singer and also Cristina's old boyfriend, whom she'd recently broken up with because he'd sold the story of their relationship to the celebrity press.

I had planned to leave Spain after the fight in Mostoles, but when I heard that Cristina was going to fight soon in a town that was easy to get to, I decided to stay a few more days. The town was called Nava de la Asunción, and to get there you head north from Madrid over the raggedy gray Sierra de Guadarrama and then onto the high golden plain where many fighting bulls are raised. The occasion for the fight was the Nava town fair. According to the local paper, "peculiar and small amateur bullfights used to be done in the fenced yards of local houses until for reasons of security it was recommended to do away with these customs." The bulls were always chased through the fields in the morning so the townspeople could see what they were like. The paper said, "Traditionally there are accidents because there is always a bull that escapes. There is maximum effort put out to be sure that this does not occur, even though it is part of the tradition." It also said, "To have Cristina Sanchez in Nava is special." "The Party of the Bulls—Cristina Sanchez will be the star of the program!" "Cristina Sanchez will show her bullfighting together with the gifted Antonio Borrero Chamaco and Antonio Cutino—a great bill in which the star is, without a doubt, Cristina Sanchez."

Nava is the prettiest little town, and on the afternoon of the fight there was a marching band zigzagging around and strings of candy-colored banners hanging along the streets, popping and flapping in the wind. Just outside the bullring a few vendors had set up booths. One was selling soft drinks, one had candy and nuts, one had every manner of bullfighter souvenir: T-shirts with matador photos, pins with matador photos, photo cigarette lighters and key chains, autographed photos themselves, and white hankies for waving at the end of the fights. Of the nine photo T-shirts, seven were of Cristina. Six were different pictures of her either posing in her suit of lights or actually fighting. The other one was a casual portrait. She was dressed in a blue blouse trimmed with white daisy embroidery, and her blond hair was loose and she appeared to be sitting in a park. A nun came over to the souvenir booth and bought a Cristina photo-hankie. Big-bodied women with spindly little daughters were starting to gather around the booth and hold up first one Cristina T-shirt and then another and finally, sighing, indicate that they would take both. Skittery little boys, sometimes with a bigger boy or their fathers, darted up and poked through the stuff on the table and lingered. After a while, a couple of men pushed past the throng, lugging a trunk marked C. SÂNCHEZ toward the area under the bleachers where the matadors and picadors were getting ready. Now and then, if you looked in that direction, you could catch a glimpse of someone in a short sequined jacket, and until the band came thundering by you could hear the hollow clunking of hooves and the heavy rustling of horses and donkeys.

The tickets were expensive whether you bought one for the sunny side or the shade, but every row was packed and every standing-room spot was taken. The men around me were smoking cigars and women were snacking on honey-roasted peanuts, and every few minutes a guy would come through hawking shots of Cutty Sark and cans of beer. Young kids were in shorts and American basketball-team T-shirts, but everyone else was dressed up, as if they were going to a dinner party at a friend's. At 5:30, in slanting sunlight, the parade of the matadors and their assistants began. Each of them was dressed in a different color, and they were dazzling and glinting in the sun. In a box seat across the ring from the entrance gate were the sober-looking judge and three girls who were queens of the fair, wearing lacy white crowns in their hair. Antonio Borrero "Chamaco" fought first, and then came Cristina. She was wearing a fuchsia suit and had her hair in a braid and had a look of dark focus on her face. When she and her assistants entered the ring, a man stood up in the stands and hollered about how much he admired her and then an old woman called out that she wanted Cristina to bless a little brooch she had pinned on her shawl.

The bull came out. He was brownish-black, small-chested, wide-horned, and branded with the number 36. Cristina, the other two matadors of the day, and Cristina's picadors and banderilleros spread out around the ring holding hot-pink capes, and each one in turn would catch the bull's attention, tease him into charging, and then the next person would step forward and do the same. It was like a shoot-around before a basketball game. Meanwhile, the matadors had a chance to assess the bull and figure out how fast he moved and if he faked right and passed left or if he seemed crazy. This bull was a sprinter, and all around the ring the capes were blooming. Then two picadors rode out and positioned their horses at either end of the ring, and as soon as the bull noticed one, he roared toward it, head down, and slammed into the padding that protected the horse's flank. The picadors stabbed the bull with long spears as he tangled with the horse. After he was speared several times by each picador, he was lured away by the big capes again. A few moments later, the ring cleared, and a banderillero sprinted into the ring carrying a pair of short, nicely decorated harpoons. He held them high and wide. Eventually the bull lunged toward the banderillero, who ducked out of the way of the horns and planted the banderillas into the bull's withers. Then a second banderillero did the same thing. The bull was panting. The band burst into a fanfare, and then Cristina came out alone, carrying a small red heart-shaped cape. She stood at attention and tipped her hat to the judge—asking permission to kill the bull—and then turned and glanced just slightly toward her father, who was standing between the seats and the ring. The bull stood motionless and stared at her.

For ten minutes or so she seduced him toward her, and just as he thought he was about to kill her, she diverted him with dizzying, rippling, precise swings of her cape—first a windmill, then a circle, then a chest pass, where the bull rushes straight toward and then under the cape. As the bull passed her, Cristina's back was as arched as a scythe. When the bull was swooning, she stood right in front of him, rubbed his forehead lightly with the flat of her sword, and then spread her arms, yelled something, and dropped down on one knee. The bull looked like he might faint.

Then she started getting ready to kill him. She walked over to her sword boy and traded him for her longest, sharpest blade. The band was toodling away on some brassy song, and after a moment she glowered and thrust her hand up to stop it. She drew the bull toward and past her a few more times. On one pass, she lost her grip on her cape and her father shot up from his seat and the crew raced in to help her, but without even looking up she waved them away. Then the bull squared up and she squared up. His fat beige tongue was now hanging out, and a saddle-blanket of blood was spreading from the cuts that the picadors and the banderilleros had made. Cristina's eyes were fixed with a look of concentration and command, and her arm was outstretched, and she lined up the bull, her arm, and her sword. She and the bull had not seen each other before the fight—matadors and bulls never do, the way grooms avoid brides on their wedding day—but she now stared so hard at him and he at her that it looked as if each was examining the other through and through.

When it was over, she got flowers, wineskins, berets, bags of olives, loafers, crutches, more wineskins, hundreds of things shoved at her to autograph, and both of the bull's black ears. The bull got two recumbent laps of the ring, hauled around by a team of donkeys, and there was a butcher with a five-o'clock shadow and black rubber hip boots waiting for him as soon as the team dragged him through the door. When the whole corrida was finally over, a leftover bull was let loose in the ring, and anyone with nerve could hop in with him and fool around. Most people passed on that and instead filed out of the stands, beaming and chatting and slapping backs and shaking hands. Just outside the front gate was a clean white Peugot van with CRISTINA SÂNCHEZ stenciled in script on the front and the back, and in it were a driver and Cristina and Cristina's father and her crew, still dressed in their sumptuous fight clothes, still damp and pink-faced from the fight. Cristina looked tremendously happy. The van couldn't move, because the crowd had closed in around it, and everyone was waving and throwing kisses and pushing papers to autograph through the van's windows, and for ten minutes or so Cristina signed stuff and waved at people and smiled genuinely and touched scores of outstretched hands. It was such a familiar picture of success and adoration and fame, but it had a scramble of contradictory details: here was an ancient village with a brand-new bullring, and here was a modern new car filled with young and able people wearing the uniforms of a sport so unchanging and so ritualized that except for the fresh concrete and the new car and the flushed blond face of Cristina it all could have been taking place a hundred years in the future or a hundred years ago.

At last Cristina whispered "no mas" to the driver, and he began inching the van down the driveway and then out toward the highway, and soon you could only see a speck in the shape of the van. The town of Nava then returned to normal. Cristina was going on to fight and fight and fight until the end of the European season, and then she planned to fly to South America and fight and then to Mexico and fight and then to return to Spain and start the season again. Once someone suggested that she try to get a Nike contract, and once she told me that she would love to bring bullfighting to America. But it seems that bullfighting is such a strange pursuit and the life bullfighters lead is so peculiar and the sight and the sound and the smell of the whole thing is so powerful and so deadly that it could only exist where strangeness is expected and treasured and long-standing and even a familiar part of every day.

It was now deep evening in Nava, and the road out had not a single streetlight. Outside town the road cut through huge unlit pastures, so everything in all directions was pure black. No one was on the road, so it felt even more spooky. Then a car pulled up behind me, and after a moment it sped up and passed. It was a medium-size station wagon driven by a harried-looking man, and there was a shaggy dappled-gray pony standing in the back. The man had the interior lamp turned on, maybe for the pony, and it made a trail of light I could follow the whole way back to Madrid.

Lillian Ross

Lillian Ross joined the staff of *The New Yorker* in 1945, during World War II, and worked with Harold Ross, the magazine's founder and first editor. She began as a Talk of the Town reporter and, over the course of her career, has written hundreds of pieces, contributing to nearly every section of the magazine.

Several of her pieces for *The New Yorker* were collected in two books: *Talk Stories,* published in 1966, and *Takes,* published in 1983. She has published more than a dozen books largely based on her work with the magazine, including *Portrait of Hemingway*; *The Player: A Profile of an Art*; *Reporting*; and her memoir, *Here But Not Here: A Love Story*, where she details her somewhat unconventional romance with William Shawn, the longtime editor of *The New Yorker* who died in 1992. Ross was also close friends with the notoriously reclusive J. D. Salinger for more than fifty years, according to her article "Bearable," which ran in February 2010.

Ross's most recent book, *Reporting Always: Writing for The New Yorker,* was published in 2015.

She lives in Manhattan.

Takes on the Town

For decades, Lillian Ross's inspired short gems have set the gold standard for *The New Yorker*'s iconic Talk of the Town section.

EDITOR'S NOTE: *While staff writer Lillian Ross has written numerous full-length articles for* The New Yorker, *among them her famous profile of Ernest Hemingway, she has a special fondness for doing Talk of the Town pieces. She explains why in the introduction to* Takes, *a 1983 collection of her Talk stories.*

I love reporting for *The New Yorker*'s Talk of the Town. In many ways, it's the most challenging kind of reporting: the most demanding, the most interesting to do, the most fun, and the most open to humor. Like the longer pieces of reporting for *The New Yorker*—Profiles and A Reporter at Large, for instance—Talk stories can take many forms. From time to time, some people have said of Talk of the Town that "it all sounds alike." As it happens, the opposite is true. For one thing, Talk stories, like any other kind of writing, vary tremendously in style from writer to writer. A Talk story reveals the very spirit of the writer, and in any given year Talk of the Town has been written by anywhere from twenty to thirty writers, each of whom has a unique, strongly personal style and feeling. Talk stories usually run to about a thousand words, but sometimes, for one reason or another, they may run twice—even five times—as long. Whatever their length, the writing requires that in a short space one build and reveal a character or a situation or an event or a moment and do so with honesty, with humor, with clarity, with freshness, and with truth.

Talk of the Town deals for the most part with life in or related to New York, and it is constantly discovering the excitement and fun in that life. Where there's life, there's humor. And usually the humor presents itself naturally, because it's part of the truth; there is no need to alter the truth to fit one's preconceptions or preoccupations. For me, the greatest opportunity for humor in writing is presented by Talk stories. In fact, they offer, on a small scale, an opportunity for working toward everything I respect and admire about reporting—what it can and should be.

Talk stories are not usually "news" stories, as many reporters define the word, and they are not "feature" stories, as newspapers use the term. Nor are they in the realm of "gossip," which seems to pervade so many books and magazines as well as newspapers these days—to such an extent that the basic meaning of "reporting" has become fuzzy.

A Talk story brings out some aspect of the truth about a person, a situation, or an event. If it is about a person, I try to build the character as one might do in fiction. Quotations help to provide insight. There are three key limitations that make this kind of factual writing difficult:

1. A reporter must have a strong sense of what should and what should not be revealed—a sense of responsibility toward the person he or she is writing about.
2. In quotations, both what is said and how it is said must be conveyed accurately.
3. What is said must be said in the presence of the reporter. It cannot be "reconstructed" from what the reporter *thinks* may have been said or from what someone else thinks he *remembers* having been said. Memory is notoriously undependable. A reconstructed quotation is not a fact; it is a pseudo-fact.

So you are limited in being bound to the *facts* about a real living person and by your responsibility not to venture too far into the privacy of that person. You must never assume that you have a right to intrude on that person's thoughts and feelings, to violate the inherent secrecy of what is going on in that person's brain. If what you select to report about the person reveals what you *think* is going on in that person's brain, that is another matter. But you must always be aware of the difference between what you know and what you merely *think* you know about a person.

The roots of good Talk reporting are to be found in the tradition of good reporting in general. Good reporting can be long or short, and I love it whatever its length. A Talk story is a specific yet mysterious literary form, of which brevity is just one element. A Talk story is not a shorter version of something else. It has its own dimensions, and is complete in itself, often compressing into inches the substance of an article of great length. It contains the essence of something. It is a distillation. For me, the definition of good reporting is good writing about real people, real situations, real events. When the reporting, whether short or long, is very good, I find it thrilling to read. Without exception, it directs my attention as a reader to *what* has been written, not to *who* has done the writing.

Davis on Dogs

Our dog-groomer, dog-partisan friend Mel Davis gave a few unsettling cries of anguish about his profession the other day while he worked—in his establishment, a cozy, warm, tidy place on East Forty-Ninth Street near the East River—on a ten-year-old small miniature apricot poodle named Goldie, who stood on a grooming table as though transfixed by the shop's windows, which were opaque with steam against the icy blasts outside. "I'm so upset about what's happening with dogs," said Mr. Davis, who is, as half the poodle owners in town know, a small, faithful, puppylike man, with a small, faithful, puppylike face, who believes that every dog has the right to look naturally beautiful, and who measures all people by the way they recognize that right. Wearing pastel-green slacks and a gaudy flower-patterned sports shirt open at the collar, Mr. Davis sat on a bar stool, his heels hooked over the top rung, and clipped away at Goldie's fluff, shaping a kind of halo on top of her head. "Every time I go out on the street and see the way dogs look, I feel so depressed," Mr. Davis said. "All around me, I see long, low dogs with haircuts shaped to make them look like walking coffee tables. Short-backed dogs look as though their heads were pushed up against their behinds. Has mass production reached the point now where all dogs are made to look alike, no matter what the breed, and with no artistry and no styling? I know it's been happening with books and with clothes and with television programs and with movies and with medical doctors and with politicians and with the faces of people. But *dogs!*"

Goldie gave Mr. Davis a look of sympathetic gloom.

"Don't the owners see the travesties that are made of their dogs?" Mr. Davis asked. "Don't they see how badly their dogs are patterned? I feel so *sorry* for the dogs—and for the owners, too. I see so many shaved bodies, with full legs but with a small, scissored head, making the dog look so unbalanced, as though he came out of a barber school on the Bowery. Can you imagine schnauzers and other terriers not being made to look like the precisely tailored creatures they should be? The other day, I met a woman whose schnauzer looked like a poodle. She didn't know how her dog should look. But the *dog* knew. He came to us so unhappy. Well, we did a complete restyling. The dog looked so serene, and the woman was hysterical with joy."

Goldie wagged her tail.

"Who knows or cares these days about how to enhance the personality or conformation of the dog?" Mr. Davis asked. "The trouble is, first of all, with the grooming schools. They appeal to the students to learn and to go out fast and earn a living in grooming. The students are dog lovers, and are sincere in their efforts. But how much can they learn in a crash course in a few months? Can an artist be taught to be an artist in the first place? We interview and audition quite a few of these graduates, but we rarely find anybody with real talent. We try to encourage the youngsters to start at the bottom, doing rough clipping, washing, drying, and brushing, and leave the styling to our talented groomers—at least, until the youngsters *learn* something. But no, these youngsters want to start immediately at the *top*. Their attitude is, once they are graduates they are immediately qualified to do it *all*."

"Sounds familiar," we said.

"To commercialize an artistic profession is to me an outrage," Mr. Davis went on. "Our clients are very fussy. When we have a new client, at first we observe the animal and suggest the correct cut. Some of these cuts are very intricate and require more than just a basic style. A Dutch clip, or a modified Dutch clip, must give the effect of a poodle wearing a jacket or pants. If you mess up on *that*, the poor dog looks as though the pants were falling down. If only these would-be groomers would attend *one* all-breed

American Kennel Club–sanctioned dog show and observe the charges of the professional handlers, they would learn more in one day than in an entire course taking months."

Mr. Davis picked up clippers to trim Goldie's nails, and she trustingly held up one paw. "Poodles are treated the worst," he said. "The textures of their coats are so varied that the formula of the shampoo has to be chosen with care. We happen to have developed our own, with high-protein content. It makes thin-coated poodles look virtually heavy-coated, while our woolly woollies become manageable, so that we can scissor and style them easily. Each poodle has an individual look. Nobody should ever forget that."

Mr. Davis looked Goldie in the eye, and she gave him a fervent wag of the tail.

"Heads have to be designed and cut to capture the true personality of each poodle," Mr. Davis said. "Every day, I go out and see dozens of horrible pinheaded dogs. When these dogs flex their ears, a horrible point appears on the top of the head. Horrible. This is what you get when you let a book-learning groomer do it. I'm so miserable when I see that Happy Hooligan look."

Goldie looked alarmed.

"It's OK, Goldie, not you," Mr. Davis continued. "I have seen legs clipped starting from incredible angles, so that they look as though they were just hanging there, defying the laws of gravity. Tails are made to look like witches' brooms. And the mustaches! Some of them only people of Diamond Jim Brady's time would wear."

Goldie cringed.

"When I do Goldie, I start from the base of the neck and work toward the shoulder line and blend it in down to the full leg," Mr. Davis said. "You're done, Goldie. I'll give you your yellow bows."

As Mr. Davis tied the bows on Goldie's head, behind her ears, he almost smiled. "I took a walk yesterday," he said. "The unhappiest walk of my life." He looked solemn again. "I started from the Forties, where every dog looked either matted or the object of a different kind of indifference on the part of the owners. I saw one Afghan hound who actually had a tied-up topknot, à la Yorkie. I saw a freshly groomed schnauzer sporting a closely trimmed poodle face and a hula skirt with legs to match. Then I saw a beautiful Yorkshire terrier with so many ribbons and bows its whole head was hidden. One head bow is sufficient for a Yorkie. Only an idiot doesn't know that. In the Fifties, I found a glut of Lhasa Apsos and Shih Tzus that had been 'economically clipped,' so the regal look of these beautifully coated breeds was ruined. When I reached the Sixties, I saw a cocker spaniel with a completely shaved skull, instead of a topknot blended into the dome. And again the hula skirt, like the one on the poor little schnauzer in the Forties, *plus* sloppy, unrounded paws. Then I saw some poodles with full puppy clips without shapings. They resembled little cigars. In the Seventies, I saw more guess-what-we-are poodles and pulis."

"All right," we said. "Specifically, what are the main faults you found with the poodles?"

"The legs were clipped so high the dogs looked as if they were walking on stilts," Mr. Davis replied. "The heads were too small and tightly cut, so the dogs looked as if they were wearing caps. The bodies were shorn too close—usually with injury to the animal, revealed by discolored hair over the skin wound. Tails sometimes looked like bananas instead of nice little pom-poms. The ears weren't blended to the side of the head, so I knew there had been deep scissoring, cutting away precious hair that had taken years to grow."

Goldie was ready to leave, looking satisfied with herself.

"*She* knows," Mr. Davis said.

Remembering Picasso

Last week, in a glassed-in office of the West Fifty-Seventh Street Gallery of Sidney Janis, eighty-five-year-old art exhibitor *extraordinaire*, who was one of Pablo Picasso's first American friends, and who helped bring Picasso's "Guernica" to this country from France in 1939, Carroll Janis, the younger of Sidney's two sons, fortyish-looking, wearing blue jeans, tan running shoes, and a tan velour sweater over a pink tennis shirt, was sitting on a corner of a desk talking on the telephone about arrangements for the gallery's opening, on October 25th—the hundredth anniversary of Picasso's birth—of an exhibition of two hundred and fifty photographs, all by David Douglas Duncan, of Pablo Picasso. In the gallery's four exhibition rooms, the white-painted walls were blank. On the floors, carpeted in beige, were rows and rows of photographs, mostly in black and white, measuring ten or twelve inches by fifteen, and mounted on rag board. Standing upright in a corner was a big photograph, in color, about forty inches by sixty; a mounted dye transfer on a thick panel, it showed Picasso in 1962, from the rear, seated in a chair in the large salon of his château at Vauvenargues, the room bare of usual furniture but with a couple of unframed Picassos on easels and one in the fireplace.

Duncan, wearing a blue-and-red checked sports shirt open at the collar, brown corduroy pants, brown socks, and no shoes, was tiptoeing among his photographs, rearranging them, studying them, straightening them, getting them ready for the walls. He picked up one showing Picasso and his second wife, Jacqueline, eating at their kitchen table and laid it beside a photograph of Picasso kidding around as he embraced his wife. Duncan, a Midwesterner who has lived for many years in the South of France, near where Picasso lived, looked the same as he has for decades: deeply tanned, thin, boyish, talkative, exuberant, and eager, as always, to share some of his endless enthusiasm for Picasso as both man and artist, which had led him to bring out four books of photographs of Picasso—*The Private World of Pablo Picasso* (1958), *Picasso's Picassos* (1961), *Goodbye Picasso* (1974), and *Viva Picasso* (1980).

An elevator door opened. Into the gallery stepped Paloma Picasso Lopez Sanchez, the thirty-one-year-old daughter of the artist, who is a jewelry designer now working in New York City. Trim, attractive, energetic, with straight black hair hanging almost to her earlobes, Mrs. Lopez Sanchez is about an inch taller than her five-foot-two father. Except for a red wool French beret with metal grommets, she was all in Saint-Laurent—navy-blue leather jacket, straight skirt of navy with white pinstripes, red-white-and-blue silk print blouse with a bow at the collar, red leather belt, black stockings, navy leather pumps trimmed with red around the instep. She also wore dark-tinted Italian glasses and a single piece of jewelry, of her own design—a gold ring set with rubellite and amethyst. She glanced at the photographs spread out on the floor and then, with a pleased smile, embraced Duncan, who grinned at her with unrestrained approval.

"This is what I wanted you to see," Duncan said. "This is our birthday present to your pop." He led her closer to the photographs on the floor. "This is not really an exhibition of photographs," he said. "The work of art here is your father."

She gave a little laugh. "Dave, it is very impressive," she said. "Very impressive." She looked up at him with large, Picasso-duplicate brown eyes.

Duncan looked as though he had just been presented with a dozen Picassos.

"And Sidney Janis is not charging one dime to get in here," he said. "This is going to be a *celebration*."

Mrs. Lopez Sanchez carefully walked along a row and looked down at a photograph of a spectacularly beautiful little black-haired girl sitting with Picasso in a café and eating an ice-cream cone. "He was always buying me ice cream," she said.

"Paloma, you know your English is astonishing," Duncan said. "Extraordinary. Perfect."

"I can do the British accent if I want to, but it's pretentious," she said seriously.

"Do you remember where that photograph was taken?" Duncan asked.

"Café des Belges, Juan-les-Pins," she said. "It was 1957."

"What a memory!" Duncan said. "You have the same memory as your pop."

"I remember it because my brother Claude and I spent so much time looking up at the Sputnik," she said.

Carroll Janis ambled over and was introduced. "It's all starting to shape up," he said.

"There are so many here I've never seen before," Mrs. Lopez Sanchez said.

"I had such an opportunity," Duncan said. "Nobody was ever self-conscious in front of the camera."

"This picture," Mrs. Lopez-Sanchez said, going over to one of the few photographs in color. "This one wearing the Indian war bonnet."

"Gary Cooper brought him that," Duncan said, with delight. He pointed to the photograph of Picasso-mugging-as-Indian-chief. "Remember when he grabbed that bull's tail that someone had given him and put it on as the Indian's hair?" he asked, with further delight. "He was the greatest mime of them all."

"I would be sitting with him, and suddenly he would put on a funny hat or a plastic nose," Mrs. Lopez Sanchez said. "They were always sending him things."

"Every day was Christmas," Duncan said.

They walked slowly and carefully between the rows of photographs.

"Here I am making faces out of leaves," she said. "He was always working on the dinner table. When I came, he would say, 'It's OK. Stay. But don't open your mouth.' I always had a second breakfast with my father. His breakfast was always the same: dry toast and Caro, a coffee without caffeine. He was homeopathic. He was careful with foods."

"He never drank anything alcoholic," Duncan said.

"I liked the big vicuña quilt he had on his bed, summer and winter," she said. "And his moccasins, with the fur inside. I'd walk in his shoes."

They looked at photographs taken at the beach. "A driver would take us all to the beach," she said. "My father never learned to drive a car. He would say that when he was poor he couldn't afford a car and then when he was rich he could afford a driver, so he never drove himself. We'd stay at the beach till five. We'd take pedal boats out."

"And here he's permitting himself to be sketched by one of those beach artists," Duncan said. "They never left him alone."

"He used to go to that beach, La Garoupe, for years before it became popular," she said. "One day, I read a book that said that my father and the Gerald Murphys and Hemingway and Chanel started going to that beach in the summer. Before that, nobody ever went there in the summer. It was too hot. They went to Deauville. Now La Garoupe is too crowded."

They looked at photographs of Picasso and his children with a goat.

"Esmeralda," Duncan said.

"I don't know how it arrived," she said. "One day, a *bull* arrived—a big fighting bull. He said, 'I don't want it here.' We sent it back." Pointing to a picture of a large boxer lying on marble steps at the front door of Picasso's house, she said, "Ian! I was sort of raised by this dog. I called him my milk brother."

"He put that dog in many paintings," Duncan said. "Do you have this one?" He indicated—in a photograph—a painting of a girl jumping rope.

"Yes," she said. "When we divided the paintings, I chose this rope-jumping painting of me, and the rope-jumping sculpture of me cast in bronze. I love it. We divided the paintings among us. I think we're six: Jacqueline, then Maya, Claude, and me—we're the children—and Marina and Bernard, the grandchildren. And the French government. It took twenty-five percent of everything." She pointed to a photograph showing a Picasso bronze sculpture of a baboon. "That is the one he made of Claude's cars," she said, laughing. "Claude's two plastic cars. My father made it so fast. He stuck the cars together to make the head. He put on a broken spring of a toy to make the tail. He made ears of the broken handles of two coffee mugs. Then he sent it all off to be cast in bronze. My brother was furious, because his toys were taken away from him."

"You can see the cars," Duncan said, outlining them with a forefinger, as Carroll Janis bent closer to see the sculpture. "The top of the baboon's head, and the bottom."

"I never knew about that," Janis said. "Toy cars," he said. "Sculptured in bronze."

"My brother has it now," Mrs. Lopez Sanchez said. "He loves it."

"The man had a perfect boxer's stance," Duncan said as she turned her attention to a photograph of Picasso pretending to box. "He was in constant motion. And here's how pure his vision was." Duncan was now pointing to a photograph of a painting of Jacqueline. "He made at least thirteen great portraits of Jacqueline, all dedicated to her. She has all of them. And there's another one. On a thin sheet of steel. He painted her profile on it and then cut it out as a sculpture. In this photograph, it's very late at night. Picasso and Jacqueline are sitting here, with the profile in metal of Jacqueline illuminated in the background."

"Did she come to the exhibition last year at the Museum of Modern Art?" Carroll Janis asked.

"Without anyone's knowing about it," Duncan said. "The week before the show closed, she came here, and we went every day."

"There's *your* dog!" Mrs. Lopez Sanchez said to Duncan.

"Do you remember Lump?" he asked as they looked at a photograph that showed Picasso, a small dachshund nearby, making one of his plates with a representation of the dog on it.

"I liked that dog," she said.

"That's the day he asked me, 'Does Lump have his own plate?'" Duncan said. "I said yes. So he asked me, 'Does he have a plate with his *name* on it?' I said, 'He can't read.' So your father said, 'How do you know?' And he made that plate for him."

"Here I am, when I was seven, at the dinner table again with my father," Mrs. Lopez Sanchez said, picking up one photograph. "He was making a linogravure with a gouging knife. And I was drawing at the same time. With crayons."

The Golden Ladies of the Golden Door

The ladies, traditionally limited to a quota of thirty-nine, arrive on Sundays at the Golden Door, a spa situated on a hundred-and-seventy-seven-acre tract of land in the Peninsula Range, about an hour's drive north of San Diego. Mostly, they come wearing designer jeans and designer blazers and carrying small bags containing their bathing suits (near-bikinis) and their sneakers (aerobic and running) and their underwear and socks and nighties. Everything else they will need for their $4,250 week is provided by the spa—shorts, warm-ups, T-shirts, terry robes, sun hats, and assorted creams and potions and pastes and a fresh toothbrush. They go quickly to their rooms, each with private bath, a perfectly mattressed queen-size bed, good lamps, a radio, stationery inscribed with the guest's name in gold letters, and reading material (*Chop Wood, Carry Water*, *Fifty Simple Things You Can Do to Save the Earth*). All the guests receive, on request, bottles of Evian and the daily newspapers of their choice. They never refer to what, if anything, they have read in the news.

The ladies emerge quickly, uniformly democratized in aquamarine-colored warm-ups and gray T-shirts. They are mostly fortyish or fiftyish, with husbands and children, but there are also a few nervous singles and hopeful fatties, and a scattering of heavy oldies (thigh-covering bathing suits), hoarse-voiced, with Barbara Bush hair, icy blue eyes, false teeth, and scads of grandchildren. Children—anybody under the age of sixteen, in fact—are banned from the premises. "We don't want to remind anybody of what she left behind," one of the spa's supervisors explains.

Most of the guests have heard that exercise increases sexuality, and they think a lot about sex and youth and health. They are immediately eager to mention their husbands, quite a number of whom are power figures in the entertainment business. The Hollywood wives have *Vogue*-cover faces and, as revealed in the Jacuzzi, large and mathematically correct breasts. The New York power wives are often good-egg types, sort of old-fashioned tomboys. There are many wealthy Eastern do-gooders with or married to a lot of money, and they quickly bring up their good works as a counterbalance to other revelations—about the country house, the tennis court, the horse that jumps, brilliant children who are going off to do admirable and hazardous work in developing countries. (The West Coasters don't bother counterbalancing anything.) As the ladies hungrily register with one another what they have in common, they still seem to be searching wistfully for something indefinable, perhaps a surprise.

The visual backdrop is inspired by Japanese culture—koi pool, rain chains, stone lanterns, sand gardens, water gardens, Zen meditation gardens, a wooden bridge that juts crookedly because "evil spirits go in a straight line." The overall ambience reflects the passions and the interests of Deborah Szekely, a cherubic, pink-cheeked, Brooklyn-born dynamo, and the widow of an ahead-of-his-time Hungarian philosopher and nature lover, Edmond Szekely. In 1939, the couple settled in the tiny village of Tecate, in Baja California, and started a health camp. People brought their own tents and paid seventeen dollars and fifty cents a week for the privilege of chopping firewood and helping to milk goats for cheese. Professor Szekely gave radical lectures lambasting cholesterol. The popularity of the camp grew especially with people from Hollywood, who then wanted a retreat with more privacy. So, in 1958, the Szekelys founded the Golden Door, with weeks limited to men only, women only, and couples only. Today, most of the weeks are for women only.

At the first dinner, the ladies introduce themselves and state why they've come to the Golden Door: "I came because I couldn't get into my bras." "I came to get away from my four children." "I came because my husband gave me this for my birthday." "I came to bond with my sister." They leave the first dinner feeling high on one another, high to be with women only, high to be away from their men, high to boast about those men. They learn an amazing lot about one another's husbands in only minutes, and then at 9:30 p.m. each goes to her room and to sleep.

The next day, reporting for the daily hike at dawn, the ladies are drinking mugs of freshly brewed coffee (black) and gulping Vitamin C tablets. They talk briefly about the howling coyote heard in the mountains. Their talk has the semblance of dialogue, but there is no back-and-forth. "Did everybody sleep through the coyotes?" one lady asks a companion, and the companion says, "I've got to call my husband's office, but it's too early in New York." "Nothing bothers me when I sleep," the first one says.

Their preoccupation with "I" and "me" seems to rule out any interest in hearing answers to questions. In pairs, as they do their hamstring and quadriceps stretches, arms around each other's shoulders, one lady says to her partner, "I was going to do the five-mile hike, but now I think I'll do the three." "I never have jet lag," the partner replies. The warm-up exercises end with an ever cheery, seemingly euphoric fitness guide reading one of Deborah Szekely's favorite Japanese-flavored aphorisms: "Success is not an end; it is a journey," or "The intellect is always fooled by the heart." The ladies listen blankly to the aphorisms, make no comment, and turn quickly to the business at hand.

As they head up the mountain, they pay little attention to the surrounding purple daylilies, the orange poppies, the baby daisies. They walk fast, seriously, heel to toe, and they continue talking, still adhering to the first-person singular. They identify further aspects of themselves. They talk more about their husbands. They outline for one another their husbands' routines—getting up early, being driven to work, outmaneuvering the other guy, obtaining courtside seats at basketball and hockey games, flying here and flying there, and running offices that efficiently deliver plane tickets and chauffeured cars to the ladies on request. Confidences abound. A West Coast lady tells an East Coast lady that her husband is Jewish and that being married to him is nice, because she's Irish-and-German, and Irish-and-German husbands are not as kind or as warmhearted as her Jewish husband. The East Coast lady responds by telling a long story about how *her* husband is afraid of cats, but she *understands* his fear of cats. Both ladies look as though they are communicating. Talking all the way up the mountain seems to take no toll on the ladies' wind or stamina. At the top of the trail, high-spirited fitness guides offer water and slices of oranges from the Golden Door's own trees. On the way back down, the ladies talk about food, about the breakfast that awaits them in their rooms on their return, at seven-thirty—today it is Baked Apple with Seven Grains, Raisins, Cinnamon, and Honey Served with Orange Slices. They talk about the lunch ahead of them—Chilled Cucumber Soup with Mint and Parsley, Green Lentil Salad on Bibb with Green Beans, Sweet Corn, Diced Vegetables, and Balsamic Vinaigrette, and Long Stemmed Garden Strawberries. "I miss chewing," one of the bonding sisters, both Golden Door repeaters, says to the other.

By Wednesday, the ladies are demonstrating much affection for and pride in one another. In fact, quite a lot of bonding is going on. Everybody seems to share in a general exhilaration; even the oldies and the fatties are getting in on it. Nobody has worn any makeup for three days. Everybody respects potassium. Everybody looks cleaner. Everybody has had a daily herbal wrap, a daily facial, and a daily body massage. Everybody will do more: country-line dancing, yoga, ballet, slide aerobics, tap dancing, self-defense, wreathmaking with herbs and flowers, nutrition lectures, and a tour of the herb garden. Digestive systems are working splendidly. Adrenaline is flowing. The atmosphere is bursting with good will. Both Easterners and Westerners express pride and joy in the oldie giving her Ruby Keeler all in aerobic renditions of "There's No Business Like Show Business" and "Give My Regards to Broadway." Nobody has as much as mentioned a husband all day.

By Thursday, though, the ladies are letting go with some negative remarks about men in general and husbands in particular. They are saying things like "Some men think that having a baby is very glamorous. Hah hah." They are saying things like "Men are from Mars; we are from Venus." Quite a few ladies are saying yoga things to one another, like "The light in me sees the light in you." Some of the powerhouse husbands on the West Coast and on the East Coast are coming in for complaints from their wives. An oldie who is also a fatty as well as a toughie says at the diner table, "At home, we have a condo. We have a big pool. Everything. Does my husband use it? No!" "The light in me sees the light in you," one of the fortyish ladies says. "You'd better believe it," the old toughie says.

On Friday, however, everybody is all business re the body. The talkers on the morning hike are muted. The bonding has become visibly loosened as each lady tends to herself. Saturday night, the ladies, manicured, pedicured, hairdressed, tighter, lighter, firmer, are having their farewell dinner of California Gold Salad with Grapefruit, Avocado, Edible Flowers, and Garden Greens and Grilled Prawns with Garlic and Ginger on Portobello Mushrooms, Wilted Spinach, and Couscous. Prizes are given out—for Hiking Maniac, for Pumping Iron Icon, for Most Active Newcomer, for Ms. Fred Astaire. There is a lot of laughter. The ladies hug, kiss, go through motions of exchanging addresses and telephone numbers. But they are retreating from one another. Almost every lady makes a point of saying loudly that waiting impatiently at home is her husband.

Susan Sheehan

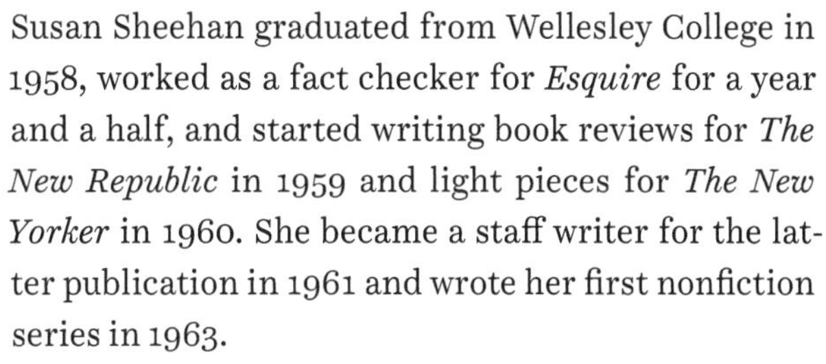

Susan Sheehan graduated from Wellesley College in 1958, worked as a fact checker for *Esquire* for a year and a half, and started writing book reviews for *The New Republic* in 1959 and light pieces for *The New Yorker* in 1960. She became a staff writer for the latter publication in 1961 and wrote her first nonfiction series in 1963.

In 1965, Sheehan flew to Jakarta to marry Neil Sheehan, a *New York Times* foreign correspondent she had met in New York a few months earlier. In the summer of 1965, he was transferred to Saigon, where Sheehan wrote her first book, *Ten Vietnamese*. Her husband was transferred to the Washington bureau of the *Times* in 1967.

Sheehan continued to write Talk of the Town stories and occasional pieces for such publications as the *Times*, *The Boston Globe*, and *Washingtonian*, but spent most of her time writing books, which were printed in their entirety in *The New Yorker*. *A Welfare Mother*, published in 1976, won a Sidney Hillman award. *A Prison and a Prisoner*, published in 1978, received the American Bar Association's Silver Gavel Award. *Is There No Place on Earth for Me?*, published in 1982, won the Pulitzer Prize for general nonfiction. Her subsequent books include *Kate Quinton's Days, A Missing Plane,* and *Life for Me Ain't Been No Crystal Stair.*

She has received fellowships from the Guggenheim Foundation, the Woodrow Wilson Center for Scholars, and the Open Society Institute. She served as the chair of the Pulitzer Prize nominating jury for general nonfiction in 1988 and 1994, and as a member of that jury in 1991.

Kid, Twelve

The Tomberlind family represents millions of America's working poor. They're not on welfare, don't live below the poverty line. And yet they struggle every day to get by.

On a brisk Saturday afternoon in March, Brian Tomberlind, age twelve, sets off for the Hickory Hollow Mall just outside Nashville, with his mother, Penny Proctor, and his best friend, Carl. Brian's father, Nathan Tomberlind, stays at home, lying on the living-room sofa wrapped in a blanket. He has hepatitis C. Five months of interferon shots, the only approved treatment for the grave illness, have not put it in remission; they just made him feel weaker. "Nathan probably wouldn't go to the mall with us even if he felt normal," Penny says. "He don't like shopping when he ain't got money to spend. Me and Brian don't go often enough to get our hopes up, but we like looking around." Brian enjoys going to places like malls with his mother, and he gives her money for gas from his earnings, if she needs it, to get there. Penny is more at ease with herself than Nathan is, and this quality translates into ease with her son. When Brian is away from Nathan, he relaxes and seems to forget the troubles of his house.

Penny parks the family's black Mazda pickup and walks with the boys to the front of the Castner Knott department store; they giggle as they pass through the women's lingerie section on their way to a tier of small shops that line the mall's interior. At Pass Pets, the boys admire a variety of pedigreed dogs in glass cages and a selection of rats; they try in vain to coax the store's parrot to talk; they stop at a showcase of Teddy-bear hamsters and an adjacent showcase of green iguanas. The showcases are open on top. Ignoring numerous "Do Not Pick Up" signs, Brian reaches in, plucks a hamster out of its cage, and suspends it over the iguana cage. "Brian, don't be doing that," Penny says. "If you drop it in with them lizards, the hamster could have a heart attack and die." The hamster wriggles, and Brian accidentally does drop it in among the iguanas. Penny looks scared.

"Them iguanas is vegetarians," Carl assures her, and then says to Brian, "Their tongues don't hurt you. They would get you with their tails." Brian reaches in for the hamster and puts it back where it belongs.

At a store called the World of Science, Brian and Carl inspect talking jigsaw puzzles, kaleidoscopes, Spin Master devil sticks, and glow-in-the-dark stars. "This is my favorite store in the mall," Brian says. "It's got cool stuff." Brian is a lanky kid (he's five feet two inches tall and weighs ninety-eight pounds) with indigo eyes, angular features, and fine long hair that has a home-cut look—Penny snips it with her scissors.

At Brian's second-favorite mall store, Spencer Gifts, he tries on a purple cap with a visor in front and a blond ponytail in back. "You look cute," Carl says, and tries on a headpiece with spiky "Wayne's World" hair in back. "*You* look cute," Brian retaliates.

The boys proceed to a shelf filled with Old Fart Slippers, X-rated greeting cards, Whipped Creme Body Topping, and bottles of PMS pills. "You-all know you can't look in there," Penny says, and then asks, "Brian, what does PMS mean?"

"Poor Man's Suffering," he replies. "I heard it on TV." He knows that PMS really stands for "premenstrual syndrome," because he studied sex ed last year in fifth grade and because his parents are forthright with him about the biological facts of life. When Brian was ten, Penny thought she heard him ask her what a condo was. "It's like a town house," she replied. "No, Mama, a condom," he said. She catalogued its virtues.

Brian asks Penny for five of the ten dollars she owes him. He earned the money two weeks ago at a construction site by picking up pieces of drywall and insulation for Sam, a man his father worked for when he was still healthy enough to work. Brian lent the ten dollars to Penny because she needed "money to run on." He buys a can of green Super String 2 for three dollars. He buys a space-age ice cream for two dollars, and offers Carl and Penny pieces of his treat.

"It ain't cold," Penny says. "You could of saved the money."

"But I wanted it," he says.

"Stuff like that amazes Brian," she says. "He ain't had money lately, so when he gets some he spends it quick."

When Penny and Brian return home, Nathan is still wrapped in a blanket on the sofa. Always a thin man—he is five feet nine and used to weigh a hundred and fifty-five pounds—he is down to a hundred and thirty-five pounds. "I got fever and chills real bad," he says. "That medicine ain't making me better, it's making me worse." He shifts to his son. "Brian, what about your multiplication tables?"

Penny Proctor, who is thirty-three, and Nathan Tomberlind, who is thirty-six, did a lot of "drinkin' and druggin'" from the time they were in their early teens until Brian was six. In March 1990, while Nathan was in jail for driving under the influence, he decided to sober up; he went through a treatment program while incarcerated. Penny stopped using on her own. She had done less drinking than Nathan after she discovered she was pregnant and after Brian's birth. Moreover, she had never injected herself with drugs. "I'll be honest with you, I think I got hepatitis C from dirty needles," Nathan says.

Nathan had always had a bad temper and was prone to moodiness, but his temper got worse after he learned that he had the illness, in the fall of 1994. His moods darkened as well, and Brian felt even more edgy around his father. Nathan's illness and his inability to work had given him more time to focus on his son. Several months ago, part of Brian's homework was to put thirty words "in 'ABC' order" and then define them. He borrowed a classmate's completed assignment, "not because I couldn't do it but to get it done faster," and went into his room after school. He sat on his bed—he doesn't have a desk—copying away. When Nathan entered his bedroom, Brian covered the paper. "Give it to me, Bubba," Nathan said. It was the second time Brian had borrowed his classmate's homework but the first time he had been caught. Nathan telephoned the school principal, who summoned Brian to his office. "You're one of our best students," the principal told him. "If we didn't have people like you at school, the school would be bad. You know your daddy loves you or he wouldn't have done this. Don't do it again, or you'll be in major-league trouble." Nathan kept Brian indoors for several afternoons after the cheating episode. Asked if he had learned his lesson, Brian answered, "Yeah. I know if I cheat I'll be punished."

Nathan's current obsession is Brian's failure to memorize his multiplication tables. He is determined that Brian will master them before the last day of sixth grade. Brian has trouble with math and is lazy about learning multiplication. On this late-March afternoon, when Nathan asks him what six times six is, he doesn't know. He seems to hope that Nathan will forget about multiplication between March and the end of May.

On Sunday morning, the Tomberlinds dress casually. Brian is wearing a green T-shirt with a white Nike swoosh logo, which he bought with most of the money Sam gave him for his birthday the previous month. Nathan drives from their house, in south Nashville, to Cumberland Heights treatment center in the city's rural outskirts, where the family attends spiritual services.

In December 1994, the Tomberlinds had a brief relapse. Nathan started smoking marijuana, Penny smoked a joint and, after an operation on her foot, started taking more pain medication than the doctor had prescribed for her; Nathan helped himself to Penny's pills. "I went back to AA on December 29—that's my birthday—and picked up a desire chip," Nathan says. "I'd been over four years sober, from 1990 to 1994, but in 1995 I couldn't get past my thirty-day chip." There was a crisis in August, 1995. Nathan hit Brian with a belt—hard. Penny left the house, taking Brian with her to the home of one of her sisters. Nathan smashed three glass tables and two lamps, broke some dishes, and drank for three days.

"I hit bottom," Nathan acknowledges. His remorse led him to spend two weeks in treatment at Cumberland Heights. After the first week, he telephoned Penny and begged her to join him. "Baby, this is our opportunity to get straightened out and work through our problems," he said. Penny's boss gave her a week off so that she could commute to Cumberland Heights for family treatment. "I learned a lot about myself at Al-Anon," Penny says. "I learned how sick I was, how much I needed to be my own person, that I had to stand up for myself when Nathan yelled at me or tried to switch words around in my head, and that I couldn't put my sobriety on his."

After two weeks, the Tomberlinds continued treatment at a Cumberland Heights center in their neighborhood. Penny asked their counselor,

Joy, if she could bring Brian with them. "At first, Joy said she didn't think an eleven-year-old would have the patience to sit still for two hours, but he was real quiet and he participated," Penny says.

"When I was asked to give a 'feeling word,' I did," Brian says. "I said I was scared when my parents started back using after four years, especially of Dad's cussing and yelling, and angry when they didn't listen to me, and glad when Dad went into treatment. I thought it would have a good result, because when he did it before it worked for a long time. And I learned that a lot of other people had troubles."

Joy told Penny that Brian astounded her—that he had handled a rough situation with a wisdom beyond his young years, and with a forgiving nature. "He's a kid hero," Joy said.

Sometimes the Tomberlinds eat a big buffet dinner at Cumberland Heights, but it costs six dollars apiece, and on this mild Sunday they don't have the money, so they go home and eat a big dinner, most of which has been simmering in Penny's Crock-Pot for five hours. Brian has an ample plateful of pot roast, turnip greens, carrots, potatoes, onions, tomatoes, peaches, and bread. "I like pickles, lemons with salt, Brussels sprouts, squash, okra, cabbage, corn, green beans, strawberries, and coconuts, and Nana's breakfasts," he says.

Nana is Nathan's mother. "She's the only relative I got who ain't messed up," Brian says. This spring, two of Penny's sisters, Nathan's only brother, and a cousin of Brian's were in jail for drug-related offenses.

Some of Brian's Super String 2 has got caught in the blades of the living-room ceiling fan. "Brian, get it off," Nathan says. "I told you not to do it, you don't listen, and you're stubborn, just like me." After Brian steps up on the coffee table, reaches up, and removes the strands, Nathan appends a "Thank you." Brian cleans his bathroom (a weekly chore), wheels his racing bike out of the storage room, and pedals across the street to Carl's house.

The Tomberlinds live in a new eleven-hundred-square-foot ranch house with gray vinyl siding, which they are buying under the auspices of a Nashville community organization that is trying to keep their neighborhood from turning as commercial and desolate as an adjacent section. The house is on a street with other modest homes, public housing, and trailers. They live within earshot of the Nashville Speedway USA, and on weekends they hear the roar of NASCAR races. Saturday nights, two neighbors tend

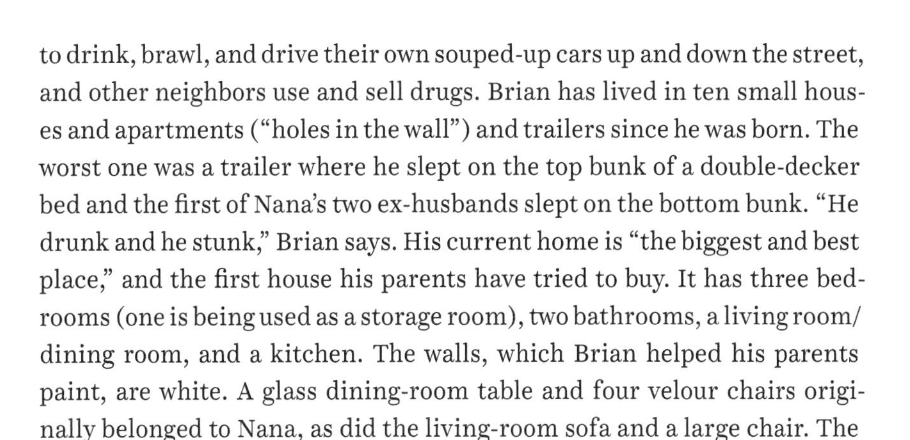

to drink, brawl, and drive their own souped-up cars up and down the street, and other neighbors use and sell drugs. Brian has lived in ten small houses and apartments ("holes in the wall") and trailers since he was born. The worst one was a trailer where he slept on the top bunk of a double-decker bed and the first of Nana's two ex-husbands slept on the bottom bunk. "He drunk and he stunk," Brian says. His current home is "the biggest and best place," and the first house his parents have tried to buy. It has three bedrooms (one is being used as a storage room), two bathrooms, a living room/dining room, and a kitchen. The walls, which Brian helped his parents paint, are white. A glass dining-room table and four velour chairs originally belonged to Nana, as did the living-room sofa and a large chair. The few books the family owns are on the bottom rung of the TV stand, next to the VCR.

On Sunday afternoon, Brian and Carl ride their bicycles until Penny and Lisa, Carl's mother, are ready to go walking. They load the bikes—Brian's Mongoose Menace and Carl's Mongoose Expert—into the back of the black truck and drive a short distance to a track at an abandoned school. Penny, who is five feet seven and has long, fluffy, layered brown hair, has been overweight since her teens. Since she and Lisa started walking for thirty minutes a day several months ago—most weekends and most weekdays after Penny gets home from work— her weight has dropped from 220 pounds to 207. Brian welcomes a brief change of scene. Sunday evening his supper is crackers with peanut butter from a large can labeled "Donated by the people of the U.S.A. for Food Assistance Program," a surplus-food commodity that Nana's first ex-husband receives and passes along to him. Brian watches a video, one of four that Penny, after attending Overeaters Anonymous, rented for the weekend for four dollars and eighty-six cents. Although Penny is more concerned about her weight than about relapsing into drugs, pills, or alcohol, she and Nathan both go to a Cumberland Heights aftercare program one evening a week, and Nathan goes alone to three AA meetings a week. At nine, Brian looks at the clock, hugs and kisses his parents, and says, "Good night, I love you, sweet dreams, and say your prayers."

On Monday morning, Nathan drives Penny to work. Since Brian was three, she has operated machines for a company that manufactures T-shirts, working "from eight-thirty to four-thirty and any overtime I can get." Then

Nathan drops Brian off at Nana's apartment for breakfast and goes on to keep a doctor's appointment. Brian quickly and quietly puts away three fried eggs, two strips of bacon, three biscuits, and a glass of milk, carries his plate to the sink, and lies down on the living-room sofa to watch TV. He likes watching TV at his grandmother's. "We don't got a cable or a remote control at home," he says, hopscotching the channels from *Family Challenge* to *Let's Make a Deal* and on to *Rugrats*. At eight-fifteen, Nana drives Brian to Glenview Elementary School, which has 363 students in kindergarten and grades three to six. Grades one and two are held at another school, because of a complicated court order desegregating Nashville's schools.

At the end of the 1994–95 school year, Glenview was 47 percent white, 44 percent black, 6.6 percent Hispanic, and 1.6 percent Asian. Approximately 25 percent of the students are bused from an inner-city housing project, and the majority of them are from single-parent homes. One of the four excuses that Glenview deems legitimate for an absence is "illness in the family requiring temporary help from the child." Glenview is a Title I school, one that qualifies for congressionally funded assistance, because it is among the schools that have a high concentration of children in poverty, meaning children eligible for free or reduced-price lunches—63 percent of the students, in Glenview's case. (Title I money and programs date back to 1965, as part of Lyndon B. Johnson's War on Poverty.)

Brian Lee Tomberlind is one of a 1.908 million twelve-year-old boys living in the United States. Like the overwhelming majority of them, he is white (80 percent) and he attends a public school (89 percent). In 1995, Penny earned $18,023 and Nathan $3,700. Those earnings, of $21,723, put the Tomberlinds in the bottom quarter of American wage earners but above the poverty line, which was $12,156 for a family of three last year. The Tomberlinds receive no subsidies from the federal government, but since Nathan's illness was diagnosed he has been on TennCare, a program that Tennessee created as an alternative to Medicaid, the federally financed health insurance for the poor and the diabled.

As a member of a three-person household with an income below $23,292, Brian qualifies for reduced-price breakfasts and lunches at Glenview, but Penny prefers to give him full-fare lunch money—a dollar and fifteen cents per day— to spare him the embarrassment that she

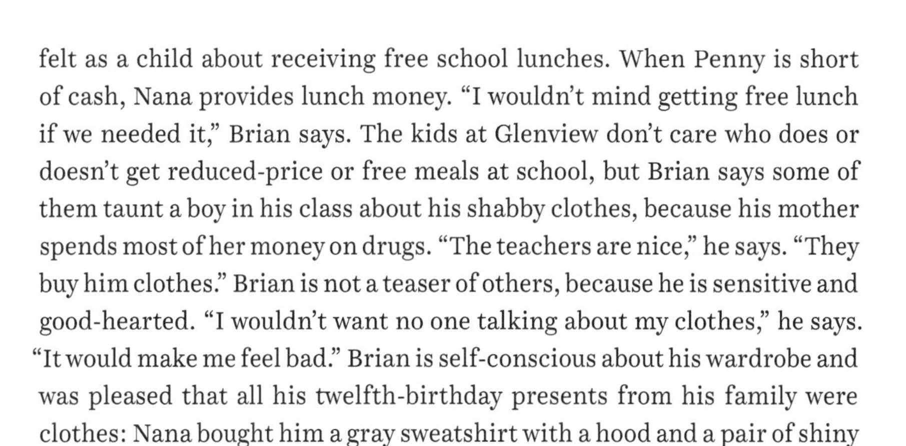

felt as a child about receiving free school lunches. When Penny is short of cash, Nana provides lunch money. “I wouldn’t mind getting free lunch if we needed it,” Brian says. The kids at Glenview don’t care who does or doesn’t get reduced-price or free meals at school, but Brian says some of them taunt a boy in his class about his shabby clothes, because his mother spends most of her money on drugs. “The teachers are nice,” he says. “They buy him clothes.” Brian is not a teaser of others, because he is sensitive and good-hearted. “I wouldn’t want no one talking about my clothes,” he says. “It would make me feel bad.” Brian is self-conscious about his wardrobe and was pleased that all his twelfth-birthday presents from his family were clothes: Nana bought him a gray sweatshirt with a hood and a pair of shiny navy nylon pants, and Penny bought him a pair of jeans. At any given time, he has about a dozen outfits in his closet and three pairs of sneakers—usually last season’s model of a name brand bought for forty dollars or less at a discount shoe store.

There are twenty-nine students in Brian’s homeroom. Two are currently in foster care—one girl because her father is in prison for murdering her mother; another girl spent last year in foster care. Several live with grandmothers, several with mothers and “bad stepfathers,” many with mothers and “mean boyfriends,” and many with single mothers. A few have been sexually abused. Very few live with their biological mother *and* father, as Brian does now. He was born Brian Lee Proctor and delivered by a midwife at Metropolitan Nashville General, a public hospital. He lived with his mother’s family off and on until he was three. His parents married when he was four and a half, and his surname was then changed to Tomberlind. His parents occasionally separated, Brian always staying with Penny, but they got back together quite soon. Glenview calls itself a “high-transit” school. Of the twenty-nine boys and girls now in Brian’s sixth-grade homeroom, only six others have been there since third grade, as he has.

Although Brian’s situation is singular, his life and the lives of his classmates are representative of the few-frills lives of children of the working poor. The farthest that Brian has ever been from Nashville is Myrtle Beach, South Carolina, where he, his parents, and Nana spent a weekend in 1993. Middle-class customs are not ones he takes for granted. So far, he has had only three “cake birthdays”—birthday parties when he could invite other kids over for cake, ice cream, and fruit punch. And yet Brian

Tomberlind is one of the three or four most fortunate youngsters in his homeroom, in that he has two parents who, despite the serious mistakes of their young years, have overcome their addictions: two parents who have stayed together and want Brian to have a better life than they have, and are working toward this goal—Penny by holding down a steady job and providing as many good times for him as she can, and Nathan by keeping him from such temptations as cheating and by trying to motivate him, sometimes by persuasion and sometimes by threats or punishment, to be a more diligent student. To Nathan, making Brian learn his multiplication tables is a symbol of the small victories that are possible in his world, and that are no less important for being small and thus perhaps attainable.

On a breezy Monday morning, Ms. Grant—an attractive fifty-three-year-old transplanted Californian, with a daughter who works as a lawyer in Pasadena—who is Brian's sixth-grade homeroom teacher and is also his reading and spelling teacher, greets her students as they arrive, with "Hi, honey" and "Hi, sweetie." She asks how their weekends went and where their homework assignments that were originally due on Friday are. Brian and a number of his classmates hand theirs in. Others make excuses: "My mother made me clean my whole room," "I had to take care of my little sister," "My mother said I didn't have to do all of it," "I don't got none."

"You don't got *none*?" Ms. Grant asks.

"I don't have any," the last kid says as Ms. Grant pencils check marks next to the names of the non-homework-doers on a piece of paper. The students know the rules: ten homework checks (or behavior checks) and they're ineligible to attend the Incentive Party held every other Friday for the virtuous. If they turn the homework in late, though, the checks will be erased. "The bottom line is I want them to do their work," Ms. Grant says.

"I can't believe a parent wouldn't let a child do his homework," Brian says, almost wistfully, in a low voice to a friend. Nathan has recently told Brian that he can no longer go out to play after school on Mondays ("He wants me to settle in after the weekend") or Wednesdays ("It's the night my parents go to aftercare and I go along and sit in the cafeteria watching TV and drawing while they're in meetings"). Less play equals more time for homework in general and math in particular.

At eight-forty-five, a student in the Glenview office asks the students over the intercom to please get ready for morning announcements.

First, the students observe "a moment of silence," mandated by the State of Tennessee. During the silence, some crack their knuckles, some doze off. After they recite the Pledge of Allegiance, they chant the Glenview Attitude Pledge, fifteen inspirational lines ("I know I'm capable of success / I am a learner and I can achieve / It's in myself that I must believe") composed by Ralph M. Thompson, who has been the school's principal since the fall of 1992. Next comes the vocabulary word of the week ("'lavish'—hard work can lead to a lavish life style"), and a few reminders ("Please bring your school-picture money to the cafeteria"). By eight-fifty-five, Ms. Grant has taken attendance, and she now asks her class to line up. The students move single file, in alphabetical order, along a hallway wall to their first Monday class—Computers.

Glenview's computer room has twenty-nine Packard Bell computers, but ten of them are in disrepair, so the kids usually "partner up." They are not proficient on the computers; like Brian, twenty-four of his classmates have no computers at home, and they attend Computer class only twice a week. Today, they are not going to use the computers, because their teacher believes they need help with capitalization more urgently. In a few weeks, they will be taking annual achievement tests that are part of the Tennessee Comprehensive Assessment Program—the TCAPs, the tests are called—and Glenview wants its students to perform well. In a booming voice, the computer teacher reminds the class emphatically that days of the week, months of the year, street addresses ("like Animal Lane"), and proper names begin with capital letters.

Tuesdays through Fridays, Brian has Math (all academic subjects are taught four times weekly), but on Mondays his next period is Reading. Ms. Grant says she wants everyone to choose a subject for a research report on an African American man or woman—"and forget Michael Jordan or Michael Jackson and any other figures from the world of sports or entertainment." She goes through the five steps of the report, which range from "brainstorming" to "bibliography." When Brian has trouble coming up with a subject, someone proposes Thurgood Marshall, the first African American on the Supreme Court. He asks what the Supreme Court is. He has heard of President Clinton but doesn't know when he was elected or which political party he belongs to. He has no idea where Bosnia and Israel are.

The students' discipline is good in Reading. If Ms. Grant doesn't like something she notices—for example, a girl wearing a low-cut dress, exposing cleavage—she tells the student that she is in violation of Glenview's dress code. The girl goes to the school office without protest, borrows a T-shirt and wears it over the offending dress the rest of the day. (Most of the girls in the class are tall, a few are overweight, all wear bras.) When Ms. Grant spots a boy chewing gum, she pronounces his name deliberately and says, "You need to spit the gum out." He complies. (The boys come in a wider range of sizes, from small and slight to tall and heavy.)

Ms. Grant, who also taught Brian in third grade, is his favorite teacher, and he considers her a friend. This February 14, he spent all the money Nathan could afford to give him on a big Valentine's Day balloon for her. On Brian's birthday, she handed him five dollars and a card in a report-card envelope. Brian doesn't realize that she gives five dollars to each of her sixth graders on his or her birthday.

On Monday, Reading segues into DARE, which stands for Drug Abuse Resistance Education, a nationwide program. It is taught by Officer Bumpas, a uniformed Metro Nashville police officer, packing gold jewelry and a .38-caliber revolver. One Monday, she leads the class—she addresses the children as "sir" and "ma'am"—in a discussion of the ways in which people are pressured by the advertising media. She mentions products that are endorsed by celebrities and moves on to those with snob appeal. A student cites an ad for Grey Poupon mustard. Brian loves commercials. He raises his hand and offers another example—a commercial for Viennetta ice cream. "It shows fancy people's hands, and the women wearing pearl bracelets," he says. "There's fancy plates on the table, like china. And crystal cups, like wineglasses. And silver—it looks real. I'd like to try the ice cream, but not for the snob appeal, just because it looks good." In the category of "Having Fun," the DARE workbook shows a boy on skis, with the caption "Have a beer." Officer Bumpas asks what the picture shows and what it fails to show. Brian's hand is air-bounced again. "It shows that in order to have fun you have to have a beer," he says. "It doesn't show if you're up on a ski slope with a can of beer you wouldn't ski well. Beer would make you mess up more or make you slower. You'd be better off without it." It is not a coincidence that Brian is more vocal in DARE than in any other class.

The last morning class is Language. One Monday, the teacher struggles to teach prepositions; another Monday, she wages a losing battle to teach the difference between "can" and "may." The students don't pay attention, and start talking to one another.

"Is there any reason you're acting like this?" the teacher inquires of a girl who has been restyling another girl's hair.

"Yeah, because we're bored," the girl answers.

The lunchroom is noisy. Brian eats his corn dog and baked potato, drinks his milk and his orange juice ("Sometimes there's Jell-O, but today orange juice is the dessert"), and talks to two classmates about basketball.

In Social Studies, the class is studying the Renaissance. Brian and his classmates read that Leonardo da Vinci painted *The Last Supper*, and Michelangelo painted the Sistine Chapel. Asked if learning about new artists in sixteenth-century Italy has meaning for him, he says "Knowing about the Renaissance makes me feel better, because it makes me feel smarter."

Science, Monday's last academic subject, has always been Brian's favorite. "I like making things and experimenting, and I collect rocks," he explains. The teacher distributes compasses, many of which don't point north. "I think some fifth graders stuck magnets in them and messed them up," Brian suggests.

From two-thirty to three o'clock every day, Brian's class goes to Physical Education. One Monday, the P.E. instructor, Mr. Majors, who is a former college football player, explains cardiovascular fitness. Brian excels at P.E. "In fifth grade, I won an award for being second-fittest in the whole school," he recalls. "We did pushups, pullups, situps, and we ran. I think I'm fit because I play a lot."

If Brian sees a fight on the way home, he avoids it. He has the gift of minding his own business—a useful gift for gliding through a Glenview day.

At the Tomberlinds' dining table in the afternoon, Brian's approach to homework is to dispose of it as quickly as possible. When his spelling assignment entails putting thirty vocabulary words into sentences, he spells the vocabulary word correctly but is careless about the spelling of other words he uses in his made-up sentences. "That pieace of cake is 'irresistible,'" he prints. (He has trouble writing in cursive.) And "Jason allways has to 'complicate' things." He avoids thinking up ways to use difficult words in sentences, and often puts the vocabulary word into a simple question, as in "What does 'predominant' mean?" and "What does 'gallant' mean?" He says he sees no point in trying harder: "Ms. Grant just looks at the homework and if you've used the spelling words you get an A. If you haven't, you get an F."

Nathan doesn't check Brian's homework, but he takes out the multiplication flash cards and asks Brian what seven times eight is. Brian hesitates, then gives an incorrect answer. Though Nathan appears angry, he doesn't preach to Brian, as he often does. Nathan was supposed to have an interferon shot yesterday and postponed it until today. Now, still dreading its side effects, he goes into the bedroom and prepares to give himself the shot.

Later, father and son discuss the fact that Glenview permits corporal punishment. Penny and Nathan have given their consent for Brian to receive it, if necessary, but Mr. Thompson has cut way back on it—from more than two hundred paddling to twenty in his first year as principal, and thereafter to below a dozen. Mr. Thompson sometimes prevails upon the parents to come to school and do the paddling, which is limited to two licks with a nine-inch-long oval wooden paddle, kept in the school office. Brian has never been paddled, but he is well informed about the ritual. "I've heard the screams from the principal's office," he says. "The kids are usually hollering before they get there. You have to bend over and put your hands on the desk. They hit you on the butt. One boy was paddled by Mr. Thompson, because his mama wouldn't do it. She tooken up for him even though her child needed correcting."

Eakin Elementary School is six miles—and a social universe—away from Glenview. It has 709 children in grades from kindergarten through six and classrooms in two old brick buildings situated near Vanderbilt University. Real-estate ads attempt to attract homebuyers to the neighborhood with the words "Eakin school district," because Eakin is among the city's most sought-after public elementary schools. There aren't quite enough local children to fill it, so parents with educational ambitions for their children enter a lottery for the out-of-zone slots. Sixteen of the twenty-nine students in Mrs. Hyde's sixth-grade class at Eakin have attended Eakin since kindergarten, twenty since third grade.

Both schools offer friendly environments and employ highly regarded principals and teachers—Glenview's Ralph Thompson was selected Nashville's Principal of the Year for 1993–94, and an Eakin teacher was chosen Tennessee's Teacher of the Year for 1994–95. The schools are distinguished in part by their differences. Eakins is less racially diverse than Glenview (it is 24.9 per cent black), and it describes the parents of its students as "middle income," with only 17 percent of the students receiving free or reduced-price meals. There is no corporal punishment at Eakin, no moving from class to class or building to building in alphabetical lines. Discipline isn't a problem at Eakin. Twenty-two of Mrs. Hyde's twenty-nine sixth graders have home computers; most are knowledgeable about current world events; and a few are already talking about going to Ivy League colleges. By seventh grade, some will be attending private schools and others selective magnet schools. Only three of Glenview's seventy-five sixth graders will go to a magnet school.

Perhaps the most precise measurement of the socioeconomic advantages that Eakin's student body has over Glenview's shows up in the annual scores on the standard nationwide achievement tests, which are part of the TCAPs. In the spring of 1996, 9 percent of Eakin's sixth-grade students and 28 percent of Glenview's tested below average in Reading, Language, and Math (the national norm was 23 percent); 47 percent of Eakin's sixth graders and 65 percent of Glenview's tested average (the national was 54 percent); and 44 percent of Eakin's sixth graders and 7 percent of Glenview's tested above average in these skills (the national norm was 23 percent).

When Brian Tomberlind was in kindergarten, most of his grades were satisfactory. A teacher commented on his report card in April 1990, that he was still "a little unsure of his letters and some numbers," and urged, "Please work with him on this. He is a precious little boy." In first grade, when Brian first took TCAPs, he had mostly 4s and 5s in each skill the TCAPs tested, although in Science he scored a 9. (Scores in stanines 1 to 3 are below average, 4 to 6 average, 7 to 9 above average.) First grade is memorable to Brian "because I discovered there was no Santa Claus and I told all the other kids." In second grade, Brian's stanines, including Science, were mostly 4s and 5s. Toward the end of fifth grade, in April 1995, his scores were all average except in Language (top of the third stanine) and Reading (bottom of the seventh). A sentence at the bottom of Brian's Tennessee Comprehensive Assessment Program report in 1995 states, "The student's total battery score is better than about 53 percent of the national sample, and falls in the average range." This spring, he scored better than 66 percent of the national sample—still in the average range.

There are two children in Brian's homeroom who test above average and may therefore have a chance to overcome their disadvantaged situations and compete with the more privileged Eakin students. One is a first-generation Vietnamese boy with a gift for math and a cultural heritage of striving for academic success. The other is a black girl who loves to read. "I read after school, I read to the kids I babysit, and I read at night," she says. "My mother's worried about the electric, so I read in bed with just a night-light until eleven o'clock—my bedtime on school nights. My mother stays up until she sees my light go off. Weekends and summers, I can read as late as I want. I'm going to go to Vanderbilt."

While Brian isn't keen on reading, and his math TCAPs, in the thirty-ninth percentile, are subpar, Mr. Thompson thinks he has a number of qualities that will enable him to succeed—with or without a college education. "Most of our kids are in bad situations none of them are responsible for, and they show it," Mr. Thompson says. "Brian senses a lot of love from his father, his mother, and his grandmother. He's a consistent and resilient child, and he knows how to insulate himself from disappointments. He's a survivor, and he's got character. Conventional wisdom has it that this generation isn't going to do as well as its parents. Brian is going to be the exception."

Asked if he expects to finish high school, Brian says "Yes," with calm but firm conviction. And what about college? "It's a long time off. But I would like to go to art school."

A conversation with Brian on a recent Friday afternoon in the Tomberlinds' living room:

"Brian, do you know what bad words are?"

"Yes. My parents use them around the house, but they told me not to."

"Are you interested in girls?"

"Yes." He turns deep red.

"In girls you see on TV?"

"Mostly in girls I know. I took one girl to the movies when I was in third grade. Me and her sat in the front of the theater, my parents sat in the back. Last year, I took another girl to a roller rink, but I stopped asking girls on dates, because I'm shy."

"Do you like to talk on the phone?"

"No. It makes me tired. It makes my ear hot. Maybe I'm not used to it. We got our first phone maybe three years ago."

"Where would you like to travel?"

"To Florida to see the Pacific Ocean."

"What effect has your father's illness had on you?"

"We don't do a lot, because he don't feel like it. And I worry he'll have to go to a hospital."

"What do you like to watch on TV?"

"Reruns of *Seinfeld* and *Home Improvement* with Mama when she gets home, and *Roseanne*, *Martin*, and *America's Funniest Home Videos*. Sports."

"How do you feel about black people?"

"Same as I do about white people. There's some good and some bad."

"Who are some of the good black people you know?"

"My friend Jonathan across the street, lots of boys in my class, Mr. Thompson, Ms. Grant, Mr. Majors, and Officer Bumpas."

"What makes you happy?"

"When someone says nice things about me. When I get finished with my homework. When we go somewhere."

"What makes you unhappy?"

"When I can't go outside, but I'm not too unhappy, because I know it's not going to help me."

"How do you like being twelve?"

"I like it. I'm older. It's better than being eleven. You're taller. You can ride the go-carts at Snookers, out at Hickory Hollow Mall. At first when I got older and taller I didn't like not being able to play on the bars at Chuck E. Cheese no more."

"Are you looking forward to being thirteen?"

"Yes. I'll be a teenager."

"Will your life be better as you get older?"

"Yes. I'm going to work at Value Plus. I think you have to be fourteen or fifteen. I'll have money, and I could get more things that I want."

"What things are you having trouble getting right now?"

"A go-cart, but they cost between six and seven hundred dollars, and my mama still ain't paid Nana back the $240 she put on her credit card for my bike. And an *NBA Jam* game for the Super Nintendo that Sam gave me one Christmas. I only have two games for it—*Super Mario World* and *Super Mario All-Stars*."

"Will your life be better than your parents' lives?"

"I think so, because I'm never going to drink or do drugs. It's dumb. I seen what they done to my parents and most of my grandparents."

"Are you worried about the future?"

"Not really, because I'm going to go to art school and be an artist, and I hope I get to do it."

Penny, who has been fixing tacos for supper, has heard part of the conversation. "Nobody ever says they *want* to grow up to be a drug addict," she puts in. "I wanted to take care of mentally retarded people. I love my job, but my first two years there I didn't know how to use the machines right and I had two carpal-tunnel operations. It's so important for me to have Brian graduate from high school. Me and all six of my siblings dropped out. Brian's said he wants to be an artist since he was three and a half and done drawings and took them to his grandfather and said, 'Pay me.' But he needs something to fall back on. He'll find his way. There's decent jobs for good people with high-school diplomas. Brian's Nana graduated high school, and she's earning eleven dollars and twenty-one cents as a security officer on the two-to-ten shift. That's good money for a woman in Nashville. I'm going to get the mortgage on this house paid off and give the house to Brian and his wife. I have a 401K savings plan. I let the company hold back 3 percent of my pay—that's nine dollars a week. The company puts in twenty-five cents for every dollar I save. The man who explained the plan to us said the money would be reinvested and would grow to fifty-seven thousand dollars before I retire."

Nathan, who is smoking a cigarette after taking a shower, has also been listening. "I ain't never had no goals at twelve, but I didn't think of sitting around AA meetings," he says. "Roofing was OK but not steady. One job finishes, you got to find you another one. I don't want Brian to do that—Lord, no. I want him to be where he's warm in winter and cool in summer. I have dreams for Brian to get the best education he could—maybe, if he wanted, to go to college. I think there's better-paying jobs if a man can use his head instead of his physical strength."

After dinner, Brian is at the cleared-off dining table. He has paper, colored pencils, and the latest issue of the magazine *Lowrider* in front of him. He is looking at a drawing of a '47 Chevy and drawing his own version of it—on a slightly smaller scale and with tires that are square rather than round. "I guess my car has flat tires," he says.

Nathan is watching a video, and Brian goes into his room. It's furnished with a double-decker bed (Brian sleeps in the lower bunk and uses both mattresses on it, to make it more comfortable), a chest of drawers, a glass coffee table (its surface is cluttered with "my stuff"), a small TV, a stereo, and a radio. The room has a wide closet and a narrow window that faces a dog pen (occupied by the family dog until it got out and disappeared in February).

In April, Nathan stops giving himself interferon shots; his doctor agrees that they have not put the hepatitis C in remission. He doesn't regain any of the twenty pounds he has lost, but the chills and fever caused by the drug diminish, and his face is less pallid. He begins to receive monthly disability benefits, for which he filed in 1995, and which cover the family's phone and utility bills.

In the spring, Nathan no longer drives Penny to work and Brian to school—some mornings he can't get out of bed in time—but when he feels up to it he starts tilling a garden, goes fishing, or does some cooking. On Good Friday, he fixes a ham, and the day after he cooks "white beans with a bunch of ham and garlic in it." For Easter, he gives Penny money. "I bought me some underthings," she says. Penny's last clothing purchase, in late February, had been "three T-shirts, brand-new, and two pairs of jogging pants, at Goodwill, for a dollar eleven each." Penny grew up hard, with a father who worked, drank, and "tried to give us kids something for Christmas, even if it was a piece of fruit." Penny is caring and likeable—qualities that Brian has inherited. When money is tight, Penny does without and doesn't complain, and when there is a little extra she is grateful for it, as Brian is, too. In late March, an acquaintance of Nathan's gives Nathan and Brian some scrap aluminum, which Penny and Nathan sell at a recycling place for thirty dollars. Nathan and Brian give Penny the money for her birthday. She buys a pair of black Lycra bicycle shorts and a black T-shirt with Garfield the cat on it, at Wal-Mart. Brian earns twenty additional dollars doing jobs for Sam, the remodeler for whom Nathan used to work. Penny drives Brian to a flea market—Brian loves flea markets. He buys Nathan a lighter on a key chain for two dollars. "I hate it when Dad smokes, but he's always losing his," he says. He spends ten dollars panning for gold flakes and gems. "I really like to go panning, and this time I came up with a cut gem, black with a little orange on it, that's ready to be mounted on a ring for Mama," he says.

In May, Sam goes out of town for a week and offers the Tomberlinds the use of his houseboat. Nathan takes Brian out of school for two days, and

Penny joins them on the weekend. Nathan nags him about his multiplication tables, but Brian studies them only halfheartedly. On May 30, after Glenview's last full day of school, Penny tests Brian on his multiplication tables. She looks at the answers on the reverse side of her flash cards; her multiplication is iffier than Nathan's, and she is embarrassed that her ability to read is so limited. Brian gets most of the answers right. "I ain't as nervous around my mama," he says.

On May 31, there is school from 8:45 a.m. to 11:30 a.m. One boy's mother fetches him at ten-thirty, and he waves goodbye. His classmates say nothing. At eleven-thirty, Ms. Grant wishes her sixth graders a good summer and asks them to visit her classroom next year. They leave nonchalantly.

Nana fetches Brian, and they go out to eat at a Po Folks. Nathan has been napping at his mother's, and they bring him back the hamburger he requested. He eats it, and she leaves for work. The television set is on, and Nathan is watching a science program. "What's seven times nine?" Nathan asks Brian as the show ends and a *Columbo* rerun begins. "Seven times nine is..." It is obvious that Brian is stalling for time, but time doesn't buy him the correct answer. "Go sharpen a pencil and write down your times tables," Nathan says.

Brian goes to the kitchen and starts opening drawers, in search of a knife. Nathan thinks that he is taking too long—that he is watching *Columbo* instead of searching with due diligence—and slaps Brian hard and noisily on the leg. "Next time, it will be with a belt, Brian," he says. Brian is sobbing. Nathan flies into a rage. "You didn't sharpen the pencil fast enough! I saw you looking at the TV! You can con your mother, but you can't con me!" he shouts.

Brian answers that he wasn't watching TV and he had trouble finding the right knife.

Back talk angers Nathan. "I've asked you your multiplication tables for the last few months," he says, and he continues firing words at his son: "You know the consequences. I'm tired of talking. I'm tired of being so patient with you. I'm tired of your crying all the time. You just talk, you don't take no action. I'm tired of your bluff. You won't go outside and play." He sends Brian, still sobbing, off to a bedroom to write the multiplication tables.

"I'm tired of Brian's bullcrap," Nathan says. "I don't think he takes me seriously. It hurts me when I hurt him. I hurt my left hand with my thumb."

Asked if he'll hit Brian with his right hand next time, Nathan answers, "Yes." Asked if he doesn't think he hit Brian a little too hard, Nathan says, "A whipping never killed me. I think kids take advantage of their parents, just like I did. They take your kindness and your generosity for weakness." And the appropriateness of slapping Brian on the last day of school? "The timing was just the way it was supposed to be. As far as I'm concerned, he's out of sixth grade and started the seventh today. Seventh and eighth grade are important years, and rough ones. Brian has to settle down and do his work hisself. The teachers won't have the time to work with him. My dad didn't care. He was only around a little when I started seventh grade. That's when my grades went down and I started getting high. I don't want Brian turning out like me. When Brian gets eighteen, it's his choice, but he's going to mind me as long as he lives with me. Brian may convince my mama or Penny that he's not capable of learning his multiplication tables, but I think he's very capable of learning them."

Asked if the only important thing in life is that eight times nine is seventy-two, Nathan, who is half-watching *Columbo* and is calming down, says "It's hard being a parent."

Half an hour passes.

"Brian," Nathan calls to his son.

"What?" Brian asks, emerging from the bedroom with several pieces of paper, on which he has printed the multiplication tables more neatly than ever before.

"Brian, did I hurt your feelings?"

"Yes."

"I'm going to ask you those multiplication tables on Monday, and if you don't know them you'll stay indoors all summer."

Brian nods.

On Friday, at 4:30 p.m., Nathan and Brian pick up Penny at work, stop briefly at a drive-in bank where she cashes her weekly paycheck—her take-home pay is two hundred and eighty dollars—and drive quickly downtown. Nashville's annual four-day Summer Lights festival started Thursday, and the Tomberlinds, Nathan included, all wanted to go. They have a nice time listening to bands, watching street performers, and eating corn dogs, roast corn on the cob, fried peppers, and sausages. Brian goes from Penny to Nathan and back easily. He is not afraid of Nathan. They get home around eleven o'clock. Brian, who is double-jointed, does marvelous acrobatic stunts in the living-room floor. All three Tomberlinds enjoy his performance. "We often have good times with each other," Penny says. "We've learned how to argue less."

On Saturday morning, after going fishing, Nathan says, "I should have counted to ten and cooled off a little bit before I hit Brian yesterday. But on Monday if he doesn't know the multiplication tables he's going to stay indoors all summer."

On Monday morning, Nathan drives Penny to work and fixes breakfast for Brian—lots of pancakes and crisp bacon. "OK, Bubba," he says as they wolf down the meal. "What's seven times nine?"

"Seven times nine is sixty-three," Brian says, with conviction.

"And six times eight?"

"Forty-eight."

"What's nine times nine?"

"Eighty-one."

Victorious, Nathan hugs Brian. Victorious, Brian goes outside to play.

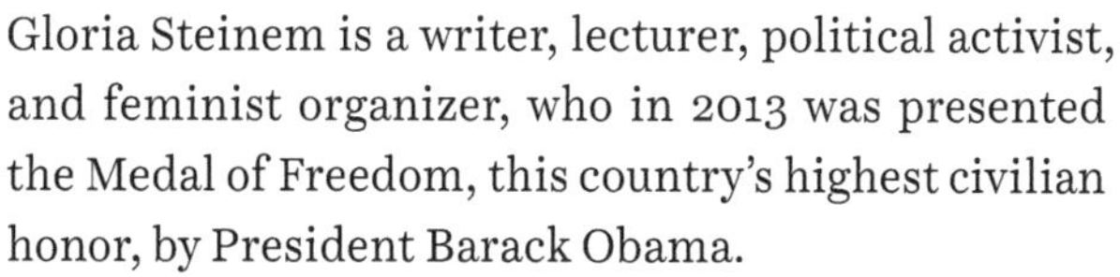

Gloria Steinem

Gloria Steinem is a writer, lecturer, political activist, and feminist organizer, who in 2013 was presented the Medal of Freedom, this country's highest civilian honor, by President Barack Obama.

Steinem cofounded *Ms.* magazine in 1972, and remained one of its editors for fifteen years. She continues to serve as a consulting editor and was instrumental in the magazine's move to join the Feminist Majority Foundation. She also helped found *New York* magazine, where she was a political columnist and feature writer. As a freelance writer, she has been published in *Esquire, The New York Times Magazine,* and publications around the world. She produced a documentary on child abuse for HBO and a feature film about the death penalty for Lifetime, and has been the subject of profiles on Lifetime, Showtime, HBO, and Makers: Women Who Make America. She is a co-founder of the Ms. Foundation for Women, the Women's Media Center, and a co-convener of Donor Direct Action. In 2009, she was awarded the Medal for Journalism by the James Weldon Johnson Institute for the Study of Race and Difference.

Her books include the bestsellers *Revolution from Within*; *Outrageous Acts and Everyday Rebellions*; *Moving Beyond Words*; *Marilyn: Norma Jean*; *As If Women Matter* (published in India); and *My Life on the Road.* Together with Amy Richards, she has produced for Viceland a 2016-17 series of eight documentaries on violence against women in countries around the world. Her writing has appeared in many anthologies and textbooks. She lives in New York.

Mrs. Kennedy at the Moment

An intimate portrait of Jackie Kennedy as she confronts difficult decisions in the year following the assassination of her husband, President John F. Kennedy.

After a privileged childhood; a reign as Debutante of the Year; an education at Vassar, the Sorbonne, and George Washington University; a brief career as an inquiring photographer; a long courtship with a man twelve years her senior who she feared "couldn't be less interested in me"; marriage to that same ambitious young senator; his several illnesses and near death; his campaign for the vice-presidency; the bearing of four children and the death of two; four years as the wife of a presidential hopeful; two years and ten months as the thirty-first First Lady of the United States; the witnessing of her husband's murder, and a full year of the rituals and restrictions of mourning, Jacqueline Kennedy, at thirty-five, must decide what to do with her life.

If Jack Kennedy had lived, the problem of how to spend the post–White House years (a problem he rarely discussed) would have been left to him, but his wife's solution was simple. "I'll just retire to Boston," she said, "and try to convince John Jr. that his father was once the president."

Her own special charisma plus the continuing political ambitions of the Kennedy family might have kept her from disappearing as quickly as a Mamie Eisenhower or Bess Truman (Robert Frost predicted after the Inauguration that Kennedy would be one of the few presidents in history who could never be thought of without also thinking of his wife), but there was nothing to indicate she would follow the Eleanor Roosevelt tradition either. Mrs. Kennedy's influence was that of a great beauty, a hostess, and a woman of taste, but she retained a certain boarding-school air ("She's the very best of that sheltered group," said a friend, "but she's still of the group") that made it difficult to take her seriously. No one was surprised when she confided breathily to a reporter: "Housekeeping is a joy to me, I feel this is what I was made for. When it all runs smoothly . . . when the food is good . . . the flowers look fresh . . . I have such satisfaction." Or when she sat, bored and unhappy, leafing through a copy of *Vogue* while her husband campaigned. Or when, in the White House, pregnancy kept her from attending a breakfast given in her honor by congressional wives, but not from going to New York that evening to see the ballet. Or when she explained at a press conference, "I really do not think of myself as the First Lady, but of Jack as president."

She seemed to be a lovely, well-bred girl who painted a little and wrote a little; whose early heroes—Diaghilev, Oscar Wilde, and Baudelaire—valued style at least as much as content; who, in the first winter she was married, took a course in American history to please her husband, but who much preferred eighteenth-century France ("American history is for men," she said); who, while First Lady, vacationed with some of Europe's less-loved capitalists; whose taste was good enough to bring a rare distinction to the White House, but no more eclectic than polite society would allow; who was, in short, the most worthwhile kind of ornament.

Sometimes, being apolitical was an asset. After a few halfhearted denouncements for her lack of involvement in women's peace groups, even the Soviets left her alone. White House correspondent Marianne Means described the galvanic effect she had on anti-American Venezuelan farmers "by appearing like a vision in a lime sheath and greeting them with a warm, simple speech in Spanish." The president was proud of "her concentration on giving historical meaning to the White House furnishings," and a little surprised that she managed the whole thing so well: "Mrs. Kennedy displayed more executive ability," he told a reporter, "than I imagined she had." (And she was working hard. Her mother, Mrs. Hugh Auchincloss, remembered a younger Jackie who wasn't interested in picking out so much as a chair for her room.) Pope John, who had been coached by his secretary to address her as "Madame," opened his arms and said "Jacqueline!" when he saw her; and Ludwig Bemelmans christened her "Cleopatra of the Potomac" after General de Gaulle put his glasses on to look at her during a state dinner, "and he is so vain that he doesn't know who is in front of him until his aide tells him." She held about twelve formal receptions a year more than Mrs. Eisenhower, entertained about twice as many state visitors, and got Pablo Casals to play in the White House in spite of our aid to Franco's Spain. "There hasn't been such a born giver of feasts in the White House," wrote Katherine Anne Porter, "since Dolley Madison."

But even when her nonpolitical accomplishments turned to pure political gold, she was still regarded as an ornament, a *salonnière* at heart.

Until the assassination.

From the moment she appeared in the bloodstained clothes she refused to change, she became a symbol of high tragedy and courage. "I'd always thought," said one rather cynical lady of the Washington press corps, "that there was nothing Mrs. Kennedy did that I couldn't have done better. I was wrong. I couldn't have gone through that funeral. For the first time, I find myself writing words like 'heroine' with a straight face."

The ceremonies ended, and she moved out of the White House and into retirement, but even her friends looked at her differently. "She's not," said one, "the brittle flower we all thought she was." ("It's just possible," said a journalist who had always scoffed at the value of good schools and "good" families, "that this country actually bred her. There's hope for us all.") Her house was surrounded by patient crowds who waited hours to catch a glimpse of her and then looked away when she appeared, as if ashamed to be caught intruding. "They just waited and waited," recalled a neighbor. "It was as if they were waiting for her to tell them what to do." More than Robert Kennedy or any other member of the family, the odd thaumaturgy of the Kennedy Administration seemed to have passed to her. "When the Kennedys lived here," said a White House guard, "nobody walked by without looking—they couldn't resist it, like people going by a mirror. It wasn't like that with the Trumans or the Eisenhowers, and it isn't with the Johnsons. Now, it's her house in Georgetown that they look at."

The thought of all that power going to waste was more than politicians could bear. Her year of mourning included wearing black and canceling all public appearances and official functions, but within a month after the assassination Mrs. Kennedy's future was being discussed nearly as much as President Kennedy's past. Dean Rusk suggested that she become a touring Goodwill Ambassador, and a Michigan lady legislator passionately advocated her appointment as ambassador to France, though the "biggest problem might be that . . . other nations might want someone of the same caliber." Clare Boothe Luce, with the questionable sincerity of a Goldwater Republican advising a Democrat, wrote an article proposing that Mrs. Kennedy rise to the podium at the Democratic Convention, make a dramatic plea, and force the delegates to give Robert Kennedy the vice-presidency. A politician from Boston suggested that Mrs. Kennedy be vice president herself. Civil rights leaders spoke of her becoming a kind of good-looking Eleanor Roosevelt who would lead Negro children into school, and give fireside, mother-to-mother talks on integration; and a few liberals daydreamed aloud, without much hope, that her marriage to Adlai Stevenson might make him a candidate again. Politicians who feared the power of her endorsement advised that she retire, as widows of other presidents have done, or stick to culture, or, at the most, run an international salon. Even those who thought her power was more moral than political had ambitious plans: an international newspaper column, a weekly show on Telstar, a campaign to beautify America, a foundation to aid young artists, an appointment as head of UNESCO.

In a pre-assassination article comparing the role of Mrs. Kennedy, then in the White House, to that of Mrs. Roosevelt, sociologist Margaret Mead wrote: "American society accords far greater leeway to widows than to wives—even permitting them to carry on activities initiated by their husbands, in whose shadows they were supposed to live quietly as long as their menfolk were on stage." The same Mrs. Kennedy who had been dismissed as an ornament was being urged to be a leader.

"This November twenty-second, when her retirement is over," said a State Department official, "Jackie could become, if she wanted to, the most powerful woman in the world."

In contrast to the attention lavished on her, the life Mrs. Kennedy was living in retirement seemed to be very simple, or at least very private. Newspapers, desperate for news of her, ran front-page photographs of her walking the dog, taking her daughter to school, or her son to his playgroup. Books and one-shot magazines on her life sold by the millions—*Jacqueline Kennedy: From Inauguration to Arlington*, and *Jacqueline*

Kennedy—Woman of Valor (Her Dreams As A Girl, Her Prayers As A Woman, Her Fears As A Mother)—and a nationwide poll showed that she was the most admired woman in the world. On the suspicion that she might have been pregnant when the president died, at least one magazine delayed a special issue for months, and gave up only after she was photographed in ski clothes in late March. *Time, Life,* and *Newsweek* wrote all they could find out about her daily routine which, minus the adjectives and padding, boiled down to the fact that she saw the children in the morning, answered correspondence or worked on plans for the Kennedy Library, played with the children in the afternoon, and sometimes had dinner with friends. The cover of a television semiannual promised "Jacqueline Kennedy: Her Future in TV" (the article said she didn't want one), and a movie magazine headlined "The Men Who Love Jackie Kennedy" (they turned out to be Lyndon Johnson, Dean Rusk, and others who had paid her sympathy calls). When she took John Jr. to a horse show where he was to ride his pony in the lead-line class, well-bred society ladies crowded around in an effort to hear what she was saying to her son. One finally managed it and reported back. What Mrs. Kennedy said was, "Keep your heels down."

Reporters were notified of what her press secretary, Pamela Turnure, called "milestone occasions"—visits to the president's grave with foreign dignitaries, an occasional appearance for the Kennedy Library, her appointment by President Johnson to the White House Preservation Committee—but the rest of her life was, as Miss Turnure said, "pretty insulated." She was surrounded by her protectors: all the members of the Kennedy family plus such old friends as artist William Walton, British Ambassador Sir David Ormsby-Gore and his wife, Mr. and Mrs. Ben Bradlee, Secretary of the Treasury Douglas Dillon and his wife, Franklin Roosevelt, Jr., Mr. and Mrs. Charles Bartlett, Secretary of Defense and Mrs. Robert McNamara, Michael Forrestal, and others.

"We all invited her to small dinners," explained one of that group, "but no matter which one of us gave it, the guest list was always pretty much the same—all friends from the old days—and the conversation always ended in reminiscing."

In the beginning, visitors noticed that her only photograph of the president was one taken while he watched a ceremony on the White House lawn shortly before he died. It showed him from the back. But, by midwinter, she was able to go through her husband's mementos to select "things I hope will show how he really was" for a touring exhibit, and to watch *The Making of a President*, a private screening of a television documentary of the 1960 campaign. (A witness said she looked teary, but "When the film showed Kennedy making wisecracks, she laughed. When he made serious points, she nodded in agreement.")

Still the small dinners continued. ("I never liked them too much before," she said frankly, "and I like them even less now.") Those close to her who felt she should be distracted as well as protected—especially her sister and almost full-time companion, Lee Radziwill—invited outsiders to entertain her, but the new guests were often so fearful of saying the wrong thing that they hung back and said nothing at all. A man described as a "young embassy type" spent an evening as her partner, and found himself reduced to asking politely if she had ever seen a bullfight. ("You just can't go through all that again," observed a guest. "It was like being right back at college.") A New York journalist who sat next to her at dinner found her starved for information. "She wanted to know if Richard Burton's *Hamlet* was good," he said, "and what Shepheard's was like, and which of several current books were worth reading and wouldn't make her sad."

By way of distraction, Mrs. Radziwill invited movie producer George Englund to stop in for a drink and some discussion of a Kennedy Foundation Dinner, on which he was an adviser. For further distraction, Mr. Englund brought along one of his actors, Marlon Brando. The three decided to go out for dinner, and asked Mrs. Kennedy to come along. ("It was very simple and spur-of-the-moment," explained Pamela Turnure. "They just didn't want to leave her there alone.") They chose what was later described by the press as "an Embassy Row Restaurant," The Jockey Club, because it was the only one in which Mrs. Kennedy, during her three years in the White House, had been able to have a private, reporterless meal. (She had lunched there with John Kenneth Galbraith, then ambassador to India, at the president's suggestion.) But this time it was not so private. Newspaper reporters were everywhere, Brando inquired about backstairs escape routes, and the restaurant manager offered to loan them his car, but it was too late. The story—down to the fact that Brando "smiled slightly as he lit cigarettes"—was carried by newspapers here and abroad.

The fact that she had chosen to make her first social appearance since the assassination with Mr. Brando (which was pretty much the way the no-explanation newspaper report made it appear) lifted the lid on other criticisms. And among those who believed that John F. Kennedy had not yet proven himself as a president, or that the Kennedy family was using the country's grief to continue its power, or that its power was not being used to advance the right causes, or that Mrs. Kennedy should have invited them to one of those small dinners, there had been a kind of underground current of criticism for some time.

That both Kennedy and Lincoln had been assassinated, for instance, was regarded as too small a basis for their identification; and some critics felt there was a clear and faintly sinister effort to identify them. (On her return from Dallas with her husband's body, Mrs. Kennedy had asked Chief-of-Protocol Angier Biddle Duke to find out how Lincoln had been buried, and the precedents he discovered during an all-night investigation were used as guideposts for the Kennedy funeral. Later, she arranged to have a Kennedy inscription added to that in the Lincoln Bedroom of the White House.) There was some resentment of the Eternal Flame she requested for his grave. When schools, bridges, airports, Cape Canaveral, a fifty-cent piece, and the National Cultural Center took on the Kennedy name, resentment grew. Fundraising for the Kennedy Library, the Telstar program celebrating what would have been Kennedy's forty-seventh birthday, the touring exhibit of Kennedy memorabilia, and the designation of his Brookline birthplace as a National Historical Landmark were all greeted as new proofs of excess.

One Washington newspaperman insisted that Kennedy himself—like the Roman Emperor who said on his deathbed, "I fear they will make a god of me"—would not have approved.

Not all the criticism was directed at Mrs. Kennedy. Some felt that the political ambitions of the Kennedy clan made them more her exploiters than her protectors; and others were apprehensive that the family's continuing devotion, however well-meaning, would bolster the group that Washington columnist Mary McGrory had dubbed "the Kennedy irreconcilables," and make the new administration's work more difficult. Robert Kennedy had tried to slow down the epidemic of renaming, and his sister-in-law had said in her first public statement that it was time people paid attention to the new president and the new First Lady, but, to some, those efforts seemed insincere or not enough.

Some complaints were more picayune. When, on January 14, Mrs. Kennedy made her first television appearance to thank the thousands who had sent messages of sympathy, it coincided with Mrs. Johnson's first White House dinner. As a result, newspapers were full of Mrs. Kennedy and printed little about the dinner. Ladies of the Washington press corps grumbled about Mrs. Kennedy's thoughtlessness, but no one could determine who had planned what first.

President Kennedy was thin-skinned to political criticism but not to personal barbs. (A writer for a national magazine recalled his reaction to a rumor, printed by Dorothy Kilgallen, that Jackie was not really pregnant during the 1960 campaign but was being kept under wraps for political reasons. "He just laughed about it," said the writer, "and added a few amusing comments of his own about what one could expect from that quarter.") For Mrs. Kennedy, the areas of sensitivity seemed to be reversed. She was disturbed by the incident of the Brando dinner and took time to explain to friends how it happened, but she seemed perfectly confident of the ways in which the president's memory would be served best. ("She's less upset by those criticisms than her staff is," said Pamela Turnure. "Once she decides something is right, she just does it.") For a woman whose combativeness, while First Lady, was usually limited to writing letters to *Women's Wear Daily* protesting the hard time given her by that trade paper about where and how she bought her clothes, Mrs. Kennedy was remarkably tough-minded in the face of charges that she was overestimating her husband's historical influence. "He changed our world," she said firmly, "and I hope people will remember him and miss him all their lives."

"She's not political," explained a former Kennedy adviser, "but she is immensely loyal. She didn't like campaigning or being a political wife, but she did it because it mattered to Jack. If he hadn't become president, it would have taken him a while to recover; the whole force of his tremendous energy was concentrated on that goal. If Jackie hadn't become First Lady, she would have smiled gently and said, 'All right. What do we do now?'"

Her loyalty was transferred to her protectors, especially to Robert Kennedy. (He is, as she explained in a now-famous quote, "the one I would put my hand in the fire for.") As a nondriver can relax with someone else at the wheel, Mrs. Kennedy seemed able to act on the political counsel of her protectors and not worry about it.

Her controversial "endorsement" of former Press Secretary Pierre Salinger, then running in California's Democratic state primary, was given at Salinger's request, but only with Robert Kennedy's permission. There had been a suggestion that she do more than make a statement: Under the guise of spending a few days at Elizabeth Arden's "Maine Chance" beauty farm in Arizona, she was to make a personal appearance in the campaign. ("There was a point there," said one of his supporters, "when Pierre was really worried that he wouldn't make it.") The trip was turned down on the grounds that the public appearance would be inappropriate. ("Can you see Jackie," said an amused friend, "at Maine Chance?") Instead, a telephone interview was granted to California newspaperman Robert Thompson, and the result for Salinger was a helpful statement that "President Kennedy valued his advice and counsel on all major matters." Reportedly, Robert Kennedy approved her giving that support only after it was apparent that Salinger was, in effect, running as a Kennedy. (His slogan was, "Let the man who spoke for two presidents speak for you," and his staff sent out four million postcards bearing a photograph of President Kennedy, the words, "In His Tradition," and a sample ballot with an "X" after Salinger's name.) But getting her to do it seemed to take very little persuading. "She feels it's natural," explained a writer friend of the Kennedys, "to serve her husband's memory by helping his men, the men who will carry on his work. I'm sure she'll keep right on doing it, but of course only if Bobby says so."

Shortly before moving to New York, Mrs. Kennedy apologized for not allowing a picture magazine to do a story on her children. She was sorry to be difficult, she said, but she really hoped her children could grow into their teens without publicity. The editor pointed out that a photograph of Caroline and John Jr. with Robert Kennedy and his children had recently appeared on the cover of *Life*. "Oh," she said, and smiled, "but that was for Bobby." In their temperament and background, Mrs. Kennedy and her brother-in-law have very little in common. (A recent guest at a Kennedy family dinner noted that they had nothing to talk about. "They share a common loss and a basic kind of guts," he said, "and that's about it.") But Robert Kennedy is head of the family now, and Mrs. Kennedy—who instructs her children that "Kennedys don't cry"—seems determined to be loyal.

Her sister, Lee Radziwill, three and a half years younger, often serves as a lightning rod for social criticism of Mrs. Kennedy in much the same way that Robert Kennedy, on political issues, often did for his brother. Any association with so-called frivolous social types (i.e., The Best-Dressed List, The Jet Set, Marlon Brando, or Europeans who don't work) as opposed to worthwhile friends who befit a First Lady (i.e., André Malraux, John

Steinbeck, Members of the Cabinet, and Americans who work) has been blamed, traditionally, on Mrs. Radziwill. As a doyenne of Paris fashion, a sometime expatriate, and the once-divorced wife of a Polish prince, she is generally regarded as the representative of café society in the woodpile.

"Lee is what Jackie would have been if she hadn't married a Kennedy," explained one intimate, "a charming, witty, intelligent woman who, as the daughter of a rich stockbroker, never acquired much experience of real life or much social conscience." Another theory is that the existing difference between the sisters was only dramatized by their choice of husbands, that Mrs. Kennedy always had been more frank and serious-minded. But they are loyal to each other. (After their joint trip to India in 1963, Mrs. Kennedy said her sister had been "marvelous. . . . I was so proud of her—and we would always have such fun laughing about little things when the day was over. Nothing could ever come between us.") "They've been through a lot together; their parents' divorce, their mother's remarriage and all that," said an old friend. "When the chips are down, it's still the Bouvier girls against the world."

It was partly due to her sister's urging that Mrs. Kennedy decided to leave the Georgetown house with the perpetual crowds outside. She spent more and more weekends in New York, and the press tried vainly to trace her movements. ("When something is published about one of them," explained an anonymous friend, "it's a game with the Kennedys to figure out who told.") She was seen inspecting a cooperative apartment on Fifth Avenue, having lunch with novelist Irwin Shaw, talking to cartoonist Charles Addams at a dinner party, walking on Madison Avenue, and going to church at Bedford Hills, New York. A local newspaper reporter spent much of that Sunday phoning around to the country homes of well-to-do Manhattan families, including that of Mr. and Mrs. James Fosburgh (whom President Johnson had appointed to the White House Preservation Committee), where Mrs. Kennedy was spending the weekend. He also phoned Broadway producer Leland Hayward and his wife—with whom Mrs. Kennedy, Mr. and Mrs. Bennett Cerf, Truman Capote, and others had just had lunch—but no one told. It was difficult for her to be anonymous anywhere, but clearly it might be a little less difficult for her and her children in New York.

In July, Mrs. Kennedy announced that her Georgetown house, whose redecoration she had halted a few months before, and Wexford, her

Virginia estate, were being put up for sale. *The Washington Post* regretted "losing a longtime resident and foremost tourist attraction." "She came among us like some wildly unexpected fairy queen," wrote *The* Washington *Star*, "and with her goes the heart of everyone who had lived in this place when she did." She was breaking her initial resolve to "live in the places I lived with Jack . . . Georgetown, and with the Kennedys at the Cape," and New York rejoiced.

"Of course, the social echelons are excited," said society press agent Mrs. Stephen Van Rensselaer Strong. "Her presence is a signal honor and will have primary salient impact; she would make any party." "She'll dress up New York," said a fashion writer. "People will go more formally to the good restaurants and theater because she might be there. It will be chic to be cultural." A spokesman for the Gray Line New York Tours promised that buses would not go off their routes to pass her apartment, "but I see no reason why, if it's on the route, our guides—we call them lecturers— shouldn't point it out." A rumor that east-side bookmakers were taking bets on Mrs. Kennedy's choice of a school for her daughter was squelched by the news that it was a sure thing: "She's enrolled in the second grade at the Convent of the Sacred Heart on Ninety-First Street," said an alumna; "just think how many tickets we can sell for our benefit next year!" With the exception of a few dissenters (a querulous writer in the "Voice of the People" column of the *Daily News* wanted to know "what part of . . . Harlem she will live in as a symbol of her husband's civil rights bill"), New Yorkers were pleased to receive her, if for rather selfish reasons. But Mayor Wagner was optimistic. "We will give her every opportunity," he said stoutly, "to have as much privacy as she wants."

In anticipation of her emergence into public life in November, some large charity events have already been postponed. (The December benefit performance, in Washington, of *My Fair Lady* was rescheduled in the hope that she could come. It is for the Kennedy Center for the Performing Arts: Mrs. Kennedy is one of the patrons.) Her social secretary, Nancy Tuckerman, has so many requests for Mrs. Kennedy to be sponsor or honorary chairman of charity-social events that she can't list them all. New York hostesses who are not optimistic enough to think that she will come to their parties ("The competition," said one, "is going to be absolutely cutthroat") are trying to spot in advance the functions she might attend. (Any Lincoln Center benefit, any premiere sponsored by the Kennedy

Foundation for Retarded Children, the Polish Ball, the National Horse Show, and the Convent of the Sacred Heart's alumnae benefit are the current favorites.)

"I hope," remarked *Glamour* editor Kathleen Casey, "that she has some good advisers and serious friends, because she's going to be set upon by café society and social climbers who will try to attach themselves to her just as they did to the Windsors."

In fact, Mrs. Kennedy has been surrounded by friends, serious and otherwise—by exploiters, distractors who vie to amuse her, and protectors who insulate her from the world—for much of her life, but she is, as William Walton said, "a strong dame." She has survived. "Jackie has always kept her own identity," said Robert Kennedy admiringly, "and been different."

Married to a strong-willed man twelve years her senior, plunged into the Kennedy clan and the role of senator's wife at twenty-four and the White House at thirty-one, Mrs. Kennedy was often in danger of being submerged. ("I feel," she said after her husband's election, "as though I have just become a piece of public property.") She was so uncertain of being able to remain "a private person" that she rarely cooperated with a press who, for the most part, adored her (she signed a photograph to Pierre Salinger, "from the greatest cross he has to bear"), and once disguised herself in a nurse's uniform and a wig in order to take her daughter out unnoticed. Some of the journalists who went along on her Indian trip had also accompanied Ethel Kennedy and Queen Elizabeth, and they complained that they had got to know "not only Ethel, but the Queen much better than Mrs. Kennedy." A writer who was a personal friend managed to get a few words with her only on the plane going home, and a photographer commented that "She barely said hello to any of us; it was hot as hell and she didn't sweat or let a hair get out of place; she didn't feel well through much of the trip but she never showed it; she was playing the great lady and total stoic."

Yet, at the end of the trip, she saw each newspaperwoman individually and presented her with a note of appreciation and a hand-painted box she had picked out herself. And on the last days NBC reporter Barbara Walters remembered that she relaxed for the first time, as if she had been let out of school: "We met the camel driver whom Lyndon Johnson had invited for a visit, and someone asked if Mrs. Kennedy would like to ride the camel. She was hesitant about it and said, 'No, but Lee would.' Her sister said something like 'Thanks a lot.' It was the first time we had seen that kind of banter between them, and it was obvious that they really liked each other's company. When Lee got off, Mrs. Kennedy got on, riding sidesaddle with her skirt up over her knees. She looked kiddish and charming and as if, finally, she was relaxed and enjoying herself."

Much of the demure, soft-voiced image she presented as she sat, hands folded and immobile through countless public functions, was evidence of the seriousness with which she took her role as First Lady. ("I'm getting good at it," she said. "I just drop this curtain in my mind. . . .") The pose concealed shyness, but it also hid a sharp wit—"It's the unexpectedness of it," said John Kenneth Galbraith, "that makes her so fascinating"—and a strong will—"I wouldn't dream of telling Jacqueline what to do," said her mother; "I never have." At her first press conference after the election, Mrs. Kennedy apologized, with a touch of whimsy, for being unable to speak "Churchillian prose," but when a reporter asked a little condescendingly if she thought she could do "a good job as First Lady," her reply was firm. "I assume," she said, "that I won't fail [him] in any way." Referring, of course, to her husband.

An interesting case might almost be made for the transference of some of the president's qualities. Robert Kennedy—who was always "the active one while Jack was the sick kid who read the books"—has taken to reading political theory and quoting Thoreau and Emerson. Ted Kennedy—the gay, slightly pampered one—is convalescing with a painful back injury and is said to be using the time to research a book. For Mrs. Kennedy, the change seems to be in attitude: she has acquired a new sense of history and a sense of her own place in it. ("Once, the more I read of history, the more bitter I got," she told writer Theodore H. White. "For a while I thought history was something that bitter old men wrote. But then I realized history made Jack what he was. . . .")

The change is not so great that she plans to accept any formal political responsibility: she has limited herself to work having directly to do with her husband's memory. Her children are still her first concern. ("I was reading Carlyle," she once told a reporter, "and he said you should do the duty that lies nearest you. And the thing that lies nearest me is the children.") She is no longer the dilettantish Bouvier girl, and New Yorkers who hope she will become the center of a glittering social scene are likely to be disappointed. She still has no real interest in politics or activism, but if she or her advisers feel that her role calls for her to act politically, indications are she will do it.

"Her public and private images of herself," explained a former classmate, "are not as different as they used to be. After a few years on her own—if she can survive all the problems and pressures—she just might emerge as the person who, up to now, only her friends have known."

Mimi Swartz

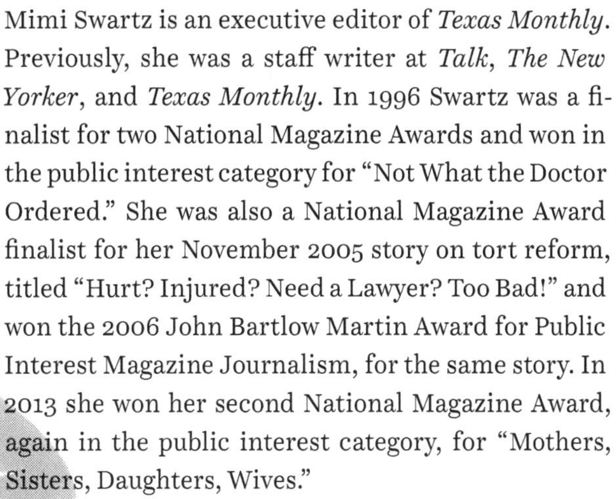

Mimi Swartz is an executive editor of *Texas Monthly*. Previously, she was a staff writer at *Talk*, *The New Yorker*, and *Texas Monthly*. In 1996 Swartz was a finalist for two National Magazine Awards and won in the public interest category for "Not What the Doctor Ordered." She was also a National Magazine Award finalist for her November 2005 story on tort reform, titled "Hurt? Injured? Need a Lawyer? Too Bad!" and won the 2006 John Bartlow Martin Award for Public Interest Magazine Journalism, for the same story. In 2013 she won her second National Magazine Award, again in the public interest category, for "Mothers, Sisters, Daughters, Wives."

Over the years, Swartz's work has appeared in *Vanity Fair*, *Esquire*, *Slate*, *National Geographic*, and *The New York Times*. It has also been collected in *The Best American Political Writing,* 2006, and *The Best American Sportswriting,* 2007. She is the author, with Sherron Watkins, of *Power Failure: The Inside Story of the Collapse of Enron*. She has been a member of the Texas Institute of Letters since 1994.

Swartz grew up in San Antonio and graduated from Hampshire College, in Amherst, Massachusetts. She now lives in Houston with her husband, John Wilburn, and son, Sam.

Mothers, Sisters, Daughters, Wives

What happens to women in Texas as the state wages war on Planned Parenthood, cuts family planning funding, and passes new sonogram laws?

There are things about women that most men would just as soon never discuss. The stirrups in a gynecologist's office, for one; the tampon aisle at the grocery store, for another; and pretty much any matter involving words like "cervix," "uterus," and "vagina." At least, that's how it was until March 2, 2011. Back in January of the same year, at the start of that legislative session, Governor Rick Perry had pushed as an emergency item a bill requiring all women seeking an abortion to have an ultrasound twenty-four hours beforehand. As Sid Miller, the legislator who sponsored the bill in the House, put it, "We want to make sure she knows what she is doing."

At a public hearing on the bill the following month, Tyler representative Leo Berman took the mic and insisted that fifty-five million fetuses had been aborted since *Roe v. Wade*—or, as he called it, "a Holocaust times nine." The author of a book on abortion rights gave a somewhat overwrought speech about the differences between "a zygote and a baby." A woman named Darlene Harken described herself as "a victim of abortion" because, she maintained, she wasn't warned about the mental and physical fallout from the procedure; Patricia Harless, a representative from Spring, thanked her for her "bravery" and "strength." Alpine's Pete Gallego countered by expressing his resentment of "people who stop caring after the child is born."

In March the bill reached the House floor, where debate raged for three days, as much as ten hours a day. Tensions ran high in the chamber, which was lit by a benevolent winter sun that glinted off the manly oak desks and supersized leather chairs. On the first day, March 2, Miller, a burly man with white hair and a sun-lined face that wrinkles into a bright, inviting smile, explained the legislation. A former school board member from Stephenville, he has a loamy Texas accent and favors a spotless white Stetson. If you stare at him long enough, you might easily forget that it's the twenty-first century.

Miller described his bill in a matter-of-fact tone, as if he were pushing a new municipal utility district. "What we're attempting to do is to provide women all available information while considering abortion and allow them adequate time to digest this information and review the sonogram and carefully weigh the impact of this life-changing decision," he began. Miller then listed everything his bill would require before an abortion could be performed. A woman would have to review with her doctor the printed materials required under the 2003 Woman's Right to Know Act. While the sonogram image was displayed live on a screen, the doctor would have to "make audible the heartbeat, if it's present, to the woman." There was also a script to recite, about the location of the head, hands, and heart. Affidavits swearing that all of this had been properly carried out according to Texas law would have to be signed and filed away in case of audits. A doctor who refused could lose his or her license.

As soon as Miller finished, Houston Representative Carol Alvarado strode up to the podium. There could have been no clearer contrast: her pink knit suit evoked all those Houston ladies who lunch, its black piping setting off her raven hair. Her lipstick was a cheery shade of fuchsia, but her disgust was of the I-thought-we'd-settled-this-in-the-seventies variety.

"I do not believe that we fully understand the level of government intrusion this bill advocates," she said tersely. The type of ultrasound necessary for women who are less than eight weeks pregnant is, she explained, "a transvaginal sonogram."

Abruptly, many of the mostly male legislators turned their attention to a fascinating squiggle pattern on the carpet, and for a rare moment, the few female legislators on the floor commanded the debate. Representative Ana Hernandez Luna approached the back mic and sweetly asked Alvarado to explain what would happen to a woman undergoing a transvaginal sonogram.

"Well," Alvarado answered helpfully, "she would be asked by the sonographer to undress completely from the waist down and asked to lie on the exam table and cover herself with a light paper sheet. She would then put her feet in stirrups, so that her legs are spread at a very wide angle, and asked to scoot down the table so that the pelvis is just under the edge."

At this point, if there had been thought bubbles floating over the heads of the male legislators, they almost certainly would have been filled with expletives of embarrassment or further commentary on the carpet design.

"What does this vaginal sonogram look like?" Luna asked, ever curious.

"Well, I'm glad you asked," Alvarado answered, "because instead of just describing it, I can show you."

And so the state representative from Houston's District 145 put both elbows on the lectern and held up in her clenched fist a long, narrow plastic probe with a tiny wheel at its tip. It looked like some futuristic instrument of torture. "This is the transvaginal probe," Alvarado explained, pointing it at her colleagues as she spoke, her finger on what looked like a trigger. "Colleagues, this is what we're talking about. . . . This is government intrusion at its best. We've reached a"—she searched for the word—"climax in government intrusion."

Those who could still focus gaped at Alvarado. No one spoke. The silence seemed to confirm for Alvarado something she had long suspected: most of the men in the House chamber didn't know the difference between a typical ultrasound—the kind where a technician presses a wand against a pregnant belly and sends the happy couple home with a photo for their fridge—and this. She locked Miller in her sights. "What would a woman undergo in your bill?" she asked.

Miller seemed confused. "It could be an ultrasound, it could be a sonogram," he began. "Actually, I have never had a sonogram done on me, so I'm not familiar with the exact procedure—on the medical procedure, how that proceeds."

"There are two different kinds of sonograms," Alvarado said, trying again to explain. "The abdominal, which most of our colleagues may think [of as] 'jelly on the belly'—that is not what would be done here. A woman that is eight to ten weeks pregnant would have a transvaginal procedure." Miller stammered a response, but Alvarado was not done with him. She continued the grilling for several more minutes, keeping Miller on the ropes with a sustained barrage of icky female anatomy talk. Ultimately, however, the room was stacked against her.

On March 7 Miller's bill passed 107–42.

Over the next few months, as the Senate passed its version of the bill, which was sponsored by Houston senator Dan Patrick, and as Governor Perry signed the legislation into law at a solemnly triumphant ceremony, the exchange between Alvarado and Miller stood as a glaring reminder of the peculiar way in which women could be largely boxed out of decisions that were primarily concerning them. (A number of female Republican legislators supported the bill too, but the overwhelming majority of the votes cast in its favor were from men.) Of course, women have rarely held the reins of power in Texas, but there has also seldom been a season as combative on the subject of women's health as the one we have experienced in the past eighteen months.

Miller's bill was only the beginning of what turned out to be the most aggressively anti-abortion and anti-contraception session in history. In the words of one female reporter who covered the legislature, "It was brutal." Not only did the sonogram law pass, but drastic cuts were made to statewide family planning funds, and a Medicaid fund known as the Women's Health Program was sent back to Washington, stamped with a big "No thanks." When the dust settled, Texas had turned down a $9-to-$1 match of federal dollars, and the health care of 280,000 women had been placed in jeopardy. And that wasn't all. Earlier this year, around the time that the new laws began to take effect, an epic, if short-lived, fight broke out between Planned Parenthood and the Susan G. Komen Foundation, pitting two of Texas's most powerful women against each other and highlighting the agonizing, divisive nature of the debate over women's health. No sooner had this conflict subsided than the legislature's decision to kill the Women's Health Program was dragged into the courts for a series of reversals and counter-reversals that is still not resolved.

These conflicts could all be seen as the latest in a long struggle, as women in Texas try to gain control over not just their own health care decisions but their own economic futures and those of their families. This is the state, after all, from which the modern abortion wars originated in 1973 with *Roe v. Wade*, a case, let's not forget, that pitted a twenty-one-year-old Houston woman and two upstart lady lawyers from Austin against formidable Dallas County district attorney Henry Wade. It's a decades-old battle between the sexes over who knows best and, more importantly, who's in charge. And over the past year, the fighting has intensified. On the one side are the Carol Alvarados of the world; on the other, the Sid Millers. The outcome will determine nothing less than the fate of Texas itself.

For most of Texas history, even during the seemingly halcyon period that was Ann Richards's governorship, the goal of Texas women to achieve parity with Texas men has been out of reach. The men who settled the state were a tough bunch. They had to survive a harsh, unforgiving climate; murderous Comanche; soil that was in many places relentlessly resistant to cultivation; rattlesnakes; bandits; long, lonely cattle drives; and more. But women—to paraphrase Richards—had to do most of that barefoot and pregnant and without any of the liberties or rights that men enjoyed. As the saying goes, "Texas is heaven for men and dogs, but it's hell for women and horses."

Many frontier women learned quickly that they were effectively on their own—the downside to hooking up with a rugged individualist far more comfortable with his cattle than with his wife. They bore, raised, and, too often, buried their kids. They figured out how to make do in the face of cruel poverty. Women had to contend with a challenging contradiction: on the one hand, the clearly defined sex roles of the nineteenth century dictated a courtliness and paternal protectiveness on the part of Texas men that survives to this day. On the other hand, the state was settled in most cases by force, fostering a worship of physical strength and a visceral contempt for anyone too weak to make it on his or her own.

Modern Texas history is filled with stories of women who were held down by what academics like to call "the patriarchy" and the rest of us might simply call "macho white guys." When trailblazing federal judge and legislator Sarah Hughes ran for reelection to the House in 1932, for instance, her opponent suggested that her colleagues "oughta slap her face and send her back to the kitchen."

Governor John Connally's Commission on the Status of Women, established in 1967, found numerous inequities in education and the workforce—but also noted that "overly enthusiastic soapboxing oratory can do the feminine cause more harm than good." It has been frequently pointed out that Kay Bailey Hutchison, one of the most successful females in recent Texas history, became a television reporter in the sixties because, after finishing law school, she couldn't find work as an attorney. During Barbara Jordan's entire term in the legislature, which lasted from 1967 to 1973, she was the only woman in the Senate; across the hall, there was only one female in the House: Sue Hairgrove, followed by Sissy Farenthold.

What their male counterparts seemed slow to grasp was that, having endured the same adverse frontier environment as their husbands, fathers, and brothers, Texas women developed many of the same characteristics: the indomitable independent streak, the persistent optimism in the face of lousy odds. But instead of speculating in cotton or oil or real estate, women focused on sneaking power from men.

The pseudonymous Pauline Periwinkle campaigned for improved food inspections in 1905 by suggesting that a woman lobby her otherwise uninterested husband after he "has broken open one of those flaky biscuits for which your cuisine is justly famous." During the Depression, when contraceptives were among the obscene materials the Comstock law deemed illegal to send through the mail, one Kate Ripley, from Dallas, used boxes from her husband's shirt company to disguise the contents of illicit packages that she shipped to women all over Texas.

As the twentieth century advanced and women began to win seats at more influential tables, several distinct types emerged. For many years, before it was considered politically incorrect, a woman in the political arena was known as a good ol' girl or a man's woman. This complimentary description meant she could drink, cuss, and cut a deal and probably never cried in public. Many of these women were what today we'd call liberals, people like Jordan, Farenthold, Sarah Weddington, Richards, and Molly Ivins. They may have endured the hollow loneliness of public scorn, but they managed to get the Equal Rights Amendment ratified in Texas in 1972. It's probably no accident that these particular heroines came from the liberal tradition—it's the one that has been most likely to let women talk, even if they weren't always heard.

But conservative women made their presence felt as well. The most successful ones, like Hutchison or Harriet Miers, played an inside game, making nice—or at least appearing to make nice—while quietly accumulating power. Beauty helped, especially when combined with a rich husband, as Joanne Herring has demonstrated. Barbara Bush took a page from sturdy Republican club women and made herself a common-sense heroine in low heels and pearls. In other words, there were various ways to get around men and grab the steering wheel, and over the years Texas women used them all.

Regardless of their politics, both Democratic and Republican women used their power to advance the cause of family planning. During the time when abortion was both dangerous and illegal—before 1973—volunteering for Planned Parenthood was a socially acceptable, even admirable, thing for many middle- and upper-middle-class women to do. It isn't surprising that Farenthold and Richards were big family planning advocates, but so were the very social Sakowitz and Marcus families, the archconservative Hunt family, and George and Barbara Bush (at least until he joined the anti-abortion Reagan team in 1980). Partisanship just wasn't in the picture.

"Over the years, everyone wrote a check," said Peggy Romberg, who worked for Planned Parenthood in Austin for seventeen years. The issues seemed very different in the sixties and seventies: women had husbands who made them remove their IUDs, or who made them quit school to tend to their babies. A woman's sexual history was allowed to be admitted in court during rape cases. Married women who wanted credit cards in their own name needed their husbands to cosign for them.

Then came that landmark moment in the history of women all over the United States. The story of *Roe v. Wade* is, in many ways, the story of Texas women. Norma McCorvey (a.k.a. Jane Roe), raised in poverty in Houston, a high school dropout at fourteen, beaten by her husband, and pregnant with her third child in 1969, tried first to lie in order to get a legal abortion—she claimed she had been raped, which would have permitted the procedure in Texas—and then she tried to get an illegal abortion, but her clinic of choice had been shut down by the authorities. Eventually, two Austin attorneys, Weddington and Linda Coffee, filed suit on her behalf, arguing that her right to privacy included her right to have an abortion. (A

San Antonio oil heiress, Ruth McLean Bowers, underwrote the legal costs of the case.) In 1973 the US Supreme Court agreed that state laws banning abortion were unconstitutional. The vote was 7–2.

Nearly forty years of legal abortion have followed, along with an endless stream of bitter arguments and toxic political strife. McCorvey, who wound up having her baby as the case progressed through the courts, later did an about-face, becoming an activist with the pro-life group Operation Rescue. Weddington went on to become an icon of the women's movement. In time, the case they launched emerged as one of the most divisive and politically expedient issues in American politics. Maneuvering from the governor's mansion to the White House, George W. Bush used it to successfully solidify conservative Republicans around his candidacy. Though Bush said he was against overturning *Roe v. Wade*, he talked about promoting a "culture of life," signed the Abortion Ban Act, in 2003, and campaigned vigorously on the issue, using it to draw a sharp distinction between himself and both Al Gore and John Kerry.

In Texas the past decade has seen a sharp turn in the rhetoric of the issue. Some of it is the result of the ferocious GOP primary wars that are now a fixture in what has essentially become a one-party state. Since there is only one election that matters anymore, it has tended to become a contest over who can move furthest to the right. Being labeled a RINO—a "Republican in Name Only"—is a fate worse than death, and what better way to establish one's conservative bona fides than by passing laws limiting abortion?

A parental notification law for minors seeking abortions passed in 1999 (later, legislators passed a law requiring that minors get permission from their parents before getting the procedure). The 2003 Woman's Right to Know Act, sponsored by Representative Frank Corte, of San Antonio, required doctors to give pregnant women a booklet—tinted pink with a daisy on the cover—that includes information about the growth and development of "the unborn child" and color photos of the fetus from four to thirty-eight weeks of gestation. (This booklet is also infamous for erroneously linking abortion with difficulties during future pregnancies and higher rates of breast cancer.)

By far the most important change came as a result of a 2005 lawsuit called *Planned Parenthood of Houston and Southeast Texas v. Sanchez*, which required the separation of all family planning facilities into two entities: one would distribute birth control and perform women's wellness checkups and cancer screenings, while the other would provide abortions exclusively. Government audits were mandated annually to make sure that no state money—no tax dollars—could ever be used to fund abortions.

"I think we all thought this was harassment—it wasn't going to improve public health. But we said OK, we'll get through this too," said Peter Durkin, who was the president and CEO of Planned Parenthood Gulf Coast for twenty-seven years. Still, despite all the conflict over abortion, there remained some restraint in the legislature over family planning. It was a given that reasonable people could differ over abortion, but most lawmakers believed that funding birth control programs was just good policy; not only did it reduce the number of abortions, but it reduced the burden on the state to care for more children.

That changed dramatically after 2010, when Republicans won twenty-five seats in the House, giving them a supermajority of 101 to 49 and total control over the law-making process. (The male-female split is 118 men to 32 women.) As the Eighty-Second Legislature began, a freshman class of right-wing legislators arrived in Austin, determined to cut government spending—a.k.a. "waste"—and push a deeply conservative social agenda. At the same time, Governor Perry was preparing to launch his presidential bid, burnishing his résumé for a national conservative audience. It wasn't a good time to be a Democrat, but it wasn't a great time to be a moderate Republican either. Conservative organizations turned out to be as skilled at social media as your average sixteen-year-old, using Twitter and Facebook to chronicle and broadcast every move of the supposed RINOs. A climate of fear descended on the Capitol. "Most people in the House think we should allow poor women to have Pap smears and prenatal care and contraception," an aide to a top House Republican told me. "But they are worried about primary opponents."

The result, in Texas and beyond, was a full-scale assault on the existing system of women's health care, with a bull's-eye on the back of Planned Parenthood, the major provider of both abortions and family planning in Texas and the country. As Representative Wayne Christian told the *Texas Tribune*, in May 2011, "Of course it's a war on birth control, abortion, everything. That's what family planning is supposed to be about."

For those with institutional memory, the most striking thing about Cecile Richards is how unlike her mother she is. The president of the Planned

Parenthood Action Fund possesses none of the folksiness and none of the bite that helped make Ann Richards an icon, maybe because neither quality is really necessary or useful anymore (and could actually be considered a hindrance for the head of a national women's organization in 2012). In fact, on the rainy day I met with Richards at Planned Parenthood's headquarters in Manhattan, she looked like someone who had come into her own. Long gone was the awkward perm she once sported. Tall and willowy, she wore a deep-purple sheath with matching peep-toe heels, a combination of chic understatement with just a hint of flash.

Clearly, she had learned her political skills not just from her mother but also from her father, labor lawyer David Richards. Before coming to Planned Parenthood, in 2006, Cecile was a labor organizer and the founder of two progressive groups: America Votes, a nonprofit designed to promote liberal causes, and the Texas Freedom Network, an organization designed to combat the Christian Right. In other words, to Planned Parenthood's opposition, she's the Antichrist.

Richards long ago learned to modulate her anger for public consumption. But when she gets to talking, she can be extremely frank. "The equity that women have now in education and wages is because of family planning," she told me, leaning forward, her voice hardening just a little. "For women, it's not a social issue. It's not political. It's fundamental—fundamental to their economic well-being." She went on, seemingly unable to believe that she was being forced to restate the obvious: birth control enables women to stay in school instead of dropping out, and to get a degree that boosts their economic status for life. It allows them to control the size of their families so that they can afford the kinds of futures they envision for themselves and for their children. A woman who once had five kids might now only have two—and send them both to college. And so on.

But why, I asked, should taxpayers be on the hook to pay for it?

"Why should we pay for Viagra?" she responded. "Why should men be treated differently? We pay for all other medications. Birth control is the most normative prescription in America. Ninety-nine percent of women use birth control. It's 2012, for God's sake!"

As for the changes in Texas, she was deeply disappointed. She had worked on the border with women who have since lost access to cancer screenings. She didn't think Governor Perry was taking the majority of

Texans where they wanted to go. "It's hard to go back home," she told me. "That heartlessness does not track with the Texas I grew up in."

Indeed, in the Texas of Richards's youth (she was born in 1958), lieutenant governors like Bill Hobby and Bob Bullock worked with Planned Parenthood to set up a network of clinics all over Texas, in both small towns and big cities. Texas Health and Human Services offered funding through a federal grant for communities willing to open new clinics for the underserved, and Planned Parenthood provided everything from breast and cervical cancer screenings to abortions. "We were encouraged to open new locations," Durkin recalled, "and the state sat right next to us when the extremist furor erupted—and it always died down."

One reason for the tolerance, Durkin said, was that twenty-five years ago there was a greater tendency to "keep out of a lady's business." "In the good old days," he explained, "the Texas Department of Health was managed by retired military doctors who focused more on afternoon golf than reproductive health care issues. And the governor's office didn't interfere either."

The expansion of family planning was crucial to the general health and future of the state itself. Texas has the second-highest birth rate in the nation, behind California. Historically, it has also had one of the highest rates of uninsured women in the country. Today, more than half the babies born each year are to mothers on Medicaid. Since the cost differential between a Medicaid birth plus postnatal care and a year of birth control pills is huge (around $16,000 for the former versus $350 for the latter), the notion that publicly funded birth control was good public policy had never been a subject of debate in the past. Prior to the last legislative session, the state's family planning program was serving close to 130,000 clients who had no form of health insurance, the poorest of the poor. And according to the nonpartisan Legislative Budget Board, the state's investment in family planning saved $21 million a year by averting more pregnancies. Ironically, before the last session began the LBB advocated for more money to be spent on family planning in order to save on the cost of pregnancies and births, which last year totaled $2.7 billion.

But that's not exactly what happened.

"We're going to be making bad decisions all day." It was the morning of April Fool's 2011, a day of important debate in the House over HB 1, the budget bill, and Wayne Christian was just getting started. Christian, from

Center, is one of the more ebullient House members, and despite his grim prediction, his mood seemed upbeat. He knew that, thanks to his party's supermajority, power would continue to rest in the heart of the Republican caucus, a place he felt very much at home. A past president of the Texas Conservative Coalition and a successful gospel singer, Christian qualified as a true believer, and on this day he was calm. He was, after all, a man with a plan.

The plan had emerged from several years of strategizing by Texas pro-life groups, and it had as its central goal the demise of Planned Parenthood. To those who oppose abortion, the separation of health care clinics and abortion clinics that the Legislature mandated in 2005 had not gone far enough. Even though organizations like Planned Parenthood are audited annually by the state to ensure that no taxpayer dollars go to pay for abortions, this arrangement remains suspect to pro-lifers.

"The separation agreement is not really enforceable," said Elizabeth Graham, an attractive, sharp-tongued brunette who is the director of Texas Right to Life. "The Legislature has never been comfortable with giving money to 1200 Main Street and 1201 Main Street isn't getting that money. The funds are fungible." So Graham's organization had been working with legislators like Christian, diligently preparing, waiting for the right opportunity. It had finally come. The tactic was to eviscerate Planned Parenthood through the family planning budget. Lawmakers, Graham later told me, "were prepared and understood where funds could go. They had assistance from agencies and information that helped them to redirect funds."

House Republicans also had a clever procedural maneuver up their sleeves. Ordinarily, budget amendments are vetted by the Appropriations Committee, which may hold public hearings on controversial issues. This time, however, the GOP legislators kept mum, intending to present these amendments from the floor, circumventing the traditional vetting process. (Unlike his iron-fisted predecessor, Tom Craddick, current House Speaker Joe Straus has proved less inclined to prevent such tactics.) This meant the amendments would come with no advice from Appropriations, so members were left without guidelines on how to vote.

Indeed, on April 1, when the family planning section of the budget came up for review, conservative legislators began attaching a blizzard of new amendments, each one designed to shrink the size of the $111.5

million budget from which Planned Parenthood drew support. First up was Representative Randy Weber, who wanted to move $7.3 million out of family planning and allocate it to an organization that seeks alternatives to abortion.

In support of his amendment, Weber, a conservative Republican from Pearland, cited a journal article from 2002 that asserted that in addition to contraception not eliminating pregnancies, it also correlated to a higher rate of pregnancy among women who use it. (In fact, the article stated the opposite.) Representative Mike Villarreal, a Democrat from San Antonio, asked Weber if he thought that birth control simply didn't work.

"Not for those that get pregnant," Weber quipped.

"Have you ever used contraceptives yourself?" Villarreal shot back.

"Well, you know, I don't think I know you well enough to go down this road," Weber cracked.

Villarreal shifted tactics, insisting that Weber's plan would do nothing to reduce abortions. Further, if they did what Weber asked, members would be moving money from programs that would save the state around $60 million into one that would not save it a cent.

Weber's amendment passed 100–44. Next up was Christian, who proposed an amendment that would move $6.6 million from family planning into a program to help autistic children. After consideration of additional proposals, Christian's amendment passed 106–34. Two more Republican representatives came forward and laid out amendments to move $20 million into early-childhood intervention programs and the Texas Department of Aging and Disability Services. Those passed too. Representative Bill Zedler asked to move funding from "the abortion industry" to services for the deaf and blind and those with mobile disabilities. Representative Jim Murphy wanted to move money to EMS and trauma care, which was operating with a $450 million surplus at the time. Representative Warren Chisum followed with an amendment to move family planning money to more-generalized medical clinics.

As the night wore on, tempers flared; sometimes it was hard to hear over the members' shouting at one another. Even a staunch Republican like Beverly Woolley found herself moving to the microphone in solidarity with the Democrats. But on and on it went. By one in the morning, the House had slashed the family planning budget from $111.5 million to $37.9 million. The final vote passed with 104 ayes. On May 3, the Senate passed its budget, with the same cuts in place—partly because House Republicans had threatened to hold up the entire budget process if they did not.

By this point, the tenor of the session was clear. As the chair of the Senate Democratic Caucus Leticia Van de Putte said, "Texas is going to shrink government until it fits in a woman's uterus." A little over a month later the sonogram bill went to the governor's desk. "This will be one of the strongest sonogram bills in the nation," declared an exultant Sid Miller. "This is a great day for women's health. This is a great day for Texas," said Dan Patrick, who had tried twice before to get such a bill passed.

Needless to say, not everyone agreed. "I went to an event with Senator [Kevin] Eltife," Patrick told me some months later, "and I parked and a car pulled up behind me and a woman started screaming at me. I've never had that happen. I've had some interesting emails too. Just amazing. But I'm a big guy. I can take criticism, because this is the right thing to do to save a life."

By his account, over time the sonogram bill will save up to fifteen thousand lives. "There will be people alive in ten to twenty years who wouldn't be alive without this bill," he told me. To Patrick, the legally mandated ultrasound isn't an invasive procedure. Critics of the bill further contend that its ultimate purpose is to limit access to abortion, especially for low-income women who may not be able to take off more than one day of work to accommodate the twenty-four-hour waiting period. Patrick rejects this argument too. As he puts it, "The purpose in sponsoring this bill was to improve women's health care." His political opponents, he says, "don't know the facts. They are dealing from emotion." He thinks the claim that most women have made up their minds long before they reach the door of an abortion clinic is "nonsense."

"Most of these women don't know," he said. "No one is trying to embarrass them, but we are trying to save a life. You want the woman to have a choice to have a baby or not, but you don't want them to have a choice to look at a sonogram? That makes no sense to me." (In fact, prior to the sonogram bill, women seeking an abortion at Planned Parenthood could elect to look at a sonogram.)

As the session reached its halfway point, many female legislators grappled with the magnitude of what had happened. Democratic women could at least enjoy the full-throated support of their male colleagues, but moderate Republican women frequently found themselves all alone, treated to a front-row seat from which to view their own powerlessness. To speak up was to be targeted for defeat in the next primary, after all. They dragged through the Capitol with heads down, making apologies to staffers and colleagues for their votes. Ultimately, both Beverly Woolley and Florence Shapiro announced their retirements. The latter told a lobbyist, "These are no longer the people who elected me."

Shapiro and Woolley weren't the only veteran Republicans to find themselves in an awkward position. Take the case of Robert Deuell and the Women's Health Program. Senator Deuell, a physician from Greenville who has held office since 2003, was known to be both pragmatic and conservative when it came to public health. He supported programs like needle exchange for addicts, but he was strongly opposed to abortion. In fact, he had worked tirelessly since 2007 to toss Planned Parenthood from the network of providers included in the Women's Health Program, a Medicaid fund for poor women started in Texas in 2006. Yet unlike many of his new comrades-in-arms, Deuell favored taxpayer-supported birth control.

If the state doesn't make birth control available, he told me, "we are going to be providing prenatal care. It's the lesser of two undesirables, and that's the point I've tried to make. Do I wish women waited? Yes, but they don't."

Deuell has always favored shifting the services provided through the WHP from Planned Parenthood to community-based health organizations and clinics known as Federally Qualified Health Centers. There were some obstacles to this, among them the question of whether the FQHCs could deliver the same quality of care. Many FQHCs were already overrun with very sick people. Jose Camacho, the head of the Texas Association of Community Health Centers, which oversees FQHCs in Texas, had insisted that, despite what Deuell wished, the FQHCs could not absorb the overflow, given Texas's soaring birth and poverty rates along with the vast number of uninsured. "We served one million patients this year, at least," he told me. "To think that any health system can ramp up to take, in effect, 20 percent more patients is not realistic."

Deuell didn't give up. The rules of the WHP had been written to exclude providers affiliated with organizations that perform abortions. This was in conflict with federal law, so in 2008, a waiver was granted that allowed

Planned Parenthood to participate. In 2010 Deuell asked Attorney General Greg Abbott, who also fervently opposes abortion, to check on the constitutionality of the waiver, and when the Eighty-Second Legislature rolled around, Deuell was prepared with a rider to the budget bill that would reauthorize the WHP while explicitly preventing Planned Parenthood from ever taking part in it. But by May, he had a problem. He could see a disaster looming—the health care of 130,000 women was already at risk because of cuts to the state's family planning budget, and now, as a result of the political climate, he saw that he didn't have the votes in the Senate to get his version of the WHP reauthorized.

"I guess what took me by the most surprise was an overall opposition to family planning," Deuell told me. The fact that such programs were statistically proven to save money by the Legislative Budget Board was not enough to change hearts and minds, even in a budget-slashing session. "My feeling is that ['the program will save money'] is what you hear every time they want to increase the size of government," said Representative Kelly Hancock, the policy chairman of the Republican caucus. He added that the caucus's opposition to such programs "had nothing to do with the women's health issue."

With time running out, Deuell found himself in the surreal position of joining forces with ultraliberal Garnet Coleman, who was trying to push a bill to save the Women's Health Program in the House. (Back in 2001, it was Coleman, the son of a prominent Houston doctor, who first carried legislation to create the WHP, which Governor Perry vetoed.) This did not go over well, especially with the folks at Texas Right to Life. After a particularly nasty budget committee hearing, Elizabeth Graham compared Deuell to Margaret Sanger, the founder of Planned Parenthood.

Finally, the bill was saved at the end of May by some last-minute politicking—it was attached as an eleventh-hour budget rider. But the victory for women was a hollow one: Planned Parenthood was no longer allowed to participate. It promptly filed suit, as many who had kept their frightened silence in the Legislature had hoped it would. By then, nearly three hundred thousand Texas women were facing the loss of birth control, wellness checkups, and cancer screenings.

And Deuell, for his part, was still stinging from Elizabeth Graham's attack. "For her to compare me to Margaret Sanger," he told me, "it's beyond the pale."

This past January, one year after the start of the Eighty-Second Legislature, the U.S. Fifth Circuit Court of Appeals ruled that the sonogram bill was legal and could stand. (The opinion was written by Edith Jones, a female judge from Texas who has never made her opposition to abortion a secret.) Many women in Texas who had perhaps not been closely following the moves of the legislature were now discovering the fruits of their representatives' labors. Others were beginning to realize that, because of the cuts to health care, they couldn't even get in to see a doctor for annual pelvic exams. Clinics were already closing, or cutting hours, or charging fees for services that had previously been covered.

The session had made it clear that Republican legislators and pro-life groups were intensifying their fight against Planned Parenthood, not just in Texas but across the country. If there was anyone who still didn't get it, the news of January 31 made it impossible to miss. That was the day that the Associated Press reported that Susan G. Komen for the Cure, originator of the pink ribbon, had decided to cancel the $700,000 annual grant it had been contributing to Planned Parenthood since 2005 for breast cancer screenings. (None of Komen's money ever went to abortion services.)

The news erupted nationwide, but in Texas it detonated like an atomic bomb. Komen, after all, was based in Dallas and was worshipped there in almost cultlike fashion. What's more, the organization's founder, Nancy Brinker, was a role model for many Texas women, a radical reformer who back in the early eighties had, as one of her oldest friends put it, "brought breast cancer out of the closet." Before she took on the cause, promising her dying sister in 1982 she'd find a cure, most people wouldn't even say the word "breast," much less "breast cancer," in polite conversation. Brinker, a former PR woman originally from Peoria, Illinois, who had married well, to the late Dallas restaurateur Norman Brinker, built Komen into a $1.9 billion philanthropic powerhouse in a relentless, but very feminine, way. She was also a highly visible moderate Republican woman, and a friend of George and Laura's who was rewarded with an ambassadorship to Hungary in 2001 and a position as White House chief of protocol in 2007.

What happened, in brief, was this: anti-abortion groups had been harassing Komen (and the Girl Scouts of America and Walmart) for years over its support of Planned Parenthood. A very vocal, if small, faction was alarming affiliates with threats to disrupt the footraces that have long been Komen's major source of funds. John Hammarley, Komen's senior communications adviser, found himself fielding more and more phone and email inquiries about the relationship between the two organizations. "It took up a sizable amount of my time," he told me.

A few years earlier, Brinker, who is sixty-five, began to step away from running the organization. She brought in a new president, who in turn brought in former Georgia Secretary of State Karen Handel. Handel, who is strongly opposed to abortion, was hired as chief lobbyist and asked to work on the problem of the protestors. Along with Hammarley, she came up with several options that included everything from doing nothing to defunding Planned Parenthood in perpetuity. Hammarley warned Komen that doing the latter would cause severe problems, so the board elected to cancel funding for one year and then re-evaluate.

Komen notified Planned Parenthood, who issued a press release decrying the decision. Immediately, social media exploded with anti-Komen messages—1.3 million on Twitter alone—that ranged from irreverent to near homicidal. Komen seemed utterly gobsmacked by the response. A campaign called "Komen Kan Kiss My Mammogram" sprang up, designed to raise $1 million for Planned Parenthood to replace (and then some) what Komen had withdrawn. Someone hacked a Komen online ad and changed a fund-raising request to say "Help us run over poor women on our way to the bank." What may have been worse were all the blog posts and mainstream media reports that exhumed negative stories about Komen's business practices—how much it spent to aggressively protect its For the Cure trademark, how much of its money actually went to research, whether the organization was supporting the right kind of scientific research, whether its pink nail polish might contain carcinogens, and so on.

There was something very retro about Komen's response—as if they didn't know how to fight like modern women. First, they hid, shutting down all interview requests. Then they tried to cover their tracks, issuing a press release that claimed their decision regarding Planned Parenthood was part of their new "more stringent eligibility and performance criteria" that eliminated any group that was the focus of a congressional investigation. (At the time, Planned Parenthood was the only Komen beneficiary to have such a problem; it had been the focus of a trumped-up investigation, spearheaded by anti-abortion forces, that had come to nothing.) On February 2, a glamorous if somewhat stressed-out Brinker appeared in a video posted on YouTube. Even though stories of internal discord and resignations were already leaking to the press, she reiterated that her decision to end the funding for breast cancer screenings for Planned Parenthood was not political but simply a way of maintaining their standards. "We will never bow to political pressure," she insisted. "We will never turn our backs on the women who need us the most."

In this particular fight, however, another Texas woman, Cecile Richards, would get the upper hand. As the head of an organization under constant attack, Richards was adept at keeping her emotions in check. At every press conference, she was the picture of empathy and calm. "Until really recently, the Komen Foundation had been praising our breast health programs as essential," Richards told *The New York Times*. "This abrupt about-face was very surprising. I think that the Komen Foundation has been bullied by right-wing groups." Meanwhile, Planned Parenthood was churning out fund-raising emails, eventually raising $3 million, far more than it usually got from Komen.

Just four days after it all began, Komen reversed itself, and Brinker, looking even more drawn, appeared before the cameras again, this time to apologize and say that the funding to Planned Parenthood would be reinstated. Handel subsequently resigned, berating Planned Parenthood for its "betrayal" in making public Komen's decision to remove their funding. Both organizations now say they are very happy to be working together again.

Other battles have not turned out the same way. In February the Texas Health and Human Services commissioner—who works at the behest of the governor—signed a rule banning from the Women's Health Program any organizations that provided abortions themselves or through affiliates. Perry declared that if the federal government didn't like it, he would find the spare $30 million for poor women elsewhere, regardless of the state's budget shortfall. In March Kathleen Sebelius, U.S. Secretary of Health and Human Services, stood among Houston's poor at Ben Taub General Hospital and announced that unless Texas relented, the WHP would not be renewed. Federal law required that women have the right to choose their own providers.

The Perry administration was still determined to stop women from being treated by abortion providers, however, so the Health and Human Services Commission distributed a flyer to clients in the WHP, saying they might have to find new places to go—even though there was an injunction in place at the time allowing Planned Parenthood to continue as a provider while the organization's case against the state made its way through the courts.

In May district judge Lee Yeakel blocked Texas from keeping Planned Parenthood out of any women's health program receiving federal funds. "The record demonstrates that plaintiffs currently provide a critical component of Texas's family planning services to low-income women," he noted in his twenty-five-page opinion. "The court is unconvinced that Texas will be able to find substitute providers for these women in the immediate future, despite its stated intention to do so." The state is currently appealing.

In June I went to a Planned Parenthood clinic in the Gulfton section of southwest Houston. Like most of the organization's ten local affiliates, the Gulfton Planned Parenthood is a modest place. It sits in a strip shopping center near a ninety-nine-cent store, a pawn shop, and an appropriately bicultural restaurant offering "Sushi Latino." Which is to say, it's about as far removed from the clubby halls of the legislature or the plush headquarters of the Komen Foundation as possible.

For more than a year, Planned Parenthood, and women's health generally, had been the subject of withering attacks and intense controversies, but the scene inside the clinic was mundane. A television on a wall of the sun-streaked waiting room played some kind of *Judge Judy* variation. By eleven in the morning, the place was filled with people of all backgrounds—African, Guatemalan, Vietnamese, browns, blacks, and whites—as well as both sexes and multiple generations, not only mothers and their teenage daughters with toddlers, but mothers and their teenage sons. Almost everyone was wearing T-shirts and jeans and staring at their smart phones.

With its encouraging posters depicting happy couples and happy families, the clinic is supposed to be a cheerful place, but the atmosphere was like any doctor's office where bad news might have to be delivered about an HIV test, breast exam, or pregnancy test. And lately, the information that clinic director Maria Naranjo has to share with her patients includes the fact that, because of the drastic cuts to the family planning budget, the clinic has had to raise its fees. The tab for a wellness checkup, formerly covered by state and federal funds, now costs $133—a prohibitive amount for someone having to choose between paying that or an electric bill. She explained to me that most people think the family planning funds have just run out until the next fiscal year, something they are accustomed to. Most do not understand they are gone for the foreseeable future.

Naranjo, who has worked for Planned Parenthood and other family planning agencies for twenty-seven years, is a bustling, efficient woman with soulful eyes and a lined face. She is the child of migrant workers and was a mother at seventeen. "This is where I can do the best service," she told me. "I know where they are coming from, and I know how difficult it is."

Naranjo has established, on her own, a pay-as-you-go program to keep the clients from staying away entirely. But some do anyway. Those are the ones who keep her up at night—the young immigrant who wanted to get birth control for the first time after having her third child, and another, not yet thirty, who couldn't afford to see a doctor about the growing cancer in her breast. "She doesn't have anyone," Naranjo said of the woman, who is also an immigrant. (Every patient has to present proof of legal status.) Naranjo found a private organization willing to provide treatment, but she doesn't know for how long—or how many more she can continue to impose on their goodwill.

And, of course, there are all the teenagers who no longer have access to free birth control: they now have to come up with $94 for an initial visit and a month's supply of pills. "That's where we are seeing a higher incidence of pregnancy," Naranjo said. She tries to work her sliding scale. She offers condoms, which are cheaper than pills, and then, she said, "you cross your fingers that their partners use them. You know they are going to be sexually active, no matter what you say."

The cycle Naranjo predicts is this: the state government prevents poor women from getting affordable health care and birth control, so there will be more abortions, more Medicaid births, more expensive complications, and more illnesses caught too late. This doesn't seem like a good outcome for anyone, much less fiscal conservatives or those who oppose abortion.

"We are going backward instead of forward," Naranjo said with a pained shrug. And then, like generations of Texas women before her, she got back to work.

Joyce Wadler

Joyce Wadler is a New York City humorist who writes the "I Was Misinformed" column for *The New York Times*, where she was a staff reporter for 15 years. Her previous newspaper and magazine work included New York correspondent for *The Washington Post*, reporter for *The New York Daily News* and the *New York Post*, and contributing editor to *New York* and *Rolling Stone*.

Her memoir about breast cancer, *My Breast: One Woman's Cancer Story*, originally a two-part cover story for *New York* magazine, was later expanded into a book. A television movie of *My Breast*, written by Wadler and starring Meredith Baxter and Jamey Sheridan, was broadcast on CBS and won the American Women in Radio and Television Excellence in Programming Award in 1995.

Five years after beating breast cancer, Wadler was diagnosed with advanced ovarian cancer, leading her to write *Cured, My Ovarian Cancer Story (Plucky Cancer Girl Strikes Back Book 2)*. It was first published as a two-part cover story in *New York* magazine.

Wadler is the author of *Liaison: The True Story of the M. Butterfly Affair*, about Bernard Boursicot, the French diplomat who was seduced into Chinese espionage and who granted her wide access to the story behind his affair with Shi Pei Pu, a male opera singer Boursicot believed to be female.

My Breast

A heartfelt, engrossing, and unexpectedly humorous account of one woman's victorious battle with breast cancer.

I have a scar on my left breast, four inches long, that runs from the right side of my breast to just above the nipple. Nick, whom I no longer see, once said that if anyone asked, I should say I was attacked by a jealous woman. The true story, which I prefer, is that a surgeon made the cut, following a line I had drawn for him the night before. He asked me where I wanted the scar, and I had put on a black strapless bra and my favorite party dress and drawn a line in ink just below the top of the bra, a good four inches below the tumor. The surgeon took it out using a local, and when he was done, I asked to see it. It was the size of a robin's egg, with the gray brainlike matter that gives it its name: medullary cancer. It rested in the middle of a larger ball of pink-and-white breast tissue, sliced down the center like a hard-boiled egg, an onionlike layering of whitish-gray tissue about it, and I looked at it hard, trying to figure it out. We did not know it was cancer until twenty minutes later, when they had almost finished stitching me up and the pathology report came back, and then I was especially glad I had looked. Mano a mano, eyeball to eyeball. This is a modern story. Me and my cancer. I won.

Whom do I introduce first, me or my breasts? Formerly, I thought of my body as a unit, indivisible, with my breasts in some small way contributing to my notion of who I am. Now that they have shown the ability to destroy me, I regard them with new respect, thinking perhaps they deserve not only separate but higher billing. As this is a breast-cancer story, maybe they should have it.

They are, anyway, good-size breasts, and though they are fibrocystic, which means the milk-producing tissues thicken and form fluid-filled sacs, and though I have what some people claim may be other predisposing factors for cancer—menstruation at an early age, no children—I did not worry about the disease. There is no history of breast cancer in my family; I do not smoke; I go to the gym. My father, the year before my diagnosis, died of prostate cancer, but I viewed this as a separate thing. Also, because I knew it would be difficult for me to spot a malignant lump given the cystic condition of my breasts, my gynecologist always examined them, and I had regular mammograms. I had my first when I was thirty. For the past five years, I had gone to the Guttman Breast Diagnostic Institute, which had been recommended to me by my gynecologist as being as good as a private service and a whole lot cheaper. In 1986, it was $45, as opposed to $125, and if a woman couldn't afford to pay, it was free. The wait was long, but there was a cozy female camaraderie, sitting in your paper hospital shirt next to ladies of all ages and seeing how many shapes we come in. One morning, when the room was exceptionally crowded, I counted and figured out there were 140 breasts ahead of me. I had a mammogram once a year, and every year the letter I got afterward began the same:

"Dear Ms. Wadler,

"We are pleased to inform you that the results of your examination were satisfactory and within normal limits. . . . "

Who I am is a journalist, forty-four, Jewish, never married, which, as everybody in New York knows, thanks to our one million collective hours of analysis, is a whole other category than single. I was raised in the Catskills, in a boarding house, in a large, noisy, opinionated family headed by my father's mother, who, rather than leaving the Russian *shtetl* of Molov Guburney, brought it to America with her. It enclosed her like a capsule, the Bubbie in the Bubble; she never learned to read English and spoke to me in Yiddish, a language I did not entirely understand. I came to New York, to the Village, at seventeen and have lived here since, working for newspapers and magazines. My closest friend is Herb, a comedy writer. We hang out so much that when I am seeing somebody, we joke about how to explain about Herb. Herb's idea is that I throw a sheet over him when he is lying on the couch reading the newspaper, and after each date I pull back the sheet a little bit, and by the time it gets serious, the guy's got the picture.

By the time this story begins, last year, I had a lot of serious dates and a lot of jobs and was working as a writer at *People* magazine. If, as research claims, tension contributes to disease, I was a good candidate: I had been working, for three years, on a book about a French espionage case, juggling six-month stays in Paris with a job in New York. Though the story, which inspired the play *M. Butterfly,* was wonderful, Paris, when I arrived, was hard: I had two friends in the city; I did not speak French; I sometimes went entire Sundays speaking only to waiters. Soon after I returned from my first stay in France, my father died an ugly death, hooked up to a life-support machine. I was a bad fit at *People* and always had been: I like forty inches just to say hello; the style at *People*, which I had come to respect as one does a skill that does not come easily, was somewhere between sausage and haiku: Reduce *War and Peace* to a snappy two-pager, and then, if Photo can't get a home take of Pierre and Natasha in the hot tub, they kill the story anyway. I was tired all the time: On weekends and evenings, I wrote my book; during the day I went to the magazine.

Also, I was in a difficult relationship. His name was Nick Di Stefano, he was a sportswriter I had known for years, and I had been seeing him, on and off, for eight months. He was Italian, which in my family is considered practically Jewish, except that (1) as children, Italians don't talk back to their parents, and (2) as adults, the men Run Around. Naturally, being so troublesome, we find them very appealing, and anyway, I had always liked Nick. He was smart; he knew all the lyrics to *The Pajama Game;* he dressed like a forties sharpie; he had the requisite newspaper Up-Yours Attitude toward authority. Also, there is something very nice about a relationship in which you have known each other a long time and are in the same business. We watched old movies from his collection, and he cooked and told me how much he loved his mother and took me dancing. Then he waltzed off to Miami for a weekend with an old girlfriend, and that was the end of Nick, Chapter One. She, it turned out, just wanted to be friends. Now when Nick is with me he is often petulant, seeing himself as the tragic hero of a doomed love affair, a role I have traditionally tried to reserve for myself.

"Why does it always have to be so serious with you?" he says. "Why can't we just live in the moment?"

And also, "You don't want me to work it out and decide what's right for me. You think if you give me enough time I'll get her out of my system."

"That's what you want in a woman, to be that selfless, you should be dating Mother Teresa," I say. "Why don't you call her up in Calcutta and see if she's available? From what you tell me, she's the only single woman you haven't nailed."

Then we break up and I go to bed for the weekend and lose two days out of my book.

That's where we're at, broken up, the morning I discover the lump. It is the first week in March, Monday, a crazy day at *People.* I am feeling particularly tense because I'm taking another leave of absence and have one week in which to finish my stories. I am so frantic I have canceled my mammogram at the Guttman, figuring I'll do it when my leave begins.

Then, as I'm showering, I feel it: a large, oval swelling on the upper inner part of my left breast. I have always wondered how women who discover lumps find them, but there is no missing this; it seems to be, as I move my hand around it, the size of an egg, slightly raised, sore to the touch. My breasts, since my mid-thirties, have been sore and swollen before my period, and as I've gotten older the soreness has increased—but I had my period two weeks ago. Another strange thing, this lump seems so big, and I don't remember it being there yesterday. I decide I should get it checked out, but am not very concerned. What I have heard about breast cancer is that except for a lump, it is asymptomatic; you don't have pain. I figure it's just another one of my fibrocystic lumps, which come and go. I'll call the Guttman and make that appointment for next week.

I go to work and forget about it. Then, in the afternoon, my breast starts to ache. I remember *People* has a staff doctor and call him. I feel a little silly about this; I am sure it is nothing, but I figure a doctor is right there in the building, so why not? He doesn't seem worried, either, until he examines me. Then his face tightens up. In the bright light of the examining room, where there is a small mirror, I see why: There is a pink flush on my breast over the lump, as if there is an inflammation, which I did not see at home. There is definitely something there, the doctor says. What it is he cannot say, but he thinks I should see a specialist. If I like, he'll be glad "to expedite it." I tell him I'm planning to go to Guttman next week. "I think it would be better if you saw somebody sooner than that," he says.

I burst into tears.

Boy, I think, I really must be strung tight today, and to him, though he hasn't mentioned the word that is now as much a presence in the room as another human being, I say, "Sorry. My father died last year of cancer."

He makes a call. An hour later, I am outside of the Time-Life Building, hailing a cab for the Upper East Side offices of a surgeon we'll call Luke. I am scared. Before I leave his office, the doctor asks if I will have health coverage during my leave, and that has added to my feeling that this is serious. I am now flip-flopping between telling myself I am overreacting and a giddy hysteria. Standing on Sixth Avenue, I have turned into Zorba the Greek. I want to *live*. The things I haven't done flash before me, a long list of "But wait, I wanna. . . ." But wait, I wanna finish my book; but wait, I wanna get married; but wait, I wanna make some money and take Nick to Paris to meet my friends; but wait, I'm just getting started. . . . I think about Nick and the time we've wasted fighting and make a deal with myself: If everything's OK, I won't worry about monogamy; I won't *hok* him about moving in; I will make the most of every moment. As unwittingly as Newton discovered gravity, I have stumbled upon the key to making me the dream girl of every uncommitting man in Manhattan: breast cancer.

In the doctor's office, there are a dozen women. They seem older than I, and oddly, they all look alike. They look like a truck ran over their faces, I find myself thinking, which I know, as soon as it crosses my mind, is an ugly thought and not correct. Then I realize what I am looking at: fear. I have never seen so much of it sitting together. It's a good thing there's nothing wrong with *me,* I think. Then, as I have to wait, I go for a walk. I have already called Herb, but now I find I want to talk to Nick too. He tells me it is probably nothing and is very sweet.

"Just tell me what you want me to do, baby," he says.

The doctor, when I get in to see him, is my age, a good listener, with the kind of Waspy calm I like to see in airline pilots and other people to whom I am entrusting my life. Speaking to him, I remember something: In the past few months, in addition to soreness before my period, my breasts have been sore afterward—so much that it was uncomfortable if Nick rested his head on my chest, and I wondered if I had had a false period and was pregnant.

Though I had called my gynecologist's office and asked a nurse if that was possible, it never occurred to me to make an appointment and have the doctor check my breasts—she had examined them four months before.

Now Luke examines me.

"I don't think this is anything to worry about," he says, and I feel relief rushing over me like a warm bath. "Malignancies tend to be hard, almost stony. You can't manipulate them. This you can. I'm 98 percent sure this is not malignant."

What he believes I have, Luke says, is an inflammation of some sort, perhaps a cyst. To find out, he would like to aspirate the lump: take out some liquid with a hypodermic, and send it to be analyzed. It's a painless procedure: All I'll feel is a needle prick. When a cyst is aspirated, a lot of liquid usually comes out, generally clear. It *is* painless, but it doesn't go as planned.

"Huh, that's odd," Luke says, and he shows me: He has been able to draw out very little liquid. What there is is thick and puslike, though that could be consistent with infection.

I get dressed. Luke tells me he still sees no reason for concern; the signs point to an inflammation, and he's prescribing Dicloxacillin, a form of penicillin. We'll try that for a week or two, and see if it reduces the swelling. If not, he will remove the lump. I am concerned: If it's a cyst, I say, how come more liquid didn't come out? And if it's not a cyst, what is it?

"I don't know," says Luke. "That's why we're doing the tests."

I go meet Nick at the Lion's Head, downtown. He's wearing his fedora low on his head and gives me that cocky Bronx grin that has always knocked me out.

"See, I knew it would be nothing," he says, and within hours we are un-broken up.

I am not a hypochondriac. I lean toward the other extreme, associating sickness with weakness and therefore denying being sick. This, I believe, is the legacy of my mother, Milly, who ran off to Florida at seventeen to paint flamingos on glass, in my childhood stole trees from state preserves insisting they were hers because her tax dollars had paid for them, and at sixty-five is still one of the great forces of nature.

"I've never been sick a day in my life," she says. "One hour after I had you, I was eating. The other women in the hospital were screaming their heads off. I made up my mind, 'How it went in, it will go out,' and that was that. This worrying you have about every little thing, *that* you got from your father. He was the worrier. Him and his mother. The Aspirin Addict."

Also, before going off at sixty-two as a volunteer in the Israeli army, "I don't fear death. Death to me is just another adventure. I can think of no greater honor than dying for the state of Israel, the Jewish homeland."

"You're an old dame, Ma," I say. "You think they're gonna put a machine gun in your hand and send you to the front? You're gonna be cleaning toilets."

"Don't even bother to bring back the body," she says.

I do fear death. Even more, I fear a bad death, strapped to machines in a hospital like my father. "Joyce," he had taken to telling me from the mountains, when I called once a week from Paris. "Your father is a very sick man. Your father is dying." I did not entirely believe him. I knew he was sick, very sick. I had been there for the early operations in the city and the last-minute flights to Florida. I knew the cancer was creeping up his spine and down his legs and was eventually going to kill him. But his blood counts were good, he was going to his business every day. It is a rotten thing to admit, but a voice in me, hearing him, was satirizing him; "Joyce, your father is dying"—Hebraic Dramatic Third Person, now replacing that previous family favorite, "You realize, of course, you are killing your father." He *was* a worrier, and critical and angry. Worrying how he and his mother and his two younger brothers would survive on a small dairy farm when he was nineteen and his father died; worrying about making a business out of nothing when he was in his thirties; worrying once he was successful it would all disappear. Then, when I got home from Paris, I saw the worrying was real: My father was sixty-seven and got up from his desk at the office like a man of eighty-five, his weight down thirty pounds, shaking, and supporting himself on a cane. Seeing me, he started to cry. "I never thought I'd see you again," he said, and I was filled with self-loathing. What the f--- was I doing in Paris all that time? I didn't even need all of that stuff. Why wasn't I here with my father? Two weeks later, he fell and broke his hip, and after that operation, his heart started to fail and they put him on life support. "You're not getting enough oxygen, Bernie," the doctor said. "Your lungs are exhausting your heart. If we don't put you on this machine, you're going to die. Do you give your consent?" My father nodded yes. Nobody in the family had any idea what life support meant, but in an hour, when they let us in to see him, we found out. An oxygen tube had been stuffed down his nose, his hands were strapped to the side of the bed, and he was pulling against the straps like an animal at auction, trying to speak but unable to because of the tube down his throat.

"We had to tie his hands to the bed because he already pulled the tube out of his nose once," one of the doctors said. "He's a little out of it now because we sedated him."

He was on the machine for two months. A few days into it, they gave him a tracheotomy so he would be more comfortable, but he could never again speak. I knew it was his life and going on the machines had been his decision, but I never changed my mind about it. I thought he would have been better off dead.

I do not, however, dwell on that memory the week of the scare. I trust Dr. Luke, and I know he's good—a friend was a patient; his reputation is excellent. I do mention the lump to my mother, who is in Florida for the winter, but I tell her I don't think it's serious, and I believe it.

That changes a little on Thursday when I talk to Luke about the test results. He tells me, in a tone indicating there is nothing to be concerned about, the results are pretty much what he expected, though there are "a number of atypical cells which could be consistent with an inflammation."

My old reporter's bell goes off.

"What do you mean atypical?" I ask. "How many cells?"

He seems a bit irritated, as if I'm worrying for no reason.

"A number," he says. "But that could happen with an infection. Keep taking the penicillin and come in in ten days, and we'll see what to do then."

The next week, I start my leave. Though *People* and I have our problems, they have been extraordinarily good to me. This is my third leave; it includes health benefits. I am perhaps eighty pages away from finishing the book, and it is a wonderful section. My twenty-four-year-old assistant, Stefan, back in Paris, has cornered a particularly evasive source. The story is reaching its climax: My hero, Bernard, a member of the French Foreign Service, has been charged with espionage and made the terrible discovery that the woman for whom he became a spy is a man.

The only thing is, I am distracted by this thing in my chest. It's so sore I cannot sleep on my stomach. The penicillin doesn't seem to be doing much after ten days. There is a very bright light in my gym locker room, and I see how vivid and delineated the area around the lump still is.

"I'm starting to feel this thing has a life of its own," I tell Herb one night, as he's stretched out on the couch. "Like it's gonna come flying out of my body any minute, like that thing in *Alien,* and run around the living room and put on a sports channel and tell me to get it a beer."

I decide it's time for independent research and pull out my medical reference books. My old standby, the AMA *Family Medical Guide,* is not very comforting: It defines "breast abscess" as a pus-filled infected area but it says that it is uncommon and usually affects women who are breast-feeding. It says, starting to make me nervous, that a cancerous lump "may or may not be painful," occurs most often in women in their forties and fifties, and is "slightly more common in women who have never breast-fed a baby." The only good news is it is also "slightly more common" in women whose families have a history of the disease. The *Professional Guide to Diseases* is worse. It adds white middle- and upper-class women to the higher-risk list, as well as those "who are under constant stress or undergo unusual disturbances in their home or work lives."

Eleven days after the discovery of the lump, I go back to see Dr. Luke. He examines my breast and in less than a minute makes a decision.

"This has to come out," he says.

I am not scared now—I am relieved. I don't think it's cancer—I'm too healthy for cancer—I just want this thing out of my body, the sooner the better. I'd be happy if Luke could do it right now in the office. He says that's out of the question. It will be done with a local anesthetic at a hospital and will take maybe half an hour. I ask if I can watch: I saw breast surgery when I did a story on a plastic surgeon in Beverly Hills, and I also hung out for a month at the New York City morgue, so I figure I won't be squeamish. Luke says he'll be glad to explain as he cuts but that most people do not want to watch when theirs is the body involved. I decide he's right.

I also realize I am concerned about a scar. I've never considered myself particularly vain; I have always thought of scars as a badge of honor, a sign of an enemy vanquished, but those, I now realize, were scars on other people. Luke says he can reach the lump from any number of spots—just show him where to make the cut. He books the surgery for five days later, at St. Luke's-Roosevelt Hospital Center, one of the hospitals where he has privileges. I have one last problem.

"I've got this deadline on this book," I say. "This isn't going to hang me up time-wise, is it?"

"Listen," Luke says, "this comes first. This is your life."

A few friends by now know I have a lump in my breast and am a bit worried about it, but it is Herb I ask to come to the hospital. He is not simply my best friend but a free lance, while Nick is on a staff. Also, after the initial enthusiasm that accompanies all our reconciliations, Nick is preoccupied with his own problems: an apartment he cannot sell; his unrequited romance. He also hates doctors. Who goes to the doctors? asks Nick. Women. Something is wrong, the best thing you can do is leave it alone, and it will fix itself. In my case, we don't even know that anything is wrong, so let's just quit thinking about it. I think I know what the real story is: his first wife, the mother of his twenty-two-year-old son, who developed schizophrenia in her late twenties. She was a nurse, she had some idea what was going on, and when a doctor confirmed it, she killed herself. I give up trying to talk to Nick and take a stroll by myself to Barnes & Noble, to the section where they have the medical textbooks. The most comprehensive seems to be *Breast Cancer, Conservative and Reconstructive Surgery,* by Bohmert, Leis, and Jackson, a surgical atlas. It's $129, too much to spend if I don't even know I have a problem, but I skim it, looking at the pictures. There are a lot of women squishing a breast like they are squeezing the Charmin. I figure it's to show how lifelike reconstructions are, but it strikes me as a man's notion of what is important to a woman. I have never squeezed my breast that hard, and if a man did it I would holler. I flip through the studies. Every one seems to include a five-year survival rate. I put the book back.

I spend the night before surgery alone. Nick calls three times, asking when I am leaving for the hospital so he can call and wish me good luck. I remember I have to make my decision about the scar. I put on a bandeau bra that is the skimpiest I own and a skinny little Nicole Miller dress, deep purple, with spaghetti straps, that I wore when Nick took me dancing at the Rainbow Room. I loved that night. I had a thirties evening bag that I had got for forty francs at a flea market in Paris and a Deco rhinestone bracelet from an estate sale in New York, and as I get dressed I wonder about the women who had owned the bag and the bracelet, and where they had worn them, and if they had been as happy as I. Then I take off the dress and turn down the top of the bra a little bit and trace the edge with a ballpoint pen. As I do, I start to cry. I don't have a perfect body by model standards, my breasts are different from what they were in my twenties, but they are my breasts, it is my body, and I like it very much. Now I am making a mark that says, "Cut me."

Next morning, I talk to Nick. "Call me with the good news as soon as you get out of surgery," he says. Then I go to the hospital with Herb. In the taxi, I remember all our strange trips; Kenya, where we eyed the lions from an open Land Rover and were scared they were seeing two New York Jews and getting an urge for delicatessen; Paris, where we went looking for Jim Morrison's grave at Père-Lachaise Cemetery and had no idea where to find it until we spotted a girl with pink hair. I tell Herb what we should do is regard this as just another weird adventure.

"You sure you don't want to ask to watch the surgery, because it could be kind of interesting," I say.

"Pass," says Herb.

Roosevelt is gloomy. A group of homeless people has set up housekeeping on the Fifty-Eighth Street side, a sofa and two armchairs arranged in a traditional living-room style. Inside, the hospital needs painting. On the third-floor short-term-stay center, Herb parks himself in a reception area, while I go to a large room, which is partitioned with curtains, and change into baggy hospital clothes. Taking off my bra, I see that the line I have drawn is very low, nearly halfway down my breast. Wonderful, I think. Now the doctor is going to think I'm fast. A few minutes later, the surgical resident who will be assisting Luke drops by.

"Whoa! You can't miss that!" he says when he examines me.

Luke comes to get me. He looks very preppy, sockless in clogs, and is very sweet, putting an arm around me as we walk to the operating room. I have a feeling this is politically incorrect behavior and I am not supposed to like it, but I do. The operating team includes a male and a female nurse, as well as the resident and Luke. Seeing the line on my breast, Luke laughs.

"You've sure made this idiotproof," he says.

They paint my breast with a red-brown ointment that smells like iodine and cover the rest of my chest with sterile cloth. I can't see the surgery, because Luke has asked me to turn my face to the right, but he has promised to tell me what I will feel and what he is doing. The anesthetic is Xylocaine. He injects it around my breast, waiting for the area to numb, then makes a cut. I have a feeling of warmth and wetness. Then there are strong sensations of tugging as he pulls back tissue and starts tunneling up to the lump, in the inner upper quadrant of my breast. Sometimes I feel a bit of pain, almost a burning sensation, and he gives me more Xylocaine.

The tunneling goes on for twenty minutes, and while it is not as unpleasant as a dentist's drilling, the more tissue that is pulled apart and clamped, the more uncomfortable I become. I am having second thoughts about being so concerned about looking good in a low-cut dress. Luke tells me they've reached the lump, but they're going to go beyond it and take a margin of healthy tissue. I'm getting worried again. I don't know whether the room is cool or I'm feeling a nervous chill, but Luke seems to be cutting a lot of flesh—I know the lump is high, but I feel he is burrowing up toward my collarbone. Then I feel some final tugging and the thing is out, and I see out of the corner of my eye a metal tray and they are cauterizing blood vessels. Luke moves away from the operating table and a few minutes later comes back. It's a tumor all right, he says, sounding serious, but what sort he cannot say. He's sending it to the lab now. I tell him that before he does, I'd like to see it.

"You sure?" he says.

"Yeah," I say. He picks it up. I am astonished at how big it is. The excised flesh is the size of a tangerine and has been sliced down the middle to expose the cross-section of the tumor—that must be what Luke did when he left the table. The tumor, which is the size of a robin's egg, is grayish white, with a layer of whitish-pink tissue. Around that is what appears to be normal breast tissue, pink and white, like very fatty, coarsely ground chopped meat. Luke points out the layering around the tumor, saying it appears to be encapsulated, and that is good. I don't think any of this is good. I can't believe this big gray glob came out of me. I have a bad feeling, a sense of unreality, as if I am in a dream or a place I had no intention to be.

"How soon will we know the results?" I say, as they start stitching me up.

"About twenty minutes," Luke says.

And then, more to myself than to anyone else.

"How am I going to tell my mother?"

"Don't get yourself worked up," the male nurse says. "We don't even know that it's anything, yet," and I try to hold on to that thought. But another part of me thinks he's patronizing me; maybe they don't want to deal with a flipped-out woman on the table if they've got to stitch up her chest. I feel lonely, unable to say what I'm thinking, and scared. I concentrate on being calm. In fifteen minutes, just as they've finished bandaging me, somebody comes into the room.

"Well, it is a tumor, and it *is* malignant," Luke begins briskly, as if he's giving a lecture to a group of medical students. "It's what's called a medullary carcinoma; it's . . ."

I am having trouble following. Thoughts are going through my head faster than I was aware thoughts could travel: This can't be real. Is he telling me I'm going to die? Should I ask for a rabbi? No, wait, I'm not a religious Jew, I'm more like an ethnic Jew—that would be hypocritical. But maybe rabbis in hospitals are more like therapists. Why is he telling me this stuff here, where I'm alone? Wasn't that the point of bringing Herb?

I interrupt him.

"Do you think we could hold off on this until we get upstairs and you can talk to my friend too?" I say.

And, as we head to the third-floor waiting room, "I think I could use a drink."

They offer me a wheelchair, but I don't want it—it is very important for me to be on my feet. Herb is where I left him. I have been formulating the idea that it will be bad to be negative, that I'm under attack and it's got to be all systems go, but as I see Herb, I give him a thumbs down and shake my head. Luke shows us into one of the little curtained-off cubicles.

"It's, like, malignant," I say.

Herb looks dazed. We find chairs. A nurse, hearing what is going on, brings me a cup of coffee, a small act of kindness that is enormously comforting. Luke starts his talk from the top. I had remembered from my father's illness that it is important to take notes when you see the doctor, because in times of stress you do not remember all you hear. My notebook is in a locker with my clothes, but I see Herb, stunned as he is, pull his little notebook from his blazer and start writing, as if it's the old days and he's at a press conference. I feel a wave of love. He's so solid. I focus in on Luke. He is saying that they've removed a medullary cancer, which is a relatively infrequent type, with "a better than average prognosis." It was "a well-circumscribed mass," 2.8 centimeters, with seemingly clean tissue around it—he'll have more detailed results in a few days. It has been caught early; clinically, it's a stage-two cancer. Provided there is no cancer in the lymph nodes under the arm, it is "quite curable." I do not entirely believe him. I was in the room with my father when a New York specialist told him that prostate cancer was curable. Four years later, he was dead. On the other hand, this is all so weird, I don't know what to believe. I don't even know, when I say what I say next, if it is me or something I picked up from the movies. I just feel it's important to get it straight.

"Look," I say, "I have no plans of dying of this thing. That's just not how I see my life. So what's the next step?"

Luke runs through them: The next thing to do is remove some lymph nodes from under my left arm and see if the cancer has spread. That's very important, the key diagnostic tool. We also have to decide how we want to treat the breast: with lumpectomy and radiation or with mastectomy and reconstruction. Lumpectomy is removing the tumor and leaving the breast, which is what he has just done, except that he would reopen the incision to take another look. The success rates for lumpectomy and mastectomy are the same. Whichever I choose, the lymph nodes have to come out.

I have another terror besides death—general anesthesia.

"Lymph-node surgery, can it be done under a local?" I ask.

"Impossible," he says.

I remember lymph nodes. When they took a sampling from my father's groin, there was cancer in eight out of eleven. I didn't know what that meant, exactly, but I knew it was bad: The surgeon, calling Dad's room after the operation, asked to speak to me, not my mother.

"What are the chances it's in the lymph nodes?" I ask.

"Twenty to 30 percent," he says.

I'm feeling dreamlike again. I don't get it, I tell Luke. I had mammograms, I had checkups, this thing was enormous; how was it missed? He says medullary is not like other cancers—it may not calcify and can appear on a mammogram as a cyst.

"So how do we know there's not another one of these things somewhere inside me? I say.

"We don't," he says. "Your breasts are a breast surgeon's nightmare. They're large and dense and full of lumps.'

I remember the pictures in the medical book. The real ones are gonna be this dangerous, let them make me a fake.

"Take it off," I say.

He explains a bit about breast reconstruction. I had assumed it was like the breast-enlargement surgery I had seen in Los Angeles, an operation in which the doctor put a silicone implant under the muscles or tissue of the breast and the patient woke up with a new breast—except that in the case of cancer, you would remove the breast tissue first. Luke says it is not that simple: You don't wake up with a new breast; they put an expander in your chest; it takes a few months. If I go with lumpectomy, in which radiation is required, it takes six weeks. Lymph-node removal involves three or four days in the hospital. There are no shortcuts—this is cancer. I do not have to decide about mastectomy or lumpectomy in a few days, but I should have surgery within four weeks. Whichever procedure I choose, lymph-node removal will be done at the same time. After that, there's a good chance I'll need chemotherapy for six months. Meanwhile, they'll be doing more tests on the tumor: DNA analysis, hormone receptors. I can take the cotton dressing off my breast tomorrow and come to his office Friday; he'll have those results and take out the stitches. I'm having trouble assimilating all this; so is Herb. We're two liberal-arts guys suddenly thrown into Columbia Medical School. I'm still back with the idea that reconstruction is a long-term process and I may be walking around lopsided for five months. Luke recommends *Dr. Susan Love's Breast Book.*

I have one more question. I am afraid to ask it, but I have to anyway.

"What am I looking at here?" I ask. "Statistically?"

He isn't any happier answering than I am asking. He doesn't care much for statistics, he says. You can still have a cancer that has a high cure rate, and if you're in the percentage that is not cured, it doesn't matter. In my case, I have a cancer that has a favorable prognosis and is "more curable than average."

I need something harder.

"When my father was diagnosed with prostate cancer, it was something like a 60 percent survival rate at four years, a 40 percent survival rate at seven years," I say.

"I would say the statistics, in your case, are considerably better than that," he says.

"How much better?" I ask.

"For breast cancer, the overall cure rate is 70 percent. For medullary, it's above that. I would say 80 percent, 90 percent."

I feel better. I like these odds. I don't entirely believe them, but I like them. This leaves me with one immediate problem: how to tell my mother. Herb has the solution: "lead with the positive." I find my notebook, and we work out the lead and phone it in. The last time I did this, I remember, I was filing a breaking story for *The Washington Post* on a Concerto for Piano and Dog at Carnegie Hall. The dog had stage fright, which was good for me, as it gave me a new top. There is a reason people hate reporters. The phone rings, and I begin the performance.

"Well, Ma, I'm out of surgery, and I'm here at the hospital and everything went great," I say.

"Oh, thank God, I'm so relieved, I don't know what to say, I was so nervous I couldn't sit still, my friends called, I told everybody, 'Get off, get off, I can't talk, my daughter is right now this minute having surgery in New York. . . .'"

I break through the wall of words, power-talking, a skill I developed from forty-three years of training with champions.

"The lump turned out to be malignant, but it's the best kind you can have," I say. "It's called medullary, it tends not to spread, they seem to have got it all. It was in one lump, I saw it, it looks like it was encapsulated, that's a good sign."

Silence. She believes me like I believe the doctors.

"I'm coming north," she says.

I tell her she is staying put, I probably won't be having surgery for at least a month, and hit her with all the other positive stuff I can think of. This cancer is very rare, hardly anybody gets it, and it has a very, very good prognosis. Yeah, it was big, but this kind grows very fast, and the doctor says we caught it early. The longer I talk, the harder it is. I am hearing my mother and my dead grandmothers and all the aunts in the family. "The worst thing in the world that can happen, the very worst thing, is for a parent to survive a child." they are saying.

"Talk to Herb, Ma," I say and walk down the hall.

Then I call Nick. Most of our relationship, I've wanted him to be more expressive. Often, when we are together, he withdraws and watches two or three old movies in a row—if he doesn't, he says, he'll think about his life, which he can't bear. In the morning, he moves the television so that he can watch *Lucy* reruns from the shower. Right now, however, I have this feeling that if he falls apart I will fall apart, and I need him to be strong.

"I'm going to tell you something, and I don't want you to get emotional, because it's going to sound worse than it probably is," I say.

I have the feeling, at the other end of the line, of a man who has been slugged in the stomach.

"You just got to give me a minute. I wasn't expecting this," he says.

Then Herb and I head downtown. Normally, a glass of wine puts me to sleep. Now we ago to the back room of the Lion's Head, where we are known as The Ones Who Only Eat, and I order a margarita. I get a second one. Then I talk tactics. The position I am taking, I say, is not that I have cancer, but that I *had* a cancer and they cut it out. I am not doing an avoidance number, we will research the hell out of this and get the best people in the business, but until it is established otherwise, I consider myself healthy. I go tottering off to my place. I am not sure whether the sense of unreality is coming from the news I have received or the drinks. The Xylocaine is wearing off, and with every step, even in a bra and bandages, my breast bounces and hurts. Luke had offered me a prescription of Tylenol 3, but I'm a little afraid of drugs, and I didn't think I needed it. Now I see I do. I call up the pharmacy to have the drug sent over. Even with the Tylenol my breast feels as if someone has stabbed me. I know I should talk to my brothers, who by this time have probably had thirteen conversations with Ma, but I am too tired. I go to bed, exhausted, wanting to be taken care of. I think of my grandmother Wadler, round, warm, and cushiony, the one member of the family who thought I was perfect just as I was, and wish she were still around. I think about Nick, who has said he will get out of work as soon as he can and pick up supper, and wonder what is keeping him. He calls, eventually, from the street near his bar. The bank must have messed up, he says, he can't get any money from the machine, he's got maybe three dollars. I go to meet him at Balducci's, bumping into Sigmund Freud on the way. "You understand the message he is sending you," Freud says. "You vill not depend on him for nossing." I banish him from my consciousness by taking him to the deli department and giving him a number and telling him to pick up some derma. There is no derma in Balducci's. By the time Freud figures it out, I'll have lost him.

When Nick and I get back to my place, just on a point of pride, I set the record straight.

"I'm still the same person I was yesterday," I tell him. "If we break up every three weeks, we break up every three weeks. I don't want you to treat me any differently."

Which, as it turns out, is the stupidest thing I will say in the course of this whole illness.

And also, as far as Nick is concerned, the least necessary.

If this were ancient Egypt, and people were buried with the things they used most often, the executors of my estate would have no problem making a decision: They would plant me with a phone in one hand and a Diet Pepsi in the other, and if it turned out there was life after death, I would be on the phone, talking to one of my girlfriends or having an emergency session with my shrink. It being late when I am prone to anxiety attacks, I would probably reach a machine:

"It's Joyce. It isn't a question of life and death—well, actually, it is, but I mean I can handle it—um, anyway, this death thing has turned out to be a little more stressful than I thought, and if you have some time, can you give me a call? If it's not inconvenient. Otherwise, I'll see you at the regular time Thursday. One good thing about this, you won't have any trouble getting me to lie down."

But when I get a diagnosis of cancer, it changes. It isn't just that I am numb from the news and the surgery. It isn't even that I need to be alone to sort this stuff out. I have spent a lifetime sorting things out with my friends. But now, I feel, I am under serious attack, and when the Scud missiles are raining on your head, you don't have time to get on the phone with your girlfriends and say you are terribly depressed. Also, there is something else—I am afraid of negativity. *Cancer* is a scary word; people hear it and think "death," and I don't want that sort of energy around me. I also don't want to hear, however well-meaning, other people's stories. Until now, I thought breast cancer was breast cancer. I had no idea there were different kinds, some more dangerous than others. I also realize that everyone's body is different. I love my friends, I want their support, but hearing a story about a friend of a friend who "had it" and is now doing fine will be a waste of my time—what I need is hard facts about medullary and information about the options. I'll tell some close friends the diagnosis, but they have to keep it to themselves. Just on a professional level, I don't want this around. Journalists are the biggest gossips in the world and the least reliable—one lunch at Orso, and three hours later word will be all over town that Wadler is dying, and I'll never get another book. I'm also making a rule: Information goes out, but unless I ask, it doesn't come in. Herb and I also ask friends to let me call them. If they want to know the details of what's happening medically, they can call Herb for briefings. Herb calls them Breast Conferences.

Wednesday, the day after the surgery, I get organized. I have an advantage: I am a reporter, and so are a lot of my friends. I call up two or three and give them a task: Herb looks for Dr. Love's book and checks on Luke's credentials (they're excellent); Heidi, a magazine editor I have known for twenty years, will call the American Cancer Society and the National Institutes of Health; Max, who is the bureau chief for an out-of-town paper, will call his contacts: we'll all get names for second opinions. There is no way, with a life-threatening disease, I am not getting a second opinion. The reference I trust most comes from an old friend who is a doctor and researcher. "You'll go to Jeanne Petrek at Sloan-Kettering for the surgery, Norton as the oncologist. He's the head of the breast-cancer department at Sloan, very sharp. He's a friend, our wives are friends. Make the call and tell him I sent you. No, wait, I'll make the call myself."

I've got other problems, too: my job and my book. My publisher has paid a bundle for this story—"Let's face it, now they own you," Ma had said when I signed the contract, and I have no idea how long this breast business is going to hang me up. I have the same concern about *People*. Neither is a problem. The publisher tells me to concentrate on my health. *People* editor Lanny Jones changes my unpaid literary leave to a medical leave—on full pay—and says the resources of the company are behind me. Within days, I've got four people from Medical calling me with the names of cancer support groups and specialists. It's a relief. But I wonder, What happens to poor women in New York who don't have medical insurance, and don't have families that can help them, and don't have friends to get them to the head of the department at Sloan-Kettering?

But I have another ongoing problem closer to home: Ma. They have an interesting way of dealing with illness in my family. They form little whispering cabals, deciding who can "take it." Or, if they must deliver bad news, they hit you in a roundabout way. "You know your uncle Murray, in the hospital in Kingston, he's not doing very well," my aunt Shirley had told me, in a phone conversation years ago. Then she asked to speak to my boyfriend. A few minutes later, he passed back the phone. "Actually," said Shirley, "he's dead."

I have never understood this, but now I do: You don't tell the people you love, because you want to protect them. But in doing that, you cut yourself off. I talk to Nick about it. He says mothers are stronger than you think, and anyway, I owe my family the full story. The day after the biopsy, I call her.

"I figured you might be worrying, and I was just wondering if you had any questions," I say.

"Yeah," she says. "What aren't you telling me?"

Trick question. Damn, these mothers are smart. I tell her there is a small possibility "it" may be in the lymph nodes, but if it is, it's not the end of the road. I say because I am concerned another lump might one day be missed, I am leaning toward mastectomy and reconstruction, but that might not be so bad—it would be fun to be able to wear cute little camisoles, and maybe, at forty-three, I could use a perkier pair.

She's scared. I can tell because she hits me with Second-Generation Wadler Cure-All One:

"You know money is not an issue."

"I know that, Ma," I tell her. "It's OK. I got insurance."

"New underwear, anything cosmetic, that's on me," she says.

"Well, I don't know, Ma," I say. "My bras are very expensive. I don't know if a poor old widow like you can afford them."

"Thirty-four B is a good size," she says. "I'll bring cash. I'll put a thousand in your account." She starts upping the amount, bargaining with some unseen force. "Three. No, five. Six. For the things that aren't covered by insurance. Taxis for back and forth to the hospital. New underwear. A wig." I'm suddenly peeved.

"What makes you think I'm gonna need a wig?" I ask her. "I didn't say anything about chemotherapy. I'm healthy. I *had* cancer. I'm just giving you some remote possibilities, because you asked. Anyway, that stuff about chemotherapy has changed—not everybody loses their hair."

"A blonde one," she says. "On me."

This is another strange thing about breast cancer: Though I have just been told I have a life-threatening disease, it's not like a cold or the flu, where you feel sick. Physically, the day after the biopsy, I feel as strong as I've ever been. My breast aches, but only mildly, and I can take care of it with the Tylenol. I can't see the cut on my breast when I take off the cotton pads, because it's covered with a row of fancy bandages, but my left breast, despite the amount of tissue that's been removed, looks the same size as the right, and somehow I knew it would. Medically, however, we're all still very confused. Herb is having trouble finding Dr. Love's book; NIH doesn't know of any medullary experts. Also, we don't understand why you would do a mastectomy at the same time as the lymph-node surgery. If the lymph-node surgery is to see if the cancer has spread, wouldn't you do that first? If it has spread, why take off a breast?

I go back to Barnes & Noble. They don't have Dr. Love's book, either, but they do have my old pal, *Breast Cancer, Conservative and Reconstructive Surgery.* I plunk down the $129 and get it. I also pick up *The Pill Book: The Illustrated Guide to the Most Prescribed Drugs in the United States,* one or two paperbacks on breast cancer, and a book by Norman Cousins, the former editor of *Saturday Review* magazine: *Heard First: The Biology of Hope and the Healing Power of the Human Spirit.* I remember hearing about Cousins's work a few years ago; he had a serious illness and cured himself by laughing. Thursday evening, before going to Luke's, I start reading the medical books. What they say is a lot stronger than what Luke said:

Cancers are classified in stages, depending on size, whether they are in the nodes, and whether they have spread to other parts of the body. There are four stages and stage two is not that great: According to one study, the five-year survival rate is 65 percent. Medullary is rare, accounting for perhaps 7 percent of breast cancers, but it can spread, and if it does, it can kill you. The worst kind of breast cancer, accounting for perhaps 2 percent, is inflammatory. The skin is flushed and has a *peau d'orange* texture—exactly what I saw the day my lump was discovered. Very few people live beyond five years with inflammatory cancer. I am petrified. I don't care that the lab reports have classified my cancer as medullary. What if they made a mistake? And even if it's only medullary, these statistics are hell. I call up Nick, convinced I am doomed. "You're driving yourself crazy," he says. "What do you care what some book says? Maybe it's out of date. Your doctor says you have the best kind." I am not interested in anything Nick has to say. I just want to be next to him in bed and hold him.

At nine the next morning, I meet Herb at Dr. Luke's. My breast, when Luke pulls out the sutures, has a thick pink scar, but I think I heal great. The problem is, I'm so frightened by what I've read in the medical books, I'm almost stuttering. When I tell Luke about my research, he is not happy. He knows some patients do this—lawyers, usually—but it's not a great thing to do if you're not a doctor because you can easily misinterpret things. I do *not* have inflammatory cancer. On the basis of size I have a stage-two cancer, but medullary is *not* the average breast cancer. I have, he repeats, a very favorable case.

We move on to the big decision: mastectomy or lumpectomy. I still don't understand why one would decide about mastectomy before knowing if cancer is in the nodes. Luke says one has nothing to do with the other. Lymph-node dissection is diagnostic; it indicates whether the cancer has spread. Mastectomy or lumpectomy has to do with treating the breast and killing any remaining cancer. If the cancer had been found in a few places on the breast, a doctor would likely recommend mastectomy. If one is worried about recurrence, one might also.

Herb wants to know the statistics on recurrence. Luke says with lumpectomy, it's 15 or 20 percent; with mastectomy, it's down to 4 percent. My chances of getting cancer in the other breast is higher than other people's, 7 percent for the next ten years, but Luke does not recommend a prophylactic mastectomy. He's sending me for a mammogram, but he sees no indication of trouble in my right breast.

I want to know about reconstruction. Luke says at the time of the lymph-node surgery, he'd remove the breast tissue, leave most of the skin, but remove the nipple—it's safer, because in one out of four times, the cancer is in the nipple. Then a plastic surgeon puts in an implant and constructs a new breast. It will look good, he says, but it won't *feel* like a breast. It's an artificial implant. I try to imagine what it will feel like. A contact lens which at first you are always aware of, then never feel? A football?

I am lost. I ask, since the current rate is the same with mastectomy and lumpectomy, what the doctor recommends.

"I think mastectomy is the better treatment for you," Luke says. "You've got difficult breasts, large, lumpy, and you're worried about recurrence. Lumpectomy is for people who say, 'I don't want to lose the breast no matter what.' That wasn't your response. The only advantage of lumpectomy is that it preserves the breast. But it's your decision."

It is true, I think, that my first reaction was "Take off the breast"—but that was before I knew what reconstruction involved. Now I'm not certain. I ask Luke if, aside from statistics and my case, he has a personal bias. He says he has had three medullary patients, and since one had a recurrence, he leans toward reconstruction. He also says that since he took so much tissue out of the breast, reconstruction will probably give me the better cosmetic result. I tell him I don't think that will be a problem; my breasts are still the same size.

"That's swelling from the surgery, and some pockets of air," he says. "When it goes down, it may be much smaller."

He suggests I talk to a plastic surgeon—there is one he thinks would be temperamentally suited for me, because he's an artist and a doctor. I take this to mean that Luke is clarifying me as a patient who is not so stable and is likely to cut off an ear or that he has been influenced by Herb's beard, but I'm happy to be seeing the artist-doctor. Maybe when we get to his office, he'll offer us an espresso. I haven't had any breakfast. I could use it.

My mammogram, which we have taken across the street, is normal, except for what the report calls "a large radiolucency, in the left breast, consistent with residual air." Apparently, Luke is right: My nice plump breast is pumped up like a Macy's balloon and may deflate at any moment.

Then, in what's turning into a cancer triathlon, Herb and I rush to the office of the plastic surgeon, Dr. Frank Veteran, in the Eighties, off Fifth. I'm a little worried about Herb. He's the sort of man who feels uncomfortable in the lingerie department at Saks; I'm remembering photos of mastectomy from my medical books and wondering how graphic this consultation is going to get. But at the same time I'm excited. In the taxi, I have come up with a wonderful idea: Rather than mastectomy, why not, after treating my breast with radiation, do a reduction? If I get rid of, say, 30 percent of breast, I remove 30 percent of potentially dangerous, cancer-bearing tissue. I won't have to run around nipple less or with a football in my chest. I could also end up with a very pretty pair of breasts. I do like my body, basically; there are times I look at myself naked and think I'm gorgeous, but as I've gotten older, or have seen skinny women with high little breasts at the gym, I have sometimes felt bad, looking at my sag, and wondered what it would be like to have a lift. I like Dr. Veteran, too. He's not slick; there's an air about him that suggests he has had personal experience with serious illness. Now, after Dr. Veteran examines me, I hit him with my idea. It's original, all right—Veteran doesn't know of anyone who's done it—but he also says it's not a good idea. Radiated tissue is difficult to work with: Some of the smaller blood vessels are destroyed; it doesn't heal as well as normal skin. If one must operate on radiated tissue, one does, but he would prefer not to. Doing the reduction *before* the radiation is not a good idea, either. Reduction is a major surgery; it takes time to heal, and that could delay radiation treatment. This is cancer; the medical considerations have to come first. My skin is good; I'm young; I can get "a very good cosmetic result" with reconstruction. The words "very good cosmetic result" disturb me. Is it a suggestion that I really could use a new pair? Is he saying, in a roundabout way, that what he has seen is awful? I have a sudden image of Joan Rivers, in an off-camera booth, feeding the surgeon lines. "She takes off her bra," she says, "she could nurse SoHo."

He explains reconstruction: At the time of the mastectomy, he would put an expander, made of silicone, under the muscles of my chest. You couldn't put it directly under the skin, as you would with breast augmentation, because all the breast tissue is gone, and there would be nothing to serve as a cushion between the implant and the skin. Over a four-to-six-week period, a saline solution would be injected into the implant, enlarging it. The muscles on top of the implant would stretch, as in pregnancy, but, as in pregnancy, you couldn't stretch them all at once. After two or three months, after the tissue around the implant has "settled down," there would be a second operation and a permanent prosthesis would replace the expander. If you're having chemotherapy, you have to wait longer because chemotherapy usually brings down the white-blood-cell count, increasing the risk of infection. Finally, in the case of large-breasted women like myself, there would be a third operation, a reduction of the healthy breast, to make it match the first and to build a nipple for the reconstructed breast.

To somebody who is terrified of general anesthesia, this is awful—I'm looking at three extra operations, not one. Then the doctor shows us the pictures and it's worse: a color Polaroid of a woman whose breast looks like a halved grapefruit. The shape is perfectly round; a thick red scar runs from one side to the other; the woman has no nipple and no areola.

"I can't walk around for six months looking like that," I say. "It's like a nuclear catastrophe."

Then I feel terrible.

"What I mean is, it just sort of throws me, the idea of walking around like that with no nipple. I'm sure when it's all finished it looks really nice," I say.

The doctor shows us more Polaroids, including women with their finished breasts, who look much better. He says there are implants he can use for a more natural look, but while they have the same texture, all breast tissue is different, so my breast may not feel the same. His patients say, however, that after a while they are not aware of the implant—it just becomes their breast. He's a lovely guy. It's running on two-thirty; we were booked at the last minute, and I'm sure he hasn't had any lunch, but he acts like he has all the time in the world.

We leave. I know now, I tell Herb, I don't want reconstruction. There is no way I am going to do those things to my body.

I also realize something else.

"You know how we're always saying we miss things," I say. "We weren't around for Paris in the twenties; we weren't reporters in New York in the forties; I had tickets to Woodstock, too much mud, I didn't go. It just hit me: All these stories about breast cancer—for this trend I'm right on time."

A week after I am diagnosed with breast cancer, I have a nightmare: I am in France with Stefan, my twenty-three-year-old assistant and translator on my book, and we are driving in my father's car, a big Chevy, in a part of the countryside that is new to us. The people are suspicious and unfriendly; the terrain is strange: encroaching on the road, perilously close, are ditches of water and irregularly shaped little lakes, some covered with ice. I don't know whether Stefan or I am driving, I only know that we have to be careful. Then, suddenly, we are on a lake. At first we are OK, driving on top of the water, and then we start to sink. I am trying to figure out how to get out and still save my father's car, which is fairly new and expensive. Should we roll the windows shut, so the car doesn't sink as fast and maybe even will float? But if we do that and the doors stick, we'll be trapped, so maybe we should just forget the car and get out. Somehow, as the car sinks, we escape, but I am left in a strange country without anything. I am supposed to be taking care of Stefan—he is younger than I, and my responsibility—but suddenly I have no money, I am more dependent than ever on Stef in this strange territory where I do not speak the language, and I am thinking that my father's car is at the bottom of this lake, and he will blame me. Then I wake up, and instead of reality being better, it is worse:

Oh, s---, I have cancer. Excuse me, that is a negative thought, cancel it. I had cancer. I had a cancer in my breast. Now it is out.

I am trying to be exceptionally positive because some of the cancer books I've been collecting claim that cancer cells are always popping up in people; on average you may "get" cancer as often as six times a year, but a healthy immune system kills the cells. Some writers, including Norman Cousins, have this theory, which normally I would consider crackpot, that stress weakens the immune system, while positive energy and laughter create, uh, endorphins or something that helps the immune system battle the disease—so don't worry, be happy. But how can you be happy when, according to some doctors, by the time a cancerous lump is big enough to be felt, around one centimeter, it contains one hundred billion cells and has been in your body ten years, and chances are there are millions of other cancer cells sloshing through your bloodstream, looking to own, not rent?

"Yes, we were very happy in Miss Wadler's left breast for a long time. It was a wonderful space—you've seen it yourself, in a T-shirt—I mean, it's enormous. But now the family is growing, and we're looking for something with a little more air and light—like maybe her lungs and the top of her head."

If there's a chance positive thinking can work, I'll try it, but I am skeptical. If my being a worrier has contributed to this disease, am I going to be able to change my outlook fast enough to stop it? I've had fifteen years of therapy trying to get married, and I still haven't been able to pull off the one space in journalism I really want: the *New York Times* wedding page.

There is also another problem: I am dealing with a growing group of specialists—breast surgeon, plastic surgeon, oncologist, radiologist. Each puts his or her field first and is somewhat ignorant, at times even disdainful, of the others.

The doctor who removed the malignant lump from my breast, Dr. Luke, has told me that the cure rates for lumpectomy and mastectomy are the same. He stresses that the decision is mine and my prognosis is good, because medullary cancer—a rare type, which accounts for 7 percent of breast cancers—tends not to spread quickly. His personal feeling, however, is that it may be safer for me to have a mastectomy and reconstruction. My breasts, he said, are a surgeon's nightmare: They are dense, large, and full of lumps, one of which was already missed on a mammogram. Also, he has had three medullary-cancer patients, and one had a recurrence. I have come up with my own ideas about treatment: If my breasts are full of potentially dangerous tissue, why not reduce the danger by reducing the size of the breasts? Instead of lumpectomy followed by radiation, the common procedure, why not do a lumpectomy and breast reduction and then have radiation? The plastic surgeon Dr. Luke sends me to see, Dr. Frank Veteran, tells me that he knows of no one who has done this, and that it is a bad idea. Reduction surgery might delay the time at which my breast could be treated with radiation. Irradiating the breast first and then doing a reduction won't work, either—radiated tissue is difficult to work with. Dr. Luke, when I speak with him later, is not aware of this problem—he suggests radiation treatment, *then* a reduction. He also does not mention that if I have a lumpectomy and radiation and the cancer comes back, I will not be able to have another radiation treatment—the breast can only take so much. If I decide I want to have a mastectomy then, reconstruction will be an extremely complicated procedure in which muscle and skin have been transferred from my stomach or back. Even if I give up my idea of a reduction, there will be three to four people involved.

"I understand that I don't see the oncologist until after the lymph-node surgery, and the radiation doctor comes in after that," I tell a nurse at Memorial Sloan-Kettering, when I make an appointment to see surgeon Jeanne Petrek for a second opinion. "But who's in charge?"

"There will be a group of doctors, who will each be monitoring you at various steps along the way," the nurse says cheerfully, "but as far as who's in charge, in a sense you are."

In a sense, that's good—I should be the one to have the final say about what happens to my body. In another, it's terrifying. I know nothing about biology or chemistry or science; I'm one of those people who still aren't sure why planes stay up in the air. What this disease needs, I decide, is a contractor—or at least one room where we could get all the doctors together.

On the positive side, it turns out that while the United States is lousy on health care, we are a great nation for booklets. Call 1-800-4-CANCER, the Cancer Information Service at the National Cancer Institute, and you can speak to a cancer expert, get fact sheets, and receive free pamphlets on everything from treatment to psychological support. Their Physician Data Query service, which is also free, sends information on cancer treatment to patients and doctors, so that even if you live in Podunk, you can still be on top of the research. I also get a lot of information from the American Cancer Society's Cancer Response System, at 1-800-ACS-2345. According to its fact sheet—which, like NCI's, is reviewed and updated frequently—medullary cancer (which I now think of as my brand) seems to grow in a capsule within the duct, and although it can become quite large, "it does not metastasize as frequently as others and has a better outlook." For the first time since the diagnosis, I have a strong sense of relief: This is not just one doctor trying to snow me. The best overview of breast cancer and therapy options comes from *Dr. Susan Love's Breast Book,* which Dr. Luke, the surgeon who removed the tumor and made the diagnosis, recommended. I wish I could have found it earlier.

Meanwhile, I'm beat. I run around town, picking up medical records and my past four years of mammograms. The mammograms are important to me. I'm hoping someone will be able to look at them and spot the tumor that was missed a year ago, when I had my last, and use it to find any other dangerous lumps. I change my mind daily on whether to have reconstruction or lumpectomy, mostly because Dr. Veteran, who has told me reconstruction involves three operations and knows I am afraid of surgery, called me with a way to reduce the number of operations from three to two: rather than use an expander that will later be replaced with an implant, he can use an expander that will remain inside the body. It sounds good, but the shape my breast will have if we use this device—"grapefruit," according to Dr. Veteran—does not. My breasts may not be saluting the sun, but they have their charm, and I'm not about to replace them with a set of citrus. I can't believe that I'm the only woman in America who's had the idea of treating cancer with lumpectomy and reduction, either. I continue reporting. I call the American College of Radiology, the American Society of Plastic and Reconstructive Surgeons. I hear of no one who has done reduction and lumpectomy to treat and prevent the disease.

I read. Though I returned my expensive breast-reconstruction text after talking to Luke, discarding research, as he has suggested, is an idea I've discarded. It's my body and my life. I read about drugs, I read about nutrition, I read about alternative therapies like visualization, where you picture cancer cells in your body and tell them to drop dead. Searching for an expert on medullary cancer, I call SHARE, a support-and-information group. They know of no one, but the volunteer I speak with does, when I ask, give me a lot of positive case histories involving women who have had cancer in the lymph nodes. My big fear, which I try not to think about, is that the cancer will be in the lymph nodes. Finally, though, our conversation, in which we discuss the possible side effects of chemotherapy—including hair loss, mouth sores, early menopause, and possibly vaginal infections—disturbs me. I understand that people with a common experience can offer a kind of special support, but at the same time, I see a club to which I do not want to belong and yet have been drafted, a fellowship of sick people. I make another decision: Rather than go to strangers, I will ask my friends to get Dr. Love's book so we will all be able to speak Cancer. If the going gets really rough psychologically, I will have a talk with the two friends who have had run-ins with the disease. I would, however, prefer not to. They both had tumors the size of peas. It's making me nervous to be the girl with the biggest one on the block.

I'm also having trouble with Nick.

"What's the good news?" he asks whenever I come back from the doctor.

When he hears rough news—the possibility of an ugly reconstruction that could go on for months, the possible problems with chemo—he brushes it off.

"The doctor says you have the best kind," he keeps saying. "You've got nothing to worry about. I wish I could exchange my financial problems for your medical problems."

I think part of this is my fault. After all, the day I was diagnosed, I told him that we had to be positive. I also know this is his way of keeping me from being overcome by terror.

"I could have a very strange look for a few months," I tell Nick one night before bed. "Scars, no nipple. . . ."

"So what's a few months?" he says. "When it's over, you have a great new pair. Maybe better."

"I thought you liked these," I say.

"I *love* them," he says. "But you know what they say—variety is the spice of life."

Meanwhile, his demand that I lead with "good news" is making me feel that he just doesn't want to hear the bad. One day, I blow up.

"There is no good news," I say to him. "This is cancer. I could lose a breast; I could die; I could be spending the summer with a hole in my chest.

If you want the good news, get yourself a twenty-four-year-old California girl. With no health problems."

Another time, I get him together with Herb.

"Could you explain to Nick this is a difficult, life-threatening disease?" I say.

"It's a difficult, life-threatening disease," says Herb, who feels that a man who spends as much time worrying about a tan as Nick cannot be taken seriously.

"Could you also say that I'm scared, especially of general anesthesia?" I say.

"What's to be scared?" says Nick. "You die on the table, you never know what hit you. I keep telling you, it's the best way to go."

"You're just saying that because you're a guy and you don't like to admit to fear of dying," I say.

"My mother isn't a guy; she wouldn't be scared," Nick says.

"Your mother is seventy," I tell him.

"Eighty," says Nick. "But she wouldn't be scared if she was forty. If she was twenty, she still wouldn't be scared."

"What is it with Italian guys and their mothers?" Herb says. "Jewish guys insult their mothers and make jokes about them. Say anything to an Italian guy about his mother and he's ready to get in a fight."

"Why would anyone say anything about my mother?" says Nick. "She's an incredible woman."

I give up and go back to research. The week before Easter, I go to Roosevelt, where they took out the lump, to pick up my biopsy slides for the new doctors. The slides are the most important medical records I have—the only specimens of my cancer—and they will be critical in determining my treatment.

Roosevelt, when I return, is even more depressing than I'd first found it. The street people who had set up housekeeping on Fifty-Eighth Street are still there in their sofa and armchairs and seem to have settled in for the long haul. Their possessions are about them in garbage bags; the sidewalk is littered with dirty fast-food containers—just what you want to see next to a hospital. They are very nice, though, complimenting me on my fedora and waving like we are old friends. I wave back. For all I know, by the time I come back for surgery, they'll be living in the waiting room.

Maybe one will have a fellowship, and I'll look up in OR and he'll be there, assisting.

The pathology department, where I have to pick up my slides, is on the ground floor, behind a door that opens onto a reception desk and a rat's run of intersecting halls. I am stumbling through them, searching for pathology, when suddenly I am hit by the smell. It is a smell I will never forget: sweet and rotting, with an overlay of formaldehyde. I see the sign just as I am on top of it: MORGUE. The door is opening, and I feel like I have suddenly split into two people, one of whom is physically turning the other's face away, so she cannot see. The corridors are like a maze in a nightmare, and although I don't believe in fate and don't believe in folk stories, I feel this is a precursor: Death has seen my face near the door of the morgue, and if I come back to this hospital for surgery, he will recognize me and think that's where I belong. If I come back to Roosevelt, they will wheel me into surgery and wheel me out to a refrigerated compartment. I manage to find the pathology department, which is, as one would expect it to be, next door, but I am now so frightened I am gulping air. A lab technician gives me a three-by-four-inch padded envelope, which she says includes my biopsy slides and the medical report. I sign for them, then beat it out for the door, looking for a phone. There is an old-fashioned one in a wooden booth. I duck into it, shutting the door behind me, crying and hiding. Hide from the Angel of Death. I call Herb. The machine answers. I call Nick.

"Oh, Jesus, you almost gave me a heart attack. I thought something had happened; you just got scared," he says.

"But something did happen," I want to tell him. "I felt my death foretold." But he is at work, and I am not a crazy person, so we just talk for a while, and I leave.

I don't know what to do. On one hand, I think I should get away from this hospital and this ugly, depressing neighborhood and go to my house and have a nice, hot bath and get sane. On the other hand, I know that when I am not dealing with cancer, I like this neighborhood a lot. It has great food stores and demented, high-energy street life and, most important, a lot of thrift shops I usually don't get to. I once got *Bells Are Ringing* around here for ninety-nine cents. I love show tunes. I took a bunch with me to Paris, and when I got scared and had to do an interview with a fancy diplomat, I used to psych myself up with *Chicago* or *Guys and Dolls.* By the end of my first hitch, my French was good enough that I could sing the first verse of "I got the horse right here" to my newsstand dealer, who always had his nose stuck in the racing form. If I stick around and hit the thrift shops, I decide, it will be much more life-affirming than panicking. Also, maybe I'll be able to find a new *Pal Joey*.

Then, walking down Ninth Avenue, I realize what I'm holding in my hand: my cancer. It seems sort of creepy, going shopping with it. If I go to the Forty-Sixth Street Salvation Army, my favorite thrift shop, will they make me check it? I could put it in my bag, but if my purse is snatched, I'll lose it. On the other hand, if somebody sees me carrying an envelope, they could think it holds something valuable and snatch that. It's the most important thing I own; if somebody steals it, what will I do? Put signs on the trees like they do in my neighborhood when somebody loses their cat? "Cancer missing; last seen in small brown envelope, vic. Ninth Avenue and Fifty-Fifth. Reward—no questions asked." Then, if I get it back, the *Daily News* will do a story like they do when a Taiwanese music student leaves his cello in a taxi and somebody returns it. They'll run a picture of me clutching my cancer, and I'll have to look grateful and teary-eyed, while all across town cabbies will be making fun of me. "Putz. Lookit this. She's carrying her cancer in her hand, and what does she do? She goes shopping. Just like a woman." I do go shopping, just to spite them, but it is unsatisfying; I stuff my cancer into my purse so I don't have to check it, and make an incredibly bad buy: a pair of navy-and-white Ferragamo flats a size too large. When you buy shoes you know do not fit, it is time to go home. When I do, I find the package with my slides unnerving me; I have a sense of them powerful and glowing, like Kryptonite, sending killer rays around the apartment. I don't know where to put them. The flowered hatboxes, where I keep my fancy underwear? The drawer with my foreign currency and passport? I'm also still shook up by the trip to the morgue. My shrink has said if I need her, call her. I do. She says she has one minute; her group is coming in. "I'm not sure I can do this in a minute," I say, but I try: my sense of death foretold; my father diagnosed with cancer at exactly this season five years ago; my fear that I will die like he did, my bones eroded by cancer, a tube down my throat. "You're not your father," she says. "This is all in your mind. You're doing this to yourself. Snap out of it." Wonderful. I get cancer—excuse me, I had cancer—and my shrink turns into Cher in *Moonstruck*. I call up my friend Heidi, who's less pressed for time. She understands why I am upset: It is insensitive and appalling that a hospital would make one pick up records next to the morgue, she says. I feel better. When I get off the phone, I decide I will demystify the cancer pack. I saw it whole, before I knew it was cancer; am I going to let it bother me now just because I know what it is? What kind of a take-charge attitude is that? I open the package: just two little slides, with a bit of translucent tissue that is stained a purple-pink, and a one-page pathology report. "Frozen Section Diagnosis: Medullary carcinoma," it says at the top. And later on, "Adeno carcinoma, infiltrating ductal carcinoma, medullary type completely excised." I give the slides some death-ray visualization, like I have read about in the books. Then I put on *Bells Are Ringing*, remembering that Judy Holliday died young, of cancer. She left her voice, anyway, that gorgeous mixture of bubble and sass, and who can't smile hearing it? In no time at all I am dancing with an invisible partner to "Long Before I Knew You," so lost in dreams it takes me a while to notice Judy has dropped in and plopped on the couch.

"So whadidya do with the slides, finally?" she asks.

"I put them in my sock drawer," I tell her.

"Oh, no," she says. "That's the first place they look.

You see the difference between Sloan-Kettering and Roosevelt the moment you walk in Sloan's York Avenue entrance: money. The reception desk is banked with pots of white narcissus; the walls are hung with tasteful prints; I haven't had so many smiling people asking if they could be of assistance since I was in Los Angeles. "This place is like Disneyland, they're so perky," I whisper to Herb. "Cancerland." A pretty nurse, warm and pneumatic, with shoulder-length blonde hair, comes out to get us. "Cancer hostess," I tell Herb after she takes my history and goes off with my cancer slides. We wait an hour and a half for Dr. Petrek, but I like her the minute I see her. She's a great-looking redhead who wears a Mickey Mouse watch with her white doctor's coat and has a smart, hyper, full-disclosure style. She enters the room with my slides in her palm, holding them as if they were just another report and not the signpost of my possible early demise. Then, cheerful as you please, she challenges my greatest-little-cancer-you-can-get diagnosis.

"This looks like medullary, but medullary carcinomas are very rare," she says. "And this report is ambiguous. 'Infiltrating duct medullary type.'"

I can't believe what I'm hearing. Neither can Herb. We exchange a frightened glance. Infiltrating ductal, I know, spreads far more quickly than medullary. I have the sinking feeling I had when I was diagnosed. Dr. Petrek doesn't seem to notice. She's picked up a pencil and straying the outline of the tumor on the slide, like a teacher who wants to make sure you get the lesson, though the lesson to me is that I may shortly drop dead.

"Cancers are very dense, packed edge to edge, and infiltrating ductal cancers have edges that look like pointy little stars—very irregular, shooting out," she says. "Medullary has a very smooth, round outline, like this, see? It looks like medullary, but I'm going to have our own people look at it."

The fear recedes. She's said "looks like medullary" twice; until the lab guys tell us different, I'll keep believing I've got it.

On mastectomy versus lumpectomy, she is far less equivocal than Luke—she sees no reason to do a mastectomy. The top medullary man in the country, Dr. Paul Peter Rosen, is at Sloan, she says. He's done a study of hundreds of breast-cancer patients over a twenty-year period and believes that medullary is much less likely to recur than other cancers. It is also less likely to be in the lymph nodes. Whether my cancer is medullary or infiltrating ductal, Dr. Petrek thinks it is best to save the breast. Given the clean margins surrounding my tumor, I am a perfect candidate for lumpectomy. She also paints a different picture of breast reconstruction from Dr. Veteran's—it can be a very uncomfortable procedure for large-breasted women, she says.

The notion of combining breast reduction with lumpectomy doesn't appeal to her at all. Nor, I gather, does reduction alone.

"Breast reduction combined with lumpectomy is a large operation," she says. "If you were ever to walk in and see it—ugh. What they do is remove a section of tissue from the lower part of the breast. Then, because they have to bring the nipple up higher, they cut the tissue all around it, and the nipple is hanging there, like on a stalk."

She pauses, giving us all time to visualize. I see from Herb's gray-green complexion he's got the picture and may never unbutton anyone's blouse again. Dr. Petrek moves along.

"There's a lot of rearranging of tissue and scarring with reduction, which could interfere with spotting another tumor on your mammogram. It would take a lot longer to heal than lumpectomy, you might have to put off radiation treatment. Combining reduction with lumpectomy . . . I don't know if you want to be the first."

She wouldn't do it, she says. But she will discuss it with the head of the breast-radiation unit, Dr. Beryl McCormick, at the next department meeting. She also suggests I get in touch with Dr. Susan Love, an "ardent, zealous" believer in lumpectomy.

Dr. Love's secretary, at her office in Boston, knows of no one who has combined lumpectomy with reduction. Still, willing to be first, I consult a prominent Manhattan plastic surgeon. Unlike Dr. Veteran, he is willing to do the surgery, as long as the reduction is done after the radiation. After talking with this surgeon, Dr. Luke is willing, too.

I decide I will do it. Then, an hour later, I decide that I will not. Then, I change my mind again. Then I talk to Ma. She has been an uncharacteristically good listener during this crisis—in her forty-three years of Jewish motherhood I've never known her to be so lacking in opinion—but five thousand years of genetic baggage happen to be working against her, and now she snaps.

"I know you said news goes out and it doesn't go in, but I'm the mother and I got a right to an opinion," she says. "My opinion is, I don't like this business of first. First is good for the doctor; he gets to write it up and be a big shot. First is good for the hospital; they get money from the government. But how is it good for you? They don't know what they're doing, they never did it before, and if something goes wrong, it's good-bye, Charlie—you're the one that has to live with it.

I give it a few days, but ultimately I agree. If reduction could result in scarring and a failure to spot recurrent cancers, it's not a good idea. If the cancer turns out to be in the lymph nodes, and reduction puts off immediate treatment, it's not a good idea either. I can't spend months trying to find someone who's had this procedure—there's a disease to beat; I'm up against time. I will stick with the basics: lymph-node removal to see if the cancer has spread; re-excision of my left breast.

That leaves me with deciding whom to go with as my surgeon. I like both Luke and Petrek; Herb has gone to the library and checked their credentials; they're both sharp, good guys. But I want the resources of a cancer-research center behind me. Luke has had three medullary patients. Rosen did a study of more than seven hundred breast-cancer patients, about 5 percent of whom were medullary. I've wanted a place where all my records, all the specialists involved, would be under one roof. I have that at Sloan. I want to know that the people who read my biopsy slides are all cancer specialists. I set the date for surgery with Petrek, for the second week in April—three weeks from the day I was diagnosed. I also ask her if she can give me some positive statistics on survival if the cancer turns out to be in the lymph nodes. She says that finding cancer in the nodes is not uncommon—it occurs in slightly less than half of all breast-cancer patients. One of those was Betty Ford. She was diagnosed in 1974, with cancer in two nodes. She is doing just fine.

Dr. Petrek also has good news about my biopsy slides. As is policy at Sloan, two doctors have examined them under the microscope. They both say I have a medullary carcinoma.

I don't spend Passover with my family. My mother, who made plans to close the Florida house the hour I told her the lump was malignant, is getting ready to drive north; I don't want to be with the clan in the Catskills. My aunt Shirley is the hostess of that one, and I haven't told Shirley the full story because I think she Can't Take It. If I go home, we may hit the next step in the Wadler serious-illness scenario: Shirley will Figure It Out.

I end up, then, spending the holidays with Nick and his family. It works out nicely, Easter falls on the same weekend as Passover, and I like Nick's family a lot, particularly his mother. She hugged me the first time she met me. She is big and soft and cushiony. She grew up in Italy and speaks with such a heavy accent that I sometimes cannot understand what she is saying, which makes me feel like I have my grandmother back. "Iiiii, *maron!*" she says, when she gets fed up. "What's this '*maron*' your mother is always talking about?" I ask Nick finally. "*Madonna,*" he says, giving it the Italian pronunciation. "Madonna, idiot." Since the death of her husband, Mrs. Di Stefano has lived with her children, spending a month here, a month there, with each one. When she stays at Nick's, he moves out of his bedroom into the den and sleeps on a futon on the floor. She arrives with a statue of the Blessed Virgin and six suitcases, one of which holds only medicine, and prays three hours in the morning and two hours at night. She prays for the dead, she prays for the living, she prays for Bush—not because she likes him but because he's president and she feels she should. When Nick tells her I have cancer, she starts praying for me too. In between, she knits socks, and says what everyone in the family is doing wrong, and tells stories about sickness.

"Whata you got, my daughter-in-law got, too," she says, lying on Nick's bed, knitting. "First she gotta one side, they cutta it out. The next year it come to the other side, they cutta it out. A cousin of mine, she got it, too."

'Oh, yeah?" I say. "You pray for her too?"

Mrs. Di Stefano nods yes.

"How'd she do?" I ask.

She does this thing with her head and her shoulder that suggest both the mortal coil and the limitations of prayer.

"*Eehhhh,*" she says.

Easter over, I move back to medical concerns. I have a bone scan and liver ultrasound to show the presence of cancer cells. They come back negative. I go to a lawyer and make a will. I sign a health-care proxy, sent to me by Sloan, giving Herb the right to make medical decisions on my behalf in case I am incapacitated during surgery, and write an outline of the last chapters of my book, assigning rights again to Herb. I have been going to the gym a lot, to strengthen my heart and lungs for surgery; now I focus on a psychic attack for my hospital stay. Most of the patients I see in hospitals, except new mothers, shuffle around like depressed shlubs. Analyzing it, I think I know why: bathrobes. Only Rex Harrison could look good in a bathrobe. Hospital pajamas aren't that great, either, though the floppy drawstring pants, matched with oversize shirts, have possibilities. Casual clothing, I decide, is what is called for. I pull out a bunch of Hawaiian shirts and bright, oversize beach tops, and flowered tights, and pink sandals. I have a presurgical session with the shrink, telling her that even if cancer is in the nodes, I will try to beat the disease, and if not, or something goes wrong on the table, I have an interesting life behind me. I have friends who love me, I got to have two grandmothers, I've been in love in Paris, I drank champagne with a spy at ten in the morning, I wrote a few things I liked, I had Herb, I had really wanted to stand with someone under a wedding canopy, but maybe it is silly to think you can have everything.

"You have a good life ahead of you," the shrink says. "It isn't finished. And if you want me, you call, and I'll come to the hospital. We've been together a long time."

The last big decision is who to take to Sloan. Though my mother is now in striking range in the Catskills, I do not want her with me the day of surgery. Part of this is superstition again. Every time my father went into surgery, the family gathered around, and I do not want death or his messenger service, seeing a bunch of Wadlers around a hospital bed, to think there's another one waiting for pickup. Another reason, the stronger one, is that I may be frightened, and if my mother is there, I will have to pretend I am not, so she won't feel worse.

I don't want to ask Nick either. The more I expose my breast to strangers, the more I am pricked with needles and scanned by machines, the more I want to be held and cherished—and Nick has made it very clear that illness or no, I am not the woman of his dreams. At night, even after making love, he still puts on a video of *Rope* and uses it to fall asleep, his face as frozen and angry as that of a little boy who feels he's been denied and always will be. I know this look because for most of my life, I have been Nick Di Stefano's psychological twin—discarding the lovers who wanted me, idealizing the ones who did not—but it's a crazy way of life and I don't want it anymore, because now I value time. "Why don't you turn off the movie and try to fall asleep with me?" I say to Nick, meaning, "The best movie is here, right under your nose; it is real, and it is me. Love me, you jerk, because now is a gift and I don't know what I'm looking at and soon I could be gone." It does no good; I can't break through the wall. I try not to rock the boat, either, with what Nick considers to be excessive demands. I have seen posters at Sloan for stress-reduction clinics. I can't risk asking Nick to come with me to the hospital. I could get too upset if he says no. I ask Herb and Heidi instead. Nick will come in the evening, after work; my mother will arrive the next day. Then, the weekend before surgery, I change my mind. I want Nick to be with me. If Heidi, who has two young children, can take a day off, so can a fifty-two-year-old sports reporter. I ask him to come. He refuses. "What is this, a test?" he says. "You know what kind of week I'm looking at at work." I try not to get too upset. I remember the posters at Sloan. Stress kills.

Mrs. Di Stefano, anyway, is solid. Sickness is her game; when it comes to life-threatening illness, she's the MVP of the Eastern Conference. She knits me a pair of socks and asks me what time surgery is scheduled, so she can launch a special prayer. Nick stays at my place the night before surgery. Next morning, as he is sleeping, Heidi and Herb pick me up. We hang out in a hospital room together, and, waiting, I am impressed with Sloan. A nurse comes by to see if I have any questions. When another nurse and an orderly come with a gurney to take me to pre-op and I tell them I would feel very silly being pushed down the hall on a bed, they go into a huddle, bend the rules, and alert pre-op on a walkie-talkie. "Patient walking," they say, and we form a nice little soaring-hospital-costs tableau: a nurse, followed by me, Heidi, and Herb, followed by an orderly and an empty gurney, parading down the hall. Heidi and Herb haven't marched since we all protested Vietnam; they think it is hilarious I am remaking the rules. "Go, Joyce!" they cheer. At the pre-op room, which is adjacent to the operating rooms, I have to tell them goodbye. The room is dim, with a row of eight or nine gurneys and three other patients. I reluctantly climb onto a bed, feeling very scared and alone, knowing there are three other people feeling exactly the same, a few feet away. It would be nice, I think, if we could all hold hands, but maybe, finally, that wouldn't help—we would each still be going it alone. I try to think how to handle the fear—and find myself, though I am not religious, silently saying the *Shema*, the prayer I was taught Jews are supposed to say when they may be facing death. If God exists and turns out to be a reefer-smoking Kerouac bebop hipster, I think, I've probably just made another disastrous career decision. An orderly comes in and wheels me into the operating room. Almost everyone is a woman, which gives me a good feeling, but I am still terrified of the anesthesia. The more scared I am, the faster I joke. "You know the movie *Coma*?" I say to the nurse anesthetist when she puts the IV in my arm and starts a saline drip. "That's my big fear. I have this feeling I'm going to, like, wake up as the featured vegetable in Gristede's." She hits me with the statistics: Twenty years ago the mortality rate from anesthesia was one in twenty thousand cases; these days it's roughly one in two hundred thousand. Then, she suggests something: a sedative called Versed, which feels like a very strong Valium. Next thing I know, I am groggily opening my eyes in a dimly lit recovery room, and then I'm in my own room with Heidi and Herb, and soon after that, Nick arrives. He has an armful of red roses and the sad look he gets when he is looking at his son or watching a Disney film. I am so doped up with morphine I can barely move my head when he bends down to kiss me, but I remember the anesthetist clearly. That lovely woman. She slipped me a mickey.

I will not know the results of lymph-node dissection for a few days. Until the lab report comes back, the surgeon herself does not know how many lymph nodes she has taken. Lymph fights infection; the nodes in the armpit lie embedded in fat like a cluster of grapes, and everyone has a different number. When nodes are removed, lymph continues to collect in that area of the body until, after a few weeks, it finds other channels. To siphon off the lymph near my left breast, I have, four inches under my armpit, a Reliavac drain coming out of my side: five feet of plastic tubing that empties into a transparent plastic canteen. The amount of pale yellow fluid that collects is the literal watermark of my release from the hospital. When I get down to fifty ccs over a twenty-four-hour period, they will remove the drain and let me go. I'm cautioned against packing my bags. Big-breasted women, the nurses tell me, have a lot of fluid.

Meanwhile, the mood on the eighteenth floor, which is known as the breast-cancer floor, is surprisingly up. Women come and go, sharing stories. After the first day, I have very little pain. I can't raise my left arm straight up over my head or touch the middle of my back, but Sloan has stretching classes to get the arm back to normal as quickly as possible, an estimated four to six weeks. My roommate, a research biochemist in her mid-fifties who had multiple lesions in her breast, has had a mastectomy but seems unconcerned: Maybe she'll have a reconstruction, maybe she won't, she says. There is no guy in her life, but if one comes along, she figures if he's a good man, he'll love her for who she is; if not, the hell with him. My mother arrives and says the food at Beth Israel is better and talks two hours at a stretch without paying much attention to anything I have to say, which makes me feel things are back to normal; Nick comes every night. Bernard, the French spy who is the hero of my book, calls from Paris; Stefan sends chocolates; my friends bring flowers and themselves. Every few hours, a different volunteer arrives. The most helpful is a former breast-cancer patient exactly my age, who also had a lumpectomy—somewhere, somebody is doing some careful matching. She's a strikingly pretty woman, in a flowered, V-neck dress, and she asks if I understand the next step in my treatment, radiation therapy. When it comes to cancer treatment, I consider myself the smartest kid in the class:

"Takes about fifteen minutes a session; you have five treatments a week for six weeks. Some people get tired; your breast can get a little swollen and pink, like you're sunburned. They mark where they're going to radiate you with ink."

"Wrong," she says. "In most places they mark you with ink. At Sloan-Kettering, they give you tattoos."

I stare at her. A tattoo? What's it gonna be? A picture of a single-breasted mermaid and SEMPER CARCINOMA on my breast?

"They're very small," she continues. "They give you four or five of them; it's better than ink, which comes off on your clothes. You can have them removed after the treatment, but I know only one person who's bothered. Can you see mine?"

I look closely at her chest. She has a sprinkling of freckles, like me, and after a minute, I can see one tattoo, above her cleavage. It's the size of an ink dot. But if someone hadn't shown it to me, and I had just heard the word tattoo going into radiation, I would have been upset.

Friday, though I'm still throwing off a lot of lymph fluid, they show me how to empty the drain, and let me go home. I wrap the Reliavac pouch in a red silk scarf, pin it to my sweater, and head out with Ma and Herb to Quatorze, on Fourteenth. I must be very distracted not to enjoy lunch, but I am not in a great mood. I want to get Ma back to the mountains as soon as I can. Dr. Petrek has told me to call her office at three, and she'll have the report on the lymph nodes. If the news is bad, I won't be able to bear my mother's face. At two-thirty, Herb and I send Ma off to Port Authority. At three, I call Dr. Petrek. Then I call my brother who is meeting Ma at the bus station, and Herb and Nick and Heidi and Max and everybody else I can think of.

"They took out twelve nodes," I say. "They're all clean."

Schlepping around with a plastic pouch coming out of my side does not make me feel particularly beautiful, but it's not a major problem. I discover that if I tuck it into a runner's pouch around my waist, no one knows it's there. It's more difficult in bed, where I pin the pouch to my T-shirt, but Nick is sweet. "You're embarrassed about the thing," he says. "You know you don't have to be embarrassed with me," and he puts his arms around me, and contented as a kitten, I go to sleep. Eight days after the surgery, the drain is pulled out. There is no pain. The area around my underarm is numb from the lymph-node surgery and will be for at least a year.

A few days later, I see Dr. Larry Norton, the oncologist who is the chief of breast-cancer medicine, to discuss the next step in my treatment. He's fortysomething, relaxed, amiable, and balding, and he has wonderful news for me: Since 1990, he says, it has been common practice to give chemotherapy to breast-cancer patients even if cancer is not in the lymph nodes At Sloan, unless a tumor is smaller than one centimeter, they follow that protocol. But "true" medullary cancer, Norton says, is "a very, very, benign disease," and Dr. Rosen, Sloan's expert in breast pathology, has done a study showing that medullary patients whose tumors are smaller than three centimeters have about a 90 percent chance of no recurrence. If a medullary carcinoma is smaller than three centimeters and the nodes are negative, the doctors at Sloan see no reason for chemotherapy. Dr. Norton is ordering additional tests on my original biopsy slides from Roosevelt to establish that I did have a true medullary carcinoma. If so, since my tumor was just under three centimeters, I will not need chemotherapy.

The tests confirm the diagnosis. I am not feeling 100 percent recovered from surgery. I still have to go to the hospital two or three days a week, so that the lymph fluid that collects under my arm can be drained. As it collects, I have a swollen, uncomfortable feeling, as if there's a volleyball under my skin. My left side and breast are also sore, but I'm very happy I won't need chemotherapy. I celebrate by going off with Nick to the Mohonk Mountain House, a rambling Victorian hotel upstate. The room has two double beds. We shove them together and open some champagne and don't get to the woods till the next day. And yet, the weekend is not a success. There is sex and there is communion, and I have the feeling that Nick is losing himself in the first, not making love to me. When we go walking in the woods, stopping to rest in one of the gazebos that circle the lake, I am not altogether surprised to run into Freud. He is on his hands and knees, carving a heart and two names into the bench. DEPENDENT LOVES NARCISSIST, it says.

"You're telling me I should break up with him, right?" I say.

"What?" says Freud. "And miss watching the two of you in bed? I wouldn't think of it. The energy you put into your lost causes."

"You may have noticed, since you've been studying everything so carefully, he doesn't exactly lie there like a lox," I say.

"Exceptional vigor for a man his age," says Freud. "And why do we think that is?"

I don't care what the answer is, I'm mad.

"I know you say there are six people in every bedroom, but you dogging me everyplace I go with this guy is too much," I say.

"In your case, darling, it's more like eight in the bedroom," says Freud. "You also got the lawyer and an agent. Plus the West Coast office of I.C.M. I'm amazed the little boulevardier has room to take off his pants."

Nick and I go back to the city. Monday morning, he switches on *Lucy*. We fight. I go off to Sloan to have a hypodermic stuck in my side. It's impossible to find a phone where you have any privacy at Sloan. I wait till I'm in the street to call Nick.

"It may seem to you like this cancer thing is over, but it's not," I tell him. "My breast hurts, my side hurts; every week I see another doctor. I just sometimes need to be held."

"Then get yourself another guy," Nick says. "We don't have that kind of relationship."

I dial Donal, my old boyfriend, at his studio. He's a big man, with a honey-colored mustache and the air of an Oxford don.

"Need a lap," I say.

I go to the studio, and Don brews a cup of tea and brings me Humphry, the fat white studio cat, who years ago lived with Donal and me. I love Humphry, though he makes me sneeze. We all curl up together.

"I know you; I know what you need," says Donal. "You're never going to get it from that man."

"I know that," I say. "It's just these treatments are making me such a baby."

Nick and I break up.

Radiation therapy, which begins in mid-May, goes off without a hitch. I have some tiredness, but I attribute that mostly to psychological factors and feel well enough to take myself off medical leave and return to my book. By the end of June, my cancer treatment is over. The medical bills come to $32,300, but almost all of it is covered by insurance. Life returns to normal. Herb and I watch TV and complain about editors. My mother re-ups in the Israeli army, as her way of giving thanks for my health. Before she flies off, we all go out to dinner and Ma and Herb reminisce about the motor pool and army life. Ma is much more enthusiastic than Herb. In September, I go back to *People*. One month later, I am among the 605 Time-Warner staffers to be laid off. "*Arrivederci,* hot tubs," I think and go back downtown, take off my pearl earrings, and finish my book. For New Year's, in celebration of life, I make a bet with Bernard that California champagne can match French, throw a few bottles in my carry-on luggage, and go to Paris for the weekend. Bernard picks me up at the airport, waving down from the mezzanine with his great felonious grin. When I get through Customs and he kisses me formally on the cheek, I start to cry.

"I didn't know if I was ever going to see you again," I say.

Between me and Nick it's over. Nick did, a while back, say, "Enough craziness; let's get rid of the other people and live together already," but it was a mood, and it passed. His mother, however, is still praying for me. She is also, Nick says, praying for Magic Johnson.

That was going to be the end of my cancer story. Then, as I was writing this piece, an extraordinary thing happened: I discovered not all of the slides of my original biopsy had been sent from Roosevelt to Sloan-Kettering.

The discovery was made by accident. Calling up Dr. Petrek, I asked if she might pull out my slides and review what she had originally discussed with me. She agreed but told me that I would have to get the slides from Roosevelt—hospital protocol, after reviewing specimens, is to return them to the institution after a procedure has been performed. Soon after picking up the slides from Roosevelt, I received a call from Dr. Norton. He told me they were two new slides—unknown to Dr. Petrek, the pathologists at Sloan-Kettering had gotten permission from Roosevelt to keep my original slides. Norton said that on the basis of the slides he had just received, he was thinking of changing my treatment. There was "an important but subtle" distinction between medullary carcinoma and infiltrating ductal carcinoma with medullary features, he said. Four pathologists at Sloan had looked at the slides; it was a close call, but on the basis of the new material, Dr. Norton felt my cancer was more likely to be an infiltrating ductal with medullary features than pure medullary. I still had, he stressed, an excellent prognosis. Nonetheless, purely as a precaution, he felt it best to give me a little extra treatment and was advising chemotherapy.

I am horrified. Infiltrating ductal is more aggressive than medullary, and if there were any cancer cells in my body before, for one year they had been getting a free ride. I am also upset that all my slides were not sent the first time. Dr. Norton says my cancer doesn't seem aggressive at all. "At the very worst, you're looking at a cancer with a very high cure rate," he says. "At the very best, you're looking at a 100 percent cure." He also explains that hospitals rarely send all their biopsy specimens—they select those that they consider diagnostic. Asked how he felt about my case, he struggles to be diplomatic.

"I'm not happy; what can I say?" he says. "I don't think there was any malicious intent. It's a difficult distinction to make, based on your pathology. Clearly, having more tissue helps you make the distinction. . . . They're supposed to send over slides which are characteristic. . . . I don't know why they chose those two slides."

I go to Roosevelt, ask for all of my slides, and talk to Dr. Bozidar Lazarevic, chief of anatomic pathology at Roosevelt. He says he stands by Roosevelt's diagnosis: I had a medullary cancer. Nor is he defensive about having sent only two slides—as Dr. Norton had said, it was protocol.

"I send the key slides I would use to make the diagnosis," he says. "I'm afraid to send all the slides—half the time I don't get the slides I send back. If there was disagreement about the diagnosis and the doctor asked to see all the slides, we would send them, but when a patient goes to see a doctor for a second opinion on therapy, we send only the diagnostic slides."

I see not only a problem with priorities here but also a Catch-22: A doctor will get all the slides only if he or she questions the diagnosis, but how will he know the diagnosis is in question if he doesn't get all the slides? I suggest to Dr. Lazarevic that he change the policy and let doctors know how many slides exist. He says doctors do know how many slides there are from notations on the pathology report, that his people may get only one of two slides from other institutions, and that in the fifteen years he's been at Roosevelt, this is the first time a doctor has challenged a diagnosis over their slides.

It all seems crazy to me, but there's nothing I can do; I have two doctors with differing diagnoses. I never, however, question Dr. Norton's recommendation for chemotherapy. If there is any risk of recurrence, I say, hit me with your best shot.

In early March, I begin a course of chemotherapy called CMF—a combination of the anticancer drugs Cytoxan, Methotrexate, and 5-Fluorouracil, as well as an antinausea sedative called Ativan. The CMF is given in an intravenous drip, which takes about forty-five minutes and is administered once every three weeks over a six-month period. My main concern about chemotherapy is that it will make me so sick it will disable me, but it does not. The first day after treatment, I am so wiped out by the Ativan tablets

I get from the Sloan pharmacy that I sleep all day; the next day I am speedy and tense, but after that everything is fine. I take my Walkman with me for my chemo treatments and listen to *Beauty and the Beast* and *La Cage aux Folles* and, because Ativan has a mild narcotic effect, get pleasantly high. In my five weeks of treatment to date, I have increased my weights at the gym to prove that I am not a sick guy. I have not had hair loss or any other physical problems. My breasts are the same size. While the doctors have said the drugs will probably put me into early menopause, I am for once going against statistics and taking the position that is unlikely to happen to me.

And even if it does, I consider myself a lucky guy. Not just because in the time of the great breast-cancer uprising, mine was so benign, but for the terror of the ride. Nothing is real until you are close to it, and for a few weeks, I was given something few people have: a dress rehearsal of my mortality. And though cancer has not made me a model of mental health, though I remain tempted by the drama and danger of gangsters and ladies' men and continue to worry about every little thing, my experience with serious illness has changed me. Death, I now see, may not come when I am eighty-five and weary, or after I have solved all of my problems or met all my deadlines. It will come whenever it damn well pleases; all I can control is the time between. So when I see something I want, I grab it. If the tulips are particularly yellow, I buy them. If I hear Pavarotti is in town, I make a run to the Met and work the crowd for a scalper. I make time for my friends the way I used to make time for work. If someone treats me disrespectfully, I leave.

As for the mark on my left breast, I am happy to have it. It is the battle scar over my heart, and if no one but my doctor and the girls at the gym have seen it lately, I am certain, believing as I do in musical comedies, that somebody will soon.

"So, how'd ya get that?" he'll ask, our first lazy morning, and I'll say, delighted he has found me, listening for the bells to ring, "Glad you asked, 'cause it's a wonderful story. . . ."

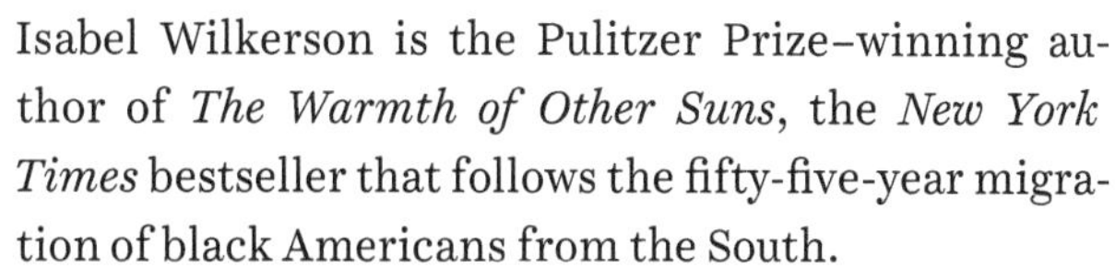

Isabel Wilkerson

Isabel Wilkerson is the Pulitzer Prize–winning author of *The Warmth of Other Suns*, the *New York Times* bestseller that follows the fifty-five-year migration of black Americans from the South.

Wilkerson won the Pulitzer Prize for her work as Chicago bureau chief of *The New York Times* in 1994, making her the first black woman in the history of American journalism to win a Pulitzer Prize and the first African American to win for individual reporting. Wilkerson has also won a George Polk Award and a John Simon Guggenheim Fellowship, and she was named Journalist of the Year by the National Association of Black Journalists.

She has appeared at universities across the country and in Europe and on national programs such as CBS's *60 Minutes,* PBS's *Charlie Rose*, NPR's *Fresh Air with Terry Gross,* NBC's *Nightly News*, MSNBC, the BBC, C-SPAN, and others. She has taught narrative nonfiction as Ferris Professor of Journalism at Princeton University, as Cox Professor at Emory University, and as Professor of Journalism at Boston University.

In 2012, *The New York Times Magazine* named *The Warmth of Other Suns* to its list of the best nonfiction books of all time. In 2016, President Barack Obama awarded her the National Humanities Medal for "championing the stories of an unsung history."

Soul Survivor

Civil rights activist Kwame Ture, formerly known as Stokely Carmichael, was a fiery leader of the Black Power movement during the 1960s.

The telephone rings, an ordinary ring in an ordinary Florida condo, and a long, lanky man you recognize from the grainy footage of the you-remember-the-civil-rights-days, the double-edged-sword-tongued soldier in the Ray-Bans and the pencil-lapel suits like the original Man in Black, spouting "Power to the people!" when the people had no power; who organized, organized, organized in the wicked Mississippi sun for the right to vote before you maybe even were born; who was rolling out of Chevy Impalas to cluck white-sheriff bullets so you could walk into a booth and check off who should be the water commissioner or the president; who had a god's face sculpted from brown velvet and could have been on the cover of *GQ* if that had been his bag, which it wasn't; who went by the unusual if patrician-sounding name of Stokely Carmichael, is now seated on his mother's white sofa in front of me, if you can believe it, unclasping his arms to pick up an impatient receiver.

He goes by Kwame Ture now, and his story unfolds between telephone rings. You rewind the spools of history. And you realize that the reason thirty-four million people call themselves black is because of the man sitting serenely in front of you, that before he got the nerve to shout "Black Power!" to a civil rights crowd in a Mississippi square in the belly of Klan country in 1966, we were neither black nor beautiful, but Negroes or worse. He was an undercover Malcolm working under Martin Luther King, Jr., professing nonviolence by day but packing a .38 just in case. Of all the civil rights generals—Malcolm, King, Medgar Evers—he is the last icon of the sixties left to set the record straight and, some wish, lead us to the Promised Land, although that in itself was never his intention.

He is fifty-six now, and sick with cancer that the doctors cannot cure. He lives in Guinea, West Africa; has not lived in the United States for nearly thirty years. Every visit here is a miracle that grows out of a patchwork budget, last-minute shuttling of boarding passes by followers around the world and the grace of God. He is here in this country for another round of chemotherapy, but never knowing how he will get here, happened to arrive this time through Cairo, where a brother from the Nation of Islam ran into him and gave him the money to get to Rome, and then New York for his chemo and then on to Miami, where his mother lives in a two-bedroom condo. He has no money, never did—got only ten dollars a week when the Student Nonviolent Coordinating Committee (SNCC, called Snick for short) could come up with the cash. Even when he was prime minister of the Black Panther Party, he was never on what you would call a payroll.

Now after all that rolling out of cars and jumping out of windows, and all those beatings in southern jails, he returns to a country that—between the drugs and the violence and the assaults on everything he worked for—may seem worse off than when he was on active duty. He heard about Rodney King and O. J. and the white backlash against affirmative action. He knows about the young brothers killing one another over rocks somebody cooked up in a basement and the bourgeois betrayals of the Clarence Thomases of the world. It has not worn him down. He had to be crazy or idealistic or both to go down South in the first place as a smart-mouthed college boy with the nerve to think he could change the world. And he does not waver.

The telephone rings again. He reaches over to answer it. His voice is West Indian molasses and rises up like a melody. He does not say hello. He greets the caller with his thirty-year-old mantra, uttered quickly and matter-of-factly as if it were a single word: "Ready for revolution."

He says it like it was the most natural thing in the world, sometimes rushed, sometimes weary, the way you would if you'd been working for years at a company with a long and convoluted name, the way you'd say

Consolidated Edison. You could say that revolution is his line of work. He still has faith in his people, no matter what's happening. "We always make progress in spite of ourselves," he tells me. "We gon' win. We gon' win. In spite of ourselves, we gon' win." He lets out a hearty laugh that rolls deep like the ocean.

Scroll back to 1966. It is June. It is hot. Malcolm is dead. Medgar Evers is dead. Countless others have been killed or beaten just because they want to vote or eat in a restaurant. And even though the Voting Rights Act is now law, most black people still can't vote in Mississippi. The foot soldiers in the Movement—the college boys running SNCC who went around trying to sign up sharecroppers too scared to even be seen with them—are restless now.

Tension was rising between SNCC and the old heads like the Southern Christian Leadership Conference (SCLC), which King ran. King preferred big marches that showed black people's perseverance and attracted national attention. SNCC liked working behind the scenes, liberating people one by one.

They also disagreed on the question of nonviolence. "Most of us in SNCC did not accept nonviolence as a principle," Ture says. "King did. We saw it as a tactic. As a principle, you have to use it all the time under all conditions. As a tactic, we could use it today if it was working fine. If it wasn't working, tomorrow we could toss hand grenades."

In every demonstration King had, he says, people would be throwing bricks and bottles. The front lines with the suited reverends were righteously nonviolent, but "the back would be snipers shooting," he says. "They'd say, 'Listen, we respect you all. Y'all nonviolent, but we ain't going for that. These honkies in here shooting, we gon' shoot back. We gon' just let you know.'" Sometimes, he says, SNCC would negotiate with the local people to hold off until after the march was over. Then, he says, "you be hearing shots all night long."

Everyone understood that guns were a part of life in the Movement. King refused to keep a gun even after his house was bombed in Montgomery. But when he came to Carmichael's turf in the Mississippi Delta, guns were everywhere to make sure he was safe. "When he came I had cars to accompany him," he says. "The first car was full of guns, and the last car was full of guns. Cars throughout were full of guns. And I had a gun."

Carmichael and others in SNCC were more militant partly because they worked behind enemy lines, deep in Klan territory. Their job was to rally sharecroppers to stand up against the caste system they lived under and register to vote. The students were like guerrillas in a war. Death was always right around the corner.

They had code names for themselves (Carmichael went by "Greenwood Sweets," after the Mississippi town). They learned how to roll out of their cars in case of a shooting and traveled their districts in souped-up sedans, each one outfitted like a poor man's James Bond. Driving along the Delta's dry-dust roads, they realized that the only way the police could track them at night was to follow their taillights. So they devised a way to switch off the taillights at a curve. "The car following us inevitably has to go off the road," he says.

They made another discovery, albeit too late to save Medgar Evers. The Mississippi NAACP leader was fatally shot by Byron de la Beckwith while he was getting out of his car at night. "It was the car light that gave de la Beckwith the target," Ture says. After that, "we made sure the bulbs were taken out."

And so by the summer of 1966, the students were growing impatient with the passive "We Shall Overcome" and "Freedom Now" rhetoric that had brought great strides but, to them, had not finished the job. They plotted a more militant approach, talking up the idea of a radical new battle cry for their followers, not knowing for sure where it might lead. It would be not only a call to take their rightful place but also a sea change in identity from polite Negroes to proud black people embracing what the world had ridiculed.

They had secretly tested the idea for years, convincing the sharecroppers of its merits. But it wasn't until June of 1966, when a major march from Memphis to Jackson was scheduled to sweep through the heart of Carmichael's territory, that SNCC thought the time was right to change the tone of the Movement. So they set out to take over the march. They sabotaged the more conservative groups like the National Urban League and the NAACP—he refuses to say exactly how—shutting them out when the march hit Greenwood. That left mainly SNCC and SCLC. Then an astonishing thing happened. "Dr. King had gone to Memphis to tape a show, I think *Meet the Press*," he remembers. "He wouldn't be there. We couldn't believe it."

With King out of the picture and the mainline groups silenced, SNCC had the march and the podium virtually to itself. It could drop the new rallying cry on the public without dissent. But a few hours before the march, Carmichael was arrested, he says, as a ploy by white officials to disrupt the protest. Supporters bailed him out just in time for the rally, where he clenched his fist in the air and for the first time publicly shouted "We Want Black Power!" to the world.

Three years later, he was gone. He moved to Guinea in 1969 after a dizzying sequence of events: He had married Miriam Makeba, the South African singer; been ousted from SNCC over divisions he believes were fomented by the FBI; and become prime minister of the Black Panther Party, which, you should know, did not start in Oakland as most people think but in Alabama with SNCC, he says. It began as an act of defiance against the Democratic Party and the white rooster that symbolized white supremacy. By the late sixties, Carmichael had become a true-blooded revolutionary. Resented by some for his celebrity and targeted by the FBI, he left the United States and joined Kwame Nkrumah's pan-Africanist All African People's Revolutionary Party in Guinea.

By the mid-eighties, he would be divorced from Makeba (the FBI pursued them, he says, and the spying took its toll) and caught up on the losing side of a military overthrow in Guinea that killed most of his comrades. The military even put him in jail for several days. He survived.

He now has two sons—one seventeen by his second ex-wife, a Guinea-born physician who now lives in Washington, and a four-year-old in Guinea by a woman he never married. He admits he is not an especially attentive father. "If I can be of help to them, I will," he says. "But they know the people are more important than them."

In between speeches and meetings with pan-Africanists around the world, he is now working on a book about his life, called *Dancing in the Fire*, with the writer Michael Thelwell, a friend from his SNCC days. The title comes from something he used to say to the ladies who caught his eye. "I'd ask them if they could inhale smoke," he says, "because I dance with fire."

The radical left-wing black militant leader of the youth arm of the Civil Rights Movement grew up middle-class in an Italian section of the Bronx and played piano at Sunday school at Westchester Methodist Church. This is not a printer's error. He was also a Boy Scout—"believe it or not," his mother, Mabel Carmichael, says grandly in her sweet West Indian brogue.

The family migrated from Trinidad to New York City in waves, completing the process in 1952 when Stokely was eleven. His mother dreamt that her brilliant only son would grow up to be a doctor like he said he would. She might have had a cushy retirement and a pool and a wealthy surgeon son she could brag about, the way middle-class mothers do. What she got was a revolutionary who was thrown into southern jails too many times to count and whom numerous entities—was it the FBI, J. Edgar Hoover himself, Cointelpro, enemy capitalistic forces, rival comrades jealous of his charms?—wanted dead and all but forced out of the country.

Through the sixties, while he was plowing through southern backwoods, trying to outrun the Klan and sign up wary black people to vote, she would sleep with the radio for word on whether he was still alive.

It was not supposed to be this way. This was an immigrant family with middle-class strivings, headed by a carpenter father who refused to let his wife work and who had big hopes for their son and four daughters. Stokely went to predominantly white schools, where, in the eighth grade, a white teacher actually spat grape seeds at him from her desk. (Oddly enough, neither he nor his family complained because they felt no good would come of it.) He made it into the prestigious Bronx High School of Science, one of few blacks at the time, where he started reading up on Lenin and Marx and feeding the charming defiance that runs on his mother's side and would carry him through The Struggle.

He went off to Howard as a premed student in September 1960, and soon got involved with the SNCC chapter there. In May 1961, Mabel Carmichael got a call from her son, the one who was going to be a doctor, announcing that he was joining one of those freedom rides, the ones you saw on the news where black and white students would board a bus or a train and ride around the South defying segregation and getting southern whites all riled up.

"I almost went crazy," his mother says. "He called me from Howard and he said, 'I'm going on one of those freedom rides,' and hung up."

"I didn't hang up," he says from across the room.

"You hang up," she says, her voice deep Caribbean now.

"No, you even said to me, 'Oh, I know you're joking. I know you're coming home.' I said, 'I'm really getting on this plane. I'm going down there.'"

"Could been," she concedes. "Then after that, he hung up."

"She hung up," he insists.

"I thought he was fooling me," she says. So on he went to New Orleans to board a train to Jackson, Mississippi, with other students, to challenge segregated train stations. "That was rough, boy," he says, laughing hard. "It was wild. It was just wild. White people were fighting each other trying to get to us. Wherever the train stopped, they broke windows. What didn't they do! Every train station we got to, it was just mobs of people."

Soon after, he broke the news to his parents that he wouldn't be a doctor after all. "He say he doesn't want to help people when they get sick," his mother recalls. "He want to help them before they get sick. I didn't know what the hell he was talking about. How you going to help people before they get sick?

"And you know what else he says?" she remembers later. "He says, if we make him become a doctor, he's going to the furthest part of Africa and help poor people. So if we're sending him to school to be a doctor 'cause we think we're going to get money out of him we're wrong."

"At least I was right there," he says. "Up to now you haven't got a penny!" They both shake with laughter.

"Money don't mean a thing to that boy," she says. "He goes around the world without a dime in his pocket."

I ask if his speeches are a source of income. "We don't speak for money," he says. His mother is doubled over now and all but rolling on the floor.

"You thought he worked for money!" she says, shrieking with laughter. She mentions a book he wrote years ago about the Movement. "All the earnings went to SNCC, and his mother was out starving. I used to tell him, 'Child, would you bring that home? How you could do this?' He leave college and never make a dime." She bursts out laughing at both of their fates.

All she asked was that whatever he did, just be the best. And he was. That first time down South, he landed in jail like a good revolutionary. His mother heard it over the radio.

By now, the neighbors were talking. "I didn't know how to face people," she says. "One friend called and says, 'You talk about everything else, but you never say your son was in jail.' I didn't know how to respond to that. Very quickly I said to her, 'It wasn't for stealing, you know.'"

This was only the beginning. "He spent the whole summer in jail," she says. "This nigger spent the whole summer in jail! When he come home, we have to send him to Harlem to cut his hair—full of lice! That," she says, pointing at Ture, "my nice son, my doctor son."

Even the death of his father in 1962 did not pull him from the revolution. "I ask him to come home; say, we're only girls here," his mother remembers. "He has to go for voter registration. Whatever he was doing down there, I don't know. But he did not come home." Her voice breaks apart. "I don't have to tell you the things which I said, which I'm very, very sorry for now."

"She didn't understand how I could sacrifice the family for the people," he says, trying to explain the situation.

Nor could she understand, until she saw Mississippi for herself years later, why he and the other would-be doctors and lawyers were down there in the first place. "You're in a class, you've got your own house, you've got everything," she says, "and I just couldn't see him coming here, going to fight for black people. Why don't they go to work? Why in heaven don't they go to work?"

It wasn't, on the face of it, the son she raised. "He's down there in Farmer Brown overalls and a pair of boots his cousin gave him, making believe he's poor." She turns to him. "What you was trying to prove?"

"Not making believe," he tells his mother, "just blending in with the South."

"Don't pay him any mind, honey," his mother says. "If you give this boy here six underwear he gives away all of them, come back with one. Say this one told me he didn't have none. That's the type of thing he was before he even got into SNCC."

Because the idea of Black Power is so central to her son's legacy, I ask her did she use the term black at home while raising her children. "At home?" she asks. "I called them niggers all the time."

She tells me it was a way of toughening them up for what the outside world might do to them. "How would you use that?" I ask her.

"I'd say, 'Nigger, come up here,'" she says. "'Didn't you hear me calling ya?'"

His own name change is still a sensitive subject. She gave him the lordly name Stokely Standiford Churchill Carmichael for a reason. It was at the suggestion of his godfather, who admired a college professor called Stokely. The Stokely we know changed his name to Kwame Ture (after Kwame Nkrumah and Sekou Toure, the respective leaders of Ghana and Guinea) in the late 1970s.

"It hurt for a while, and up to now I still curse him," she says, smiling. She calls him both names now.

His life as a revolutionary made her one by association. As he was stalked, so was she. Her house in the Bronx was under round-the-clock surveillance until he left the country. FBI agents followed her wherever she went and tapped her phone, she says.

Sometimes agents would call and ask her where her son was. "I would say that's your problem," she says. They sent black agents posing as Stokely's friends to fish information out of her. They followed her to the market when she bought her fish and green bananas.

Soon, she had had enough. She picked up the phone and spoke into the receiver. "'Mr. Hoover,'" she would say to the man who ran the FBI, "'I know you are listening to our conversation right now. But I wish you the slowest, eating-up cancer that will take time to die.' Every single day I pick up my phone, I used to curse Mr. Hoover. And here now my son have cancer. How you like that? God, how I'm sorry for that one."

Ask Ture what happened to the Movement and you get a dose of radical speechifying about the corruption of the petite bourgeoisie with their self-serving class-action suits, FBI sabotage, and the relationship of the people to the means of production. He holds in particular contempt the beneficiaries of the Movement who forget that people died so they could be a judge or an assemblyman or senior vice-president of such-and-such. He calls people like Ward Connerly, the black conservative who led the charge against affirmative action in California, "reactionary garbage." He says, "My grandmother used to say, 'When you boil dirty water, the first thing to rise to the top is the scum.'"

On politics and The Struggle: "The enemy seeks to take us out of the streets to the ballpark of electoral politics, which solves nothing. . . . We have more mayors and worsening conditions. We've had to admit as a people that reform cannot solve our problem; only revolution can."

On drugs in the black community: "In revolutionary history, drugs are usually the last go-round before the defeat of imperialist forces. . . .

I think most people don't recognize we're in a war. . . . At certain times, they heat up certain fronts, so the drug war is heated up the last two decades."

On the disproportionate number of black men in prison: "It's to be expected. The system is going to do everything possible to suppress us. But those prisons are going to turn out Malcolm X in mass."

On the perils of integration: "It's an insidious subterfuge for the maintenance of white supremacy. Because it makes you think that for things to be better, you gotta go to whites. You want a better school, you gotta go to a white school. You want a better neighborhood, you gotta go to a white neighborhood. It instills an inferiority complex in the minds of Africans."

On his infamous quote about the position of women in the Movement being prone: "You can't judge a person's position on women by a phrase. It was a private joke inside of a private SNCC meeting during a debate on the role of women within SNCC. We laughed. We were all laughing. You couldn't say it and really mean it. This phrase was taken up by white women who were put out of SNCC when I was chair. They were mad at me and trumpeted it everywhere."

On the need for unity: "I want Julian Bond to meet with Farrakhan. I want a united front."

On why we keep looking for a savior: "It says we're disorganized therefore powerless, so we look for shortcuts, whether a King or a Mandela."

One night last fall, Kwame Ture sat in a den in Miami surrounded by teachers and librarians and community activists and other working people with children and car notes talking about the situation in South Africa. They listened to the master dissect the state of race relations, suggesting that here, like there, blacks in position is not the same as blacks in power.

The hour grew late and still the people drank in his words. Then the master, weary, went to another room. And then as often happens when black people meet, the subject turned to why black people can't get themselves together, and the discussion toured all the suspected reasons—from self-hate to apathy. The people in the room, their leader departed, were left groping, searching, arguing and sometimes agreeing, on their own. It was Black America itself—Dr. King dead, Malcolm X dead, Medgar Evers dead, Stokely Carmichael gone to the Motherland, the people left wandering alone, convinced they need a leader. The man who left the country left the group. The group would have to figure out the situation on its own. There would be no Messiah with a miracle.

In December 1995, Kwame Ture went to visit his mother in Miami. She had just gotten the new condo and, since he didn't have any money and she was so anxious to see him, she paid for his plane ticket herself. When he got there, she noticed he walked with a limp. And his son noticed he walked with a limp. And his nephew noticed it, too. "Yes, Uncle Kwame, you not walking so good."

The doctor in Guinea said it was a pinched nerve. His mother wasn't convinced. She told him to see another doctor. He saw one in New York. He was hospitalized right away. It was the prostate. It was cancer. The prognosis was not good. "The cancer was already started in his bones," his mother says. She still found reason to be glad. "I was really thankful to God that he was letting him stay on this time with us."

He has an everything-is-everything calm about him on these days. He laughs loud and easily. Seems at peace. The smooth face has white stubble now, and a straight white buzz cut above. He rests his swollen legs and feet on his mother's glass coffee table during hours of interviewing, leaning back against the cushy spine of his mother's white sofa, the one with the lace doilies on the armrests, tired not so much from the fight for your civil rights but from a cellular invader.

His line of work means no medical insurance, no pension. There is a resignation in his mother's voice when she speaks of how others seemed to make the most of their civil rights fame. "Every last one of those boys used that freedom ride to climb," she says. "So Stokely could have climbed, too. So this is really what he wanted."

He lived his life hoping his devotion would bear fruit. "If you struggle for the people, the people won't let you starve," he insists.

The fruit falls in unlikely places. One black doctor treating him in New York volunteered his services out of respect and gratitude. He said he might not have been a doctor had Stokely Carmichael not done what he did. "I told him, 'Don't ever worry about a bill from me,'" said Dr. Gerald Hoke, his urologist. "The honor of being associated with him is payment enough. This is the least I can do."

Ture believes that the FBI gave him the cancer—how exactly, he doesn't know. "The cancer still has not gone into remission—the FBI was serious with this one," he says soberly, but managing to smile at the paradox. "The chemotherapy and the other treatments have been able to calm the pain. That's all. They can't stop the cancer."

In the meantime, he's still talking about revolution, making calls from his bedside if he has to, giving speeches when he can, meeting with his band of believers on several continents, talking about straws and slingshots, and how eventually there will be enough of them pointed and piled together to end injustice. "We never know which straw will break the camel's back," he says. "But we do know a straw will break the camel's back. Just keep putting the straw on. The camel's back will be broken sooner or later."

Permissions

"They Were Commandos" by Madeleine Blais, first published by *The New York Times*, April 18, 1993. Reprinted with permission of the author.

"The Cheerleaders" by E. Jean Carroll, first published by *Spin*, June 2001. Reprinted with permission of the author.

"Some Dreamers of the Golden Dream" by Joan Didion, first published by *The Saturday Evening Post*, April 1966. Reprinted with permission of the author.

"Wonder Dog" by Melissa Fay Greene, first published by *The New York Times Magazine*, May 2, 2012. Reprinted with permission of the author.

"Holy Days: The World of a Hasidic Family" by Lis Harris. A version of this story was first published by *The New Yorker*, September 23, 1985. Reprinted with permission of the author.

"The Last Day" by Robin Marantz Henig. This story was first published with the title "The Last Day of Her Life" by *The New York Times Magazine*, May 14, 2015. Reprinted with permission of the author.

"On the Bus with B.B. King" by Gerri Hirshey, first published by *Rolling Stone*, December 25, 1998. Reprinted with permission of the author.

"Nureyev Dancing in His Own Shadow" by Elizabeth Kaye, first published by *Esquire*, March 1991. Reprinted with permission of the author.

"The New Face of Richard Norris" by Jeanne Marie Laskas, first published by *GQ*, August 27, 2014. Reprinted with permission of the author.

"The Troubled Life of Boys" by Adrian Nicole LeBlanc, first published by *The New York Times Magazine*, August 22, 1999. Reprinted with permission of the author.

"Prodigal Daughter" by Jill Lepore, first published by *The New Yorker*, July 8, 2013. Reprinted with permission of the author.

"The Split" by Suzannah Lessard, first published by *The New Yorker*, December 8, 1997. Reprinted with permission of the author.

"Yuja Wang and the Art of Performance" by Janet Malcolm, first published by *The New Yorker* on September 5, 2016. Reprinted with permission of the author.

"The Bullfighter Checks Her Makeup" by Susan Orlean, first published by *Outside*, May 2, 2004. Reprinted with permission of the author.

The following stories have been reprinted with permission of the author:

Excerpts from "Introduction" by Lillian Ross, from *Takes: Stories from the Talk of the Town*, published March, 1983 by Congdon and Weed. All rights reserved.

"Davis on Dogs" by Lillian Ross, first published by *The New Yorker*, January 26, 1981. All rights reserved.

"Remembering Picasso" by Lillian Ross, first published by *The New Yorker*, October 19, 1981. All rights reserved.

"The Golden Ladies of the Golden Door" by Lillian Ross, first published by *The New Yorker*, June 2, 1995. All rights reserved.

"Kid Twelve" by Susan Sheehan, first published by *The New Yorker*, August 19, 1996. Reprinted with permission of the author.

"Mrs. Kennedy at the Moment" by Gloria Steinem, first published by *Esquire*, October 1964. Reprinted with permission of the author.

"Mothers, Sisters, Daughters, Wives" by Mimi Swartz, first published by *Texas Monthly*, August 2012. © 2012 by *Texas Monthly*. Reprinted with permission of *Texas Monthly*.

"My Breast" by Joyce Wadler, first published by *New York Magazine*, April 13, 1992, and April 20, 1992. Reprinted with permission of the author.

"Soul Survivor" by Isabel Wilkerson, first published by *Essence*, May 1998. Reprinted with permission of the author.

About the Editor

Patsy Sims is the author of three nonfiction books, including *The Klan* and *Can Somebody Shout Amen! Inside the Tents and Tabernacles of American Revivalists,* named a noteworthy book of 1988 by *The New York Times Book Review.* She is also the editor of *Literary Nonfiction: Learning by Example* and coauthor of the narration for Academy Award–nominated documentary *The Klan: A Legacy of Hate.*

Prior to writing books, she worked as a staff writer and editor for the New Orleans *States-Item, The San Francisco Chronicle,* and *The Philadelphia Inquirer.* Her work has appeared in *The New York Times Book Review, The Washington Post Magazine, Oxford American, Texas Observer,* among other publications. She has been a recipient of creative writing fellowships from the National Endowment for the Arts and the District of Columbia Commission on the Arts and two Associated Press Awards for investigative-interpretive reporting. "No Twang of Conscience Whatever," about the 1964 murders of three civil rights workers in Mississippi, was named a Notable Essay of 2014 by *The Best American Essays.* She directed Goucher College's MFA program in creative nonfiction from 2001–2014.

About the Publisher

The Sager Group was founded in 1984. In 2012 it was chartered as a multi-media artists' and writers' consortium, with the intent of empowering those who create art—an umbrella beneath which makers can pursue, and profit from, their craft directly, without gatekeepers.

TSG publishes books; ministers to artists and provides modest grants; and produces documentary, feature, and commercial films. By harnessing the means of production, The Sager Group helps artists help themselves. For more information, please see www.TheSagerGroup.Net.